A WORLD
WITHOUT
WOMEN

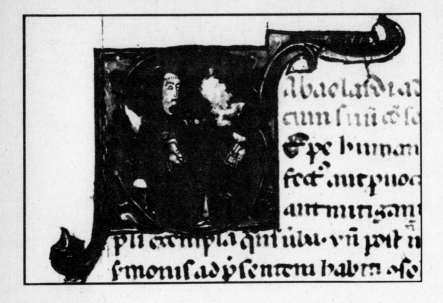

A WORLD WITHOUT WOMEN

❧

The Christian Clerical Culture of Western Science

DAVID F. NOBLE

OXFORD UNIVERSITY PRESS
New York   Oxford

Oxford University Press

Oxford   New York   Toronto
Delhi   Bombay   Calcutta   Madras   Karachi
Kuala Lumpur   Singapore   Hong Kong   Tokyo
Nairobi   Dar es Salaam   Cape Town
Melbourne   Auckland   Madrid

and associated companies in
Berlin   Ibadan

First published in 1992 by Alfred A. Knopf, Inc., New York,
201 East 50th Street, New York, New York 10016,
and simultaneously in Canada by Random House of Canada
Limited, Toronto.

First issued as an Oxford University Press paperback, 1993

Oxford is a registered trademark of Oxford University Press

Library of Congress Cataloging-in-Publication Data
Noble, David F.
A world without women : the Christian clerical culture of Western
science / David F. Noble.
p.   cm.
Originally published: New York : Knopf, 1992.
Includes bibliographical references and index.
ISBN 0-19-508435-7 (pbk.)
1. Women in science—Europe—History. 2. Science—Europe—
History.   I. Title.
[Q130.N63   1993]
306.4′5′082—dc20

2   4   6   8   10   9   7   5   3   1
Printed in the United States of America

For Mary Ann
and our daughters,
Clare, Helen, and Alice

*At the Resurrection, sex will be abolished
and nature made one. . . . There will then be
only man, as if he had never sinned.*

JOHANNES SCOTUS ERIGENA

Contents

Acknowledgments

A World Without Women is the first part of a larger inquiry into the origins and implications of the masculine culture of Western science and technology. (A second volume on the development of modern technology, *The Masculine Millennium*, is under way.) I began to think about such an undertaking in 1975, at the insistent urging of sociologist Sally Hacker, with whom I shared an office at MIT. Hacker's pioneering efforts to penetrate the masculine mystique of engineering forced me for the first time to confront the gender dimension in science and technology, a belated and at the time still rather dim insight reflected merely in a footnote in my own book on the history of engineering. My subsequent study of the history of industrial automation convinced me of the need to explore the underlying compulsions of the male engineering culture, but here too the matter, which I still found unwieldy and elusive, gained only a footnote, albeit a somewhat longer one. I thereafter resolved to concentrate my efforts on this difficult but crucial subject.

In the meantime, of course, others well in advance of me have been pointing the way. This study could not even have been imagined without the path-breaking work of a generation of feminist scholars who cast a new light on the whole of Western history. I am especially indebted to those feminist students of science and technology who, like Sally Hacker, welcomed me into their ranks and encouraged my efforts, among them Cynthia Cockburn, Ursula Franklin, Sandra Harding, Evelyn Fox Keller, and Autumn Stanley. In researching and writing this study, I benefited from the support of the Library of Congress, Drexel University, the American Council of Learned Societies, and Mary and Stan Weir. I also want to thank Mike Cooley, David Dickson, Thomas Ferguson, Paul Forman, Michaelangelo de Maria, Leonard Minsky, and Douglas Noble for their advice and encouragement, and in particular Edward Reed, who shared with me his knowledge of the history of modern science and carefully reviewed the entire manuscript. I owe a great debt to historian George Ovitt, a patient and generous guide into the mysteries of the Middle Ages and the somber world of the Latin Church. This study could not have been done without his help and friendship. Nor could it have been done without the companionship of that other lapsed Catholic and abortion-rights activist Mary Ann O'Connor. With an intelligence enriched by a spirit of defiance, she helped me grasp the full significance of the masculine culture of the church. And into my arid reflections upon that womanless world, she cast three daughters.

Introduction

WESTERN SCIENCE EVOLVED only half human, in a world without women. As philosopher Sandra Harding has noted, "women have been more systematically excluded from doing serious science than from performing any other social activity except, perhaps, frontline warfare." Heralded time and again as a heroic break from a more primitive past, the scientific enterprise nevertheless bore within it the enduring and deforming scars of a more ancient rupture, in the relations between the sexes. The scars are visible still.[1]

"I recall very vividly my first day in class," mathematician Marian Boyken Pour-El told a 1973 New York Academy of Sciences conference on women in science. "Three seats in front of me, three seats in back of me, and two seats on either side were left vacant. I was a complete pariah in that social setting [the graduate school of Harvard University]. . . . The men were positively unable to interact with me." Physicist Betsy Acker-Johnson recalled that she was viewed as a "weirdo because I was a woman studying, of all things, experimental physics." Joanne Simpson remembered that her professor, "the greatest living meteorologist, was a model to me whose creativity, expansiveness, and ability to . . . inspire people I am still seeking to emulate. He had no use for women in meteorology, however."[2]

"I was not prepared for the discovery that women were not welcome in science," that their presence would be viewed as "an outrageous violation of the social order and against all the laws of nature," experimental psychologist Naomi Weisstein explained in a later forum. "We were shut out . . . we were shown we didn't belong. . . . I was completely isolated. I did not have access to the normal channels of communication, debate, and exchange in the profession—those informal networks where you get the news, the comment, the criticism, the latest reports of what is going on. . . . I had been exiled [from] the 'inner reaches' of the profession." Mathematical biologist Evelyn Fox Keller likewise recounted her initial estrangement from the culture of science and the classroom "sea of seats" which surrounded her. "Perhaps the most curious, undoubtedly the most painful, part of my experience was the total isolation in which I found myself. . . . I was clearly a serious threat to my fellow students' conception of physics as not only a male stronghold but a male retreat."[3]

This book examines the evolution of this anthropologically "curious" culture of science, which has somehow come to appear so normal. Though there have been notable recent efforts to recruit women into so-called traditionally masculine scientific fields, there has been noticeably little reflection about how these fields became "masculine" in the first place—and with what significance. In recent years, there have been important pioneering attempts to understand the nature and origins of this "masculine" scientific tradition, such as in the work of Carolyn Merchant, Brian Easlea, Evelyn Fox Keller, Sandra Harding, and Londa Schiebinger, but for the most part the exclusive identification of science with men has been taken as a given, something to be overcome, perhaps, but never really explained. Yet any genuine concern about the implications of such a culturally distorted science-based civilization, or about the role of women within it, demands an explanation. For the male identity of science is no mere artifact of sexist history; throughout most of its evolution, the culture of science has not simply excluded women, it has been defined in defiance of women and in their absence. Thus, predictably, the world of science has remained an alien world for women, and a hostile one, a world where women are not merely marginalized but anathematized, where they face not just discrimination but dread. How did so strange a scientific culture emerge, one that proclaimed so boldly the power of the species while at the same time shrinking in such horror from half that species? This is the question before us.[4]

THIS BOOK is an effort to explain historically how, when, and why the culture of Western science evolved in the strange way it did. To pose these historical questions serves not only to acknowledge the peculiarity of that culture but also to imagine things being otherwise. The chief obstacle to such historical imagining is the belief that there has been something natural, or at least inevitable, about the world without women, because it presumably has always been this way. There is a widespread assumption that the culture of learning in the West, out of which Western science emerged, has always excluded women, an assumption that rests upon the allegedly enduring legacy of ancient Greece, with its homosocial Platonic academies and Aristotelian misogyny. But facile interpretive leaps, say, from Aristotle to Aquinas, leave out too much history, including history in which women came to play a far more prominent part in the culture of learning than they did in either ancient Greece or the High Middle Ages. Part one is meant to provide a corrective to this common ahistorical assumption of continuity, and the fatalism it engenders, by fleshing out in some detail the very different situation for women that existed during the first millennium of the Christian era, a period when priests were married, an androgynous Christian ideal was taken seriously, aristocratic women gained significant control over property, and, not incidentally, Aristotle's writings were all but lost to the West. (It should be emphasized at the outset that, with its focus upon the culture of learning, this study concentrates almost exclusively upon the relatively privileged members of society, those with the means, and the associated expectations, to devote themselves to study.) The experience of these centuries, as well as the recurring episodic revivals of this experience in later centuries, constituted the historical reality out of which, and against which, the world without women was constructed.

And it was constructed. Part two challenges the assumption that the Western masculine culture of learning evolved automatically and inevitably as a mere extension of ancient patriarchy. It traces in detail the historical development of this culture from the early centuries of the Christian era to the scholasticism of the High Middle Ages. The focus here is upon the evolution of the Latin Church and, in particular, of the clerical ascetic culture of its male hierarchy. As historian Henry Lea long ago pointed out, "the Latin Church is the great fact which dominates the history of modern civilization. . . . All other agencies which moulded the destinies of Europe were comparatively isolated or sporadic in their manifestations. Nowhere do we see combined effort, nowhere can we detect a pervading impulse, irrespective of locality or of circumstance, save in the imposing machinery of the church establishment. This meets us at every point, and in every age, and in every sphere of action." It is here, in the struggle of the Latin clergy to impose itself between God and the rest of humanity, that the curious culture which spawned Western science took shape. For it is here, as orthodoxy invented heresy and then identified it with women, that a world without women emerged: a society composed exclusively of men, forged in flight from women, and intent upon remaking the world in its own half-human image.[5]

Rooted in the male monasticism of the fourth century and distinguished above all by its emphasis upon total clerical celibacy, the clerical ascetic culture of the Latin Church hierarchy had become by the High Middle Ages the culture of the entire priesthood, as well as of the culture of learning. But the consolidation of this clerical ascetic culture required a millennium of struggle and even after that the struggle never really ceased. Once entrenched, the defenders of orthodoxy had perpetually to deal with periodic revivals of anticlerical religious heterodoxy, which time and again reopened spaces for women. The fate of women in the Western world of learning was thus tied to the recurring tension between orthodoxy and revival which marked the entire history of the Christian West.

In secular retrospect, Western science has been portrayed as the opposite of, and in opposition to, religion, a dramatic departure from Christian, and clerical, tradition. Part three challenges this fundamentally ahistorical view of Western science, placing it instead squarely within the Christian, and clerical, culture from which it emerged. It suggests that, especially with regard to women, the history of Western science must be understood in the context of the history of Latin Christendom, with its enduring tension between orthodoxy and revival. As an essentially sacred activity, science took shape in an epic social struggle over access to divine knowledge. Chapter eight traces the link between science and anticlerical revival in the wake of the Reformation, which created new but temporary openings for women in the Western culture of learning. Chapter nine describes the scientific revolution of the seventeenth century as an aspect of the restoration of clerical authority. Finally, chapter ten describes the (perhaps) permanent entry of women into Western centers of learning in the nineteenth century, especially with the advent of coeducation, as the result of yet another anticlerical revival, this time combined with a sustained political-economic challenge to clerical culture from outside religion. Women at last gained entry into the world without women, however, only to be confronted by another clerical restoration, in the form of a male scientific professionalism that betrayed the same misogynistic and, indeed, monastic habits of the clerical culture it superseded.

. . .

THIS STUDY draws more upon the work of other scholars than upon primary sources, for sound scholarly reasons. As every historian knows, primary materials can be properly interpreted only through a full appreciation of the context in which they are embedded, and the wrenching of details here and there from original sources does havoc to historical accuracy. Thus, daunted by the prospect of adequately mastering two thousand years of history, I decided early on in this study to lean heavily upon the authority of scholars who have mastered the history of particular periods. The text is therefore replete with quotations from such scholars. What I have written, however, is not merely derivative. Although it builds upon the work of many specialists, this study asks of old material questions rarely posed, much less answered. Indeed, given the wealth of knowledge readily available and the seeming obviousness of the questions, it is rather disconcerting that such an inquiry had to await someone as unprepared for it as I. As a trespasser on the turf of so many scholars, I offer the present work less as a definitive history than as a plausible framework for further investigation.

Part One

A WORLD WITH WOMEN

One · *Mothers, Daughters, Sisters, Wives*

THE HISTORY OF IDEAS is not the same as the history of people. Western philosophy, and by extension Western science, might well be a mere footnote to Plato, but the masculine culture of Western science is not simply a legacy of Plato's Academy. In search of the historical origins of modern scientific culture, we might begin by tracing the evolution of the institutions that are today associated with science, the scientific professional societies and academies and the universities. If we go back to the creation of the professional societies in the nineteenth century or of the academies in the seventeenth, we find that at their inception both already bore the stamp of a world without women. Similarly, if we return to the beginnings of the Western universities in the twelfth and thirteenth centuries, we see that the familiar patterns were already established here too. And the same is true for the cathedral schools, seedbeds of the universities, during their intellectual pre-eminence in the eleventh and twelfth centuries. Beyond the cathedral schools, we come to the monasteries, the chief centers of learning in the West during the so-called Dark Ages, between the fall of Rome and the high-medieval period. In the tenth and eleventh centuries, we again find a world without women, but if we go back a bit further, a quite different world suddenly confronts us.

Ely Cathedral, north of Cambridge, England is a former abbey dating from the seventh century. The front row of pews today bear embroidered cushions which silently recount the illustrious and long history of this monastic center. Each cushion bears the name of an abbot, beginning with the founding of the abbey. One is immediately struck by a startling fact: the earliest abbots were all abbesses, starting with the foundress of the abbey, Ethelreda. The next cushion bears the name of Ethelreda's sister Sexburga, and that is followed by cushions embroidered with the names of Sexburga's daughter Ermenhilda, and *her* daughter Werburga. Then there is a huge pillar, tacitly symbolizing a historic interruption in gender relations (although tradi-

3

tion has it that there were several additional abbesses after Werburga).
Chronologically, the pillar coincides roughly with the period of Viking
invasions in the ninth century, during which time, in 870, the abbey
was destroyed. On the far side of the pillar, the embroidered cushions
continue, but now they bear the names exclusively of abbots. The
first is that of Brithnoth, who became head of the abbey in 970, after
it was restored as part of the monastic reform movement of the tenth
century. Here at Ely, then, we have a clue about the origin of a world
without women, which was apparently much more recent than the
alleged ancient Greek antecedents of Western scientific culture.

"In the great period of monastic foundation from the early tenth to
the early twelfth centuries," medievalist and church historian R. W.
Southern has observed, "the position of women in the monastic life
suffered a sharp decline." But before this juncture—and long after the
demise of the ancient academies—something quite different seems to
have existed, raising doubts about simple continuity. For Ely was no
convent of cloistered women. It was a double monastery, inhabited
by both men and women, headed by a woman. Nor was it unique in
either regard. Double monasteries dotted the early-medieval land-
scape throughout Anglo-Saxon England and elsewhere, and were
quite commonly headed by an abbess. Bede, in his history of the
church in England, refers not only to Ethelreda of Ely but also to
other powerful abbesses of the time. Such institutions, Bede records,
were important centers of education and learning, as well as political
affairs. In marked contrast with the institutions that arose later, here
men and women worked together in their common pursuit of knowledge and salvation.[1]

Proponents of the concept of patriarchy emphasize continuity in
history rather than change, to demonstrate the persistent power of
men over women. Certainly female subordination is a recurring fact
of human history, and the presence of women in these centers of
learning reflected neither a reversal of such gender domination nor an
end to it. But it is important to remember that, within this overarching
patriarchal pattern of gender relations, there have been significant
variations of experience, variations that have shaped particular cultures and lives. Although it is possible to recount recurring misogynist
themes in apostolic and patristic writings, for example, which echo
classical disdain for women, it would be a serious mistake to regard
the experience from late antiquity to the High Middle Ages as merely
a realization of them. Clearly, woman's fate was not ordination but

subordination; however, women remained present, and indeed prominent, within both church and society. For, as the cushions of Ely attest, these misogynist voices, while no doubt influential, were not the whole of reality. Indeed, as calls for a world without women, these voices themselves remind us that such a world did not yet exist. What did exist was something quite different.

At the dawn of the Christian era, a world without women existed in embryo, but it was dwarfed by an elite Christian world of both sexes. In 70 A.D., the year the Romans destroyed Jerusalem and a few years after the death of St. Paul, Pliny the Elder described a small community of male ascetics, the Essenes, living on the west side of the Dead Sea; they are "a solitary race," he observed, "and strange above all others in the entire world. They live without women, renouncing all sexual love." The very strangeness of the lives of these radical Jewish militants, with whom Jesus himself was perhaps briefly associated, highlights the quite different social milieu in which the new religion emerged. First, it was in the Jewish and Roman household that early Christianity took root. From this familial foundation arose two lasting legacies which would endure for a millennium: a married priesthood and the presence (and at times prominence) of pious women as clerical and lay wives and widows. Second, alongside this material or institutional foundation stood an ideological one, the androgynous ideal of Christian piety inspired by Paul's preaching to the Galatians that "there is neither Jew nor Greek, there is neither slave nor free, there is neither male nor female, for you are all one in Christ Jesus." This pronouncement sanctioned and encouraged female participation in Christian leadership, both within the household congregations and especially among the communities of celibate ascetics who increasingly abandoned the household in pursuit of the Kingdom of God. If the household institution guaranteed the presence of both sexes within the elite circles of the emerging church, the androgynous ideal promised an unprecedented equality between the sexes, and indeed, in the view of many Christian ascetics, a transcendence of the sexes altogether. Thus, from the outset of Christianity, both the married household and its opposite, celibate asceticism, fostered a noticeable female presence.[2]

Jesus led a celibate life as an aspect of his prophetic calling but, true to his Hebrew heritage, upheld for his flock the sanctity of marriage and the commandment to multiply. In addition, he welcomed women among his disciples, most of them either married or widowed.

Although the apostles had become celibates in order better to fulfill their function as roving missionaries, they had been married themselves and rejected calls for a celibate church. The general practice of the emergent church "judged the married state as the normal way of life for all Christians," including the leadership. This view adhered not only to biblical precept but also to contemporary Roman laws enacted by Emperor Augustus that, in a period of population decline, penalized celibates and rewarded families for having children. Thus, even as the numbers of nomadic celibate Christian preachers continued to swell, the "silent majority" of Christians, as Peter Brown reminds us, remained unswayed by their call; these were "careworn and decent householders . . . secure in their moral horizons . . . and in no position to allow the painfully assembled fabric of their social person—their wives, their children, their kinfolk, and the few ancestral fields that they would inherit when they buried their father—to evaporate at the call of the wandering few."[3]

St. Paul had himself abandoned marriage for the celibate apostolic calling but rejected celibacy as the basis for building the church, believing that it would lead only to cultic isolation. Intent upon enlarging the church through the conversion of gentiles and Jews alike, he upheld the centrality of marriage and relied upon the authority and resources of the household to spread the gospel. The result was a household church and a married church leadership. "During the first generation," as historian JoAnn McNamara has explained, "certain persons were evident to whom the administrative and liturgical leadership of the newly established Christian communities had been entrusted. These were married persons whose households served not only as gathering places for Christian worship but as hospices for itinerant and fugitive Christians."[4]

This pattern persisted in both the East and the West, despite a growing ascetic challenge to the settled world of the household, to clerical marriage, and to marriage itself. In the urban centers where Christianity flourished, clerical marriage became the norm; the Christian clergyman "continued to earn his living, to care for his family . . . and was not distinguished by his style of life from his fellow Christians." At the end of the second century, Clement of Alexandria defended the value of marriage not only for laymen but for deacons, priests, and bishops as well, and the fourth-century Apostolic Constitutions "recommended that the fitness of the clergyman to govern his church be judged by his success in governing his household and his family." In short, as Henry Lea noted in his pioneering history of sacerdotal celibacy, in the early church "marriage was freely permitted to the ministers of Christ." This assessment has been confirmed in a more recent study by Anne Barstow, who concludes that "it is now generally agreed that the majority of the clergy in the early church were married." The fathers of the church, while increasingly extolling virginity as the epitome of Christian virtue in the wake of the monastic movement, nevertheless avoided denying the sanctity of marriage. The First Ecumenical Council of the church, held in Nicaea in 325, rejected an earlier call for clerical continence by the Spanish bishops at Elvira and defended marriage as an "honorable state," for clergy as well as laity; forty years later, the Council of Gangra condemned those who refused the sacraments of a married priest. As Lea observed, according to "the doctrines accepted at this period . . . there was no authority admitted for imposing restrictions of any kind on the married clergy."[5]

In the East, although it was the original locus of the monastic movement, no sustained, much less successful, challenge to clerical marriage ever emerged—for reasons that will be discussed in the next chapter. Thus the Eastern Church, in Lea's words, "preserved the traditions of earlier times." To this day, Orthodox canon requires celibacy of bishops only and leaves the secular clergy free to marry.

In the West, clerical marriage persisted—albeit increasingly on the defensive—for a millennium. A serious challenge to it emerged only in the fourth century, with the development of monasticism. Thereafter, papal and conciliar demands for clerical continence and celibacy intensified but, it appears, with little effect. At the close of the sixth century, St. Columban observed the clergy in Merovingian Gaul living "either openly or clandestinely with their wives," and the letters of Gregory the Great "leave no doubt that ecclesiastical sanctions were defied by both clerks and their wives." Gregory of Tours testified that "even wives of bishops were reluctant to leave their husbands and that some openly rebelled against their husbands' abstinence."[6]

"Most authorities agree," one church historian has pointed out, "that the great majority of clergymen in the West from Gregory the Great to the tenth century were married men." To explain this, Barstow refers to Friedrich Kempf's speculation that the "unsettled conditions" of late antiquity and the early-medieval period "made family life all the more necessary for parish priests." But whatever the reason, clerical marriage persisted. Indeed, as Lea pointed out, the perpetual legislation against it "betrays the fact that it was not only practically impossible to maintain separation between the clergy and their wives, but that at times marriage was not uncommon even within the prohibited orders." Thus, Barstow notes, "the tenth century is claimed to be the high point of clerical marriage in the Latin communion. . . . It is generally agreed that most rural priests were married, and that many urban clergy and bishops had wives and children. . . . Clerical marriage was so widespread as to be the usual condition of the parish clergy; it was frequently found in every level and branch of the church, even on occasion in monasteries. Despite six hundred years of decrees, canons, and increasingly harsh penalties, the Latin clergy still did, more or less illegally, what their Greek counterparts were encouraged to do by law—they lived with their wives and raised families." It was only in the eleventh and twelfth centuries, in the wake of the Gregorian reforms, that clerical marriage was decisively discouraged in the West.[7]

Just as the household origins and familial foundations of Christianity left an enduring legacy of clerical marriage, so they also offered an array of openings to pious women. At first, the church and the household were essentially one and the same, and women influential in the household were influential in the church. Later, when the church became a separate institution, and as males monopolized clerical positions, women played several roles, as clerical wives within the clerical household and, most important, as influential wives and widows within the lay household. Among the first generation of urban Christians, as Wayne Meeks has explained:

> there were women who headed households, who ran businesses and had independent wealth, who traveled with their own slaves and helpers. Some who are married have become converts to this exclusive religious cult without the consent of their husbands, and they may . . . initiate divorce. Moreover, women have taken on some of the same roles as men's within the sect itself. Some exercise charismatic functions like prayer and prophecy in the congregation; others . . . are Paul's fellow workers as evangelists and teachers. Both in terms of their position in the larger society and in terms of their participation in the Christian communities, then, a number of women broke through the normal expectations of female roles.

Such possibilities stemmed from a gradual but steady breakdown of the Roman family during the late-Hellenistic period, which had

yielded a greater independence for respectable women and upset
traditional gender roles. The predictable tensions which resulted
aroused the anxieties reflected in the satire of Juvenal and some of
the more notoriously misogynist Pauline letters such as those to the
Corinthian congregation.[8]

At a time before any strict division had emerged between clergy
and laity, the leadership of the church fell to those who oversaw the
household, including women. Paul refers to Priscilla and Aquila, for
example, a married couple who apparently presided over house
churches and perhaps catechetical schools in Ephesus, Corinth, and
Rome; judging by the fact that Paul consistently mentions Priscilla's
name before that of her husband, Meeks speculates that "certainly
Prisca is at least her husband's peer in this activity." In Corinth,
Meeks points out, there was apparently "an equivalence of role and
a mutuality of relationship between the sexes in matters of marriages,
divorce, and charismatic leadership of the church to a degree that is
virtually unparalleled in Jewish or pagan society of the time." As Peter
Brown has noted, moreover, "Some women were heads of households
in their own right and effective protectresses of the new churches."[9]

As the church separated from the household and men increasingly
monopolized clerical status, some women continued to play a leading
role in church affairs because of their position as clerical wives. Although the precise role of clerical wives in the early church is a
matter of some controversy among historians, JoAnn McNamara has
concluded that

> there is some fragile evidence that the priest's wife may have been
> vested with some ecclesiastical functions. A long persistent tradition
> has connected the priests' wives with the office of deaconess, which
> appears in early Church literature, though there is no clear text to
> prove the argument. . . . In any case, it seems safe to assume that
> many of the subsidiary and nonsacramental administrative functions
> may have fallen on the marital partners of clergymen.

Whatever their paraclerical role, however, the presence within the
clerical world of the wives of clergy is indisputable, and this presence
would persist, along with clerical marriage, for a millennium.[10]

Wives, moreover, whether clerical or lay, often became widows,
and, given the growing ascetic tendency within the church, they were
increasingly discouraged from remarrying. These permanent "postmarital celibates," as Peter Brown refers to them, including growing

numbers of women who had abandoned their husbands, became early and influential participants in church leadership. Their influence stemmed not from their relationship to clergymen but from their lay families' wealth, social status, and political power. The prominent and visible role of such women in the early church made Christianity, especially in the eyes of its pagan critics, "notorious for close association with women." Again, it was the household, now the lay household, that afforded women such access. Even as pressures mounted for the creation of an ascetic priesthood, in part to insulate it from undue lay influence, the lay household remained unchallenged as the crucial material foundation of the church. For it was "the loyal support of . . . well-to-do, married householders," conscientiously cultivated by church leaders, that "provided the wealth and the children." The centrality of the wealthy lay household to the fate of the church offered many opportunities for the women of these households, especially when, as widows, they came into control over its resources. By remaining unmarried, moreover, they retained such control while at the same time fulfilling growing ascetic expectations. Thus, as Brown observes, "the Christian clergy of late antiquity found that, in their community, influential women were there to stay." The clergy therefore "welcomed women as patrons and even offered women roles in which they could act as collaborators," and, because of their postmarital continence, some women even "edged closer to the clergy." "By 200 A.D., the role of women in the Christian churches was quite unmistakable."[11]

Peter Brown offers a telling composite portrait of such women. "She was a woman who had been the head of a Christian household and the mother of Christian children. She frequently controlled property. Her wealth enabled her to impinge on the local church as a benefactress. . . . She was no demure creature"; by the time she embraced continence, she was "mature, financially independent, and already influential." She was able to enjoy "the enviable mobility associated with the apostolic calling" and also to exercise "paraclerical roles," offering advice, instruction, prayer, and prophecy. In the role of prophetess especially she "could sometimes overpower clergy," despite her lack of ordination.[12]

Most important for the present study, with regard to "the intellectual life of the churches," "in any Christian community that boasted upper-class members and well-wishers, women were prominent." As Sarah Pomeroy has indicated, the intellectual, educational, and professional opportunities for aristocratic women had expanded steadily throughout the Hellenistic period, leaving the pederastic Platonic academies in the distant past. The literary-minded "high born Roman matrons" satirized by Juvenal "were following a pattern established by Hellenistic ladies." The well-to-do lay Christian woman profited from this legacy in that, as Brown notes, "the world of the great Christian teachers was close to that of the upper-class study circles of pagan philosophers. Like the philosophers, Christian teachers assumed that women might be present at their gatherings, that they would raise questions, and that they were entitled to receive careful answers." The participation of women in the circle around Origen in the third century, for example, and their prominence within that of Jerome in the fourth, bear this out. "Altogether," Brown concludes, "the Christian intelligentsia of the age took the presence of women, as disciples and patronesses, absolutely for granted."[13]

For the "silent majority" of Christians and the early church leadership alike, the household, and its correlates marriage and the family, defined the life of the church. But this was not the case for all Christians. During the same first three centuries of the Christian era, a quite different and, indeed, opposite Christian tendency emerged which would eventually come to dominate the culture of the Western Church: celibate asceticism. Christian asceticism entailed a thoroughgoing renunciation of settled society, whether pagan, Jewish, or Christian, and, as such, it too offered unprecedented possibilities for women. If the household provided a material, institutional foundation for female participation and influence, the androgynous ideal of celibate Christian asceticism which arose in opposition to the household provided an ideological one.

The Christian ideal of asceticism grew out of the militant apostolic energies of the first Christian generation, who set out to live life anew in the spirit of Christ. In keeping with Christ's teaching, they believed that the Kingdom of God was already in their midst and that by their example the world could be reborn. As Peter Brown has suggested, the physical symbol of such social renewal was the transformation of the body: renunciation of the flesh, especially sexuality (and hence reproduction), constituted at once a rejection of the existing society and the realization in the present of the new Kingdom. "Sexual renunciation might lead the Christian to break the discreet discipline of the ancient city," with its hierarchy of social relations and expectations. "Only by dissolving the household was it possible to achieve the priceless transparency associated with a new creation." The family household would thus be replaced by a community of celibates, who would literally embody a spiritual and social revolution. "Through the drastic gesture of perpetual chastity," Brown writes, they "used their bodies to mock continuity" of the established order, and thereby "announced the imminent approach of a 'new creation.'" In the words of Wayne Meeks, their existence thus symbolized at once "metaphysical rebellion" and "realized eschatology." And their example gave rise to "the great hope which, in all future centuries, would continue to flicker disquietingly along the edges of the Christian church."[14]

If celibacy challenged the household and the perpetuation of the family, it also profoundly challenged the gender categories of late antiquity. As Meeks observed, "in late Hellenism, especially in the period immediately following the consolidation of Rome's imperial power"—which saw the emergence of Christianity—"there were many pressures exerted on the traditional roles of men and women . . . ; the identification of what was properly masculine and properly feminine could no longer be taken for granted, but became the object of controversy. The differentiation of male and female could therefore become an important symbol for the fundamental order of the world, while any modification of the role differences could become a potent symbol of social criticism." The androgynous ideal of Christian asceticism was just such a symbol.[15]

In renouncing their sexual lives, the Christian celibates renounced as well their sexual identities. They thus became an altogether new type of being—a "third race," according to pagan critics. The celibates themselves believed that, in Christ, following Paul's pronouncement to the Galatians, "man is no longer divided—not even by the most fundamental division of all, male and female"; through baptism, "the believers were considered to have recaptured a primal, undifferentiated unity." In their ascetic renunciation, they sought to embody this new unity, "a new genus of mankind," or "the restored original mankind." To this end, they aimed to overcome the demands not only of propriety but of procreation, to become neutered souls beyond both the conventions of gender and the compulsions of sexuality. This quest was reflected in the words of Clement of Alexandria. The Greek philosophers taught continence as a means of rendering instincts subservient to reason, he pointed out, but for Christians, "our ideal is not to experience desire at all." Early ascetic Christians were convinced that, by transforming their bodies through rigorous renunciation of the flesh, they could hope in their lifetime to transcend sexual attraction and achieve the Kingdom of God. They could thus live, men and women together, like the angels, in innocent spiritual communion.[16]

The Christian apologists of the second century, though divided over the relative merits of marriage and celibacy, heralded Christian asceticism, with its emphasis upon sexual renunciation, as the single most distinctive characteristic of the new religion, a powerful symbol of cultic identity. Justin Martyr viewed total chastity as a form of heroism equivalent to martyrdom, and Athenagoras maintained that "remaining in virginity and in the state of a eunuch brings one closer to God." Brown suggests that, since sexual desire defined "a common human condition," sexual renunciation offered a means whereby Christianity could achieve universality. It also had an "elemental simplicity" about it, making it in essence accessible to all, male and female alike. "As Christians, women . . . could achieve reputations for sexual abstinence as stunning as those achieved by any cultivated male." The androgynous ascetic ideal thus held a powerful attraction for women, promising them an unprecedented independence from patriarchal bonds and an equality in the image of God. Some have even suggested that the celibate ideal originated with women, who used it to create for themselves a new social space beyond the confines of the family and marriage. But whether or not women invented it, the androgynous ascetic ideal certainly enabled women as never before to join in community with men outside the family. As with the Christianity of the household, therefore, early ascetic Christianity too was a world with women, a spiritual mingling of the sexes.[17]

The androgynous cast of early-Christian asceticism was apparent already in the apostolic generation. Portrayed in the Gospels as an eschatological family, those who gathered around the apostles included both men and women; though some were married, others were postmarital ascetics and chaste married couples. Among the latter, Paul refers to Priscilla and Aquila, Junia and Andronicus, and Claudia and Linus. In addition, there were women who lacked any apparent attachment to either men or families. Judging from the Pauline letters and the Acts of the Apostles, the new phenomenon of permanently unmarried women had already made its appearance. As JoAnn McNamara suggests, "there were virgins before there were patristic proponents of virginity. . . . The virginal life was only fully sanctioned by orthodox writers after women had made it a practical reality." The "popular piety" of early mixed ascetic communities is reflected in the so-called Apocryphal Gospels, which were written in Syria and Egypt during the second century. The Acts of Paul, Peter, Thomas, Andrew, John, and Xanthippe recount the heroic conversions of women to Christianity, and virginity, in rebellion against family and society. Their experiences emboldened later Christian martyrs, men and women alike, for whom chastity had become emblematic of the new faith. Also portrayed in the Apocryphal Gospels were such chaste couples as Paul and Thecla, Maximilla and Andrew, Thomas and Mygdonia, and Andronicus and Drusiana, who exemplified at once a radical rejection of society and a new type of bond between the sexes.[18]

The Apocryphal Gospels describe a Christian world quite different from that of the household, a "grass-roots movement" which began in the East between Greece and Mesopotamia and spread west to Rome and beyond. "From the second century onward, and almost certainly from an earlier, less well-documented period," Peter Brown has written, "little groups of men and women scattered among the Christian communities throughout the eastern Mediterranean and the Near East." There was considerable diversity in the beliefs and practices of these groups, the Montanists, Marcionites, Encratites, and Gnostics. But they all preached renunciation of the flesh as a means, and a sign, of redemption, and they all embraced men and women together in joint spiritual pursuit. For them all, "renunciation and baptism into the Church declared the power of sex null and void."[19]

The Montanists, "one of the first grass-roots movements in the history of the Church," originated in Phrygia in Anatolia. "Women sat in the highest ranks of the movement"; they taught and prophesied in public and also baptized and conducted the Mass. Among the members of Montanus' immediate circle were Priscilla and Maximilla, who apparently had an influence on the church father Tertullian. In stark contrast to the "household-based core of the Church," Marcian and Encratite leader Tatian "both demanded full sexual abstinence from all baptized Christians," a celibate or at least continent church. The Marcionites, who began their mission in Pontus beside the Black Sea and moved west to Rome, believed that through such renunciation they "attained the world beyond and the resurrection" and became "already equal to the angels." Such views, Brown points out, were not merely idiosyncratic but, rather, "circulated in many churches of

Palestine, Syria, and in parts of Asia Minor, as . . . variants of a well-established 'radical consensus.' " The Marcionites included female priests, prophetesses, and teachers, and their prominence within the movement prompted an attack by Tertullian. "These heretical women—how bold they are! They have no modesty; they are audacious enough to teach, to engage in argument, to perform exorcism, to undertake cures, and maybe even to baptize." Tertullian was equally vigorous in denouncing a movement of young women in Carthage who defiantly stood unveiled in the church, firm in the belief that, in their virginity, they had eclipsed the stigma of womanhood. "I am not veiled because the veil of corruption is taken from me," read the Acts of Thomas.[20]

The Encratites likewise brought continent men and women together in common cause, and their vision was thus a "binocular vision," "an attempt to join male and female perceptions." The followers of Tatian were "quiet little groups of men and women" for whom "baptism had brought an ability to live at ease with each other." Because the power of sexuality had been thereby "disconnected," these proponents of "group celibacy" were able to live and even travel together without fear of temptation. Hence they "could once again stand together as couples, linked in a chaste communion that astonished and appalled observers in this and in all future centuries. . . . By the end of the third century, little groups of continent men and women, called 'the Sons and Daughters of the Covenant,' stood at the core of the married Christian communities in the Syriac-speaking regions of the Near East." Firm in their belief that in their continence they had already transcended the present age, they were not bands of "wild ascetics" but ever-widening "pools of quiet confidence."[21]

The Gnostic Valentinians in Rome and Alexandria also believed that the transcendence of all divisions, including that between the sexes, "was the surest sign that the redemption offered by Christ had come," and, in the sexual terms of their mythological imagery, strove to make the two one by absorbing the inferior female into the superior male. The Apocryphal Gospels similarly speak of celibate women as having become men, a notion later echoed in the church fathers' paeans to virile virgins. But, as Elizabeth Clark has suggested, the experience of women in early ascetic, and even later patristic, circles, belies such misogynist mystification and might rather be labeled "androgynous"; if the ideal of "unisexuality," the symbolic reunification of male and female, was often expressed as a reduction of the female to the male, the practical expression was a close spiritual companionship between men and women in which sexual identity had all but lost its significance. The experience of the "coed" study circles or *didaskaleion*, which formed the core of the Gnostic and other ascetic communities of late antiquity, bears this out. According to Brown, such "small study circles were the powerhouses of the Christian culture of the second and third centuries. The extraordinary intellectual ferment of the period is unthinkable without them." "By claiming that the redeemed had overcome sexual desire," Brown noted, the Gnostics, like other groups, "were able to accept women as equal partners in the intense group-life of a Christian intelligentsia." The mythology of realized eschatology, however it was articulated, made possible an unprecedented "spiritual friendship" between men and women, and upon this basis they together undertook a common intellectual and spiritual, rather than physical, rejuvenation of society.[22]

In addition to the *didaskaleion*, which left a lasting legacy of male-female intellectual companionship, the androgynous ideal gave rise also to another enduring institution: syneiactism or spiritual marriage. Derek Bailey has described it as "the cohabitation of the sexes under the condition of strict continence, a couple sharing the same house, often the same room, and sometimes even the same bed, yet conducting themselves as brother and sister." Such couples apparently believed that "God had already given them the impassibility of the angels," enabling them to cohabit without sin.[23]

The earliest evidence of such arrangements comes from the late-second-century *Similitudes of Hermas*, and subsequent accounts, mostly in the form of attacks, continue into the early Middle Ages. The women in these chaste unions were known as *agapetae* or *virgines subintroductae*, and they were likewise the subject of sustained critical attention. Despite the condemnation of syneiactism by such early bishops as Irenaeus, Cyprian, and Chrysostom, as well as by church councils beginning in the fourth century, the practice continued throughout Christendom. One possible indication of its popular acceptance is the notable omission of canonical strictures against it in penitentials, which otherwise reflected canonical concerns. As Hans Achelis noted in his pioneering study of *virgines subintroductae*, "of one thing we can be sure, there was hardly a church province in ancient Christianity in which spiritual marriages were unknown." One student of the practice in the Celtic Church similarly maintains that the Irish experience "was the continuation of a Christian practice which dates from the origins of Christianity and which was spread throughout the early Church, both in the East and the West." Such chaste unions were common not only among the more radical celibate groups but also among the orthodox, including the clergy in the West, up until the eighth century. Spiritual marriages probably survived thereafter under the cover of double monasteries or under the more disparaging name of "concubinage." The mutual benefits of such arrangements for the couple were both practical and spiritual and varied from place to place and from couple to couple. But, whatever practical advantages had made these unions attractive, the androgynous ideal of sexual transcendence had made them possible. Without it, such intimate heterosexual companionship outside the bounds of normal marriage would have been unthinkable. In the third century, the perhaps quint-essential expression of this ideal was formulated by one of the greatest early-Christian philosophers, Origen.[24]

The son of an Alexandrian Christian martyr, Origen grew up under the protection of Christian ladies, in particular a wealthy woman who had also patronized a famous Gnostic teacher. He later secured the patronage of a former Valentinian, Ambrosius, who lived in continence with his wife, his "pious companion," Marcella, and his sister, Tatiana. With such support, Origen at an early age became the spiritual guide of a "coed" study circle in Alexandria. His work reflected the influence of Plato as well as the myriad movements of early Christianity. Central to his outlook was a compelling belief in the merely transitory nature of the human body, which made it possible for people to overcome their physical "bondage," through ascetic renunciation, and become one with God. "Look now at how you have progressed from being a tiny little human creature on the face of this earth," Origen wrote. "You have progressed to become a Temple of God, and you who were flesh and blood have reached so far that you are a limb of Christ's body."[25]

Inherent in this teaching was the conviction that underlay the androgynous ideal, that sexuality itself could be transcended once and for all. As Peter Brown has explained,

> Origen bequeathed to his successors a view of the human person that continued to inspire, to fascinate, and to dismay all later generations. He conveyed above all a profound sense of the fluidity of the body. Basic aspects of human beings, such as sexuality, sexual differences, and other seemingly indestructible attributes of the

physical body, struck Origen as no more than provisional. . . . Origen was prepared to look at sexuality in the human person as if it were a mere passing phase. It was a dispensable adjunct of the personality that played no role in defining the essence of the human spirit. Men and women could do without it even in this present existence. Human life, lived in a body endowed with sexual characteristics, was but the last dark hour of a long night that would vanish with the dawn. The body was poised on the edge of a transformation so enormous as to make all present notions of identity tied to sexual differences, and all social roles based upon marriage, procreation, and childbirth, seem as fragile as dust dancing in a sunbeam.[26]

Origen apparently practiced what he preached; at age twenty he had himself castrated. Contemporaries believed that he did this to avoid charges of promiscuity between him and his female disciples, but Peter Brown suggests another interpretation consistent with his teaching. Just as celibate women, in their "boycott of the womb," had given up those reproductive capabilities which ancient society used to define womanhood, so Origen determined to give up that which made him a man. Although celibate women were categorized by men as spiritual males, they themselves believed they were, rather, becoming a new type of androgynous being, at once both male and female and neither male nor female. Origen sought to join the ranks of this "third race." "The eunuch was notorious," Brown points out, "because he had dared to shift the massive boundary between the sexes. He had opted out of being male. He was a human being 'exiled from either gender.' " In having himself castrated, Origen became "a walking lesson in the indeterminacy of the body."[27]

For Origen, sexual renunciation was not just a negative act, the repression of sexual drives; it was a positive act, an act of freedom. Virginity stood for the "pre-existing purity of the soul"; it "preserved an identity already formed in a former, more splendid existence and destined for yet further glory." Sexual renunciation, therefore, "meant the assertion of a basic freedom so intense, a sense of identity so deeply rooted, as to cause to evaporate the normal social and physical constraints that tied the Christian to his or her gender." In the work of Origen, then, the androgynous ascetic ideal which arose among the celibate communities of early Christianity had gained an articulate champion. And in the wake of his influence, the notion gained ever wider acceptance, not only at the fringes of the church but within its orthodox core as well.[28]

As Brown noted, the androgynous ascetic ideal of early Christianity gave rise to a "great hope which, in all future centuries, would continue to flicker disquietingly along the edges of the Christian church." At the close of the fourth century, the height of the patristic age, when the church fathers were busy drawing their trenchant distinctions between orthodoxy and heresy, the Priscillian movement in Spain and southern Gaul attracted anxious attention. In 380, "little groups of men and women" withdrew from the city on the eve of great festivals "to hold 'retreats' in mountain villas, under the guidance of inspired, self-styled 'teachers' of the Scriptures." Priscillian himself, ascetic bishop of Avila, settled outside Bordeaux in the household of the widow Delphidius. "Doubtless influenced by the Apocryphal gospels and acts," he preached virginity and continence. For Priscillian, as for earlier ascetics, all division denied the unity of God. "As the most obvious and far-reaching division is that between the sexes, Priscillian tended to deny that there was any significant difference between men and women" and hence stressed their equality in access to instruction and perhaps even ordination.[29]

The movement inspired by Priscillian prompted a violent reaction, which resulted in the executions of both him and his patron on charges of sorcery and immorality. It also led to an intensification of official condemnation of "spiritual friendship" among ascetic men and women. But such strictures were hardly sufficient to snuff out all hope of "realized eschatology." The Manichean Elect, for example, both men and women, took their heroes and heroines from the epics of the Apocryphal Acts and, like the apostles, "walked the roads of Syria together." Moreover, "they brought a touch of the terrible, high freedom, associated with the radical Christianity of Syria, out of its distant homeland and into the streets of Antioch, Carthage, and Alexandria."[30]

As late as the twelfth century, in northern France, the hope continued to flicker. Georges Duby describes a movement of "heretics" in the 1120s in Champagne, Orléans, and Arras who "regarded the clergy as superfluous" and condemned marriage and sex. "As they were preparing for the return of Christ, their ambition was to abolish sex altogether. So they allowed women to join them, treating them as equals and claiming that everyone in their communities lived together as brothers and sisters, in perfect purity and in the caritas that reigned among the angels in heaven." Although it received support from priests still living in concubinage, the movement was condemned as heretical. Critics focused their attention on the prominence of its women; "it was seen by its contemporaries, and represented to them by its enemies, as a kind of feminist movement." But, "above all, the detractors of heresy branded as hypocrisy the heretics' claim to reject sex while living in mixed communities." Finally, at the end of the twelfth century, the sexually mixed Catharist community of Languedoc still reflected the spirit of androgynous asceticism, perhaps because of its possible Manichean origins. Catharist *perfectae* enjoyed great esteem and performed functions similar to those of their male counterparts. "The Catharist faith, by denying the 'reality' of the sexes—as it denied the reality of all life in the flesh—was at least implying an equality between men and women." Thus, as R. I. Moore has shown, an ideal which originated among the earliest Christians persisted at the margins of the church for a millennium, despite centuries of condemnation and persecution.[31]

Within the core of the church also, the ideal took root; conjoined with the household legacy of postmarital celibate female patronage, it fostered a millennium of mixed monastic communities. By the beginning of the fourth century, despite protestations by the marriage-based local leadership of the church, sexual renunciation had become "a widely acclaimed feature of Christian life." Thus, as Peter Brown has observed, "Antony and the monks of the fourth century inherited a revolution, they did not initiate one." Nevertheless, the example of the desert hermits and monastics, heralded in Athanasius' immensely popular *Life of Antony*, had a profound influence upon the lives of Christians in both East and West. At the same time, the legalization of Christianity by the Edict of Milan and Constantine's abrogation of the Augustan laws against celibacy encouraged aristocratic urban Christians as never before to adopt the ascetic spirit.[32]

Foremost among these new ascetics were well-to-do Christian women, both widows and young virgins. "Women with ascetic vocations emerged in upper-class circles, where they had the wealth and prestige needed to make a permanent impact on the Church." These female "household ascetics" formed intense friendships with one another and "coagulated into small groups" for support and study. At the same time, because of their vows of celibacy and especially their wealth and social status, such "ascetic women were free to seek the protection and spiritual guidance from males of any kind—from relatives, from ascetic soul mates, and from men of exceptional insight and learning." Such men became, as Brown suggests, "Origens of a new age" who "gained no small part of their public reputation by giving spiritual guidance to devoted women. . . . It was in such circles that the cultural and spiritual ideals of the *didaskaleion* of the Early Church survived into a harsher age." Thus, at the dawn of monasticism, "an intense sense of spiritual companionship drew male and female ascetics together."[33]

Spiritual companionship between men and women marked the earliest moments of Eastern monasticism, and reflected to some extent the "radical expectations" of the earlier Encratite movement. Hierakas, for example, following Origen, sought to establish within the settled community a federation of cells of continent men and women. Those who opted to abandon the settled society did so also in mixed company. Pachomius, founder of cenobitic (or communal) monasticism, established monastic communities along the Nile for both men and women (including his sister). In a similar fashion, in Cappadocia—where "groups of consecrated, upper-class spinsters were a force to be reckoned with"—Basil of Caesarea and his sister, Macrina, created monastic communities for men and women along the Iris River. For Basil, as for his brother, Gregory of Nyssa, who wrote her biography, the virgin Macrina was the supreme symbol of Christian purity, "the root that had blossomed," an "uncut meadow." From her sheltered piety, moreover, whether in her widowed mother's household or her convent at Annesi, she passed on the culture of the Scriptures. In time, the example of Basil and his sister prompted other groups of men and women to set out together upon the monastic life.[34]

Olympias and Melania the Elder were two other aristocratic ascetic women, from Constantinople, who had a powerful influence on the emergent monastic movement. Both were "great heiresses" and early widows, which gave them the independence and the independent means to become patronesses of monasticism. Melania, granddaughter of a consul, was widowed at twenty-two and went into self-imposed exile, first to Rome and then to Alexandria. She had taken all her portable wealth with her and used it to support monastic settlements outside Alexandria. She then moved on to Jerusalem, where she established and oversaw a monastic community for men and women on the Mount of Olives. "Bishops, monks, and pilgrims from all over the Roman world were supported by her when in Palestine," Brown notes. "By this means, Melania was able to live at the center of the Christian imagination of her age." In this capacity, she became the friend and patron of Jerome's learned companion Rufinus of Aquileia, whose unwavering dedication to Origenist ideals outstripped even that of his colleague. Olympias was the granddaughter of a major politician at the court of Constantine who was raised by a sister of one of Basil's episcopal colleagues. Widowed at twenty with an enormous fortune, she became a deaconess of the Church of Constantinople and used her wealth in support of the church. Renowned for her ascetic piety as well as her money, she founded perhaps the first monastery in Constantinople and, most important for the present subject, became the patroness and "soul mate" of John Chrysostom.[35]

In the West, the prominence of women in the ascetic and monastic movements was even greater than in the East, as Melania the Elder's experience in Rome demonstrated. The fourth-century Italian aristocracy was marked by "a new and assertive alliance between noble women and the Christian clergy." Here was "an ascetic movement whose principal exponents and patrons were noble women," both widows and their virgin daughters. And because of their substantial means, their influence upon the Latin Church was "far out of proportion to their numbers." Moreover, "as distributors of wealth and patrons of individual writers, aristocratic Latin women acted as arbiters of intellectual life to a degree unparalleled in the Greek East." This enabled them also to mix freely and intimately with their chaste male spiritual and intellectual companions, such as the scholar Jerome.[36]

The arrival of Athanasius in Rome following his exile from Alexandria stimulated tremendous interest in monasticism, especially among noble women. One of these women was Marcella, who, together with other senatorial women—Albina and Marcellina, sister of Ambrose of Milan—had established a salon devoted to the study and practice of ascetic Christianity. Jerome came to Rome in 382 after having studied in Antioch and Constantinople and having spent two years in a hermit's cell in Syria. He used his monastic and intellectual reputation to advantage and soon became the spiritual guide for Marcella's circle, which eventually included also the widow Paula and her daughters, Eustochium and Blesilla, as well as several other widows and virgins, Furia, Fabiola, and Asella. They all met together at Marcella's house on the Aventine, which had become a retreat for ascetics. For these women, as Peter Brown suggests, "Jerome adopted the persona of Origen," having translated for them Origen's *Homilies on the Song of Songs*.[37]

In the persona of Origen, Jerome "took for granted the profound identity of the minds of men and women." Moreover, like Origen he had come to believe that "bodies endowed with the sexual characteristics of men and women were ephemeral things . . . that it was possible for 'spiritual' persons to live as if the restraints and perils of the body did not affect them." Hence "they could form companionships based on the meeting of like minds." According to Brown, Jerome adopted this Origenist model of the person "because it enabled him to live at ease with gifted and influential women such as Marcella . . . and . . . Paula." This androgynous ideal also enabled these aristocratic women to take part in the most exciting intellectual enterprise of their day. Just as Melania had mastered Greek and had studied Origen as well as other Christian authors, so Paula and some of the other women had learned Hebrew the better to appreciate the Old Testament. As Elizabeth Clark observed, "when we consider how rare was the knowledge of Hebrew among male churchmen of the fourth century, their accomplishment is truly astounding." According to Brown's assessment, Marcella's Greek was "probably as good as that of Ambrose, and her library as well stocked in up-to-date Greek books, . . . a rarity in fourth-century Rome." Jerome considered Marcella the foremost student of Scripture in Rome, after himself.[38]

Three years after his arrival in Rome, Jerome was driven into exile by men opposed not only to his growing influence but, perhaps more important, to the independence of the ascetic women he served. The spiritual and intellectual bonds established in Rome were not so easily broken, however. Jerome settled in Bethlehem and was soon followed there by Paula and her daughter Eustochium. In Bethlehem, they established a monastic community for men and women and resumed their intellectual labors. A fifth of Jerome's letters are addressed to his female colleagues, in response to their detailed, erudite questions. Moreover, "the constant literary preoccupation with female companionship showed that such practices were common among the privileged expatriates of the Holy Land." "The unbelieving reader may perhaps laugh at me for dwelling so long on the praises of mere women," wrote Jerome. "He had better look on himself as conceited than on me as a fool; I judge merit by mind, not by sex."[39]

The author of the famous Augustinian Rule for monastics similarly corresponded with pious and learned women and, indeed, wrote his Rule for a community of women at Hippo. Recounting the difficulty of his conversion to celibacy after living thirteen years with the woman who bore his son, Jerome's near contemporary Augustine described sexual renunciation, in androgynous terms, as but the formation of a new and more sublime bond between men and women. In his tortured imaginings, celibacy itself came forth as female, to relieve him of his torment.

> On the side to which I turned my face, and which I feared to pass, the chaste majesty of continence disclosed herself. . . . She stretched out to receive and embrace me, her hands full of good examples; children, young girls, youth in abundance, all ages, venerable widows, women grown old in virginity, and continence was not barren in these holy souls: she produced generations of celestial joys, which she owed O Lord to thy conjugal love. And she seemed to say to me, with a sweet and encouraging irony: What! Canst not thou do a thing which is possible to these children, these women?

Augustine's identification of Christian asceticism with women was more than mere sexual sublimation. Like other patristic writings which exalted female virginity as the height of Christian perfection— those of Ambrose, Chrysostom, and Jerome—Augustine's reverie reflected not only the androgynous spirit of early monasticism but also the profound presence of women as patrons and paragons of ascetic culture. It was a presence that would leave its mark upon the monastic movement for centuries to come.[40]

Two · *Revivals*

T HE MEDIEVAL MONASTIC WOMAN, as Derek Bailey suggested, represented a "merger" within the church of the earlier female roles of widow, virgin, and deaconess. "As the Church developed a male-dominated hierarchy," Suzanne Wemple has noted, "monasticism offered a special appeal to women, for it permitted them to retain a degree of influence in the Church and participate actively in the service and worship of God." As in the early church, the position of women in the monastic movement rested upon the household legacy of lay patronage and the enduring spirit of androgynous asceticism. Both together guaranteed not only a continued place for women within the church but also the continued mingling of ascetic men and women within the medieval monasteries, the new centers of education and learning. This proximity of monastic women to monastic men perpetuated the presence and participation of women within the cultural mainstream.[1]

Materially speaking, women's importance within monasticism was grounded upon their possession of inherited fortunes. In the estimate of historian Elizabeth Clark, the power of female monastics as founders and leaders of monastic communities "derived ultimately from their family wealth and status" rather than from any formal offices or rules. The persistence of the androgynous ascetic ideal, moreover, provided ideological legitimation for a continuation of the intellectual and spiritual companionship between men and women which had been cultivated in the *didaskaleion* of late antiquity. The monastic movement provided an important new locus for such companionship, the double monastery. Within this new institutional setting, especially as spiritual marriages and nonconformist practices came under increasing attack from the church, the tradition of the "coed" study groups was carried forth into the Middle Ages.[2]

Although there was considerable variation in their physical structure and social and religious practice, double monasteries were distinguished by the close association of men and women. The men and women lived in adjoining or neighboring houses; they sometimes but not always shared a common church and a common cemetery, followed the same rule, participated together in common services, and obeyed the same leaders—male or female. Double monasteries were not merely a "peripheral phenomenon," as Sharon K. Elkins has pointed out in her study of twelfth-century English monasticism. "Considered alongside other monasteries . . . these houses do not appear as anomalous as formerly assumed. . . . In certain regions and during certain decades, most of the new religious establishments for women also included men."[3]

In practical terms, the existence of double monasteries reflected the need of female monastics for the services of male priests, to celebrate the Mass, and for male protection in troubled times. But they also reflected the sustained belief in the androgynous ideal, which surfaced again and again in the wake of monastic revivals. In her study of double monasteries, Mary Bateson noted that "double monasteries arose in many countries and at many times as the natural sequel to an outburst of religious enthusiasm." Such enthusiasm revitalized androgynous ascetic aspirations, the "primitive idea" of the early church. "With almost all the great movements of spiritual revival, there was a recrudescence of the conception of a purer form of chastity in the shape of a fresh development of this particular method of monastic organization." In Bateson's view, double monasteries were "moral experiments" which "could live only in the purest spiritual atmosphere" and entailed a "struggle after a particular form of chastity," a transcendence of sexual division.[4]

Double monasteries emerged in the very first wave of monastic enthusiasm. A close association of the houses for men and women marked the monastic communities established by Pachomius and his sister in Egypt, Basil and Macrina in Cappadocia, Melania the Elder and Rufinus in Jerusalem, and Paula and Jerome in Bethlehem. In the East this tendency was retarded by the combined resistance of the church and the empire, which viewed it as a threat to both traditional marriage and monastic purity. In 529, the Emperor Justinian issued decrees calling for the abolition of double monasteries; they "forbade all [men] who dwelt in monasteries with nuns to converse with them" and mandated that "the sexes were to be separated" and that property held in common be divided. Priests were to be appointed to celebrate Mass for the nuns "but should not dwell with them." Although the establishment of double monasteries apparently continued in the

East, even as late as the fourteenth century, they remained a peripheral and relatively insignificant phenomenon.[5]

If double monasteries foundered in the East, they flourished in the West. "In the West, there was no systematic opposition from church and state as there was in the East." Compared with the Eastern Empire, which was within easy reach of the imperial and ecclesiastical authorities in Constantinople, the West was a frontier, a "wild" West beyond the reach of the centers of imperial power. "It may well be doubted," Bateson opined, "whether [double monasteries in the West] would be suppressed as a consequence of the Byzantine Emperor's decree." The absence of an all-powerful Western secular authority, moreover, was coupled with the relative weakness of the Latin Church. As R. W. Southern explained, "the affairs of the Church [in the West] received very little direction from Rome. Monasteries and bishoprics were founded, and bishops and abbots were appointed by lay rulers without hindrance or objection." This relative absence of church and state authority, and the disarray engendered by the great barbarian migrations, encouraged in the West an institutional independence and diversity unknown in the East, and provided a fertile ground for "moral experiments."[6]

Barbarian society, so called, also fostered a relative independence for the propertied clerical and warrior classes from centralized authority, an independence rooted in the landowning family. This familial context, moreover, provided wives, daughters, and widows of warriors and married priests with considerable power and influence, especially as changes in Germanic law guaranteed women greater rights to inherit, own, and administer property. Visigothic and Burgundian laws were especially liberal in this regard—which accounts for the sustained prominence of women among the propertied classes of southern France and Spain—but Frankish, Alemannian, and Bavarian laws also gave wives and widows enlarged property rights. Thus, as historian David Herlihy has observed, "women appear with fair consistency as land owners and land managers and apparent heads of their families at all times and places in the early medieval period," and, as a result, "social customs as well as economic life were influenced by [their] prominence."[7]

Property ownership and control afforded some women considerable influence within the church. David Herlihy has illuminated "the prominence that women could achieve amid a largely nicholaite [married] clergy," especially as clerics sought advantageous liaisons with propertied women. More important, perhaps, propertied pious lay women patronized the church and, adopting celibacy, became foundresses and abbesses of monasteries. Such upper-class and religious women, moreover, on the continent as well as in Ireland, were known for their "knowledge of letters" and were even viewed as "repositories of literacy." The combination of their wealth, their virtue, and their intellectual abilities gave these women a formidable presence within the church and guaranteed them the enduring respect, and the spiritual and intellectual companionship, of their male counterparts. Institutionally, such companionship spawned, and was sustained by, the double monastery.[8]

Although it was not the sole source of double monasteries, as once was believed, Ireland nevertheless provided fertile ground for their development and played an important role in their subsequent proliferation elsewhere. Ireland had escaped Roman domination and, hence, never knew "the rationalizing influence of Roman administration and law." Irish Christianity, moreover, was "a Christianity which . . . was quite independent of the Roman hierarchy," its spirit "dominated both morally and administratively by monasticism rather than by clericalism." Irish monastics were renowned for their independent, nomadic, missionary zeal as well as for an intense, uncompromising asceticism. These "primitive" characteristics of Irish Christianity were coupled with another: spiritual marriage between male and female celibates. As one student of the subject has noted, "*syneiactism* was a common phenomenon in Celtic Christianity." The combination of a relative independence from centralized authority, a spirit of heroic asceticism, and a tradition of spiritual companionship between men and women made Ireland, in Mary Bateson's view, an "environment . . . peculiarly favorable" to the development of double monasteries. Herbert Workman has suggested also that such institutions flourished in Ireland "because they were a survival of the old clan system when men and women alike belonged to the same religious community."[9]

If the Irish of the early-medieval period were known for their independence, their ascetic rigor, and their evangelical earnestness, they were known above all for their great learning. In this period, Ireland "was a veritable land of scholars. . . . Her monasteries were world renowned as institutes of learning" and for centuries drew a stream of students from England and the continent. Here alone in the Christian West, scholarship had continued uninterrupted from the fourth century, and Irish scholars were unrivaled in their command of Greek and their knowledge of classical and early church literature. Irish double monasteries carried forth this learned tradition, for women as well as men.[10]

The most famous of the Irish double monasteries was Kildare, established by St. Brigit in the fifth century. Like the monasteries instituted by men, it served as both a religious house and an educational center. According to a study by Mary Pia Heinrich, Kildare "was renowned as an institution of learning and was probably a double monastery." Brigit herself provided counsel to eminent leaders of the Irish Church, and abbots as well as saints sought instruction at Kildare. In the south, the "Brigit of Munster," St. Ita, established the double monastery of Cluain-Credhuil, which was also well known as an educational center. St. Brendan, St. Cummian, St. Fachtna, and the abbot Mochaemoch all received instruction there. No doubt because of the existence of such institutions, and hence the proximity of women to the Irish centers of learning, women in Ireland found opportunities "to acquire an education corresponding to the status of Irish intellectual culture during this period."[11]

Given their experience in Ireland, it is hardly surprising that, when the great Irish missionaries traveled to spread the pious and learned teachings of Irish monasticism, they shared also an enthusiasm for double monasteries and for the spiritual and intellectual companionship of women. "Irish monks seem to have greatly promoted the establishment of double monasteries on the continent," Heinrich, like many others, noted. And, in the spirit of Irish monastic tradition, they carried their message to women as well as to men. St. Columban, for example, whose sixth-century mission to Gaul sparked a monastic revival on the continent, "did not harbor prejudices against women. Instead of shunning their company, he sought their friendship. Instead of emphasizing their impurity, he recognized their spiritual equality." His example "inspired a new attitude toward women among his Frankish collaborators and disciples" which paved the way for a golden age of medieval "coeducation."[12]

It is likely that double monasteries existed in Gaul before Columban's arrival. The first monastery in Gaul was established by Martin of Tours and Hilary of Poitiers in 360, but it was not until the sixth century, following the conversion of the Merovingian King Clovis in 496, that monasticism began to flourish. Women played a central role in sixth-century monastic development, beginning with Clovis' wife, Clothilde, who is credited with having secured Clovis' conversion.

"Through her efforts," Lina Eckenstein wrote in her study of women under monasticism, "the Franks became the first tribe to embrace orthodox Christianity [and] many Frankish monastic foundations and churches owed their existence to her generous and ready good-will," including the double houses of Les Andelys and Chelles. After Clovis' death, Clothilde herself retired to the abbey of St. Martin of Tours. Caesarius of Arles and his sister, Caesarea, established adjoining monastic houses for men and women in 506, and Caesarius wrote the first Western monastic rule for women ascetics. St. Radegund left her husband, King Clothacar, to establish the Abbey of the Holy Cross in Poitiers in 566, a female house separated only by the town wall from St. Mary's monastery for men. Radegund's "spiritual companion," the poet Fortunatus, was probably a monk of St. Mary's and, according to Mary Bateson, was "undoubtedly the teacher of the nuns in the study of poetry." The existence of early Frankish double monasteries is indicated by the sixth-century conciliar legislation forbidding the close association of houses for men and women.[13]

Monastic growth in the Frankish kingdom took place not in the urban centers, under episcopal dominion, but, rather, in rural areas, under the auspices of local elites. Here monasticism became "seigneurial, agrarian, aristocratic and royal," in the words of Friedrich Prinz, and thus independent and diverse. "The monastic rules of this primitive epoch were very numerous," according to Heinrich. "It might, in fact, be said that there were as many rules as monasteries. Founders enjoyed an absolute liberty in the selection of rules for their monastic establishment." In this environment, moreover, aristocratic women were able to wield considerable influence over monastic development. As historian Suzanne Wemple observed, "in the Merovingian period, when both royal and ecclesiastical authority had been feeble and decentralized, women could exercise considerable power as members of the landed aristocracy and as heads of monasteries." The monastic revival of the seventh century, which was sparked by the arrival of the ascetic missionaries from Ireland, reflected both the independent aristocratic initiative and the prominence of women characteristic of the Frankish kingdom. The intense asceticism brought by Columban and his associates contributed decisively to this social mix, creating a remarkably fertile environment for the full flowering of double monasteries.[14]

Columban arrived in Gaul in 591 and immediately established the famous monastery at Luxeuil, which became the educational center of the Irish movement. Before too long, through the efforts of Frankish bishops and abbots trained at Luxeuil, the androgynous ascetic spirit of the Irish began to spread among the Franks. These influential men

> cultivated spiritual friendships with women and sought feminine cooperation in building a network of monasteries throughout the kingdom. As a result of their efforts, men and women began to work together in partnership, promoting the contemplative life and discovering a practical solution to the problem of instituting female communities outside the cities. To protect nuns, help them run their vast establishments, and provide sacerdotal services, these enterprising men and women attached a contingent of monks to some of the newly founded communities. They created thus a new institution, the double monastery, which had some precedents in the East and in Ireland. They also set up separate, affiliated communities for men and women in close proximity to each other.

Double monasteries were, according to Eckenstein, "the most popular type of establishment for women in the seventh century," in both the English and Frankish kingdoms. Practice varied, but nuns and monks typically occupied separate living quarters and shared common functions in the scriptoria, in the schools, and during the divine service. Women performed administrative, spiritual, and even some "quasi-sacerdotal" functions. Usually the double monasteries were directed by an abbess.[15]

The double monastery of Brie was founded by Burgundofara, who had been converted as a child by Columban himself and had taken her vows from the abbot Eustace, Columban's successor at Luxeuil. Living with her at Brie were her brother Chagnoald, a former monk at Luxeuil; Waldebert, a future abbot of Luxeuil; Jonas, writer of Columban's life; and other monks. The houses of men and women were ruled by an abbess, who heard confession and had the power to excommunicate. Bateson notes that, according to Jonas' biographies of the nuns, "no distinction between the sexes was recognized; the abbess treated male and female equally." The double monastery of Remiremont was established by Romaric, a former monk at Luxeuil; here the abbess Mactefeld governed the women and the abbot Amatus directed the men. Donatus, a disciple of Abbot Eustace of Luxeuil, created the double monastery of Besançon for his mother, Flavia. The first abbess, Gauthstruda, was succeeded in turn by Flavia and her daughter. The convent of Jouarre was founded by two brothers, Ado and Dado, disciples of Columban, for their cousin Theodechild, who had been a nun at Brie. It was closely associated with Rebais, a monastery for men, and the two houses jointly attracted monks and nuns from Ireland and England as well as France.[16]

Following her conversion by the abbot Eustace of Luxeuil, Salaberga established the double monastery at Laon. Although the houses for men and women were some distance apart, they were both governed by the abbess Salaberga, who was succeeded by the nun Anstrude. The monastery of Chelles, instituted in the sixth century by Queen Clothilde, was re-established by Queen Bathilde in 662 and became one of the most famous of double monasteries, under the abbess Bertile. According to Bateson, "many English came to Chelles to learn the discipline of a double monastery." At Nivelles, under the abbess Gertrude—daughter of the foundress, Ita—"many Irish and English monks congregated" and "the nuns were noted for their learning, and imitated monks in wearing the tonsure." The double monastery at Soissons was originated by Ebroin, mayor of the palace of Neustria, and his wife, Leodutrud; the one at Montierender was founded by a former monk of Luxeuil, Bercarius, and his niece Waltilda; at Hasnon, "a brother and sister presided over their respective sexes." Other double monasteries were established in the seventh century, among them Pavilly, Chamalières, Fécamp, Vienne, Hamay, and Maubeuge.[17]

Many of these double houses were distinguished as centers of learning and education, for women as well as for men. The double monasteries served as "coeducational schools," as Suzanne Wemple observed, and, as such, they carried on the tradition of the early-Christian study circles. Abbess Gertrude of Nivelles, a distinguished teacher herself, obtained books from Rome and invited Irish monks to teach her and her sisters "chant, poetry, and Greek." Abbess Aldegonde of Maubeuge was known for her "rare knowledge of sacred learning," and Abbess Anstrude of Laon "was famous for her learning and teaching." Abbess Bertile of Chelles was widely renowned as a teacher; her biographer noted that "kings from across the seas . . . beseeched her to send her disciples as teachers and to establish similar monasteries for men and women." At the same time, men and women from Britain as well as the Frankish kingdom flocked to Chelles for instruction, among them two future Frankish kings, Dagobert III and Theodoric IV, the Northumbrian Princess Hereswitha, and, later, the sister and daughters of Charlemagne.[18]

The educational and intellectual opportunities for Frankish women in this period owed much to the existence of the double monastery, which guaranteed a female presence within the centers of learning. Heinrich, for example, noted "the special benefit that a community of women might derive from the contiguity of a community of men, especially if the latter abounded in educational opportunities." "It is a noteworthy fact," she observed, "that the flourishing period of double monasteries in Gaul coincided with that of feminine eminence in learning." And the same was to be true elsewhere: "feminine culture itself, apparently, shifted with the movement [of double monasteries] from Gaul to England and from thence to Germany."[19]

As in southern Gaul, the property laws and customs of Anglo-Saxon England favored aristocratic and royal women and accounted for their prominence. "The evidence which has survived from Anglo-Saxon England," Doris Stenton noted, "indicates that women were more nearly equal companions of their husbands and brothers than at any other period before the modern age." In her study of women in Anglo-Saxon England, Christine Fell has confirmed this assessment. A dowry, or "morgengifu," Fell notes, was given by the husband to his wife, and she retained "personal control over it, to give away, to sell, or bequeath." Wives also shared the joint property of the marriage and, upon its dissolution, retained half of it.[20]

The laws thus recognized "an element of financial independence and responsibility in the wife's status." Inheritance laws, moreover, did not follow primogeniture and thus did not give preference to male heirs; they allowed daughters to inherit and also reflected considerable concern for the economic well-being of widows. From wills, Fell explains, "we get the clearest indication that women—wives and daughters—inherited and held property independently from husband or father. . . . It is clear that within the legal framework the rights of maidens, wives and widows were protected, and that women in the upper classes at least were potentially powerful." Records of gifts of land make it clear as well that women "moved in the world of landed property with as much assurance and as full rights as the men of their family," and that they were able "not only to inherit, . . . but also to dispose of estates and goods according to their own wishes." The elite women of Anglo-Saxon England were thus in an excellent position to foster and gain from the seventh-century ascetic religious revival.[21]

"From the very earliest times," Angela Lucas noted, "women are known to have played a part in the evangelizing of England." In the south, the Frankish Christian Bertha, daughter of the Merovingian king, played an important role; she married King Ethelbert of Kent in 597 and promptly converted him to Christianity. Shortly thereafter, with their blessings, Pope Gregory's missionary St. Augustine arrived in Kent and established Canterbury as a base for his mission. In the north, Ethelberg, the daughter of Bertha and Ethelbert, played a key role through her marriage in 625 to King Edwin of Northumbria, who was baptized two years later. Whereas in the south the movement was influenced by Rome through Augustine, in the north it was influenced by Ireland through Aidan. A monk of Columba's famous Celtic monastery on the island of Iona, Aidan was brought to Northumbria by King Edwin's successor, Oswald, who had himself spent some years at Iona. Under Oswald's auspices, Aidan established the monastery of Lindisfarne, which became a famous missionary center, episcopal see, and monastic school in the Irish tradition. It was this Irish influence which spawned the earliest double monasteries in England, and it was here, in Bateson's view, that the institution realized its "full perfection."[22]

Hilda, Edwin's grandniece, had been baptized with him in 627 at the age of thirteen. Her sister, Hereswitha, had left England to become a nun at Chelles and, apparently, Hilda intended to do the same. But she was persuaded by Aidan to remain in England and promote monasticism there. She became abbess at Hartlepool, established earlier by the Irish Princess Heiu, and then founded the double monastery at Whitby. King Oswy of Northumbria, whose wife, Enfleda, dedicated their daughter, Elfleda, to the religious life after his victory over the heathen Penda, placed her under Hilda's charge and provided the money and land to build the new monastic community. Hilda organized the monastery along Irish lines and followed the Rule of Columban. According to Bateson, the men and women were required to live communally, sharing all property, and in accordance with a strict ascetic regimen "after the example of the primitive church."[23]

Hilda's monastery at Whitby became an important educational as well as political center of Northumbria and, indeed, of England as a whole. One writer has described Whitby as "the most noted center of learning and culture in Britain." According to Bede, five future bishops received their education at Whitby, including Wilfrid of York. Montalembert suggested that the monks and nuns knew some Greek as well as Latin, most likely because of the Irish influence. As a center of literary activity, Whitby is perhaps best known as the home of the celebrated poet Caedmon, whom Hilda befriended and patronized. Nicholson wrote that the monastery "played a major intellectual role in a newly literate society," alongside such male houses as Canterbury, Jarrow, Wearmouth, and Malmesbury. As a royal monastery, Whitby was visited often by princes and kings as well as by bishops, priests, and missionaries. Attesting to its political significance is the fact that Whitby was chosen as the site of the historic Synod of Whitby in 664, at which controversial differences of practice between the Roman and Irish churches (such as the dating of Easter) were resolved in favor of Rome. (Hilda herself sided with the Irish.) After Hilda's death, leadership at Whitby was passed first to Enfleda and then to her daughter, Elfleda. According to Eckenstein, Bede's accounts of English monasteries indicate "how natural he felt it to be that the rule of a settlement should pass from mother to daughter," and that it was the Anglo-Saxon custom for double monasteries to be headed by an abbess.[24]

Another important English double monastery was Barking, founded by the bishop of London, Earconwald, and his sister Ethelburg, who became the first abbess. Ethelburg was succeeded by Hildelith, who had received her monastic training in France. Barking's reputation as an intellectual center is associated with the scholar and bishop Aldhelm. Aldhelm had studied under the Irish scholar Maidulf at Malmesbury and at Canterbury under Archbishop Theodore and Abbot Hadrian, knew Greek, and was described by Bede as a "wonder of erudition." Aldhelm's celebrated writings on virginity were addressed to the nuns of Barking, whom he instructed and befriended. According to Aldhelm, the women at Barking knew, in addition to sacred literature, the liberal arts, ancient law, history, and poetry, among other things; he addressed them not as inferiors but as his sisters and "scholarly pupils." Eckenstein noted that, as with the early Jerome, "the interest Aldhelm took in women was so great that posterity pictured him as continually in their society."[25]

Another seventh-century double monastery was created at Coldingham, by King Oswy's sister Ebba, who had been veiled by Aidan's successor, Finan. The monk Cuthbert, future bishop of Lindisfarne, spent time at Coldingham instructing the monks and nuns; in keeping with the ancient spirit of androgynous asceticism, Nicholson noted, "Cuthbert's sanctity was never threatened by the women with whom he was so friendly." Abbess Ebba was herself the teacher of Ethelreda, the foundress and first abbess of the double monastery at Ely, with which we began our exploration.[26]

Ethelreda, the daughter of King Anna of East Anglia, was married to King Ecquith of Northumbria, Oswy's son and successor. Her sister Sexburga had founded the double monastery on Sheppey and her two other sisters had become nuns at the Frankish double monastery at Brie. Eager to leave her husband for the monastic life herself, Ethelreda befriended Wilfrid, the archbishop of York, and gave him a large gift of land in return for his providing her with the veil and hence freedom from her marriage. Wilfrid, who had himself been educated under Abbess Enfleda at Whitby, sent Ethelreda to Ebba's monastery at Coldingham. But since Coldingham was still within her husband's domain, she soon fled south to Ely, land given her as dowry by her first husband, Tunberht, and here, in 673, joined by the priest Huna, she established her double monastery. Upon her death just six years later, she was succeeded by her sister Sexburga, foundress of the monastery on Sheppey. As the cushions on the pews of Ely Cathedral still testify, Sexburga was followed by her daughter, Ermenhilda, a former nun of Sheppey, and then by *her* daughter, the influential Werburga. According to later chroniclers, "other abbesses followed Werburga," until Ely was sacked by the Danes in the second half of the ninth century. Ethelreda's example, meanwhile, inspired two other Northumbrian queens, Cyneburg and Cuthburg, to found double houses, at Castor and Wimbourne.[27]

Wimbourne Monastery in Dorset was one of the last houses to be established during this golden age of double monasteries; it was founded in the eighth century by Queen Cuthburg, who had earlier left her husband, King Aldfrith, to become a nun at Barking, and was headed by Abbess Tetta. Wimbourne is perhaps best known as the place from which Winfrith, or Boniface, solicited assistance and recruited companions for his mission in Germany. While in England, Boniface had taught both men and women at his monastery at Nursling, and, as a missionary in Germany, he corresponded with women at several monasteries. The abbess Bucge, a former student of his at Nursling, and Abbess Eadburg of Minster at Thanet provided him with books, and Lioba and Walpurga of Wimbourne joined him as his evangelical companions in Germany. Boniface's correspondence attests to the intellectual abilities and accomplishments of such women. Moreover, as in Aldhelm's writings for the women of Barking, the tone of Boniface's correspondence "is rarely that of instructor to pupil; it is that of brother to sister." There is "no hint whatsoever of the patronizing tone concerning the inferior abilities and status of women" characteristic of a later period. It was this spirit of Anglo-Saxon monasticism, the legacy of earlier Irish and Frankish traditions and the androgynous ascetic ideal of the early church, that Boniface and his male and female companions initially carried with them to Germany.[28]

Several double monasteries had already been established in Germany before Boniface's arrival, at Säckingen, Babinchrora, and Pfalzel. Abbess Adela of Pfalzel had corresponded with Elfleda of Whitby in the seventh century. But the full development of the institution in Germany was the work of Boniface's disciples in the eighth century. The two best known of these houses were Heidenheim and Bischofsheim, headed by Walpurga and Lioba, respectively. Heidenheim was founded in 752 by Walpurga and her brother Wunnibald, also a missionary in Germany, along the lines of Wimbourne. It was ruled by brother and sister together until Wunnibald's death, at which time, at Boniface's request, Walpurga was made abbess of both houses, in the Anglo-Saxon manner. According to one authority, the monastery became an educational center and "soon became famous as a center of culture." Bischofsheim was founded by Boniface's companion Lioba, whose house was in close association with Boniface's monastery at Fulda (where she was buried). Although it is uncertain that this was a double monastery, Bateson suggests that "it is natural to expect that the system to which they had been accustomed at Wimbourne would be used by them abroad."[29]

The distinguished double monasteries of the seventh and eighth centuries fell into decline and all but disappeared in the following centuries, in the wake of Viking invasions and a succession of monastic reform movements. Although no longer a part of the monastic mainstream, double monasteries reappeared briefly during the religious revival of the twelfth century. The powerful new Cistercian Order was the major institutional outgrowth of this revival, but other new orders emerged as well. And like the earlier episodes of religious enthusiasm, this twelfth-century spiritual reawakening provided fertile ground for moral experimentation.

The Order of Fontrevault was founded at the start of the century by Robert d'Abrissel, an itinerant preacher from the Loire Valley in France. Robert's preaching attracted a following of both men and women, the women including, in the words of Robert's biographer, "rich and poor, widows and virgins, old and young, prostitutes and man-haters." Robert believed that "women should live with men" but "scrupulously, without scandal." Accordingly, Fontrevault was from the outset an order of both monks and nuns; its abbeys were communities of both sexes, headed by an abbess, whom the monks were sworn to obey. Within a generation, the Order of Fontrevault had spread throughout northern France and England, and became "a refuge for women from the greatest families."[30]

Norbert of Prémontré founded the Premonstratensian Order in 1120 and, initially, also created double monasteries, though headed by men rather than women. The Premonstratensian Order owed much to its female members, "from whom, or on whose behalf, it had received a large part of its property." Nevertheless, here the moral experiment was short-lived. Three years after Norbert's death in 1134, the double-monastery organization was abandoned, and by the end of the century the Order was no longer admitting women.

As Sharon Elkins has demonstrated, a variety of forms of mixed monastic communities emerged in twelfth-century England. Perhaps the most striking example of such collaboration between celibate men and women was the Order of Gilbertines in the north. Like the first Cistercians in France, Gilbert of Sepringham was the son of nobility, destined for the life of a knight; instead he went to study on the continent, began a school for boys and girls, and then became a priest in the service of the bishop of Lincoln. Inspired by the rigorist ideals of the Cistercians, Gilbert originally intended to establish a monastery for men. But, like Jerome in Rome, Gilbert found his only disciples to be women. Thus he created his house for them, soon adding a contingent of lay sisters and brothers. He attempted to gain support for his effort from the Cistercians, but they rejected him because his monastery included women; to provide priestly services for his community, he therefore added a group of male Augustinians. By the time of Gilbert's death in 1188, fifteen hundred Gilbertines lived in nine houses for both sexes and four for males only.[31]

As was the case with the moral experiments of the other orders, it was not long before this mixing of the sexes aroused suspicion and hostility. Unlike the Premonstratensians, however, the Gilbertines vigorously defended their practices and even went on the offensive, boldly proclaiming their vision in terms strikingly reminiscent of the declarations of ascetic Christians a thousand years earlier. The Gilbertines insisted upon the "apocalyptic meaning" of their daring arrangement and provided an "eschatological justification" of their efforts. Their order constituted "a new creation," "an apocalyptic sign" which "signalled the beginning of a new age"; their mixed celibate communities offered "a foretaste of the coming of the Kingdom." As Paul had declared to the Galatians, the Gilbertines announced that they had achieved "a marvelous unity" before God in which "all lived as one." In the words of the Gilbertine author of Gilbert's life, "there young men and young girls, the old and the young, will praise the name of the Lord, because all ages, every condition, and both sexes exalt not their own but the name of the Lord alone." "With images of the millennial kingdom," Elkins observed, "the Gilbertines propounded an ideological justification for their distinctive way of life." It was a way of life a thousand years in the making, a way of life in which men and women moved history together.[32]

Given the evangelical enthusiasm of the previous century, as Elkins points out, the "nuns and sisters of the early thirteenth century had no reason to expect that their monasteries would cease to exist." Nor did the early-medieval abbesses before them, the proud bearers of an eight-hundred-year tradition, given the world to which they had grown accustomed. In retrospect, Suzanne Wemple has written, "it is tempting to speculate on what would have happened if the independent forms of female monasticism had been allowed to grow. . . . What kind of creativity might have burst forth from the communities of women if their members had not been . . . isolated from the mainstream of religious, political and intellectual life." But hindsight is the privilege of those who write the history, not those who live it. These women did not foresee, nor perhaps could they have, that a world without women would ultimately take hold of Western culture for a thousand years.[33]

Part Two

A WORLD
WITHOUT
WOMEN

Three · *Saints: The Ascent of Clerical Asceticism*

A WORLD WITHOUT WOMEN did not simply emerge, it was constructed. It did not follow inevitably from the inherited patriarchal norms of pagan and Jewish society, with their assumptions of female pollution and women's subordination to men, much less from some inexorable logic of misogynistic Aristotelian discourse. Rather, it was brought about through the rise of clerical asceticism within the church. As we have seen, though early Christianity no doubt reflected ancient traditions and ideas, it also held out an eschatological promise of gender equality and spiritual companionship which was seized upon by many Christians in their pursuit of new social relations. This ambiguous potential of the early church is well reflected in the contradictory statements of St. Paul. On the one hand, in the interest of attracting a broad following, he announces the transcendence of social divisions, including those between the sexes; on the other, in the interest of unity and order, he admonishes church members to adhere to the norms of established authority, including the strict subordination of women to men. This mixed message was exploited by different people for different, and indeed contradictory, purposes during the early-Christian centuries. Beginning in the second century, however, with the emergence of clerical asceticism, we can identify certain incipient institutional and ideological developments which would not only reinforce the second side of this contradiction at the expense of the first, but would ultimately overcome the contradiction altogether in a world without women.[1]

It has been suggested that a hardened and hostile attitude toward women within the church resulted from a change in the composition of its membership in the second century, with a shift from lower to middle class, and with the influx of Hellenized Jews, since both populations upheld the traditional patriarchal patterns of female subordination. At the same time, in the face of persecution and by means of persecution, leaders of the church struggled to formulate a coherent and unifying Christian identity and to consolidate their own position within pagan as well as Christian society. In both regards, by the mid-second century the role of women in the church had become a focal point of their effort and hence, in Elaine Pagels' words, "explosively controversial." Out of this struggle, there emerged not only a powerful new ecclesiastical institution and a canon of orthodoxy which pre-scribed the Christian woman's proper place, but also a new and differ-ent social caste—an orthodox ascetic male clergy—intent upon remaking the world in its own peculiar image.[2]

The remarkable expansion and diversity of Christian communities during the first two centuries confronted church leaders with a serious internal challenge as they sought to withstand episodic but intense persecution from without. "Since to profess Christianity was still sus-pect and potentially dangerous throughout the Roman Empire, many Christian churches owed their coherence and their survival to the astuteness and courage of their leaders, the bishops." At the same time, the bishops and clergy demanded greater unity and discipline on the part of their beleaguered flock and struggled to establish and extend their authority, to forge a tighter hierarchical organization, a common doctrine of belief, and an enforceable code of behavior. En route to his trial and execution in Rome, Bishop Ignatius of Antioch urged all Christians "to stand together under persecution and to main-tain unanimous loyalty to the clergy." "In a word," Henry Chadwick noted, in the eyes of church leaders, "the central issue was that of authority."[3]

According to historian Elizabeth Fiorenza, the second century saw the beginning, in prescription if not yet in actual reality, of a shift "from charismatic and communal authority to an authority vested in local officers who . . . absorb not only the teaching authority of the prophet and apostle but also the decision-making power of the com-munity." "We ought to regard the bishop as the Lord himself," Ignatius insisted. During the next three centuries, these bishops, embattled against both pagan persecution without and rival Christian leaders within, "came to assume responsibility for specific areas, or dioceses, a pattern," Pagels reminds us, "modeled on the organization of the Roman army."[4]

In this effort to strengthen the Christian movement against the perils of pagan persecution and, not incidentally, their power within it, the bishops spent much of their energies defining and enforcing "orthodoxy" (right thinking) against what they came to call "heresy" (literally, choice). "To the bishops, nonconformists and dissidents, even when they seemed to be sincere Christians intent on striking out on their own spiritual paths, were dangerous to the movement." The notion of heresy, one scholar has suggested, defined "an entirely new kind of internal enemy, invented by Christianity," which made the persecuted church leadership persecutors in their own right. It probably originated, according to Peter Brown, among the second-century apologists, perhaps with Justin Martyr. Within a diverse and divisive Christian movement, "one group, connected with the bishops and the clergy, wished to present itself as representing the 'Great Church.' They claimed not only that they alone had preserved the authentic teachings of Christ . . . but also that they represented the views of an overwhelming majority of 'right-thinking' believers."[5]

The orthodox leadership maintained that they alone stood in the order of apostolic succession and that their authority was thus divinely ordained. They thus formulated the Peterine Doctrine, the "concept of the monolithic church, universally extended in space and with unbroken continuity in time, unanimous in its possession of immutable revelation." From this posture, the leaders labored to distinguish between orthodox and heretical texts, teachings, and practices and, in the process, condemned and destroyed many of the otherwise flourishing Christian sects. Like Justin Martyr and Ignatius of Antioch, Irenaeus of Lyons and Clement of Alexandria vigorously attacked the Valentinian Gnostics, the Montanists, Encratites, and Marcionites whose faith in immediate redemption through renunciation had led them to believe that "they no longer needed the bishop or the clergy." Denouncing the ascetic rigorists who proclaimed the possibility of such "instant redemption," Hippolytus of Rome maintained that the "mediated authority of the church" and not the "immediate inspiration" of the Montanists was essential to salvation, whereas Clement insisted upon "the long, moral, and intellectual discipline required of every Christian," under strict clerical authority and guidance.[6]

By the latter half of the second century, sexual renunciation had already begun to be seen, by pagan observers and Christian apologists alike, as a distinguishing mark of Christian identity. While they extolled the virtue of Christian purity to defend their movement from slanderous propaganda and to distinguish it from pagan society, however, within the church the orthodox leadership still defended the superiority of marriage and the household against the rigorist claims of the ascetic "heretics." The emergence of episcopal authority at the expense of prophetic authority, and the gradual replacement of the "house church" by the "Church as household of God," Fiorenza emphasized, resulted in a "patriarchal" restriction of church leadership to "male heads of households." Intent upon retaining the devotion, and thus the material support, of married householders and upholding the authority of married clergy, the bishops defended the sanctity of marriage and the patriarchal family against "heretical" demands for clerical and lay celibacy as well as the leadership of women.[7]

Irenaeus, in his polemics against the Marcionites and Valentinians, dismissed the appeals of those ascetic teachers and prophets who claimed to have transcended desire, whereas Clement wrote against the Encratites and Gnostics in order "to block the rise of a dangerous mystique of continence." These orthodox bishops, Peter Brown has argued, were engaged "in a social struggle . . . fought on the issue of marriage and continence within the Church. Insistence on continence would have opened the leadership of the Church to very different figures from those for whom Clement wrote"—to ambitious lower-class talents rather than rich and cultured heads of families, to continent aristocrats who arrogantly disdained the pedestrian lives of the married clergy, and, most important of all, to women.[8]

In their conservative defense of the Christian patriarchal household, the orthodox bishops condemned the male heretical teachers not only for their ascetic ways and their eschatological excesses, but also for their iconoclastic relations with women. The close companionship of men and women in these groups and the active participation of women in their religious practice, in defiance of the norms of both church and society, aroused the concern and wrath of orthodox leadership. As Elizabeth Clark observed, "since the 'mainstream' church was in competition with these sects for adherents, it distressed orthodox churchmen that women found these groups appealing." Indeed, from the earliest times the idea of heresy and the independence of women were inextricably linked. The generally prominent role of women in these otherwise disparate groups became, in the eyes of the orthodox leadership, their chief identifying characteristic, from which the orthodox church had to distinguish itself. "In the second and third centuries," Clark explains, "the Christian church was engaged in the quest for its own self-definition. Striving to define itself over against non-Christians without and dissenters within, the church drew firm lines, precise boundaries, between itself and these heretical . . . movements." Moreover, in order

to demarcate the boundaries between "us and them," the church fathers singled out for attack various features of the sects' allegedly misguided teaching and practice, such as the leadership roles of Gnostic women. Over against the blasphemies and permissiveness of the sects, no orthodox Catholic woman should teach, preach, baptize, exorcise, offer the Eucharist, or prophesy. Thus the mainstream church's limitation of women's roles can be understood in part as an aspect of its quest for self-definition—that is, for an identity that clearly distinguished it from rival movements.[9]

"In the light of the emergency caused by the persecutions," JoAnn McNamara noted, "Clement of Alexandria viewed the independent Christian women of his city with dismay," fearing that the women might be the "weak link in the chain of resistance to the persecutors." He attacked the heretical preachers, prophets, and sects and sought "to bring women back under the . . . instruction of approved representatives of the church." Bishop Irenaeus likewise thought it seriously divisive "that women especially [were] attracted to heretical groups" which "accorded to their women members respect and participation increasingly denied to women" in the patriarchal-household-based orthodox churches.[10]

Tertullian of Carthage also attacked Marcion for allowing women to become priests and even bishops within his church, and railed out against the women themselves as well. "These heretical women—how audacious they are! They have no modesty; they are bold enough to teach, to engage in argument, to enact exorcisms, to undertake cures, and, it may be, even to baptize!" To contrast orthodox practice with such heretical habits, Tertullian prescribed what he regarded as "the precepts of ecclesiastical discipline concerning women," according to which "it is not permitted for a woman to speak in the church, nor is it permitted for her to teach, nor to baptize, nor to offer [the eucharist], nor to claim for herself a share in any masculine function—not to mention any priestly office."[11]

The hierarchy's condemnation of female independence, and its corollary ascetic rigorism, continued unabated. But in its struggle with "heresy" for a durable Christian identity and survival in a pagan society, and for political and doctrinal leadership within the church, the orthodox clergy itself gradually came to reflect some of the very tendencies it denounced. Slowly and subtly, the church appropriated and transformed the ideals of its rivals. "A younger generation of leaders were simply not interested in rethinking the issue of the sanctification of the married, as Clement plainly felt himself obliged to do," Peter Brown observed. "Their slogan was 'virginity.' The rise to prominence of the Christian Church in Roman society in the course of the third century was a process that . . . was accompanied by the emergence of what can best be called a 'sensibility,' almost an 'aesthetic,' of virginity. The ideal of the untouched human body came to the fore."[12]

"In this acceptance of the ideology of virginity," JoAnn McNamara pointed out, "the church was moving dangerously close to the heresies of the second century which their foremost theologians had expended so much effort to suppress." Several scholars have tried to account for this striking reversal. Anthropologist Mary Douglas drew a connection between "purity" and "danger" in the formation of cultic identity, and suggested that the church's belated adoption of asceticism was a response to persecution. In her view, "the idea that virginity had a special positive value was bound to fall on good soil in a small persecuted minority group. For [such] social conditions lend themselves to beliefs which symbolize the body as an imperfect container which will only be perfect if it can be made impermeable." McNamara suggested that the orthodox adoption of the celibate ideal reflected another concern, the need of the clergy, during a time of crisis, to reintegrate within the church independent women whose alienation rendered the church more vulnerable and whose wealth and influence were considered invaluable to its survival. In the process of co-opting such women, the clergy was compelled to honor their code of celibacy, came to recognize its ideological power, and ultimately appropriated this power for themselves.[13]

Brown argues that the advent of orthodox clerical asceticism reflected the clergy's need "to define their own position against the principal benefactors of the Christian community." On the one hand, the clergy had to defend the sanctity of marriage to ensure the piety and, hence, benevolence of the married laity. On the other, the clergy had to distinguish themselves as somehow superior to the laity to safeguard their leadership positions and prevent any usurpation of clerical power by wealthy and powerful lay benefactors. To this end, the clergy early on monopolized the celebration of the Eucharist, the central Christian rite, and subsequently adopted the ideal of clerical continence and celibacy as evidence not only of their ritual purity but also of their "charismatic calling." Unlike some of the heretical sects, which called for a totally celibate Christian community, the clergy resolved the "eminently practical issue" of both providing for the continued material and biological reproduction of the church and protecting their privileged place within it by upholding the sanctity of marriage for the laity and adopting the ideal of celibacy for themselves. The second and third centuries thus witnessed what Brown calls a "silent revolution"—"the creation of a strict division between the clergy and the laity in the Christian church."[14]

Whatever the proximate reason for the rise of orthodox asceticism, it can hardly be disputed that the orthodox clergy were belatedly coming to recognize the value of sexual renunciation, for purposes of both Christian and clerical identity, to guarantee clerical discipline and loyalty, and perhaps also to prevent the alienation of church property through clerical inheritance. But in their exaltation of virginity the clergy had come to resemble the very heretics they continued to condemn. Thus, whereas before they had pitted the sanctity of marriage and the patriarchal dignity of the household against ascetic rigorism to distance themselves from heresy, they now pitted their own ideal of asceticism against another, an orthodox clerical asceticism against the androgynous asceticism of the heretical sects.

If the latter was an ideal shared by both men and women alike in their common pursuit of Christian salvation, the former was to be an ideal, like orthodox clerical status itself, for men only. And if sexual temptation posed a threat to androgynous asceticism, the greatest danger to clerical asceticism was more narrowly defined: the presence of women. Whereas the androgynous ideal had fostered a chaste mingling of men and women, the clerical ideal instead drove men into frightened flight from women. As never before, then, the struggle against the heretical groups identified the threat of heresy with the proximity of women. At this early stage in the formation of the church, the contrast of orthodoxy from heresy already implied a world without women. The inherited patriarchal assumptions of the household-based clergy had subordinated women; the new ideals of the ascetic clergy eliminated them.

In the first two Christian centuries, although male asceticism certainly existed, celibacy was associated with women in Christian writing. But, as McNamara points out, in the early third century, "male writers began to address themselves to questions of male celibacy."

Along the same lines, whereas in the first two centuries the threat to virginity was identified with the ardor and violence of the male sex, in the third century, "with the promulgation of male virginity, . . . a note of misogyny" emerges in the literature. It is already there in the work of Tertullian, the first—one might say premature—orthodox champion of clerical celibacy (he ultimately abandoned orthodoxy for Montanism rather than give up his opposition to digamy). In his *Exhortation to Chastity*, addressed to a widower, Tertullian issued the "first consequential statement, written for educated Christians and destined to enjoy a long future in the Latin world," and offered the earliest indication of "those in the clerical state opting for the celibate life in great numbers."[15]

For Tertullian, women were not merely disqualified for the priesthood by their sex; they were indelibly and irrevocably identified with temptation and were thus the "devil's gateway," in Brown's words, "a breach in the defenses of the Church, by which the world might gain an entry into the somber assemblies of the male saints." In attacking the Carthaginian women who dared stand unveiled in church, claiming that in their asceticism they had transcended their sex, Tertullian derided their claims as heresy and thereby identified such heresy with women. Moreover, he viewed their nakedness as a threat not to their own virtue but, more important, to that of the men who looked upon them; he insisted upon female modesty, yes, but for the sake of male chastity. Tertullian's hostile reaction to the bold women of Carthage stemmed from his firm belief that sexual desire was a permanent human affliction and that women were naturally and dangerously seductive, views that "clearly foreshadowed the future development of the Latin church." Two third-century treatises on virginity mistakenly attributed to Clement of Rome, written to denounce the practice of spiritual marriage, cautioned, "with maidens we do not dwell, nor have we anything in common with them. With maidens we do not eat, nor drink; and where a maiden sleeps, we do not sleep. . . . With us may no female, whether young maiden or married woman, be there at [the time of prayer]; nor she that is aged, nor she that hath taken the vow; nor even a maid-servant, whether Christian or heathen, but there shall only be men with men."[16]

"As orthodox Christianity came more and more to embrace the ideal of celibacy and to clamp down on the heresies where women were most involved," Averil Cameron observed, "it excluded women more completely from the organization of the church." By the time Cyprian had become bishop of Carthage, this transformation was already well under way. Cyprian was bishop for a decade in the middle of the third century, during the persecutions of Emperor Decius. Like the other powerful ascetic bishops of Rome and Antioch, Cyprian believed that only those who had demonstrated "virginal continence" could be entrusted with such power. His career "shows very clearly the extent to which . . . virginity was harnessed to the needs of the Catholic clergy," and the dire implications for women in the church. In the face of imperial persecution, Cyprian emphasized above all the need for a military discipline. To his mind, the Christian communities of Rome and Carthage were "in the fighting line against pagan authority," and the church was a "bond of brotherhood" braced against persecution. He thus praised virgin women only to exhort them to discipline, took pains to ensure that their personal wealth would not be used to influence the clergy, and issued stern warnings against "the polluting waters of heresy" and any "effeminate weakening of the hard resolve of the Christian." Clearly, as Brown points out, he "was the last person who would have treated continent women as partners."[17]

"By the year 300," Brown observes, "Christian asceticism, invariably associated with some form or other of perpetual sexual renunciation, was a well-established feature of most regions of the Christian world." In the Latin West, he adds, it "tended to gravitate around the clergy of the Catholic Church," giving rise to a "holy priesthood." For the fourth-century church historian Eusebius, "the victory of Christianity in the Roman world implied, also, the victory of an elite within the Christian church," the rise of an ascetic corps of apostolic heirs charged with the salvation of humbler lay souls. They are "above nature, and beyond common human living," wrote Eusebius. "Like some celestial beings, [they] gaze down upon human life, performing the duty of a priesthood to Almighty God for the whole race." Over the next centuries, this cadre of clerical ascetics would undermine all of the foundations of women's presence, participation, and prominence in the Christian community. By successively demolishing their heretical androgynous rivals, displacing the married clergy, and diminishing lay influence over the church, they steadily paved the way toward a world without women.[18]

The "victory" announced by Eusebius was more potential than actual. The majority of clergy were still married, including many bishops, and there remained a heavy clerical dependence upon female lay patronage. But the ascent of the ascetic clergy was gaining momentum, as Eusebius observed, in the wake of the monastic movement of the fourth century. Of course, Brown points out, "Anthony and the monks of the fourth century inherited a revolution, they did not initiate one. . . . Total sexual renunciation had [already] become a widely acclaimed feature of the Christian life." Nevertheless, the new movement of the desert "became the powerhouse of a new culture," one that would irreversibly exalt the new ascetic tendencies of the orthodox clergy and hence fuel their struggle against both clerical marriage and the androgynous aspirations of women alike.[19]

The monastic movement actually began in part as a lay revolt against the corrupt church of bishops and priests, but it quickly became aligned with orthodoxy against heresy. Herbert Workman described this crucial transformation. "At the outset, over against Cyprian's conception of a great imperial institution as the channel of grace, with its apostolically descended bishops, presbyters, and deacons, its elaborate system of sacraments, and its idea of solidarity in a common organization, the monk opposed the life of the soul, face to face with God, in direct not intermediate communion with Him. . . ." Thus, in both East and West, the movement was initially identified with heresy and was "bitterly opposed [by the church], especially by the bishops."[20]

Yet "this antagonism between the ideals of the cleric and the monk could not last. . . . By a strange accident a movement which in its early days had been, at times, identified with Marcionism and Origenism, became allied with orthodoxy," in common opposition to the widespread antitrinitarian heresy of Arianism. "One consequence of the alliance . . . between orthodoxy and monasticism . . . was the support [subsequently] given to monasticism by all the great leaders of the Church. . . . Basil, Chrysostom, Jerome, Augustine, never weary in singing its praises." The fullest embodiment of this alliance was Bishop Athanasius of Alexandria, a former hermit and disciple of Anthony and stalwart champion of trinitarian doctrine, who, "more than all others, united in himself all that was most virile in the Christianity of the age." Friend of Pachomius and of Anthony's companion Serapion, Athanasius became the most influential orthodox proselytizer of monasticism, not only in the East but in the West as well. Thus, as Workman emphasizes, "the alliance between orthodoxy and monasticism was completed by Athanasius writing *The Life of Anthony*, a book that henceforth set the standard of conduct of the whole Church and established the new ideal of monasticism."[21]

The monastic ideal reflected and reinforced the chief characteristics of the ascetic orthodox clergy: sexual renunciation, a disciplined bond of brotherhood, and, on both counts, distrust of women—in short, the characteristics of a military culture. Anthropologists have amply documented the ascetic, misogynist, and male homosocial orientations of warrior societies, marked as much by their distance from women as by their bonds between men. The fourth century witnessed the formation of such a culture within Christianity. This new culture bore the legacy of early Essenic militants and later Christian martyrs, on the one hand, and the stamp of Roman militarism and an imperial orthodox church, on the other. Though it grew out of the experience of a persecuted minority, it was consolidated by a now dominant institution in its wars against heresy and heathen invasion. Monasticism in its later communal if not its initial eremetical expression, was the supreme and lasting outgrowth of this culture.[22]

In the face of persecution, Christians like Cyprian adopted a rigorous ascetic discipline which mirrored that of the Roman army; and just as Roman soldiers had been forbidden to marry, so they too avoided the company of women and guarded themselves against any feminine erosion of Christian resolve. This tendency became even more pronounced once Christianity became the imperial religion and the two swords, spiritual and temporal, became one. Constantine's conversion to Christianity was, as Chadwick has noted, in essence "a military matter"; he believed that the new religion could further his imperial purposes and had his cross inscribed with the words "in this conquer."[23]

The imperial conversion resulted in what Philippe Cantamine has called a "sacralization of war"; by the beginning of the fifth century, an imperial edict excluded non-Christians from the Roman army. The reverse side of this process was the militarization of the church. The pacifism of Tertullian and Origen gave way to a new Christian defense of war against heretics and barbarians, by Athanasius and, later, Ambrose and Augustine. If the clergy and monks were not themselves to fight on the temporal field of battle, they were to man the equally vital spiritual field of battle, *milites Christi* armed with the weapons of "prayers and fasts, meditations and good works, justice and piety, meekness, chastity, and abstinence."[24]

The monks, as Workman suggests, were the inheritors of the martyrs' mantle, perpetuating in their life of renunciation the eternal combat against evil. Thus the monks above all "engaged in spiritual imitation of the military." Indeed, the father of communal monasticism, Pachomius, the author of the first monastic rule and organizer of the first monastic community, had been a soldier under Constantine before becoming a monk. Not surprisingly, his community at Tabennisi, on the Nile, the model for the movement, was renowned for its militarylike regimen, with its emphasis upon ascetic rigor, order, and efficiency. "Obedience in Pachomius' organization," Chadwick pointed out, "was military and complete." Cassian, the fourth-century proselytizer for Egyptian monasticism, likened the monk's discipline to that of the soldier, and Chrysostom, another great champion of the movement, "sternly reminded the monks that Christ had armed them to be soldiers in a noble fight, to cast down demons and wage spiritual warfare, not to devote their days to waiting on girls." It was understood, Workman argues, that the monks, as soldiers of Christ, were bound "by the same restrictions as the soldiers of the emperor at Constantinople or Rome." He offers the example of Martin of Tours, founder of monasticism in Gaul and an ex-soldier himself. Martin forbade a monk to live with his wife, even though she too had taken vows. " 'Tell me,' said Martin, 'have you ever stood in the line of battle?' 'Frequently,' he replied. 'Well then, did you ever in the line of battle see any woman standing there or fighting?' By this 'true and rational analogy,' Martin convinced the monk that he must abandon his wife."[25]

This military orientation of monasticism was reflected in its asceticism, which emphasized above all chastity for men. Lewis Mumford noted that the "sexual one-sidedness of monastic organization" resembled that of the "archetypal bachelor armies." "The great myth of the desert . . . had given new meaning to male asceticism in Egypt and elsewhere," Peter Brown observed. Unlike the androgynous ascetic communities—now identified as heretical—the new monastic movement, like the military, was homosocial in nature and was marked by distance from and dread of women. Women had come to symbolize all that the monks were struggling against: sexual temptation, the corruption of settled society, and heresy.[26]

For the monk, sexual temptation was identified with women. The solitude of the desert had convinced the monks of the "intractability," in Brown's word, of lust; it could not be transcended in this world, as earlier ascetics had believed, but remained a resilient reminder of the body's innermost defiance of the will. Hence a chaste mingling of the sexes was an impossibility, and the monk was bound to eternal vigilance against desire, and thus against women. The monastic "emphasis on the infinite preciousness and fragility of a monk's virginity generated a new sense of peril," Brown notes. "In the fourth and fifth centuries, the ascetic literature of Egypt became a repository of vivid anecdotes concerning sexual seduction and heroic sexual avoidance. In this new monastic folklore . . . women were presented as a source of perpetual temptation," the chief danger to monkish virtue. Anthony overcame the "sensual ardor of his youth" by "fasting, macerations, and, above all, prayer." His desert follower Hilarion likewise struggled in torment against his "recollections of the beautiful women of Alexandria," reducing his body through hunger and thirst in order to subdue his passions. During his brief desert sojourn, Jerome too was haunted by "the remembrance of the delights of Rome, and of its choirs of young girls, who came to people his cell and to make it an accomplice of his own burning imagination."[27]

In order to maintain their virtue and hence their militant spiritual vigor, "monks were supposed to put an unbridgeable distance between themselves and the women of the settled land, and even between themselves and nuns." But the "studied misogyny" of ascetic literature expressed more than just a simple reflex against sexual temptation. As Brown suggests, "it was mobilized as part of a wider strategy" by church leaders to contain and control the monastic movement. First, a heightened fear of women served to keep the charismatic monks away from settled society—identified with marriage, reproduction, and thus with women—and so out of direct competition with the established clergy. Hence, as Brown describes it, "a fog of sexual distrust gathered along the edge of the desert at exactly the same time as we find monks increasingly involved with the settled world. . . . Fear of women fell like a bar shadow across the paths that led back from the desert into the towns and villages." "The disciple of Apa Siosoes said to him, 'Father, you have grown old. Let us move a little closer to the settled land.' The Old Man said, 'Where there is no woman, that is where we should go.' "[28]

The "studied misogyny" of ascetic literature served also to distance the monks, who were allied with orthodoxy, from the heretical ascetic communities, because these communities typically included women. Indeed, the same ascetic movement which produced monasticism also "threatened to revive the radical expectations long associated with the Encratite movement." The Egyptian spiritual guide Hierakas, for example, a younger contemporary of Anthony, tried to establish groups of continent men and women along the lines of the earlier androgynous ascetic communities, "men and women [gathered] together into little confraternities, bound by personal vows of chastity." "As in Encratite Syria," Brown noted, "spiritual fathers of Hierakas' persuasion shocked their opponents by boasting of the close ties of service and spiritual companionship that linked them to their continent women disciples. . . . Throughout the Roman world, the situation created by tenacious and vivid groupings of pious women provoked studiously fostered sexual alarm. . . . A steady flow of circumstantial evocations of the perils of sex were a byproduct of the rise of women's asceticism and the consequent search, by men and women alike, for spiritual companions of the opposite sex." Thus "a haze of anxiety" settled over the monastic communities. As Brown suggests, "the words of the prophet Nehemiah, 'make to yourselves separate booths' [became] the motto of the day," fostering a strict segregation of the sexes within the ascetic movement.[29]

Basil of Ancyra, an older contemporary of Basil of Caesarea, wrote an exhaustive cautionary treatise *On the Preservation of Virginity*, "conjuring up the facts of sex so as to keep the female ascetics of his region at a safe distance from male soul-mates." ("Cordoned off in this way, the continent women would look only to their true spiritual friends, the [orthodox] bishop and his clergy.") Athanasius likewise wrote his *On Virginity* against the dangerous teachings of Hierakas. Among the Pachomian communities, just up the Nile from those of Hierakas, these strictures were heeded with high walls and strict vows, and an "explicit sense of sexual danger . . . pervaded many of the rulings and exhortations of Pachomius' successors." According to Cassian, one Apa Paulus "had made such progress in purity of heart in the stillness of the desert, that he would not suffer, I will not say a woman's face, but even the clothes of one of that sex to appear in his sight." In his *Institutes* Cassian himself warned future monks that "when the Devil, with subtle cunning, has insinuated into our hearts the memory of a woman, beginning with our mother, our sisters, or certain pious women, we should as quickly as possible expel these memories for fear that, if we linger on them too long, the tempter may seize the opportunity to lead us unwittingly to think about other women."[30]

Invoking the military male spirit underlying monasticism and the combatants' fear of feminine weakening, Chrysostom insisted that "the monk acquired 'womanish' traits by his constant association with the female sex." Arguing vigorously against spiritual marriage and chaste companionship between the sexes—despite his own relationship with Olympias—Chrysostom maintained that "the monks who live with virgins have abandoned their 'crosses' like cowardly soldiers who, instead of marching steadfastly into battle, toss away their shields and retreat to the women's quarters." If such military metaphors served to strengthen the monk-warriors' chaste conception of masculinity and to heighten monkish anxieties about feminine enfeeblement—common characteristics of warrior subcultures— it also reinforced the homosocial norms of the monastic community, to the point of fostering a homoerotic ethos reminiscent of the academies of classical Greece. Brown noted that older men harassed the novices; "with wine and boys around, the monks have no need of the Devil [woman] to tempt them." In the Pachomian communities, "the individual monks had to be separated from each other," and recurring monastic and penitential injunctions against pederasty and homosexual practices in general betray their prevalence. Indeed, in his virulent condemnation of heterosexual mingling, Chrysostom himself "fell back on an ancient rhetorical argument in favor of homosexual love, wherein pederasty was exalted as the 'final refinement of lovemaking.' "[31]

The new male-centered monastic subculture was destined to have a profound influence upon Christian asceticism and the church, not to mention Christian society as a whole. The nature of its influence in the East, however, differed significantly from that in the West. Although "it is exceedingly difficult to know how much and in what manner the sexual codes, elaborated to such a pitch of caution in the desert, trickled back into the churches," Brown observed, "the sexual codes that governed the relations of men and women in the Christian East undoubtedly hardened in the course of the fourth and fifth centuries." In the wake of the church fathers' stern condemnation of spiritual companionship between ascetic men and women, the Eastern monasteries themselves pushed male exclusivity to the extreme; not only women but females of any species were excluded from the peninsula of Mount Athos. Although the traditional patriarchal household which formed the basis of the church had already given it a misogynist orientation, the monastic movement reinforced this tendency, as evidenced above all by a "growing segregation of the sexes in the churches."[32]

The acceptance of celibate women within the orthodox church (like the acceptance of women within science a millennium and a half later) was gained at the price of their subordination to the male clergy and their relegation to a separate and restricted place. Increasingly, holy women were permitted to minister only to women, and their church duties were carefully distinguished from the sacerdotal functions monopolized by the clergy; the ceremonial consecration of virgins and widows was not to be confused in any way with ordination. Perhaps most important, the consecration of celibate women was likened to a marriage ceremony; the women became "brides of Christ" and hence the subordinates of their husband's earthly representatives, the male clergy. As JoAnn McNamara has explained, "the idea of the virgin as the bride of Christ suggested a way of defining her position that freed the clergy to praise and admire her without fearing her competition. . . . As brides of Christ, [celibate women] were to hold an honored but circumscribed place."[33]

As women religious were strictly being excluded from sacerdotal rituals, particularly the Eucharist, these all-male rituals, like those of other warrior cultures, were becoming deliberately more elaborate, awe-inspiring, and mysterious. According to Chadwick, the clergy intentionally fostered a lay "attitude of fear and trembling" during the rituals, and "before the end of the fourth century it began to be thought necessary to screen off the holy table with curtains," thereby making for dramatic clerical "entrances" at the reading of the Gospel. By this time too, even church music was being reorganized. Although they had been excluded from the priesthood, women had until then been "important as singers both as members of the congregation and in choirs." During the latter half of the fourth century, however, congregational singing was gradually abandoned in favor of professional choirs restricted to men and boys. Women could continue to sing their praises only within the walls of their segregated convents.[34]

Paradoxically perhaps, although monasticism had its earliest influence where it began, in the East, that influence never became as far-reaching as in the West. Most important, the celibate monastic culture never became in the East the model for the church itself, which retained clerical marriage except for bishops. As Workman phrased it, "in the East, in fact, the separation between the two ideals became complete, a married clergy over against a celibate monasticism." Here the charismatic challenge embodied by the monks was decisively confronted and contained by a powerful state. Although the monks were exalted by church and state alike as the supreme symbols of Christian virtue, they were kept at a distance from the awe-inspired population of settled society, and in their place politically. As a result, in maintaining the practice of clerical marriage, as Henry Lea noted, the Eastern Church "preserved the traditions of earlier times."[35]

Charismatic hermits and monks were perceived very early as a potential threat to both clerical and imperial authority.

> In the East both church and state began to feel the necessity of reducing to subjection under some competent authority the vast hordes of idle and ignorant men who had embraced the monastic life. . . . The solitudes of the deserts had become peopled with vast communities, and as the contagion spread, monasteries arose everywhere and were rapidly filled and enlarged. The blindly big-oted and the turbulently ambitious found a place among those whose only aim was retirement and peace, while the authority wielded by the superior of each establishment through the blind obedience claimed under monastic vows, gave him a degree of power which rendered him not only important but dangerous. The monks thus became in time a body of no little weight which it behooved the Church to thoroughly control. . . .[36]

The General Council of Chalcedon was called in 451, as Monta-lembert noted, "to bring a remedy to these . . . dangers, and with the formally acknowledged intention of restraining all of those vaga-bond and turbulent monks." Thus the council decreed, at the behest of Emperor Marcian, that "the monks should submit to the episcopal authority in everything, under pain of excommunication," and they were expressly forbidden to leave their cloisters to take part in ecclesi-astical or secular affairs. Such legislative control over the monks by the church, however, did not in itself suffice. The monks, as Lea points out, "were fast becoming not only disagreeable but even dan-gerous to the civil power . . . [and] finding the Church unable to enforce a remedy, the civil power was compelled to intervene." Fifth-century imperial edicts restricted monks to their cloisters and prohib-ited them from participating in religious disputes or presiding over assemblages of any nature; in the sixth century, hermits were required to join monasteries and thus be subject to the same restrictions.[37]

These imperial decrees were confirmed and permanently instituted by means of the so-called Quini-Sext canons, issued by the Trullan Synod held in Constantinople in 691. The purpose of the canons, according to historian Judith Herrin, was "to keep bishops in their sees, priests in their churches, and monks in their monasteries, that is, to maintain the hierarchical arrangement and geographical division of the Church." The Quini-Sext "formed the bases for all later canon law" and marked "a decisive separation between East and West" by upholding the "Byzantine respect for the marriage of holy men."[38]

According to the Quini-Sext canons, bishops had to observe strict continence, although not necessarily celibacy. If a bishop was married before election, he could remain married, but his wife was compelled to live in a remote monastery with his continued support. In practice, most bishops tended to be unmarried men, and ambitious clerics aiming for episcopal office tended to avoid marriage and even to become monks. "For all other clerics, however, the Synod permitted marriage before ordination and the use of marriage rights afterward." Moreover, the synod insisted that, "if anyone should attempt to deprive a married priest, deacon, or subdeacon of his marriage rights, or if one of the aforesaid should renounce his wife 'on the pretense of piety,' he was to be condemned and deposed." After the Trullan Synod, "no further legislation on celibacy or clerical marriage was issued by the Eastern Church throughout its history." Indeed, in the Byzantine and Russian Church, "a priest attached to a country parish was required to marry." In short, despite its early influence in the East, the monastic movement did not here transform the world of the church itself into a world without women. The West followed a different course.[39]

Four · *Fathers: Patristic Anxiety to Papal Agenda*

I N THE WEST, as we have seen, the relative weakening of imperial, and hence ecclesiastical, authority in the wake of barbarian
incursions made possible the persistence for centuries of diverse
and even androgynous ascetic experimentation, despite the masculin-
izing trends in the monastic movement as a whole. Paradoxically,
however, the same relative decline of imperial authority allowed the
new monastic ethos to enter the soul, if not yet the body, of the
Western Church as it never did in the East. For here there was no
desert to distance the monks from settled society, nor a powerful state
intent upon keeping the monks at bay. Here, then, the elite clerical
culture evolved largely as part of the monastic movement rather than
in contest with it. The great fathers of the Western Church—Ambrose, Jerome, and Augustine—were all profoundly imbued with the
monastic spirit and strove incessantly to claim it for the church itself.
They inspired a new monastic-minded church leadership at a time in
the late fourth century when the Roman see was emerging as a "pre-
eminent centre of both leadership and juridical authority."[1]

This inspired generation challenged the experience of three centuries of Christianity. Against the household, they exalted the monastic
ascetic ideal—which was first associated in the West with aristocratic
women—as the highest form of Christian life. Against the androgynous "radical" ascetics, they appropriated that ideal for men, mirror-
ing the monastic developments in the East in their celebration of an
exclusive male asceticism. Finally, against the married clergy, they
became champions of clerical asceticism, and undertook to impose
the male monastic ideal upon the church as whole, particularly in the
form of clerical celibacy. Thus, as Peter Levi described it, "the celibacy of the monasteries slowly extended like an ice age to cover the
ordinary clergy. . . . The monks were meant to make everyone more
monk-like." In the process, meanwhile, pious women, initially
embraced by these men for their "manliness" and "virility," were
increasingly subordinated and segregated, kept out of the celibate

cadre and away from the cloisters and cathedrals of their brave new world.[2]

"The introduction of Monasticism to the West," Herbert Workman noted, "may be said to have been due to the great Athanasius," the influential champion of orthodoxy and monasticism. Exiled from Alexandria, he journeyed to Rome in 339 and stayed for three years. There he met Marcella and told her of the works of Anthony and Pachomius and of the virgins and widows in the monastic movement. Marcella, as we have seen, became the first aristocratic proponent of monasticism in Rome, and soon established the house monastery on the Aventine which became the breeding ground of the ascetic study circles associated with Jerome, who established himself as an authority on monasticism. The dissemination of the *Life of Saint Anthony*, attributed to Athanasius and translated into Latin by Jerome's friend Evagrius, had a particularly profound influence in fostering Western monasticism, along with Jerome's translation of Pachomius, the monastic accounts of Rufinus, Sulpicius Severus' *Life of Saint Martin*, the paeans to asceticism by Ambrose, Jerome, and Augustine, and the proselytizing of Cassian. By the end of the fourth century, Italy abounded with monasteries, and monastic missions had been established in southern Gaul.[3]

The role of the church fathers was critical to the rise of asceticism in the West, and their influence proved enduring. Ambrose, bishop of Milan, early seized upon the ascetic movement and turned it to the advantage of the church. "The notion of virginity served him as a sounding board. By preaching on virginity, and especially by upholding the perpetual virginity of Mary, Ambrose made resonantly clear the position that he wished the Catholic Church to occupy in the Western territories of the Empire." By analogy to the virgin, he envisioned a powerful yet pristine church, seemingly untouched by the corruption and pollution of the secular world, which drew its authority from its purity. In the face of a dangerous and dissolute society, he was "dominated by a need to assert the position of the Church as an inviolably holy body." He thus placed the virgin body at the pinnacle of human perfection and identified the church with it: "like the virgin, the Catholic Church was an intact body."[4]

Although virginity at the time was associated with female virtue and Ambrose theologically exalts the virgin woman above all else, in practice his preoccupation with male asceticism is clear. Like that of his predecessor Cyprian, who similarly strove to consolidate church power in the face of a hostile world, there is much of the militarist and misogynist in his call to holy purity. His imaginative world, like that of Cyprian, "was a tensile system . . . built up through a series of potent antitheses—Christian and pagan, Catholic and heretic. . . . To be a Catholic Christian was to keep these antitheses absolute. . . . To surrender any boundary line was to court the ancient shame of the Roman male—it was to 'become soft,' to be 'effeminated.' " His was a "harsh, defensive view of the world [which] caught only too well the mood of northern Italy in the 380's and 390's, after the collapse of the Danubian frontier and a series of civil wars had thrown the region into a state of perpetual mobilization." According to Brown, "Ambrose reacted instinctively. . . . Like Cyprian" he presented the Christian as "tensed against the saeculum," which he characterized as "beguiling female figures who threatened always to 'effeminate' the male resolve of the mind." This warrior orientation, with its emphasis upon unpolluted masculinity, matched the growing tendencies of the monastic movement, but it conflicted with the prominent role played by aristocratic women within Western monasticism, which heightened gender anxieties. As Brown points out, "we should not underestimate the impact on Italian society of an ascetic movement whose principal exponents and patrons were noble women." Ambrose, whose own sister, Marcellina, had joined Marcella's monastic house, was very much aware of this feminine role and the challenge it presented to both the monastic movement and the church. Like other proponents of the new monastic tendencies, he denied the possibility of any human transcendence of sexuality in this world, anticipating Augustine's doctrine of original sin. He thus opposed as dangerous any monastic mingling of the sexes such as that practiced by the radical ascetic Priscillians, whose teachings Ambrose condemned. He praised ascetic women as the embodiment of the highest Christian virtue yet insisted upon their segregation.[5]

Within the church, as Brown points out, "the prominence accorded to consecrated women in the basilica raised the explosive, because male, issue of the quality of the clergy of the Latin churches." If ascetic women were the quintessence of Christian purity, and the church, in Ambrose's view, had to become pure to survive and grow in a hostile world, then what role should such women play in the clerical hierarchy? Ambrose was not about to allow such women to be ordained; women clerics were the mark of heresy. Another question posed itself with perhaps greater insistence: ought not the clergy be pure to guarantee the purity of the church? "In the 380's," Brown notes, "it was an open question whether the *integritas* traditionally associated with consecrated virgin women would spill over into the ranks of the clergy as a whole, in the form of lifelong clerical celibacy."[6]

Ambrose became a champion of such clerical purity, insisting upon the superiority of celibate clerics over their married colleagues. Intervening in a dispute among the congregation of Vercelli over whether to choose a monk or a married landowner as bishop, Ambrose strove to persuade Christians "to choose as their leaders and moral guides only men who had maximized their own control of the sexual urge—those who had lived lives of perpetual celibacy." When the ascetic Jovinian argued for the spiritual equality of celibate and married, Ambrose attacked him as a dangerous foe of the church and urged that even married laity should strive to lead continent lives. For Ambrose, the virgin state of women was "the model of a state of sexual intactness that men and especially members of the clergy should strive to make their own." Although continence on the part of the higher clergy had long been prescribed, if rather unsuccessfully, as a sign of the sanctity of the priesthood, the notion of lifelong celibacy for the clergy as a whole was a startling new idea which had just begun to take hold in the West among "an increasingly vocal group of ascetics" in Spain, Gaul, and Italy. While distancing himself from the more extreme ascetics, Ambrose became a champion of clerical continence. "You must remain strangers to conjugal intimacy," he counseled clerics, "for you know that you have a ministry, whole and immaculate, which must never be profaned by any sexual relations." He warned also that women were never to be allowed in the homes of the clergy.[7]

As a champion of clerical asceticism, Ambrose was an inspiration and adviser to the papacy at precisely the time that the Roman see was trying to enlarge its authority and impose a uniform discipline upon the Western Church. The earliest papal pronouncements on clerical continence, by Popes Damasus and Siricius, were means to this end and bear the clear mark of Ambrose's writings. In their wake, the rebellious androgynous ascetic ideal of early Christianity, which had already begun to give way to a male-oriented monasticism, was now to be co-opted and monopolized by the established male-only clergy itself. As Brown emphasizes, "the long history of the Catholic Church makes it easy for us to forget the novelty of such a claim. Never before had Roman public men been expected to appropriate, in this way, virtues usually delegated to women." The tensions associated with this shift from androgynous to clerical asceticism are perhaps most clearly visible in the life and work of Jerome.[8]

"In Jerome," Brown observes, "we can follow the unresolved tensions of a man who had defined himself as the spiritual guide of upperclass women." After his brief sojourn in the desert, Jerome became the major advocate of asceticism in Rome, serving as secretary and later spokesman for his patron Pope Damasus, who had begun to claim unprecedented papal authority over the Western Church. At the same time, he assumed the role of a latter-day Origen to his wealthy female spiritual companions. Like other radical Christian ascetics, such as his friend Rufinus, Jerome strove "to find a place for intimacy with devout women as colleagues, disciples, and mentors," inspired and justified by eschatological myths of sexual transcendence. He embraced such women not as women *per se* but as women who, in their chastity, had overcome the deficiencies of womanhood enough to become manly. It was this transcendence of their sexual identity, through ascetic renunciation, that made possible female companionship with ascetic men, who likewise struggled to overcome their sexual selves.[9]

As a former desert monk, however, Jerome had already confronted his seemingly ineradicable lust for women. "He who, in fear of hell, had banished himself to this prison," he later wrote to Eustochium, "found himself again and again surrounded by dancing girls! My face grew pale with hunger, yet in my cold body the passions of my inner being continued to glow. This human being was more dead than alive; only his burning lust continued to boil." His recognition of the persistence of desire despite heroic feats of denial is reflected in the notes of sexual caution which pervade his letters. As Brown observes, even though he celebrated the eschatological promise of female chastity and continued to cultivate intimate relations with pious women, "he himself had contributed handsomely . . . to the sharp tone of sexual anxiety that stressed the irreducible sexual differences between male and female bodies, and that lingered with studied alarm on the dangers that stemmed from these differences." Hence Jerome was already well "aware of the changing temper of the times."[10]

The condemnation of Priscillian and his execution in 386

was a chilling reminder that, outside a few privileged milieux, intimacy with influential and militant Christian women might lead to

65

violent death and, at the very least, to the lasting stigma of sexual innuendo. In the West, as a generation earlier in the East, the clergy came to learn that true Christian courage lay in cultivating a holy timidity with regard to women. . . . Spiritual friendships . . . were condemned, . . . branded as a form of "clandestine subversion," of the "wall of moral vigor."

"By the late 390's," Brown concludes, "the clouds that these fears had silently generated in Italy, Spain, and Gaul came to darken Jerome's horizons."[11]

As an ardent champion of asceticism with close ties to Pope Damasus and his successor, Siricius, Jerome lobbied for clerical celibacy. Insisting, like Ambrose, upon the superior virtue of virginity over marriage, Jerome argued that the clergy should embody the higher virtue. Whether this advocacy of clerical celibacy followed from his growing sense of sexual caution or simply from his exaltation of virginity, the effect would have been the same, given the male monopoly of ordination: a clerical world without women. He argued, in his attack on Jovinian, "that priests were holy only in so far as they possessed the purity of virgins. The married clergy were mere raw recruits in the army of the church, brought in because of a temporary shortage of battle-hardened veterans of lifelong celibacy." Jerome's immoderate assault on Jovinian's defense of the equality of marriage and virginity—he had likened Jovinian to a latter-day Epicurus, "wantoning in his garden with his favorites of both sexes"—brought down on himself accusations of extremism and, worse, heresy. He had become caught up in the so-called Origenist controversy, which had begun in attacks upon Origen's teachings by Bishop Epiphanius of Cyprus two decades earlier and would culminate in the official condemnation of Origen in 553. As the foremost champion of asceticism, Jerome had spearheaded the ascetic opposition against the married clergy. His identification with radical asceticism, however, had now become a serious liability. As Brown puts it, "Jerome was forced to choose."[12]

Having challenged the married clergy, on the one hand, Jerome chose to distance himself also from the radical ascetics, on the other. He abandoned his support of the now unpopular Origen, whom he had earlier described as "an immortal genius," and condemned the Origenist notion of transcendence of sexual difference through renunciation. After 395, he "came down firmly on the side of views that stressed the lasting differences between the sexes and the irremovable risk of sexual temptation between men and women." Consequently, he endorsed the somber Augustinian notion of original sin and viciously attacked Pelagius for his continued insistence upon the freedom of the will. He broke with his friend Rufinus, who continued to defend Origenist teaching, and derided Rufinus' companion Melania, whom thirty years earlier he had likened to a "second Thecla," as "the crazy old woman." Although he himself continued to his death to maintain his relationships with his female companions and even to be buried beside his beloved Paula and Eustochium, Jerome advised against female companionship for monks and clerics and adopted a "fashionable misogyny." Rufinus denounced Jerome for having betrayed his early promise as the mentor of Marcella, Paula, and Eustochium. But Jerome was more attuned to the times. As Brown notes, "the drift of theological attitudes, though limited to sheltered circles of monks and scholars, coincided with a marked hardening of official attitudes." These new theological and official attitudes were fully reflected in the work and life of Jerome's younger contemporary Augustine of Hippo.[13]

Twelve years younger than Jerome and the product of patriarchal North African society, Augustine escaped the tensions that beset Jerome. He grew up in a world in which women presented less of a challenge to male society. In keeping with established practice for men of his class, Augustine had taken a concubine, with whom he lived for thirteen years and had a son. He had also become an auditor in a Manichean sect. At the age of thirty he traveled from Carthage to Rome and then to Milan, where he hoped to put his talents as a teacher of rhetoric to advantage at the imperial court. His mother, meanwhile, arranged for a suitable marriage that would have gained him entry into Milanese society, and Augustine abandoned his mistress in anticipation of his new life. In Milan, however, Augustine encountered Ambrose, whose Platonic sermons so excited his philosophical interest that he began to consider conversion; he also encountered for the first time the *Life of Saint Anthony* and, through it, the monastic ideal of celibacy.[14]

In Milan as in North Africa, Augustine traveled in a tight circle of male companions. Despite his relationship with his mistress, Augustine's closest attachments were to his male friends. In his *Confessions* he recounted that "he had no doubt that, in his early twenties, the sweetest joy of his life had been an ever-deepening friendship with a fellow student." "For a young intellectual of the fourth cen-

tury," Brown points out, "male friendship opened the door to deeper satisfactions" than relations with women. For Augustine, a "woman's company was plainly less stimulating than a man's." "To talk and laugh. To do each other kindnesses. To read pleasant books together," wrote Augustine, "these, and such like things, proceeding from our hearts as we gave affection and received it back, and shown by face, by voice, by eyes, and by a thousand pleasing ways, kindled a flame which fused our very souls together, and, of many, made us one."[15]

In Milan, Augustine "joined a circle of hard young careerists"; his friends Alypius, Verecundus, Nebridius, and his patron Romanianus had hoped "to found some kind of philosophical community" around Augustine, and his prospective marriage "would have caused their ideal of a shared life to crumble." The allure of the "continent sociability" of monasticism proved irresistible for Augustine and his friends and afforded them a way out of their dilemma. Augustine's conversion to Catholicism thus entailed from the outset a commitment to a life of perpetual continence—however difficult it was for him to adjust—and it was, moreover, a "group experience"; to consider conversion collectively, Augustine retired with his friends in a "quasi-Platonic retreat" at an estate outside Milan. Not long after his baptism at the hands of Ambrose, Augustine returned with his friends to Africa, where they established a small ascetic community at Thagaste. "From the moment of his conversion in the summer of 386," then, as Chadwick explains, "Augustine's ideal was monastic."[16]

Shortly after establishing his monastic community, Augustine was pressed into service as presbyter, and later bishop, of nearby Hippo. But even as a cleric and high-ranking church official, Augustine's ideal of church organization remained monastic. Relocating his monastic community to Hippo, he strove to bring the church into line with the devout practice of a monastic community. Augustine believed, according to Chadwick, "that the really serious work of dedicated servants of God was done within the framework of monasteries." He "saw the monastic movement as a protest against the infiltration into the churches of the secular loves of power, wealth, a defiance of materialist values and disordered sexuality." The monastery was for him a "battle school for the soldiers of Christ"; "monks were there to show the Church that discipline is actually possible."[17]

Augustine's dedication to clerical celibacy followed naturally from his monastic orientation. "In the West," Workman observed, "the consciousness of opposition between cleric and monk" never became "so pronounced as in the East, [owing] in no small degree to the influence of St. Augustine." Thirty years earlier, Bishop Eusebius of Vercelli had required his clerics to live according to a rule; Augustine introduced the same custom at Hippo and several other sees and thereby contributed to the creation of a clerical caste, distinguished from the laity by monkish dress and habits. The monastic ideal, including celibacy, was in effect imposed upon the clergy. "Although he submitted to the call to serve as presbyter and then as bishop," Chadwick explained, Augustine's "ideal for the life of the 'secular clergy' . . . remained deeply ascetic; he took it for granted that his clergy, even if married, would no longer live with their wives, and that celibacy was part of the priestly calling." In contrast to the ascetic milieu of Rome, among the clergy of the African Church there were "no examples of spiritual companionship with gifted and influential ascetic women." Indeed, Augustine "imposed strict codes of sexual avoidance on himself and his own clergy. He would never visit a woman unchaperoned, and did not allow even his own female relatives to enter the bishop's palace." Thus Augustine maintained a rigorously "continent household at Hippo," where "the little groups of monks and continent clergymen gathered around him in the bishop's palace." "Compared with Jerome, and even with Ambrose," Brown points out, "Augustine moved in a monochrome, all-male world." And it was from within this all-male world that Augustine formulated his new theology, the austere and pessimistic precepts that would henceforth dominate the Latin Church.[18]

Augustine's teachings were informed by monastic asceticism in general and in particular by his own belated and therefore ardent renunciation of sexual life. But they also reflected his official position in a social hierarchy and his confrontation with opponents within and without the church. First and perhaps foremost, he represented the views of a new breed within the church. His *Confessions*, for example, "were written to address—and, in addressing, to help to form—a distinctive group," the clerical ascetics who were assuming positions of leadership in the churches of Africa and Italy. His defense of celibacy and assertion of the superiority of virginity over marriage were at the same time part of an ideological offensive against the married clergy, with whom the ascetics were competing for power and position within the church. Second, as a spokesman for what was now a state religion, he represented imperial as well as ecclesiastical authority. His substitution of the essentially predestinarian idea of original sin for earlier Christian ideals of salvation through freedom of the will corresponded not only to his own preoccupation with ineradicable concupiscence but also to the needs of established authority.[19]

As Elaine Pagels has forcefully argued,

> Augustine's theory of original sin . . . proved politically expedient, since it persuaded many of his contemporaries that human beings universally need external government—which meant, in their case, both a Christian state and an imperially-supported Church. . . . The political and social situation of Christians in the early centuries had changed radically in Augustine's time. Traditional declarations of human freedom, forged by martyrs defying the emperor . . . , no longer fit the situation of Christians who now found themselves the emperors' "brothers and sisters in Christ."

Augustine's new theory "made religious sense of the new political realities." His church "was the new, expanding church of Ambrose . . . established in the respect of Christian emperors . . . , a church set no longer to defy society but to master it." Nor did Augustine merely theorize. In his effort to unify the Catholic Church by "validating Roman society," he urged that "the bonds that held subjects to emperors, slaves to masters, wives to husbands, and children to parents could not be ignored [or] abandoned"—thereby reinforcing the existing social order, including "the rule of men over women."[20]

Just as Augustine was prepared to use his authority against rival married clergy and a restive laity, so was he willing to employ both ecclesiastical and imperial power against other, more radical, Christian ascetics. This is evident in his dealings with the Donatists and the Pelagians, both of whom shared an early-Christian insistence on free will as essential to salvation. The Donatists were a formidable Numidian schismatic group which for nearly a century had challenged Catholic authority in the African Church. The rigorously ascetic Donatists, who were supported by Berber "bands of wandering ascetics of both sexes," claimed to be the only true church. As a leader of the Catholics and an ascetic himself, Augustine vigorously denounced them as a heretical sect, a danger to both the church and the ascetic movement. In addition, he secured and condoned their suppression by secular imperial authorities.[21]

Pelagius was a British monk living in Italy who insisted that free will was essential to both morality and salvation. He thus opposed

Augustine's idea that concupiscence eliminated the possibility of free will and denied his gloomy claim that sin was inherited from the fallen Adam through the procreative process. After considerable controversy, in which Pelagius' ideas were attacked, by Jerome as well as Augustine, as heretical and dangerous, Pelagius was condemned by Pope Innocent I. This papal condemnation was soon reversed, however, by Innocent's successor, Zosimus. Augustine thereafter took the matter to the secular authorities, arguing that Pelagian ideas encouraged social revolution, and secured an imperial condemnation with which Zosimus was compelled to comply. In the Pelagian controversy, and especially in his dispute with the married Pelagian Julian of Eclanum, Augustine was forced to formulate a full exposition of his new theology of grace. "This work offered an analysis of human nature that became . . . the heritage of all subsequent generations of Western Christians," while those "Christians who held to more traditional views of human freedom were . . . condemned as heretics."[22]

Augustine's theology both signaled the end of the traditional household church of married clergy and denied the eschatological promise of early-Christian asceticism. By unequivocally exalting virginity over marriage, Augustine paved the way for the enforcement of clerical celibacy. At the same time, with his doctrine of original sin, he undermined the possibility of individual pursuit of salvation. Earlier ascetics held that Adam and Eve had been chaste before the Fall and that sex was the curse of the fallen state. The story of Adam and Eve thus offered an original state of perfection which could be restored to humanity, by will and grace, through sexual renunciation. This myth also underlay the notion of sexual transcendence and the possibility of both sexual equality and the chaste mingling of the sexes. Augustine rejected this view, arguing that Adam and Eve had not been chaste before the Fall. Rather, their sexuality had originally been bound inextricably to their will. The curse of the Fall was not sexuality *per se* but the divorce between sexuality and the will. Sexual desire now raged independent of the will defying and thus delimiting it. In short, the Fall had led to the loss of free will; in violating God's will, Adam and Eve had sacrificed their own.

This curse of concupiscence was carried forth, generation after generation, to each newborn through the sexual act of its parents in which it had been conceived. The loss of will was thus inescapable and irrevocable. All that was left for Christians was a faith in the grace of God and an utter dependence upon the authority and guidance of the church. Of course, not everyone accepted this startlingly pessimistic formulation; Julian and Cassian, for example, strongly resisted its somber message. But precisely because it fit so well with the needs of those in power, a fact that became clear enough after the condemnation of Pelagius, the new theology of Augustine prevailed, reversing the consensus of three centuries of Christianity. "By abandoning the ascetic myth of a pre-social Paradise," Peter Brown wrote, "Augustine had validated . . . the secular society . . . whose coercive powers he had come to accept [in] justifying the official suppression of his religious rivals." As the barbarian tribes poured down into Italy and Spain, sacking Rome and preparing for the siege of North Africa, Augustine of Hippo abandoned his faith in a Christian empire and sought contemplative refuge in an otherworldly City of God. Yet he had already bequeathed a "heavy legacy" to later ages, for all Christians the lifelong burden of original sin, for the clergy the "hard male puritanism" of clerical asceticism.[23]

The writings and lives of the fathers of the Western Church reflect the decisive movement among church leaders toward an unambivalent embrace of asceticism. At the same time, they reflect the shift within the ascetic movement itself away from the androgynous ideal of early Christianity and toward the exclusive masculine ideal of fourth-century monasticism. Both tendencies are evident in the church fathers' advocacy of clerical celibacy, which signaled the eventual elimination from the elite circles of the church of both married and ascetic women alike. Within monasticism, which they viewed as the engine of ecclesiastical reform, the church fathers insisted upon the strict segregation of the sexes for the protection of male purity. Within the church, they identified consecrated women as the subordinate and marginal brides of Christ, and clerical wives as a threat to the purity of the clergy. Surely they had themselves for a time embraced ascetic female companions, but only as "angels" or symbolic men, not as women. Tertullian had observed that the African Church of his time was "afire with the question of whether or not virgins were still women," and it had become a commonplace among male ascetics by the fourth century to praise their female companions for their virility, their military virtues, and their manliness. However much this symbolic realm might have been viewed and exploited by women as the opening of a new space of female independence and gender equality, for their male companions it was, in theory at least, already a world without women. It was destined to become one in fact as well.[24]

The church fathers contributed substantially toward this end with their actions as well as their words, and their righteous resolve served to solidify official attitudes. In large part through their efforts, the heretofore unheard-of notion of clerical celibacy had already gained official respectability and sanction by the close of the fourth century. No doubt it would soon have taken hold in the church as a whole but for the collapse of the Roman Empire and the corresponding crisis of church authority that followed.

The earliest official recognition of the monastic concern for clerical purity came in Spain, at the local Council of Elvira, near Granada, in 306. In its famous Canon 33, the synod of Spanish bishops "for the first time demanded [explicitly] in a canonical decision sexual continence of its married clergy." The canon read as follows: "bishops, presbyters, and deacons and all other clerics having a position in the ministry are ordered to abstain completely from their wives and not to have children. Whoever, in fact, does this, shall be expelled from the dignity of the clerical state." This oft-cited canon was directed at the majority of married clerics, and demanded of them not celibacy but continence; it did not forbid marriage itself but, rather, conjugal intercourse. Peter Brown suggests that the Spanish bishops thereby took a middle road between the radical ascetics who demanded complete celibacy, on the one hand, and the wealthy married laity and influential married clergy who insisted upon the sanctity of marriage, on the other. Clerical continence was, in effect, a compromise position "between the shrill ascetics and the new men of power" within the church. In officially adopting it, the church sought at once to co-opt the ascetic movement and to lessen the worldly corruption of the married clergy, in the process creating a new legitimacy for the ecclesiastical hierarchy.[25]

The concern of the Spanish bishops about the worldly corruption of the church was a clear indication of their own ascetic inclinations, but they were equally concerned about the growing influence of radical asceticism. Their move toward clerical continence was thus also, as Daniel Callam noted, "the most effective means by which the hierarchy could establish and maintain its ascendancy over the laity against the increasing power and competition of the ascetics." This is made plain by Canon 27, in which the already ascetic clergy are expressly forbidden to have contact or alliances with women unrelated to them, an explicit condemnation of spiritual companionship among celibates. Indeed, one scholar has suggested that the canons of Elvira were the product not of a single synod in the beginning of the fourth century but, rather, of a series of councils much later in the century, and represent official reaction against Priscillianism.[26]

The restrictions the Spanish bishops imposed upon the male clergy and religious—prohibiting sexual relations with women for those who were married and forbidding spiritual relations with women for those who were celibate—were expressions not only of the new ecclesiastical embrace of asceticism but also of the dread of women that had come to characterize the masculine asceticism of the fourth century. A leading authority on the canons of Elvira, Samuel Laeuchli, observed that the "flight from heterosexuality can be read everywhere in the century before and after the synod of Elvira. . . . Man no longer defined himself in relation to woman. . . . Instead, he defined himself in separation from women . . . , [by] the need to escape from direct, concrete relationship to women." The misogynist core of the canons is evident in the fact that more than a quarter of them "are directed expressly against women" themselves. In Laeuchli's view, "the aggressiveness, hostility, and ambiguity in these decisions, the clerics' need to punish and tease the women of their churches, are fully comprehensible as a natural result of the sexual restrictions which they imposed on themselves."[27]

Frazee has argued that Canon 33 of Elvira "set the tone for further action to preserve the sacredness of the ministry," but the immediate impact was nil. The Spanish Bishop Hosius of Cordova, who had been a leading figure at Elvira, became Constantine's ecclesiastical adviser and president of the assembly at the First Ecumenical Council, at Nicaea, in 325. Yet, when he attempted there to secure general legislative sanction for the local canon on clerical continence, he was unsuccessful; the subsequent Council of Gangra in 362 actually condemned those who sought to impose "restrictions of any kind on the married clergy." But the Council of Nicaea, while not yet daring to intrude itself into the marriage relation, was willing nevertheless to prohibit clerical marriage after ordination, an important step toward a celibate priesthood. Equally important, with regard to the tradition of androgynous asceticism, the council upheld the Elvira restrictions against celibate clerical companionship with women. In the meantime, Anne Barstow points out, ascetic Spanish bishops began to come often to Rome in the mid-fourth century. By the end of the fourth century, in the wake of the monastic movement, in the face of barbarian invasion and heretical challenge, in the interest of an enlargement of papal authority, and under the guiding influence of Ambrose, Jerome, and Augustine, the Western Church was finally prepared to embrace in full the strange new spirit of Elvira.[28]

"Whatever the practicality of the ideal of total clerical celibacy," Peter Brown observed, "appeals to it became surprisingly vocal at the end of the fourth century. . . . In Spain, Gaul, and Italy small and increasingly vocal groups of ascetics wanted a place in the clergy of the cities." Henry Lea attributed the intensification of interest in clerical celibacy to the increasing influence of monastic asceticism and related concerns about the growing corruption of the clergy. Certainly, as the church became a prestigious and amply endowed imperial institution, assuming the authority of the empire, the influx into the clergy of wealthy and well-connected Romans fueled such concerns. Moreover, as Daniel Callam pointed out, the unprecedented dogmatic exaltation of virginity over marriage, such as was evident at Elvira, was "bound to raise objections." Indeed, it triggered a strong and, for a time, successful reaction in support of the sanctity and virtue of holy wedlock and the dignity of clerical marriage. The defiant and popular positions put forth by Helvidius, Bonosus, and especially Jovinian during the last two decades of the fourth century had the effect not only of defending the *status quo* for the majority of clergy but also of encouraging, or at least condoning, the return of continent priests to their wives' embrace, of already celibate clergy and bishops to their concubines, and even of monks to married life.[29]

"When an increasing laxity of morals thus threatened to overcome the purity of the Church," Henry Lea wrote, "it is not surprising that the advocates of asceticism should have triumphed over the more moderate and conservative party, and that they should improve their victory by seeking a remedy for existing evils in such laws as should render the strictest continence imperative on all who entered into holy orders." Lea also suggests that, with the great enlargement of church property under imperial auspices, some churchmen lobbied for clerical celibacy as a way of eliminating clerical family inheritance and thus securing the "inalienability" of ecclesiastical possessions; certainly such a motive was acknowledged in later centuries. In 370, no doubt at the urging of ascetic church leaders, Emperor Valentinian issued sanctions against ecclesiastics who visited the houses of widows and virgins. Soon thereafter, the works of Helvidius, Bonosus, and especially Jovinian provoked the well-known vituperative ascetic responses by Ambrose and Jerome, which spurred the involvement of Popes Damasus and Siricius.[30]

These patristic responses lent considerable force "to the zeal for the purity of the church and to the undoubting belief in the necessity of perpetual celibacy," and their impact was more than theoretical. For example, they prompted conciliar support of clerical celibacy in both Milan and Rome during the papacy of Damasus, Jerome's patron. Ultimately, the ascetic bonds between the church fathers and the papacy—in particular those between Ambrose and Siricius—culminated in papal decretals which constituted "the first definitive canon prescribing and enforcing sacerdotal celibacy, exhibited by the records of the Church." This came, again, at just the moment in which, as church historian Frazee points out, "the Roman bishops were intent upon strengthening their power within the church," and thus must be viewed as but one important sign of "the rapidly progressing sacerdotalism of Rome."[31]

The immediate stimulus for the papal decrees on clerical celibacy was a letter to Damasus from Himerius, Spanish bishop of Tarragona; it arrived after Damasus' death and was thus answered by his successor, Siricius. Himerius had written to Rome for advice about, among other things, how to deal with the breakdown of both monastic and clerical discipline in Spain. Siricius' reply indicates that "a crisis in the observance of continence and virginity had arisen in Spain"; priests had resumed conjugal relations, digamists (remarried widowers) were being ordained, and monks and nuns had taken to marrying, "secretly at first, but eventually quite openly." Siricius covened a synod of bishops to formulate his reply to Himerius, the papal defense of clerical continence. He also wrote two subsequent letters along the same lines, to the bishops of Gaul, and of Africa. Siricius employs many lines of argument in his defense of clerical continence; he draws heavily upon general cultic demands for the purity of the priesthood (whom he likens to the celibate soldiers in the imperial army) as well as specific rules on clerical ritual abstention. But, as Daniel Callam has shown in his careful analyses of these letters, such arguments tend to be inconsistent, logically problematic, and otherwise unpersuasive. Callam concludes that, although Siricius employed such arguments in order to try to convince married clergy of the need for continence, the main force of his argument was ascetic. "The anomaly of these decretals," Callam notes, "lies in their attempt to derive total continence from the principle of ritual purity in situations where this can justify only occasional abstinence," and not even for all clergy. "Siricius accepts both the principle of ritual purity and the perfection of the state of continence or virginity. He is willing to use arguments from either one to convince clerics that absolute continence is required of them, but since the state of celibacy or continence cannot be arrived at by the principle of cultic abstinence, it is better seen as primarily the result of the Christian ascetic ideal of virginity."[32]

The ascetic philosophical conviction of the absolute value and necessity of continence and the elevation of virginity above marriage is evident in Siricius' letters, and it stems, no doubt, partly from his close association with Ambrose and his sympathy with the monastic movement. Although he commands that all bishops, priests, and deacons be continent, without thereby condemning clerical marriage altogether, "it is more accurate to say," Callam suggests, "that Siricius is more interested in opposing clerical marriage than in defending ritual abstinence." Indeed, as Lea pointed out, Siricius urged that monks vowed to perpetual chastity ought to be ordained as priests in order to ensure the purity of the clergy.[33]

But if the decretals of Siricius did not reflect a simply ritualistic renunciation of sexuality, neither did they reflect merely a Christian ascetic contempt for marriage. They signaled in particular the triumph of clerical asceticism, over both clerical marriage and its own androgynous ancestry. In taking this first official step toward an ecclesiastical world without women, the papacy formally incorporated within the church the male monastic flight from women. In the words of Henry Lea, "the Western Church was thus at length irrevocably committed to the strict maintenance of ecclesiastical celibacy, and the labours of the three great Latin Fathers, Jerome, Ambrose, and Augustine, were crowned with success." "By the time that Augustine laid down his pen, in 430," Peter Brown concluded, "the leaders of the Christian Church already carried in the back of their minds a deposit of assumptions that marked them off irrevocably from the elites" of late antiquity. "By insisting that its leaders no longer beget children, the Catholic Church in the West made plain that it enjoyed a supernatural guarantee of continuity that no ancient city could claim. If they were to be respected as the leaders of a 'holy' institution, bishops and priests had to remain anomalous creatures."[34]

The doctrines on clerical continence laid down by Siricius were subsequently confirmed in a series of fifth-century papal decretals;

moreover, Innocent I "ordered that anyone wanting to be a cleric must promise he will never marry," and Leo I extended this prohibition of marriage to subdeacons. According to Callam, there was in all of this legislation "a desire for uniformity" of practice throughout the Western Church. And, indeed, in the fourth, fifth, and sixth centuries, "local councils in the West supported the Roman rulings." "The usual canons for admittance to [clerical status] required married men to practice continence and unmarried candidates to pledge they would never contract matrimony." Following the pattern established a century earlier at Elvira, the councils at Carthage, Turin, Orange, and Tours also included prescriptions on the place of women in the church which restricted their access to the altar and regulated their dress and behavior. In the fifth century, the civil law had begun to reflect this ecclesiastical legislation. The Theodosian Code of 438 "incorporated the Nicene canon forbidding women, except wives [and close relatives] to live in the same house with clerics"; subsequent Justinian legislation seconded this prohibition and "further forbade a married man with children to become a bishop and ordered that any childless married priest, elected to the bishopric, must no longer have sexual relations with his wife."[35]

CERTAINLY THE ASCETIC CLERGY had gained considerable ecclesiastical influence and, in the political and economic vacuum created by the fall of the Roman Empire, their views came increasingly to the fore within the church. But, at the same time, though "vociferous," "magnetic," and papally supported, as Brown notes, they remained still a small minority. The majority of clerics, beyond their reach, continued to follow the time-honored tradition of clerical marriage. As the ancient Roman centers of established power gradually gave way to a multitude of land-based barbarian fiefdoms, church power and property became more diffuse, localized, and proprietary. Now the importance of marriage, family, and inheritance was reinforced rather than diminished, within the church as without it. If landed elites patronized and dominated their churches, they also retained, or gained, private hereditary control over ecclesiastical property. The major clergy of this "proprietary church" inescapably became officially involved in the disposition of church property. However much they might insist upon the holiness of their institution, "the undeniable message of vast private wealth and family power" was "congealed in the splendor of [their] buildings." Moreover, they were bound to develop a personal stake in church property, in the form of benefices, which they could pass on to their heirs. There is ample evidence in the Western Church of married bishops passing on church property to their children, and even of bishoprics themselves becoming hereditary. Later, the secular investiture of bishops bound the church even further into the feudal relations of power and property. Thus, while the influence of the ascetics increased within the upper hierarchy of the Latin Church, the actual authority of that hierarchy over the church as a whole was diminished by the dramatic transformation of European society. The ascetic reform of the clergy was therefore delayed.[36]

From the fifth century on, local councils continued in vain to support and elaborate on papal policy regarding clerical continence and celibacy. "Over the next four centuries there was constant lawmaking in councils and local assemblies concerning the sexual life of the priest, giving evidence of the inability of church authorities to make effective the ban on marriage for clerics in major orders. Efforts were pushed to have the secular clergy in the towns live with the bishop or share a common residence, but again the frequency of the laws shows the weakness of the practice." In Lea's view, "this perpetual legislation . . . betrays the fact that it was not only practically impossible to maintain separation between the clergy and their wives, but that at times marriage was not uncommon even within the prohibited orders" of bishops and even monks. Frazee concludes that, despite the succession of ecclesiastical pronouncements and legislation, "most authorities agree that the great majority of clergymen in the West from [the sixth] to the tenth century were married men." Barstow adds that prohibitions against conjugal sex were also notoriously difficult to enforce. Thus neither celibacy nor even continence had come to characterize the clergy of the early-medieval Western Church.[37]

"In almost all countries" of feudal Europe, Friedrich Kempf observed, "the rural priests cohabited with women, either in concubinage or in a real marriage. Not a few clerics or canons attached to urban churches followed their examples. There were even isolated cases of bishops [and] monks, who had wife and children." In addition, as we have seen, the earlier ascetic spiritual companionship between churchmen and royal and aristocratic women re-emerged in the monastic revival of the seventh century, once again enlarging the female role in the evangelical church and giving rise to the durable and venerable double monasteries of France and England. In short, as Kempf concluded, by the ninth century the prohibitions "to which the Western Church had bound major clerics since the fourth and fifth centuries had to a great extent fallen into oblivion."[38]

As Workman noted, the Western Church had modeled itself organizationally along the same military lines as the empire. As the Western Empire deteriorated during the fifth century, a semblance of Roman order was for a time maintained through the episcopal organization of the church. During the fifth-century barbarian migrations, for example, the Catholic bishops of Gaul strove to maintain the fourth-century ecclesiastical reform momentum, issuing conciliar legislation on clerical continence and placing restrictions on women. In the sixth century, most of the Western Empire fell into the hands of barbarian tribes which either resisted conversion or had been converted to Arian Christianity. Under Clovis, however, the Franks became Catholics and hence the mainstay of Western support for both the empire and the Latin Church. The clerical ascetic reform campaign thus continued in earnest under royal Merovingian auspices. As Suzanne Wemple explained, "Merovingian bishops, supported by their rulers, engaged in vigorous conciliar activity in the sixth century. They strengthened male domination of the hierarchy by abolishing the office of feminine diaconate, defining the order of widows as a religious state devoid of clerical status, and barring priests' wives from pastoral service."[39]

The Merovingian Church councils denied the traditional mutuality of marriage vows and permitted prospective clerics to withdraw unilaterally from conjugal relations—earlier, such ascetic commitment had to be taken by both husband and wife together—thereby lowering both the status and freedom of wives. Increasingly portraying the presence of women as a threat to ritual purity, the sixth-century councils of Orléans, Tours, Macon, and Lyons moved toward depriving women of any role in parish affairs. Up to this point, requirements of clerical continence had not necessarily entailed the actual severing of family ties, but by the end of the century, priests' wives were officially barred from sharing their husbands' homes. Such legislation, in Wemple's view, "amounted to a de facto requirement of clerical celibacy in the Frankish church." "The banishment of deacons', priests', and bishops' wives from the presence of their husbands had a dual consequence," Wemple noted; "it may have ostensibly removed a source of temptation from the [clerics'] lives, but it also decreased the influence of women in parish affairs." In addition, since female performance of clerical functions was identified with Priscillianist heresy, the Frankish bishops prohibited women from the diaconate and also ordered that "women could not receive the Eucharist in their hands or touch the altar cloth, and they must be veiled when they took communion." In short, during the sixth century, "the political power that the Merovingian bishops gained from the patronage of their kings enhanced the effectiveness of their opposition to the feminine diaconate" and clerical marriage, and hence their ability to "assert the exclusivity of male authority in the church." The royal advantage enjoyed by the episcopal hierarchy did not last long, however.[40]

By the close of the sixth century, the ultimate failure of Emperor Justinian's effort to reconquer the West, the fragmentation of the Merovingian dynasty into competing royal and aristocratic fiefdoms, and the ascetic revival inspired by the Irish missionaries under Columban effectively put an end to the Roman episcopal campaign. The imperial hold on the Mediterranean gave way to that of the Visigoths in Spain and the Lombards in Italy, while England fell prey to the Angles and Saxons. In the Frankish kingdom, because of what Georges Duby termed the "long-term tendency" of warfare-based barbarian kingship to strengthen the aristocracy, "the mayors of the palace, the court nobility, and the territorial aristocracy . . . gained ascendancy over the kings." The Frankish Church rapidly became "part and parcel of the age"; bishops shifted their allegiance from the papacy and the king to their regional lords, amassed control over great wealth, and their bishoprics became bastions of the local aristocracy.[41]

The prominent role played by wealthy noblewomen in the development of this aristocracy-based church reversed for a time the clerical campaign for an ecclesiastical world without women. In addition to their patronage of the local bishop, these women were especially active in the Irish movement which had revived the androgynous ascetic ideal of the early church. In cooperation with the Irish monks, they aided evangelical missions and, perhaps most important, founded and ruled over double monasteries and nunneries. Thus, although women were excluded from the diaconate, they once again began to exercise quasi-clerical functions; nuns assisted priests in the distribution of sacraments and looked after the altar, and abbesses heard confession and gave benediction to both male and female members of their monastic communities. In short, prohibitions against women's participation in and performance of ecclesiastical services were neither enforced nor, perhaps, enforceable. Indeed, inspired by the new ascetic movement themselves and beholden to their wealthy women benefactors, the bishops of the Frankish Church now cooperated and even collaborated with the powerful women of the church. As the authority of the papacy, the king, and the Roman Empire eroded and diminished, the stern admonitions of the fathers of the church were all but forgotten.[42]

Although seventh-century synods continued to reiterate earlier demands for clerical continence and the physical separation of clergy from their wives, the observations of Bishop Gregory of Tours, historian of the Frankish Empire, and of Columban, in his letters to Pope Gregory I, "leave no doubt that ecclesiastical sanctions were defied by both [clerics] and their wives." Wemple also points out that "there is sufficient evidence to suggest that the councils did not insist on the enforcement of celibacy and that the church did not monitor the lives of priests and deacons." As the church became bound up increasingly in local feudal relations, the clergy married, had children, and bequeathed church property in the aristocratic manner. Married priests again shared homes with their wives and resumed conjugal relations, and their unmarried brethren often lived with concubines. "During the seventh century," Wemple observed, "we find married men in the highest echelons of the Frankish church handing down bishoprics to their sons [while] certainly among lesser clerics the rule of continence was disregarded." The ascetic clergy, meanwhile, in the wake of the Irish monastic revival, once again cohabited with virgins or widows, or enjoyed the chaste companionship of women within the walls of double monastic communities. By this time too, a similar situation had come to prevail in Anglo-Saxon England, the scene of barbarian conquest and conversion, warring kingdoms, and Irish evangelism. In short, the vigorous male monastic and clerical ascetic reforms of the fourth and fifth centuries to which the church fathers had given voice had, by all appearances, faded into a distant past.[43]

Five · *Brothers: The Militarization of Monasticism*

THE RUDE REALITIES of early-medieval Western society defied the clerical ascetic ideals of Rome and the fathers of the Latin Church. By the seventh century, however, those ideals gained renewed force in an alliance between the papacy and Benedictine monasticism. Benedict of Nursia, the scion of a Roman patrician, retired from the world at the age of thirty, around the year 500, to become a hermit at Subiaco. There he endured the trials of rigorous ascetic renunciation in the Eastern fashion. As with Anthony before him, his greatest temptation took the female form.

> The allurements of voluptuousness acted so strongly on his excited senses, that he was on the point of leaving his retreat to seek after a woman whose beauty had formerly impressed him, and whose memory haunted him incessantly. But there was near his grotto a clump of thorns and briars. He took off the vestment of skins which was his only dress, and rolled himself among them naked, till his body was all one wound, but also till he had extinguished forever the infernal fire which inflamed him even in the desert.

Eventually, Benedict's heroic asceticism attracted a following, and he established around him at Subiaco twelve monasteries of twelve monks each. "Driven from Subiaco by an irruption of shameless women" sent down on his flock by a dissolute priest, according to Workman, Benedict relocated his community in 529 to Monte Cassino, the hallowed center of what became known as the Benedictine Order.[1]

It was at Monte Cassino that Benedict composed his famous Rule, which followed upon the earlier efforts of Pachomius and Cassian to establish a regular discipline for monastic life. Before Benedict, each monastery was a "rule unto itself," as Workman phrased it. Although Benedict himself had no intention of founding a monastic order, his Rule inspired a sense of solidarity among monks while preserving self-government in each community. Emphasizing self-surrender and humility rather than self-mastery and mortification, Benedict insisted above all upon the unqualified obedience of monks to their abbot, as well as a commitment to permanent residence in their first community and adherence to a regular daily discipline. In the place of arbitrary authority, Benedict instituted rule by law and system. With its emphasis upon ascetic moderation, his Rule was designed to correct for both the ascetic excesses of the East, on the one hand, and the ascetic laxity of the West, on the other. Benedict's communities were also characterized by their communal principles and their sanctification of manual labor. His contemporary Cassiodorus contributed another element for which the Order would become renowned in the centuries ahead: the preservation and pursuit of learning.[2]

Benedict's foundation owed its great success not only to the soundness of its principles but also to the enduring support of the papacy. Toward the end of the sixth century, monasticism in the West gained considerable momentum when monks, who were also ordained clergy, were for the first time chosen as bishops of Rome. As Charles Frazee explained, "this meant that the ideals of the monastic life would be even more emphasized for the clergy as a whole." The first of these monk-popes was Pelagius II, who attained the papacy in 579. Ten years later, Monte Cassino was burned by the Lombards, and the Benedictine monks fled to Rome for protection. Pelagius established them in a monastery near the pope's residence, which was to remain the headquarters of the Order for more than a century. It was here that Gregory the Great, who succeeded Pelagius the following year, first came under their influence.[3]

Gregory had been a well-to-do prefect of Rome before becoming a monk and a founder of monasteries. He subsequently was a deacon, the papal ambassador to the imperial court at Constantinople, and, finally, pope. As a monk himself, Gregory was convinced that "the strictness of the monastic life is the only possible mode of salvation for the greater portion of mankind," and insisted upon mandatory clerical celibacy, even for subdeacons. In Peter Levi's phrase, he was "fired with the conviction that the hope of Christianity lay in monastic communities," and his contact with the Benedictines fueled that flame.[4]

Given his ambitions, Gregory had become pope at a propitious moment. The receding influence of the Byzantine Empire in Italy and the West afforded him a degree of autonomy unknown to his predecessors, as well as what had become in effect an international parish. He recognized that the future of the papacy was tied no longer to the empire but to the successful conversion of the barbarian kingships, and he accordingly established an alliance with the Lombards. He also understood that the pope's most reliable allies in such an endeavor were not the bishops but the monks. Indeed, he would deploy the monks to challenge the princely pretensions of the bishops; "if the bishop was the king's man," Workman noted, "the monk was the pope's." In monasticism, then, Gregory saw a potent vehicle for evangelism, for restoring discipline to both ascetic communities and the church itself, and for establishing in the place of the vanishing empire "the temporal power of the papacy."[5]

Benedictine monasticism, with its emphases upon law, regularity, discipline, and obedience, was made to order for such an ambitious papal reformer. As pope, Gregory devoted himself to the promulgation of the Benedictine system and sought to impose the strict enforcement of Benedict's Rule upon the whole of Western monasticism. He authored the first *Life of Benedict* and showered the Order with protection and privilege. Perhaps most important, he conferred upon the Benedictine monasteries a partial papal exemption from episcopal control, thereby minimizing the bishops' interference in monastic affairs and strengthening the ties between the monks and the papacy. The Benedictines benefited immensely from the pope's blessings, gaining greater internal control over their order and a vastly extended reach for their operations throughout the West. In return, the pope secured their unwavering allegiance; the monks became, Workman noted, "the watch dogs in every land for the pope." "Gregory was a Benedictine in almost all but name," Levi suggested. His promotion of the Benedictine Rule as the Western standard "was the keystone of monastic reform for centuries . . . and it was through him that the monastic movement became a papal instrument."[6]

The conversion of the Anglo-Saxons in southern England was perhaps Gregory's greatest triumph, and to achieve it he relied upon the monks from his own monastery at St. Andrew's, led by Augustine. After the conversion of the Kentish King Ethelbert in 597, largely through the efforts of his wife, these monastic missionaries established an outpost of the Roman Church at Canterbury and from there carried the papal program of reform throughout southern England. For centuries thereafter, the archbishop of the English Church would be chosen by the Benedictine monks of Canterbury. These agents of Rome were, however, not the only Christian missionaries in England.

The Irish, through the evangelism of Columba and later Aidan, had succeeded, likewise through the efforts of royal women, in establishing Northumbria as the English stronghold of the Celtic Church. In the ensuing contest between these rival churches, the Benedictine alliance with the papacy proved decisive. Benedict Biscop, a Benedictine monk who founded several new monasteries in England, traveled five times to Rome and became a leading promoter of Roman practice in the English Church. Wilfrid of Ripon, a Celtic bishop educated at Aidan's monastery at Lindisfarne, was attracted to the work of Biscop, introduced the Benedictine Rule at Ripon, and became a champion of Latin practice in Northumbria. At the Synod of Whitby in 664, held in the Celtic double monastery of the abbess Hilda, Wilfrid led the Roman party to victory over the Celtic; although the synod merely approved the use of the Roman date for Easter over the Celtic, the decision signaled the Roman eclipse of the Irish Church in England.

On one of his trips to Rome, in 668, Benedict Biscop accompanied to Canterbury the newly appointed Archbishop Theodore of Tarsus and his colleague Hadrian, soon to be abbot of the Peter and Paul Monastery. Theodore had been sent by the pope to carry out the reform of the English Church, and Hadrian was sent along to keep Theodore to the task. Together they sought to bring the English Church into line with Rome and the Benedictine movement. Theodore immediately sought to outlaw the establishment of any new double monasteries, although he acknowledged that he was powerless to close down those already existing. At the Synod of Hertford in 673, over which Theodore presided, special stress was placed upon Benedictine requirements such as the permanence of monastic domicile. By and large, these attempts at reform were disregarded—new double monasteries were established, such as Wimbourne—and the established practices of the Anglo-Saxon Church would persist until the devastation of the Danish invasions of the ninth century and the revived Benedictine reforms of the tenth. Nevertheless, the papacy had regained its foothold in England. Equally important, the ecclesiastical reform campaign was now to be carried from England back to the continent of Europe by a product of the English effort, the Anglo-Saxon Benedictine missionary Boniface. Brought up in a Benedictine school near Exeter and trained at the Benedictine monastery of Nursling, Boniface carried the torch of Rome and Benedict into Germany and the Frankish kingdom.[7]

As an apostle of Benedictine reform, Boniface undertook to bring the Frankish bishops and monasteries into line, not just with Rome but with the leaders of a new Western Empire. The deterioration of the Merovingian dynasty had enabled the mayors of the palace to rule on behalf of the impotent descendants of Clovis, in effect usurping their royal authority. At Tours in 732, Charles Martel halted the Arab advance north from Spain, thereby laying the basis for renewed Frankish security and expansion. On the death of Charles Martel in 741, his son Pepin assumed the illegitimate mantle of Carolingian authority, his other son Carloman having retired to a monastery. At this time, the Lombards in Italy were again laying siege to the papal state. When the pope appealed to the Franks for military assistance, Pepin successfully intervened; he thereupon placed the Lombard territories under Frankish control, rendering the papal state, in effect, a Frankish dependency. In return for his protection, Pepin secured papal sanction for his rule and thus legitimacy for the new Carolingian dynasty, as well as church support for Frankish expansion and internal order. The church in Rome had gained security and also a means of greatly extending its reach by sword as well as by word, but the pope was now compelled to accept a secondary role in ecclesiastical reform.

If Boniface and the pope saw in the Carolingians powerful support for their missionary activities, Pepin and his successors Charlemagne and Louis the Pious saw in the church and its Benedictine mission effective vehicles for securing greater royal authority over the Frankish aristocracy, church, and monasteries. In pursuit of these political ends, meanwhile, the Carolingian kings also wittingly and unwittingly lent their might to the clerical ascetic reform agenda of the Roman Church. New church-sanctioned marriage regulations weakened noble alliances and concentrated dynastic power, and Carolingian reform of the secular and regular clergy, through control of the episcopate and renewed enforcement of Benedictine discipline and celibacy, ensured that ecclesiastical and monastic allegiance and property would accrue to royal rather than aristocratic benefit. But in the wake of these changes, many aristocratic and lower-class women, clerical wives, and female religious were increasingly marginalized. If, as Suzanne Wemple suggests, "the early Carolingians' attempt to regulate relations between the sexes was prompted . . . by political considerations," the effect was to invigorate the clerical ascetic campaign to create an ecclesiastical world without women.[8]

Pepin found in Boniface an invaluable aid in gaining church sanction for his crown; moreover, Boniface's ideas about the reform of Frankish sexual norms, which entailed polygamy, divorce, concubinage, and incest, "strengthened Pepin's position against the aristocracy network of alliances among the great [aristocratic] families." Royal invocation of the church's far-reaching prohibitions against incest—which extended to the seventh degree of consanguinity as well as to relationships of affinity and spiritual kinship—enabled the Carolingian kings to narrow the definition of lawful wedlock and hence restrict the range of possible aristocratic alliances through marriage. Further restrictions on these alliances were sanctioned by ecclesiastical taboos against adultery, polygamy, and concubinage (which included so-called trial marriages and quasi-marriages). The most important contribution of the church in this regard, and Boniface's primary concern, was the principle of the indissolubility of marriage. This idea rendered divorce difficult if not impossible—except in the case of adultery by the wife—and gave supreme sanction to the monogamous conjugal couple. As the prohibition of polygamy eliminated multiple marriages, so the prohibition against divorce diminished the likelihood of serial marriages.

All of these notions, which derived from the church fathers, ran against established Frankish custom and tradition, and some, such as the prohibition against divorce, were resisted by Pepin. But, insofar as they enabled the Carolingian dynasty to concentrate royal-familial relations while weakening the web of aristocratic ties, they were endorsed by the Frankish rulers. Boniface introduced incest restrictions in the Frankish Church councils, and Pepin ratified them in royal capitularies. Pepin's son Charlemagne, who ascended the throne in 771, had led a robust sexual life and had himself many wives and concubines, and eighteen children. Yet in 789 he prohibited remarriage of divorced men and women, and in 796 decreed that even adultery could not dissolve the marriage bond. Perhaps because of this enforcement of the principle of the indissolubility of marriage, and the grave significance it gave to marriage, Charlemagne permitted his own daughters to engage in sexual alliances outside of marriage and hence avoid the lock of wedlock.[9]

Charlemagne's successor, his son Louis the Pious, was, as his name suggests, of a "more puritanical temperament" than his father. In the spirit of the church fathers, he viewed marriage as a guard against concupiscence. After having had several alliances with concubines, he married, driven by the fear, according to his biographer, "that otherwise, overcome by the innate heat of his body, he would be forced against his will to seek multifarious sexual pleasures." From within the haven of his marriage, he gazed with contempt upon the dalliances of his sisters. Thus, "immediately upon ascending the throne in 814, he excluded the entire female company from the palace" and thereafter "tried to rid the imperial palace and royal residences of women of questionable conduct." In addition, he barred men who lived with concubines, the women themselves, and their illegitimate children from testifying in court, a decision later ratified by episcopal-conciliar canons. When, following his wife's death, Louis remarried the young and influential Judith, his advisers tried desperately to separate them. They accused her of adultery (with Louis's closest adviser, Bernard of Septimania) and even arranged for her abduction and confinement in a convent. But belief in the indissolubility of marriage had by this time become so entrenched that Louis prevailed in maintaining his wedlock.[10]

By the second half of the ninth century, the new Christian ideal of monogamous marriage "was enshrined in secular and ecclesiastical legislation," with myriad consequences. Aristocratic marriages had become more carefully arranged and exclusive, greatly diminishing the opportunities for lower-class women. Moreover, with the ascent of monogamy as the only lawful relationship between laity, the gap between bona fide wives and all other women widened considerably. And, given the narrowing notion of marriage and the restrictions against polygamy and divorce, there were fewer wives. The only other church-sanctioned option open to women was the cloister; indeed, the cloistering of widows had become "an integral part of the church's effort to enforce monogamy." The growing proportion of women outside of marriage or the cloister, meanwhile, was increasingly liable to insult and injury. Allegations of women engaging in sorcery and bewitching men, for example, increased.[11]

If the advent of monogamy transformed the nature of the family, it also altered the "descent of property." The lawful conjugal couple and their children were now the "dominant economic unit" which alone acquired, controlled, disposed, bequeathed, and inherited property. The new laws certainly guaranteed aristocratic wives greater security and power, but those living outside of lawful marriage, such as concubines and their children, were now economically disenfranchised. The reduction in the number of wives and the exclusion of concubines from control over property are reflected in the decline of female ownership and alienation of property in the second half of the ninth century, even though Frankish inheritance laws remained unchanged.[12]

"By the ninth century," Wemple argued, "legal principles and social customs that were to define women's role in the highest and lowest echelons of European society were clearly enunciated." And the church-inspired Carolingian reforms initiated by Boniface had "opened a new chapter not only in the history of marital relations but also in the history of the ownership of land." "In the open and fluid society of the Merovingian period," Wemple observed, "more women had access to wealth and status through marriage than in the ninth century"; as a consequence of Carolingian legislation, "fewer women had the opportunity to gain control of property through marriage." And, in the absence of such economic power, fewer women than before were in a position to exercise landed authority over ecclesiastical and monastic affairs. Ironically, in the tenth and eleventh centuries, following the collapse of the Carolingian Empire and the re-emergence of the feudal nobility, some aristocratic wives ultimately benefited from the familial concentration of aristocratic wealth and were once again able to wield considerable economic and political power. But these were the exceptions. For the most part, "the formalization of wifely duties in the ninth century, while enhancing the wife's influence in aristocratic families, strengthened male dominance in all other spheres," including the church.[13]

From the beginning of the Carolingian dynasty, the church and state were bound together in mutual dependence and obligation. Just as the kingship of Pepin had originally been blessed by Pope Zacharias and anointed by Boniface, so Charlemagne was later crowned emperor by Pope Leo III. Indeed, for Louis the Pious, "not the person, not the force of the Emperor, but the Church was . . . the center and the mainspring of the state." This symbiosis between church and state meant, for the Carolingians, both that religious pursuits served secular ends and that secular pursuits served religious ends. But, given the preponderance of Frankish power over that of the papacy, once the state had secured its divine legitimacy, the church became more a creature of the state than vice versa. The Frankish Church had become another imperial church, a *Reichskirche*, and its clergy were obliged to serve the state as both a religious and a secular institution. The royal interest in church affairs was thus a fundamental aspect of church governance; reform of the church had become an important end of the state.[14]

As R. W. Southern observed, the Benedictine creed had "that in it which must appeal to anyone who values order and discipline. . . . The main element in this ideal was the practice of obedience." It is hardly surprising, therefore, that such virtues as these, so evident in the practices of the Anglo-Saxon missionaries, were seized upon by Pepin and his Carolingian successors in their struggle to secure royal control over the Frankish Church. And if, as Wemple suggested, "the ecclesiastical reform movement initiated by Boniface called for the reassertion of episcopal authority," Boniface also understood that such episcopal authority would depend upon the bishops' becoming obedient instruments of the state. "Just as it was a bishop's duty to assist the ruler in his secular task," Southern added, "so it was the responsibility of the ruler to direct the bishops toward their proper end."[15]

The effort by the Anglo-Saxon monk-bishop and his royal masters to reform the church thus produced "the first substantial body of legislation in the West about the spiritual duties of a bishop. . . ." During his long reign, Charlemagne issued a series of detailed and exhaustive directives to the bishops of their realm—which were summed up in a treatise on episcopal guidance by Archbishop Hincmar of Rheims—and revived the office of metropolitan to enforce them. Thus, by the end of the ninth century, the Carolingian bishop "was a man," in Southern's description, "endlessly exercised in the care of temporal and spiritual things, a chief agent in the royal government of the kingdom."[16]

The obedience of the church to the state was further guaranteed by the status of bishops and abbots as vassals within a warrior kingdom. The Frankish Empire was, after all, essentially a military enterprise; during Charlemagne's reign alone, there were major campaigns against the Lombards, Avars, Saxons, Frisians, and Arabs. In keeping with Gallic conciliar legislation, Charlemagne prohibited clerics from bearing arms and going to war. The lower clergy were expected, rather, to serve as spiritual soldiers, chaplains attending to the religious needs of the combatants. But the higher clergy were another matter. Since the church was one of the largest owners of land in the realm, its leaders were subject to the same imperial requirements as other nobility. Charlemagne required the approximately one hundred bishops and two hundred abbots to provide armed men and supplies for imperial campaigns. Moreover, whereas in Merovingian times the higher clergy had on occasion been combatants themselves, "under the Carolingians . . . all this was institutionalized. . . . Charlemagne expected bishops and abbots to follow him in his campaigns," despite their protestations that priests should fight only with spiritual arms. The result was, in Philippe Cantamine's phrase, the "militarization of the higher clergy." "Intimately engaged in the wars of the period, the church hierarchy experienced . . . an inevitable secularization of its habits, training, and even appearance." At the same time, in fealty to the king and obedience to military commanders, "it was led to sacralize and sublimate warrior values," thereby sustaining the masculine clerical habits born of persecution and an earlier imperial identity.[17]

In following the prescriptions laid down by Boniface, Charlemagne sought religious conformity to the established usage of the Roman Church. Given its importance to the identity and well-being of the kingdom, religious practice had to be made to adhere to an unprecedented discipline: correct observance had to be codified and enforced, dogma precisely defined, ritual purified and standardized. Charlemagne's innumerable decrees on religious practice emphasize authenticity, uniformity, and order. "The conception of religion, not simply as a means of personal salvation for the individual, but as a social force moving and transforming society, owes its strength to Charles the Great," Geoffrey Barraclough observed.[18]

One of Charlemagne's personal preoccupations in this regard was the detailed reform of the liturgy, which was ultimately codified by Amalarius of Metz. Boniface had early insisted upon the importance of liturgical reform, as had Pope Zacharias. Following their advice, Pepin had revived the Roman imperial tradition of the *laudes regiae*, a public ceremony of intercessory prayers conducted by the clergy on behalf of the king. Under Charlemagne, this practice was given a "separate liturgical form" with a new "unique form of litany," and was sung in processions, at coronations, and in the introductory section of the Mass. Most important for the warrior-kings of the Carolingians was the "liturgy of war." If Frankish kings "attached great political as well as spiritual significance to prayers performed on their behalf," this was especially true of prayers offered in preparation for and commemoration of military campaigns. Again, this practice began at the behest of Boniface and Pope Zacharias, and henceforth Pepin and his son Charlemagne both played an active role in arranging special religious services on the eve of military expeditions and in times of military crisis.[19]

Charlemagne "took active measures to organize litanic processions by noncombatants on behalf of a specific undertaking of the Frankish army" in order not only to secure divine assistance but also "to involve his kingdom's noncombatants in his wars." On the eve of a campaign against the Avars in 791, he decreed that "every single priest was to perform a votive Mass" and "every clergyman . . . was to sing fifty [psalms] and walk barefoot while performing the litanies." "By the early ninth century," Michael McCormick has written, "the performance at royal command of special propitiatory services, particularly in times of military danger, was an established tradition [and] it would continue at least down to the end of the century." The practice was promoted by the higher clergy, especially by those who sought to escape from the burden of actual combat "by invoking the contemporary institution of special propitiatory services as a kind of liturgical substitute for military service."[20]

If the Carolingian transformation of the church began with episcopal and liturgical reform, it ultimately depended for its success on the reform of the entire clergy. This entailed not only the enforcement of clerical obedience to episcopal, and hence royal, authority, but a revolution in clerical education and renewed imperial insistence upon clerical purity, especially with regard to celibacy. If the clergy were to conform to the new practice, they would have to be educated in it, and if the correct rituals were to have their intended effect upon the heavens, they would have to be performed only by untainted male souls. At the heart of the so-called Carolingian Renaissance was the royal determination to establish officially correct religious practice and to educate the clergy in conformity with it. Because of the depletion of literacy among the upper strata of secular society, moreover, Charlemagne depended upon an educated clergy to staff his imperial bureaucracy. To these ends, he established his famous palace school under the direction of the Anglo-Saxon Alcuin of York and ordered that clerical schools be created in every episcopal cathedral and monastery. He set Alcuin to revise and correct the text of the Vulgate and write against the Adoptianist heresy, encouraged a revival of Latin Christian learning and the seven liberal arts, fostered the creation of libraries, and even introduced a new standard form of writing, the "minuscule." Although the emperor had "certified the final demise of Latin as a living tongue" among the laity by requiring the use of the vernacular in preaching, he insisted upon clerical literacy in Latin, thereby making of the clergy a linguistically distinct elite caste. The Carolingian Renaissance, then, as Barraclough has argued, "was simply a byproduct of Charles' efforts to raise the standards of clerical education, not as an end in itself, but to reform religion."[21]

Equally important as education to the reform of the clergy was the Carolingian effort "to enforce a regular discipline and a collegiate life among the clergy of the great cathedral churches, so that the priests would love a purer life and therefore better perform their function." The Carolingians sought to transform the clergy into a "corporate body distinct from and superior to the laity" which derived its authority through the ritual of the sacraments. To ensure both the viability of the ritual and the authority of the clergy vis-à-vis the laity, the reform effort demanded clerical continence and justified it in the name of ritual purity. As in the past, Carolingian church synods forbade clerics to live with women, but now "the goal was not to prevent clerks from sleeping with their wives . . . but to transform the clergy into a celibate body." Following a plan of Bishop Chrodegang of Metz, "the cathedral clergy was organized into chapters of canons and discipline was tightened."[22]

With imperial support, "the church censured married priests who had resumed sexual relations with their wives, as well as unmarried priests who had sex." Such clerical reform efforts were more effective under the Carolingians than they had been under Merovingian and Gallican auspices, because now, in the wake of the ecclesiastical reorganization, "the episcopate could unite more readily and could count on royal cooperation." Indeed, under the Carolingians, "clerical incontinence became a criminal offense." If such imperial support of clerical celibacy reflected a concern for ecclesiastical discipline and ritual purity, it also furthered royal interests vis-à-vis the aristocracy— an aspect of the reform that would become increasingly clear. Just as the church sought by means of clerical celibacy to prevent the alienation of its property, through clerical marriage and inheritance, into the hands of the clergy, so the kings sought to prevent the loss of church property, through clerical marriage and inheritance, into the hands of the nobility. Indeed, under the Carolingians, "clerical incontinence became a criminal offence, equal to theft and perjury, punishable with loss of office and inheritance."[23]

If episcopal and clerical reform was essential to the Carolingian reorganization of the church, monastic reform was its core. From the outset, the monastic spirit inspired imperial reforms, and these reforms in turn ultimately, and irrevocably, transformed the spirit of Western monasticism. The Carolingian dynasty was, in a sense, rooted

in the monasteries. Both Pepin and Carloman had received their
early schooling in Frankish monasteries, and Carloman retired to one.
When Boniface the Benedictine "turned his attention to the state of
the Frankish church, he first proposed the reform of all monasteries
according to the Benedictine norm." The Anglo-Saxon missionaries
"introduced the Benedictine Rule into [their] new foundations, subjecting abbots and abbesses to strict episcopal control. As the reforms
progressed, all forms of religious life were brought under episcopal
control. . . . [This] extension of episcopal jurisdiction over the monasteries was carried out with the help of the new dynasty." "In fact,"
Wemple suggests, "increased episcopal authority [over monasteries]
was the bishops' reward for cooperating in the creation of the Carolingian *Reichskirke*." In the process, the monasteries lost their independence, and their practices and assets came under imperial control.[24]

Charlemagne, who sent his daughters to monasteries for their
schooling, secured a copy of the Benedictine Rule from Monte Cassino, "recognized no other rule," and tried to enforce its universal
and correct observance. At the time, discipline in the Frankish monasteries was diverse or lax: monastic assets had often been alienated to
lay nobility, the Irish influence was pervasive, and monks and nuns
lived—in double monasteries, together—according to other rules
(such as that of Caesarius of Arles), their own unique rules, a combination of rules, or no rules. Not given to asceticism himself, Charlemagne nevertheless sought to bring the monasteries under episcopal,
and hence royal, control and encouraged reform; in the last year of
his reign, at the Council of Tours, "the Frankish bishops rebuked
abbots for living 'rather as canons than as monks.' "[25]

The seriousness with which Charlemagne regarded royal monastic
reform is indicated by his insistence upon the new monastic liturgical
duty of performing intercessory prayers on his behalf. A decade after
the Frankish annexation of Lombard territories in Italy, for example,
a controversy over this monastic obligation arose at the monastery
of San Vicenzo al Volturno, near Monte Cassino. The head of this
monastery, the abbot Potho, refused to sing a required psalm for
Charlemagne—the daily prayer, Psalm 53, which had been incorporated into the monastic office—and "was reported to have remarked,
'if it weren't for my monastery and [its] land, I'd treat him like a
dog.' " Acknowledging that the monastery's survival depended upon
allegiance to the king, the abbot nevertheless refused to participate
in the new liturgy. Accused by one of his own monks, he was subjected

to an inquiry by the duke of Spoleto and other high officials, including the pope himself. He was eventually exonerated, but only after he had been "forced to swear that he had never been unfaithful to the lord King, nor would he ever be." As McCormick explained, this controversy illuminates not only the extent to which the Carolingians had gained control over the monastic practice, but also the function of even monastic prayers "as a political litmus test, as a public manifestation of loyalty. . . . Failure to perform them was grounds for an accusation of 'infidelitas.' " In 783, the monk-chronicler Paul the Deacon sent a letter from Charlemagne's court to Monte Cassino expressing his "confidence that the Benedictine community was ever zealous in pouring forth prayers 'for our lords and for their army.' " Like the rest of the clergy, the monks had become, in effect, the king's spiritual soldiers.[26]

Although in most other regards he paled in significance next to his all-powerful and long-lived father, Louis the Pious was without a doubt the chief Carolingian champion of monastic reform. He advanced substantially Charlemagne's campaign for tighter episcopal and royal control over the monasteries, and he further encouraged what might best be called the "militarization of monasticism," the historic shift in monastic priorities from personal salvation to imperial service. He fully understood, as did his father, that, as long as monks were merely pursuing their own perfection, their indiscretions and errors of practice were of little social consequence; but now that the well-being of the emperor and his subjects depended upon their purity and their prayers, these became matters of grave imperial concern. (In our seemingly secular age, it is all too easy to overlook the genuineness of such concern; as G. E. M. de Ste. Croix reminds us, at the time such prayers were "believed to be a necessity.") Emperor Louis's success in this regard, in imposing upon the monasteries a conformity to approved standards of behavior and a uniformity of correct practice, far surpassed that of his father, and left an enduring legacy for subsequent monastic reformers.[27]

Louis the Pious was so moved by monastic ideals that historians have often described him as "monkish." Such ideals, it has been suggested, "were, perhaps, the preponderant influence upon him, . . . the driving force behind much of what [he] thought and did." As the ruler of Aquitaine, he had already begun a campaign to reform the monasteries there and had been involved in the foundation of a dozen new houses. Once he became emperor, "monasticism possessed Louis' most consistent and concerted attention," to such an extent that Ardo—biographer of Louis's chief monastic adviser, Benedict of Aniane—referred to this ruler as the "father of all monks."[28]

It was in Aquitaine that Louis became attracted to the work of Benedict of Aniane, later known as the "second founder" of Western monasticism, who became the emperor's "principal and most intimate advisor." On assuming the throne, Louis immediately established for Benedict a new monastery near Aachen, beside the Inde River, at Kornelimunster, so that he could be closer to the imperial palace. Within but two years of his coronation, Louis had called and, together with Benedict, presided over the famous Councils of Aachen, which imposed the Benedictine Rule upon all of the monasteries in the realm and produced the most important monastic reforms of the Carolingian era. Beyond the monasteries proper, Louis adopted the Benedictine Rule as his guide for imperial rule. "The remarkable agreement between the monastic spirit and the ruling ethos adopted by Louis cannot be coincidental," one close student of Louis the Pious has suggested. "The occasional adumbrations of the RB [Benedictine Rule] to say nothing of more direct borrowings, in the legislation of Louis the Pious, indicate a deliberate adaptation and application of the RB to the governance of the empire." In short, Louis embodied the reform spirit of Boniface: "from the essentials of Benedictinism . . . [he] did not deviate."[29]

If Louis provided the political authority for the reform of the monasteries, Benedict of Aniane provided the religious conception and justification. Like Pachomius and Martin of Tours, Benedict was yet another soldier turned monk, and his reforms bear the mark of a military disposition. The son of a noble cup-bearer at the court of Pepin, Benedict served for five years in Charlemagne's army during the campaign against the Lombards. After a narrow escape from drowning, he entered a Benedictine monastery in Burgundy, but remained there only a short time. To his mind, the Benedictine monasteries were in a sorry state: discipline was lacking, the wealth of many of the houses had been alienated to laymen, and there was considerable conflict over which rule was to be followed. In desperate pursuit of salvation through renunciation, Benedict thus turned instead to the Eastern experience and became a hermit in Aquitaine. His piety and ascetic zeal soon attracted a following, however, and before long, by 782, he had become the head of a stately abbey with over one thousand monks. It was here that his efforts at monastic reform first attracted the attention and support of the ruler of Aquitaine, Louis the Pious, and he thereafter became, in the apt description of his biographer, "the emperor's monk."[30]

The emperor and his monk shared a commitment to the Benedictine ideal and militarylike organization. Benedict himself was a tireless "routinizer, organizer and centralizer," with a passion for rigid uniformity. Thus, after establishing Benedict in his new monastery near Aachen, Louis placed him in charge of the monastic reform. The process was described in detail by Benedict's biographer Ardo. "The emperor . . . set Benedict over all monasteries in the realm, that as he had instructed Aquitaine and Gothia in the standard of salvation so also might he imbue Frankland with a salutary example." "That there might be one wholesome usage for all monasteries, as there was one profession by all, the emperor ordered the fathers of monasteries to assemble" with their monks to receive instruction from Benedict on prescribed practices. "Benedict then prepared for the emperor a chapter by chapter decree for confirmation to enjoin observance in all monasteries of his realm." Thereupon, "Louis appointed inspectors for each monastery to oversee whether those practices that were enjoined were observed and to transmit the wholesome standard to those unaware of it. [In this way] all monasteries were returned to a degree of unity as if taught by one teacher in one place. Uniform measure in drink and food, in vigils and singing, was decreed to be observed by all." Benedict's own monastery at Kornelimunster became the model, that all monks "might see the standard and discipline of the [Benedictine] Rule portrayed in usage, walk, and dress of the monks at Inde."[31]

Benedict had precise specifications for everything, from dress, talking, and movement to the ringing of the bells, "the products," in Workman's phrase, "of an almost mechanical will." He dictated that monks were to maintain strict celibacy, that they were to remain steadfastly in their cloister, that they were to avoid obligations which might bring them in touch with the world, and that they were to teach in their schools none save oblates in training for the monastic life. "Obedience was to be immediate and entire," and "a special promise of subjection was required before the novice might be tonsured, in addition to the regular vow of profession." In his famous *Concordia Regularum*, he compiled extracts from twenty-six different rules in his quest of the surest way to salvation—for the empire as well as for the monk. "Even prayer and praise did not escape his machinery." Indeed, he gave special attention to the liturgy, and here bent the Benedictine rule itself to imperial purpose.[32]

Because of the many intercessory prayers incorporated into the monastic office, to be performed on behalf of the king, his armies, and his subjects, "offices were multiplied until they became almost continuous." In addition, special attention was taken to ensure that the prayers were performed with regularity and "exact precision." Hence the Opus Dei of the Benedictine Rule had become much longer and more elaborate; moreover, "as time went by, the Mass was celebrated not only on Sundays but every day." This imperial transformation of the liturgy had three important consequences. First, the Benedictine requirement of manual labor was sacrificed in the interest of adequate performance of the liturgy. Thus, "more and more in these Frankish monasteries of the ninth century manual work was being transferred to lay servants, leaving the [monks] free for prayer."[33]

Second, it compelled monks to become priests as well. Only priests could preside over Mass; as the services became more elaborate and continuous, the number of priests available in the monastery had to increase—that is, monks had to be ordained as priests. In the wake of Benedict of Aniane's reform, "most monks were priests." This entailed a dramatic change in monastic custom and epitomized the imperial transformation of Western monasticism. Traditionally, priests and monks represented opposite tendencies in Christianity, the first toward pastoral care in the world, the second toward renunciation of the world. The imperial insistence upon the obedient service of monks to the state had turned monasticism outward as never before, thereby creating a new clerical breed, the monk-priest.[34]

Third, unlike abbots and bishops, monks were not obliged to perform military service for the king. Indeed, like other clergy—including abbots and bishops—they were canonically averse to such bellicose activity. But, in the performance of their liturgical function, the monks too had been conscripted into the king's armies. They were not simply warlike, in that their regimen resembled that of the camp; they were warriors. If they did not fight battles against earthly enemies, they fought equally important battles against heavenly foes. As Ardo explained, they served, like Benedict, "in God's knighthood," on behalf of the emperor's knighthood. Alan Cabaniss, translator of Ardo's biography of Benedict of Aniane, noted his striking and repeated "use of military terminology for monastic service." Just as military activity in the Christian state had been sacralized, having taken on "a spiritual and redemptive value," so prayer had been militarized, having acquired a martial function. The monks had become priests, therefore, to become soldiers. The twelfth-century abbot Anselm of Havelberg noted in his *Dialogues* the by then obvious link between the "*disciplina militaris*" of the army and the "*disciplina regularis*" of the monastery. It was a link that originated with the Carolingian reforms, the religious contributions of a warrior state.[35]

The imperial reform of the Frankish Church had a profound impact upon the lives of both the secular and regular clergy. But the most dire effects of ecclesiastical and monastic reform were experienced beyond the courtly clerical circles, by religious women. If religious practice was now a form of warfare, the church altar and the monastery were battlefields and thus, as Martin of Tours had argued, no place for women. The militarization of the church, in short, was also a masculinization. As Suzanne Wemple explained, "the imposition of the Benedictine Rule, advocated by Saint Boniface, gave the Carolingian bishops the opportunity to bring all forms of religious life, male and female, under episcopal control. But, unlike the monks and canons who were incorporated into the Carolingian *Reichskirche*, nuns and canonesses were isolated from the mainstream of religious, political and intellectual life."[36]

Certainly this had not been Boniface's intention. As an Anglo-Saxon churchman, he knew well and had high regard for the contributions made by religious women; his letters attest to this. In his evangelical endeavors, he depended upon the support solicited and received from the nuns of Wimbourne, relied heavily upon Lioba and the other female missionaries who accompanied him, and helped to transfer the Anglo-Saxon double monastery to the continent of Europe. Nevertheless, as Wemple points out, Boniface and his colleagues "were careful to guard the prerogatives of the male clergy [and], as bishops, the Anglo-Saxons supervised feminine communities more closely and interpreted the Benedictine Rule more rigorously for female than for male monasteries." The Council of Verneuil, for example, following Boniface's reform initiatives, issued detailed instructions for bishops on how to deal with women who failed to accept the Rule, including excommunication and imprisonment, but "that uncooperative monks might be coerced in this manner was not considered."[37]

In the church proper, the reformers' renewed emphasis upon ritual purity likewise turned the bishops against women. Reawakened to the alleged polluting nature of the female half of the species—a danger to the efficacy of both prayer and combat—"the councils insisted upon clerical celibacy and the exclusion of women from any ecclesiastical authority or active participation in sacred rites. In tones reminiscent of their sixth century predecessors, the Carolingian bishops reaffirmed the disability of women to perform clerical functions and persuaded the rulers to include these admonitions in the royal capitularies." In order to safeguard the purity of the already married clergy, the church councils and imperial edicts forced the wives of priests to take a vow of chastity and subjected them to criminal punishment and banishment to a convent if they violated it.[38]

Although Charlemagne had entrusted his own daughters' education to the abbess of Chelles, he nevertheless "invoked ancient prejudices against women" and maintained that "the weakness of her sex and the instability of her mind forbid that [woman] should hold the leadership over men in teaching and preaching." Accordingly, he prohibited abbesses from blessing the male members of their congregations or veiling nuns, while the nuns themselves were once again forbidden to approach the altar, touch the sacred vessels, or help distribute the sacrament. In short, in ecclesiastical as well as secular legislation, "ritual purity served as the rationale both for excluding women from the clerical hierarchy and for eliminating their influence from parish affairs as the wives of priests." Thereafter, for centuries to come, orthodox religious women "made no attempt to claim a share in pastoral or ministerial functions . . . [and] henceforth, women would appear in ministerial roles only in heretical sects." Such was the lasting consequence of the new Carolingian "organization of the clergy as an exclusively male hierarchy."[39]

If the Carolingian reformers excluded women from the knightly realm of the *Reichskirche*, they also undertook to drive them from the scene of masculine monastic combat. Here they strove especially "to keep women religious locked in convents" in order to keep their militarized "clerks segregated from the company of women." Charlemagne, in addition to prohibiting the quasi-clerical functions of abbesses and nuns (while, at the same time, encouraging monks to become priests), "legislated against too close association of the sexes in monasteries"—in keeping with a general prohibition on the establishment of new double monasteries that had been issued in 747 by the Second Council of Nicaea. He insisted also that nuns and abbesses had to be strictly cloistered and placed under firm episcopal, and hence male, control. Bishops could interfere in all decisions regarding life in the convent and the admission of new members. Indeed, bishops were now given the exclusive right to consecrate nuns. Moreover, in keeping with the segregation of the sexes and the restriction of monastic education to oblates, the emperor prohibited abbesses and nuns from teaching boys in their convents; future monks were to be taught only by monks.[40]

Charlemagne's monastic policies with regard to women were developed further by Louis the Pious and Benedict of Aniane. Despite his monogamous attachment to his second wife, Judith, Louis the Pious' anxieties about the dangers of women were amply demonstrated when, immediately upon assuming the throne, he banished his legitimate but unmarried sisters and all other women—except those required for housekeeping—from the palace at Aachen. In Eleanor Duckett's description, Louis "ruthlessly ordered [his sisters] to leave Court for the convents to which, he declared, they properly belonged. With them he drove out the many women who on one pretext or another were living in the Palace; only those entirely necessary for its round of work would he keep. His three illegitimate brothers he allowed to remain." Benedict of Aniane and his fellow monks apparently shared similar anxieties. Ardo describes one episode early in Benedict's monastic life in which the small oratory used by the monks was momentarily occupied by a group of impudent women. "Jeering at the residence of the monks, they said to one another, 'you take the abbot's position and stand in his place.' But as each one, who took turn in the prayer stall as though praying, knelt down, she had difficulty in rising." Providentially, Ardo reports, "suitable punishment overtook the women at once. They began to be wracked with jerks and twists" which ceased only with the belated prayers of the monks, offered grudgingly at the behest of the women's desperate husbands.[41]

When Louis and Benedict together undertook their ambitious program of monastic reform, their misogynous tendencies gained an earnest religious expression. Under their regime, all women religious outside of convents and marriage were compelled to join female communities. In keeping with the campaign against lay control, proprietary female houses were discouraged, existing small foundations were consolidated, and all female communities were placed under strict episcopal control. The abbots of male monasteries were able to lessen the impact of such episcopal control through their close association with bishops and kings; abbesses enjoyed no such associations and, as a result, their houses "declined in power and influence." Moreover, the women in these communities were strictly cloistered—that is, they were confined to, or imprisoned in, their convents.[42]

The establishment of new double monasteries was prohibited, and the communities of monks attached to existing double houses were replaced by a small chapter of canons. A few canons were not only less expensive to maintain than a community of monks but "were less likely than monks to share with the sisters a sense of common endeavor." Thus "ended a period in the history of Western monasticism when feminine and masculine communities had been considered fully equal and coordinate institutions," Wemple explained. "Henceforth, it became more difficult for male and female ascetics to draw inspiration from each other for their parallel . . . pursuit of spiritual perfection." Along similar lines, abbesses and nuns were permitted to instruct no boys, just girls, and church councils "cautioned [women religious] against unnecessary visits by men, including bishops, canons, and monks."[43]

The rude treatment accorded women religious reflected the new imperial, and hence ecclesiastical, priority placed upon the male monasteries, which received the lion's share of religious, political, and economic support. With the advent of a military, strictly masculine, ideal of monasticism, women religious had become peripheral, their presence viewed, if at all, as a danger. The purity and able performance of the kingdom's new spiritual soldiers, grounded upon the "unique sacramental and juridical powers of the priesthood," were first and foremost in the mind of the monastic reformers. Thus "abbesses, unlike abbots, did not participate in reforming assemblies," and Aniane's detailed reform of monastic life ignored women entirely. "No attempt was made to adapt the Benedictine Rule for use by nunneries. Whereas monks were sent to Inde to be trained in Benedictine observances, Louis the Pious did not designate a model Benedictine abbey for the training of women." Of the fifty-three abbeys that are recorded as having adopted the Benedictine Rule under the auspices of the reform movement, only five were for women.[44]

"The new and more exacting conception of the monastic duty of liturgical specialization and of the intercessory value of monastic masses necessarily emphasized the importance of monks who could more efficiently perform these duties," R. W. Southern argued in explanation of the decline of female monasticism. Indeed, as the monastic office came to be seen as a form of spiritual warfare, monks became priests so as to be more effective soldiers. In the process, several critical time-honored distinctions—between the warrior and the minister of peace, and between the worldly clergyman and the otherworldly religious—collapsed. And as these heretofore antithetical identities fell together, women religious, neither soldiers nor priests, were squeezed out of the picture. It is hardly a wonder, therefore, that, in the wake of such an epochal transformation of monastic identity, "council after council [had] to inveigh against nuns wearing male attire."[45]

THE ISOLATION OF WOMEN from the mainstream of Carolingian clerical and monastic life had as its inevitable corollary their exclusion from the Carolingian world of learning and education. As Wemple points out, "the Carolingian revival of learning, which began at Aachen under the sponsorship of Charlemagne and was later introduced into the cathedral and monastic schools, bypassed the communities of women. . . . The new literary products, the textbooks, Biblical commentaries, sermons, theological treatises, letters, encomia, and moral instructions addressed to kings, and the interpretations of canon and civil law were written by men." Indeed, Charlemagne's instructions on the promotion of scholarship expressly indicated that such work would be done only by men.[46]

The new cathedral and monastic schools, like the cathedral chapters and monastic communities themselves, were restricted to celibate men and male oblates. The schools were housed by the church, were run by clergy, and were dedicated to clerical training. Since women were barred from clerical ranks, there was no justification for their inclusion; besides, the presence of females would have only endangered the purity of the students and their teachers. And, within the female communities, "the strict cloistering of women religious . . . limited the opportunities for nuns to keep abreast of the new learning. Abbesses were not allowed to go to the leading centers of learning to master the new skills. The restriction that convents could educate only girls undoubtedly served to justify the exclusion of nuns from the mainstreams of education and intellectual life. . . . Because women could neither preach nor participate in the liturgy, there was no need to introduce this new program in female communities." Thus "the strict cloistering of women religious and the separation of the sexes in the monastic schools of the ninth century," Wemple concluded, "resulted in the exclusion of women religious from the main-stream of education. . . ." In short, the mainstream had become, to borrow Mary O'Brien's felicitous phrase, the "malestream."[47]

Although the participation of the emperor's daughters had at times to be tolerated, the palace school of Charlemagne was, in its essence, a world without women on the ancient model. "In Charles' 'Academia Palatina,' " Johan Huizinga noted, "the avowed ideal was the estab-lishment of an 'Athenae Novae.' . . . The leading lights adorned themselves with classical and biblical names: Alcuin as Horace, Angil-bert as Homer, and the Emperor Charles himself as David." More-over, here at the epicenter of a warrior society, disputations naturally took the form of knightly jousting as learned couriers competed with one another in "pompous display of erudition, poetry, and pietistic sententiousness."[48]

The Carolingian revival of classical learning revived also the homo-social subculture of the ancient philosophers. Only now that subcul-ture was legitimated in orthodox Christian theology as an earthly approximation of the world to come after the resurrection. This was most clearly articulated by the great Carolingian scholar Johannes Scotus Erigena, court philosopher of Charlemagne's grandson Charles the Bald. "At the Resurrection," Erigena wrote, "sex will be abol-ished and nature made one. . . . There will then be only man, as if he had never sinned." As Georges Duby explained the passage, "in this life such a reunification was impossible. It had [only] to be waited and hoped for [and] man must prepare for it by abstinence." Then, with Christ's return, "the end of the world would do away with dual sexuality or, more precisely, with the female part of it. When the heavens opened in glory, femininity, that imperfection, that stain on the purity of creation, would be no more."[49]

In the shadow of this imperial paradise sat the women who still darkened the earthly realm, women whose wretched lives cast in relief the masculine ethos of Carolingian society. The experiences of two of them, Gerberta and Dhuoda—sister and wife, respectively, of Bernard of Septimania—well illustrate the fate that might befall even the most highly and properly placed women in the wake of the ninth-century social and ecclesiastical reforms. Bernard, the son of Charle-magne's cousin William of Genone—a monastic follower of Benedict of Aniane—had become one of Emperor Louis's most trusted advisers and, as such, an ardent participant in the internecine struggles among the emperor's sons. It was also Bernard who had been accused by

Louis's aristocratic enemies of being the Empress Judith's lover. Bernard's intrigues and military adventures placed him in constant dangers, and he was ultimately executed by Charles the Bald. But the earliest casualties of his imperial career were his sister and wife.

Gerberta, a nun, was charged with having bewitched her brother, the empress, or perhaps the emperor himself. Her accusers were the same group of noble conspirators who had tried unsuccessfully to slander, abduct, and imprison Judith in order to diminish her influence over Louis. "Gerberta appears to have been an innocent victim, a scapegoat upon whom Judith's enemies vented their frustration and hatred." Whatever the motives of her accusers, however, Gerberta was in fact executed as a witch. According to Wemple, "this is the first known instance in the Latin West of witchcraft being used as a legal ground for the execution of a woman."[50]

Dhuoda had married Bernard in 824 in the imperial palace at Aachen. When Louis entrusted Bernard with authority over the Spanish Marches, Dhuoda at first accompanied her husband on his imperial adventures. But, some time after the birth of her first child, William, in 826, Dhuoda was dispatched to the hinterlands to attend to Bernard's property and remained isolated there until the emperor's death in 840. Bernard then paid her a brief visit, and she thereafter bore him a second son. In the bitter fighting among contenders for the throne, Bernard had allied himself with Aquitaine, the losing side; to reconcile himself with the new king, Charles the Bald, he had his teenage son, William, sent to the imperial court as, in effect, a hostage. Soon he summoned to Aquitaine his infant son, less than half a year old and not yet christened. Dhuoda, abandoned by her husband and robbed of her sons, was left alone and desolate. Yet she dutifully accepted her husband's commands and struggled heroically to maintain his patrimony, following the precepts of monogamous marriage. In her "tragic solitude" she turned to writing to assuage her grief over the loss of her only children, and in 843 composed a manual of instruction, a guide for living, for her first son, William. (William, it turned out, could make little use of his mother's manual. Like his father, he was executed for treason five years later.)[51]

Apologizing for the frailty of her sex, her woeful ignorance, and her impudent pursuit of the male craft of writing, Dhuoda affirms the masculine ethos of Carolingian society. She exhorts her son to fulfill his dual obligations to God and king, to obey the new emperor (no doubt out of fear for his safety), the clergy, and, above all, his own father, who had abandoned him—to serve, to remain loyal and stead-fast, to have courage, to be a man. But she writes also to exalt the gentler virtues and to remind him of a different kind of bond, more powerful even than those between brothers. She writes, above all, to remind him of his mother, and in so doing lays bare the desperate plight of a woman in this man's world:

> Certainly I also, though an unworthy woman and frail as a shadow, seek [God] as best I can, and incessantly implore his help, as far as I know how. For indeed that is absolutely necessary to me. Some-times it happens that a persistent puppy, under his master's table, can snatch the crumbs and eat them even among the taller male whelps. For he who made the mouth of the dumb creature speak has the might to open my understanding, in keeping with his clem-ency of old; and he who prepared a banquet for his faithful in the desert . . . can also fulfill his wish in me, his handmaiden, because of my longing for you. . . . What more shall I say? Your Dhuoda is always there to encourage you, my son, and when I am gone, which will come to pass, you will have the little book of moral teaching here as a memorial: you will be able to look at me still, as into a mirror, reading me with your mind and your body and praying to God; you will find there too, in full, what tasks you owe me. My son, you will have teachers who will give you more lessons, and more valuable ones—yet not in the same way, with the heart burning within, as I with mine, my first-born one. . . .[52]

Six · *Priests: The Monasticization of the Church*

T HE DEATH OF LOUIS THE PIOUS in 840 signaled the demise of the Carolingian Empire. A decade before Louis's death, the struggles among his heirs—Lothar and Louis from his first marriage, and Charles (the Bald), son of Judith—had already fostered a fragmentation of dynastic authority, along with splits within the *Reichskirche* (the abbots Ebbo of Rheims and Agobart of Lyons, for example, had been exiled for siding with Lothar against the emperor). Meanwhile, the menacing raids by Vikings from the north and Saracens in the Mediterranean had begun to intensify (to be joined at the end of the ninth century by the Magyar incursions from the east). The result was a dissolution of centralized government and imperial organization into smaller feudal dynasties which congealed around those most able to provide military protection. "From the anarchy produced by the Viking invasions," Geoffrey Barraclough noted, "a new free class emerged, a class which was at one and the same time free and noble, and which claimed its freedom and nobility because it could devote itself entirely to the profession of arms. Thus France saw, in the ninth and tenth centuries, a profound social revolution, the creation of a new society" based upon the fiefdoms of counts and dukes. The new feudal aristocracy had become the arbiters of social order.[1]

The collapse of the Carolingian Empire meant the demise also of the imperial church. Unable to maintain their wealth and strength, kings could no longer protect the church and bishops were thus compelled to seek support from the aristocracy. The episcopal organization hence devolved once again into lay-controlled bishoprics. The process of feudal territorial consolidation, Barraclough points out, "did not stop at the laity but also embraced the church." Dukes began to usurp royal authority over the church, and bishops became the vassals of aristocratic lords rather than kings.

The monarchy lost that direct connection with the church which had been so great a source of strength to the Carolingians; it lost its ability to place royal nominees in the majority of monasteries and episcopal sees. . . . The ordinary ecclesiastical benefice . . . was turned into a fief owing homage and service. Thus the clergy, like the lay nobility, were subjected to feudal bonds. The churches of the land were brought within the feudal hierarchy, and feudalism became the dominant principle in every sphere of life.[2]

In the wake of such sweeping social disturbance and realignment, the Carolingian reforms lost their hold. Without royal authority behind them, bishops could no longer "take concerted action to enforce clerical and monastic discipline." Priests once again lived with their wives and concubines, and even some bishops married and passed on church property and episcopal office to their children. As Friedrich Kempf wrote,

> The German Emperors observed with great anxiety how everywhere great and petty lords were taking possession of ecclesiastical property in an increasing measure. So long as this involved monastic property, the bishops also helped themselves. Further losses occurred because of the widespread disregard of celibacy. Bishops, abbots, and priests provided for their illegitimate children as far as possible with clerical property.[3]

In this dissipation of royal and ecclesiastical authority, lay and religious women regained for a time some of what they had lost to the Carolingian reforms. Ironically, owing in large measure to the imperial promotion of monogamous marriage and the concentration of aristocratic family wealth it engendered, aristocratic women were momentarily able again to wield considerable social and economic power. Thus they reasserted some measure of influence over the church, as patrons of feudal churches and foundresses of proprietary monasteries. Clerical wives and concubines once more participated in pastoral affairs—if not quasi-clerical functions. Moreover, in the absence of episcopal and royal power, monasteries re-established their independence, and abbesses of nunneries—though no longer double monasteries—exercised anew wide authority, while the effort to impose strict enclosure on nuns was abandoned. Nuns again won respect as teachers, writers, and contemplatives (and mystics). This was especially true in Germany, which remained relatively immune from coastal raids. In the tenth century, Gandersheim, "a small, proudly independent principality ruled by women," became renowned as a center of learning and as the home of the playwright and poet Hrotswitha. This intellectual tradition was carried forth in the next two centuries by the encyclopedist Herrad of Heidenheim and the mystic Hildegard of Bingen.[4]

The clerical reforms of the Carolingian dynasty were largely eroded by the close of the ninth century. The spirit that had inspired those reforms, however, Benedictine monasticism, remained alive. Indeed, the self-sustaining monasteries, though shorn of royal patronage and protection and forever embattled in this time of troubles, survived as oases of Carolingian continuity under aristocratic auspices. By the beginning of the tenth century, a Benedictine revival was under way, and the reforms of Benedict of Aniane found new and even more potent expression. Out of the ashes of empire, and the beneficence of counts, dukes, and princes, a new reform movement arose to herald the opening of Christianity's second millennium.

At the core of the movement was a renewed monastic reform effort along the lines developed by Benedict of Aniane. In a time of social turmoil, millennial uncertainty, and a spiritual pessimism reminiscent of the fourth century, monasticism appeared the only refuge and hope for reform-minded churchmen. "In an age when the monastic life offered one of the very few alternatives to the life of war and the chase," Christopher Brooke wrote, "it is hardly surprising that the monasteries drew many talented recruits." (The monasteries also became an outlet for aristocratic sons disinherited by strife or, later, by primogeniture.) Relatively unchallenged in a preoccupied world, these new monks would become an ecclesiastical vanguard as never before, with "an influence in the Church out of proportion to their numbers." First, in the tenth century, under secular auspices, they would reform the monasteries. Second, their reformed monasticism would gradually fill the episcopal void, and then the papal see itself, and overtake the church. Third, under the command of a revitalized papacy, the monasticized church would fill the imperial void to reign supreme over European society.[5]

At the close of the ninth century, the former Frankish kingdom was gripped by terror and destruction. During the dismal reign of Charles the Simple, the bishops of the Frankish Church, meeting in Trosly, catalogued the horrors of the age—"fornication and adultery, sacrilege and manslaughter"—and their dire impact upon monasticism: cloisters burned, pillaged, and destroyed; utter corruption of the Benedictine Rule; religious houses brought under arbitrary lay authority;

monks and nuns in dire need and confusion falling prey to sin. "In consecrated houses of God lay abbots are living with their wives, their sons and their daughters." Along with chastity and ritual rigor, education and learning had also fallen by the wayside. It was hardly an auspicious beginning for what Georges Duby has called "the age of the monks." In their misery, the bishops asked, "how shall our monks be reformed without the care of a Father of true religious calling?" Not long thereafter, out of the fertile Burgundian soil of Frankish monasticism, their answer arose. The Benedictine reform spirit once again burst forth when, "to counteract this decay," Duke William IX of Aquitaine founded the monastery of Cluny.[6]

Founded in 909, Cluny became the bastion of monastic stability in a desperate age; with a missionary zeal worthy of Boniface himself, the monks of Cluny soon spread their monastic reform to independent houses throughout France, Germany, Belgium, Italy, and Spain and, in the eleventh century, incorporated them as "daughter" houses into a single international organization centered at Cluny. In one important respect, Cluny signaled a radical departure from feudal monasticism, although the full impact of this departure would not be felt for another century. Cluny was a secular foundation, but Duke William sought in its charter to immunize the affairs and resources of the abbey from future lay control and pronounced a curse upon those who would violate his injunction. By the close of the tenth century, William's grant of secular exemption was matched by the pope's grant of episcopal exemption, leaving the monks of Cluny uniquely independent of external constraints. Thus, before long, the Cluniacs had "set before themselves the dream, if it were possible, to impress upon the whole Church the ideals of the cowl. Instead of seeking to realize the monastic ideal as heretofore by fleeing from the world, it were better to infuse the ideal into the world [starting] with the Church itself."[7]

If the unprecedented autonomy and ambitions of Cluny heralded a new "age of the monks," its monastic practice reflected a conscious continuation of the Carolingian reform. Berno, the first abbot of Cluny, had been abbot at Baume and was deeply imbued with the spirit of Aniane. As Christopher Brooke pointed out, the reform houses of Cluny, like those of the subsequent reform order emanating from Gorze, "all looked for instruction to Benedict of Aniane." "Its rule," Workman noted, "was the strictest interpretation of the Rule of Benedict; obedience was absolute and total chastity understood." Cluny also inherited the unique Carolingian emphasis upon the liturgical (*opus Dei*) function of the monks, at the expense of manual labor (*opus manuum*); following Benedict of Aniane, the Cluniacs forsook Benedict of Nursia's original religious exaltation of manual labor, relegating this function to lay workers, in order to concentrate upon the all-important monastic office. For the monks of Cluny, as for their predecessors at Inde, the monastic office represented "work of a very practical kind"; the enlarged and elaborate liturgy, which incorporated intercessory prayers on behalf of noble and royal founders and bene-factors, constituted an indispensable service. If, under the Carolingian emperors, royal monasteries had become the spiritual counterpart of imperial armies, now, amid social upheaval and heathen advance, the monastic performance of the liturgy had become a spiritualized form of feudal combat.[8]

Southern emphasized,

> It is important to understand that the monasteries did not exist solely or even mainly for the sake of the monks who sought within their walls a personal salvation. This motive could never have filled more than a small proportion of the numerous monasteries of the period, nor could founders and benefactors have been induced to part with a large proportion of their wealth to make provisions for the aspirations of the few. In the period of their greatest expansion, Benedictine monasteries were founded and filled for political, social, and religious purposes of which we hear nothing in the Rule. These purposes cannot be clearly distinguished from each other, but very broadly founders and benefactors saw in the "cowled champions" of the monasteries the spiritual equivalent of secular soldiers. The monks fought battles quite as real [as], and more important, than the battles of the natural world; they fought to cleanse the land from supernatural enemies. To say that they prayed for the well-being of the king and the kingdom is to put the matter altogether too feebly. They fought as a disciplined elite, and the safety of the kingdom depended on their efforts.[9]

"Cluny hoped to militarize prayer," Georges Duby suggested. Like the Carolingians before them, the Cluniacs "looked upon the monastic office as a kind of combat and the monk as a variety of soldier." Berno's successor, Abbot Odo, in his *Life of Gerald of Aurillac*, gave religious sanction to the military activity of the feudal nobility by calling them "knights of Christ," a novel and still-incipient notion which would spark and spur the Crusades in subsequent centuries and give rise, ultimately, to actual warrior-monks (such as the Knights Templar, Hospitalers, and Order of Calatrava). But until then there remained a tension between the feudal and the religious life. This tension, Barbara Rosenwein has suggested, was acute among the aristocratic monks who were born to be knights. As the sons of the feudal nobility, they had been reared to fight, yet, as Christians and especially as monks and priests, they had also been called to pray for peace on earth. The contradiction between these identities, Rosenwein has suggested, generated intense conflict within the lives of these noble youths, a conflict that was sublimated through the ritualized aggression of spiritual monastic warfare. Thus the monastic liturgy provided the outlet at once for both impulses: Christian love and feudal combat. Adalbero of Laon described the Cluniac monk as a knight not only because he mingled with knights but also because, as Rosenwein argued, "the life of the Cluniac monk even inside the cloister was unconsciously a ritualized re-enactment of the life of a knight."[10]

Knights were men. Like the Carolingian reform upon which it was grounded, the Cluniac reform was masculine to the core and all but ignored women. To the extent that women religious were given any attention at all, they were viewed as potential threats to the ritual purity, and thus to the knightly effectiveness of the monks; they were either excluded altogether or placed under rigid restrictions and male control. Cluny thus contributed significantly to the decline of female monasticism that was to mark the tenth-century monastic reform movement. Indeed, as Peter Levi wrote, following the breakup of the Carolingian Empire, "the first definite move to exclude women from the monastic life, or at least from the old double monasteries, was under the influence of Cluny, the first major Benedictine reform of the high middle ages in the tenth and eleventh centuries."[11]

"In the great period of monastic foundation from the early tenth to the early twelfth century," Southern observed, "the position of women in the monastic life suffered a sharp decline. The institution of double monasteries, and more especially the dominant position of the women in them, came under attack." Southern acknowledged that "nunneries of course continued to be founded, but in contrast to their earlier importance they played only a small part in the monastic development of the period. The evidence of Cluny, where the ideals of the new monasticism were most fully displayed, is particularly striking in this regard. In the tenth and eleventh centuries scores of monasteries were founded in association with Cluny, but they included only one foundation for nuns.''[12]

In the twelfth century, Abbot Hugh of Cluny established on his brother's property the nunnery of Marcigny, to provide a chaste retreat for the wives of men who had been induced by Hugh to become Cluniac monks. As Southern notes,

> the circumstances and terms of the foundation illustrate the lowered esteem of women in religion. They no longer directed their own affairs; still less did they rule monks. On the contrary, those who entered "this glorious prison" were placed under the rule of a prior appointed by the abbot of Cluny. The nuns were strictly enclosed lest "in appearing in the world they either made others desire them, or saw things which they themselves desired."

The fostering of the female religious life was thus no longer the androgynous ascetic celebration of asexual perfection or even the patristic exaltation of female sanctity as a surrogate form of masculinity. Rather, it had become but a deliberate defense of clerical sanctity against feminine dangers. In keeping with the spirit of this again ascendant clerical asceticism, moreover, the cynical promotion of female monasticism was just one aspect of the renewed ecclesiastical condemnation of clerical marriage. According to one contemporary account, the Marcigny nunnery "was to be 'a place where mature women who were tired of matrimonial license might purge their past errors and be worthy of attaining the embraces of Christ. Noble-women who had been freed from matrimony chose this place, resigning themselves the more patiently to the loss of matrimonial joys as they had discovered how short and full of sorrows are its pleasures.' " Cluny, in carrying forth the reform of Western monasticism, thus pushed forward the ecclesiastical campaign for clerical celibacy as well. As Duby observed, "the condemnation of marriage emerged more clearly in the course of the tenth century, when the disintegration of the Carolingian order was accompanied by a rising tide of monasticism, which gradually submerged the whole church hierarchy."[13]

If the so-called Benedictine age stretched in time from the eighth-century Carolingian reforms of Boniface to the eleventh-century papal reforms of Gregory VII, it also stretched in space from one end of Western Europe to the other. The Cluniac reforms spread first within France; in 930, the celebrated monastery of Fleury (St.-Benoit-sur-

Loire) came under the reform influence of Cluny at the hands of Abbot Odo himself. Fleury had already claimed to be the head of all Benedictine monasteries because it presumably contained the bones of Benedict of Nursia and his twin sister, the nun Scholastica. Early on it had come under the sway of Aniane's reform and held in its library the original manuscript of Aniane's *Concordia Regularum*. Thus, Fleury, like Cluny itself, readily became an internationally known site of Benedictine pilgrimage and instruction, and its visitors and disciples went forth to spread the Cluniac reform beyond France.[14]

The French Benedictine monastery of Gorze was reformed by Adalbero of Metz in 933, in the wake of the Cluniac revival, but developed somewhat differently and independently of Cluny. Like Cluny, Gorze followed the patterns pioneered by Benedict of Aniane and adopted a military style. Indeed, Adalbero was himself not only a bishop but also a feudal warrior. Gorze never enjoyed Cluny's exemption from secular authority but, rather, epitomized the lay-proprietary monastery of feudal society. Its reform spirit was borne by both nobility and monks, and by the end of the tenth century had been carried not only to other houses in France but also into Belgium, Switzerland, Austria, and especially Germany. The influence of Cluny was felt primarily in southern France, but also in Belgium, Italy, Spain, and England. Following the decline of Italian monasticism in the wake of the Saracen raids, the Cluniac reform was carried into Rome by Abbot Odo in cooperation with Prince Alberic, whose family controlled the papacy for much of the later tenth and early eleventh centuries. The Italian monastic reform movement followed the established pattern in most respects; however, because of the influence of the noblewomen of the powerful House of Theophylact, which played a leading role in the reform effort, the movement here resulted in the restoration of a greater number of houses for women, five all together. In the eleventh century, the Cluniac movement was carried down into Reconquista Spain by Kings Ferdinand I and Alfonso VI of León-Castile. It was England, however, that experienced the greatest impact of the Cluniac movement outside of France. Just as the Carolingian reform had been sparked by the channel-crossing of the Anglo-Saxon Boniface, so now the channel would be crossed in the other direction, bringing the Benedictine reform spirit, as it were, back home.[15]

The waves of Viking raids and invasions during the ninth century had all but destroyed the monastic and ecclesiastical world of Anglo-Saxon England, leaving what remained in lay hands. With the defeat and settlement of the Danes by the early tenth century, and the consolidation of English power by Alfred the Great and his successors, a revival began under royal auspices. Unlike on the continent, where the erosion of the Carolingian Empire had left church reform to the aristocracy, here the royal reconstruction mirrored more faithfully the original Frankish reform movement. "It had begun, in part at least, as a protest against lay ownership of monasteries, seen as the principal cause of their decline." Inspired and directed by a new breed of monk-bishops nurtured by the continental reforms, the kings of England boldly displaced lay and noble control over the church and pushed forward the clerical ascetic agenda of the two Benedicts.[16]

Lamenting the demise of English culture and monastic life, King Alfred recruited a community of monks from France and installed them in a new monastery at Athelney, built on Carolingian design, to try to rekindle the flame, but the effort failed. He had more enduring success with the nunnery he built at Shaftesbury for his daughter Ethelgifu, mother of the future king and monastic reformer Edgar. Alfred also recruited the monk Grimbald from the reformed abbey of St. Bertin's in Flanders and placed him in the cathedral at Winchester. Grimbald later encouraged Alfred's son Edward the Elder and, thereafter, his widow, Easlswith, to construct New Minster together with the Nunnaminster for women. Alfred's efforts, however, proved premature. The real English reform effort began a half-century later, under the auspices of King Edgar and his three monk-bishops Dunstan, Ethelwold, and Oswald.[17]

Dunstan was born in 924 of the highest rank of Wessex nobility, his family enjoying close ties to the court, and was brought up by the Irish-inspired brothers of the ancient abbey of Glastonbury, the only English monastery still worthy of the name. After his uncle Athelm became bishop of Wells, Dunstan briefly pursued the life of a courtier, but, at the urging of the "priest and monk" Aelfheah, bishop of Winchester, he returned as a monk to Glastonbury and was then ordained a priest. In 940, King Edmund appointed him abbot of Glastonbury, and he undertook the cause of monastic reform while serving also as court counselor. After King Edmund's death, he came under royal disfavor and was forced to spend a year in exile at the monastery of St. Peter in Ghent, where he was able to study in detail the austerely ascetic reform movement of Gorze. In 957, Dunstan was recalled from exile by the young King Edgar to become bishop of both Worcester and London, and was consecrated by another early reform enthusiast, Archbishop Oda of Canterbury. Three years later, Dunstan himself became archbishop of Canterbury.[18]

Ethelwold was a close contemporary of Dunstan and also of high noble descent. They had become friends at the court of King Athelstan and were ordained priests together on the same day by Bishop Aelfheah. When Dunstan was appointed abbot, Ethelwold joined him as a monk at Glastonbury and there acquired a passion for Benedictine reform. He was made prior at Glastonbury and then abbot of Abingdon, near Oxford. Here "he slowly brought into stern reality of practice the immature Benedictine life which Dunstan had fostered anew in Glastonbury." While Dunstan was in exile, Ethelwold became the standard-bearer of monastic reform; he dispatched one of his monks to Fleury to learn the correct reform discipline, and his monastery thereafter followed the Cluniac pattern. Before long, "men were flocking to Ethelwold in their desire for that regular life which had [been] reawakened in southern England." With the ascent of King Edgar, who had been educated by Ethelwold at Abingdon, Ethelwold was made bishop of Winchester. The third monk-bishop was Oswald, nephew of Archbishop Oda of Canterbury. Inspired by his uncle, he early became a reform enthusiast and entered the monastery of Fleury. In 971, Archbishop Dunstan appointed him bishop of Worcester, where he undertook to establish the new Benedictine discipline of Cluny. He thereafter became archbishop of York.[19]

Like Charlemagne and Louis the Pious before him, King Edgar sought to return order to his realm by returning order to the church. To do this he had not only to revive ecclesiastical organization and loyalty but also to wrest control over church property from the lay nobility, and he saw in the monastic reform movement a means to these ends. The monastic reformers Dunstan, Ethelwold, and Oswald likewise wanted to restore monastic and church life to the chaste discipline of the Rule, forcing out of the monasteries and cathedrals the dissolute clerics and their families and replacing them with celibate monks. They clearly understood that the wealth and power of the king provided them with the means to achieve their ends. To their indigenous efforts was added the momentum and prestige of Cluny (through Oswald's and Ethelwold's links with Fleury) and Gorze (through Dunstan's ties with Ghent), and thus the authority of Aniane.[20]

Though their early efforts had been slow and difficult, within fifteen years of Dunstan's appointment as archbishop of Canterbury the monastic reformers had brought thirty-five monastic houses under strict Benedictine observance. By that time, in 973, they were prepared to convene the Council of Winchester, which they modeled explicitly on Louis the Pious' great Council of Aachen. "The reforms resulting from the Council of Aachen were well known in Anglo-Saxon monastic circles," one historian of the reforms has noted, "and are probably the conscious basis upon which the Council of Winchester was called and the Regularis Concordia drawn up." In the place of Emperor Louis the Pious sat King Edgar; in the place of Benedict of Aniane sat the monk-bishop Ethelwold; in attendance, in addition to the English monks, bishops, and royalty, were invited guests from the monasteries of Ghent and Fleury. As the Council of Aachen produced the Rules for Canon and Capitula for monks, so the Council of Winchester produced the *Regularis Concordia*; stressing the "need for uniformity in the observance of 'one Rule and one country,'" its provisions regulated all ecclesiastical affairs, including "the discipline of the common life of abbots and monks, of abbesses and nuns, [and] of boys in abbey schools."[21]

The Council of Winchester in effect ratified reforms already well under way in Edgar's England. Just as royal authority was seen as a means of extending the monastic reform, so monastic reform was seen as a means for undermining lay influence within the episcopate and clergy, and thus enhancing royal authority. The monastic hold on the episcopate was first and foremost. The royally appointed monk-bishops Dunstan, Ethelwold, and Oswald served as exemplars of the new ecclesiastical regime, their dual roles reflecting both the monasticization of the church and the subjection of the church to the authority of the king. The Council of Winchester urged that "episcopal and abbatical elections are to be carried out according to the Rule and with the consent and advice of the king"; henceforth bishops should best be drawn from the reformed monasteries, as a guarantee of both episcopal purity and loyalty. Throughout much of the following century, monks held the important sees of Worcester, Winchester, Canterbury, York, and Ramsbury, and the majority of these men were close associates of the reform leaders. "It has been calculated that until 1042 nine-tenths of the bishops were monks, and over the century before the [Norman] Conquest . . . three-quarters of them were monks." As monks became bishops, they also became collaborators of the king. "The central fact of Edgar's reign cannot be denied: the close and constant co-operation between king and bishops who were members of the monastic order, for the good of both kingdom and Church. The interests of both were believed to be best served by the multiplication of new foundations, by the promotion of monks to the episcopate, by the prominent part in local government taken by monastic bishops and abbots and by monastic influence at court, especially in formulating laws."[22]

Consistent with their effort both to monasticize the church and to bring it under royal control, the reformers sought to eliminate lay dominion over and presence within the cathedrals and monasteries, through concerted campaigns against clerical marriage and simony. "Rejection of simony and insistence on celibacy and chastity pointed the way to moral reform under royal direction for the good of the Church." Early in the reform movement, the monk-bishops strove to eliminate secular canons and their families from the monasteries and married clerics from the cathedrals, replacing them with monks. At the same time, they used royal might to expropriate church properties from the noble landowners who had come to control them. "The obstacles in the path of the reformers were tremendous," D. J. V. Fisher has written. "It is impossible to write with anything like certainty the history of the monasteries which had fallen into decay during the eighth century, or had been destroyed by the Danes, but it seems that often their temporal possessions had been . . . acquired by private landowners. Those that had survived were . . . occupied by clerks. Whether the project was to reform or to refound, vested interests were strongly entrenched and vehemently hostile." Thus, in the wake of the reform movement, "many laymen must have suffered." Moreover, "the clerks in the houses reformed by Edgar . . . were powerful largely because a high proportion of their inmates came from noble families. . . . To eject a community of this kind was no easy matter." Many of these royal reforms had to be "accomplished by force." "At both Winchester and Worcester monks replaced the cathedral clerks. To accomplish this, royal intervention was necessary because it involved endowments being transferred from individual clerks and their families to the monasteries as communities."[23]

The most vigorous and feared of the reformers was certainly Ethelwold of Winchester. He "was a man full of rushing energy, impetuous, driven by a single purpose, unencumbered by scruple. . . . To him the cause dominated all. . . . To those who resisted the course he held necessary and right, he was fearsome; in his wrath, men said, he leaped like a raging lion, like a bolt of thunder from heaven. And his standard of obedience, his ideal for his monks, was extremely high." With such personal resources, plus his own considerable wealth and the ever-present threat of royal violence, Ethelwold assailed the proud clergy at Old Minster, demanding discipline, obedience, and celibacy. "They heard, but they were in no state of will or readiness to cast away, then and there, clothes, possessions, homes, wives, even their whole way of life." So Ethelwold, backed by Dunstan and Edgar, "forced them out," replacing them with monks from Abingdon and imposing upon these a stern regular discipline. In this way, at Winchester, Worcester, Canterbury, and other reform centers, the monastic way of life was extended beyond the monasteries proper to embrace the cathedrals as well, giving rise to the "peculiarly English institution of monastic cathedrals." There the Carolingian Renaissance flowered again on English soil; in the new male-only environment, schools were re-established for oblates only, the Carolingian minuscule was employed in the copying of manuscripts, the ancient glory of English learning was revived in Athenian style. The *Regularis Concordia* took note of both the promise and the perils of this heady new classical world: "Master and scholar are to be together and to go about together according to the requirements of reason and necessity [but] not even the master himself may be in company with any boy without a third person being present as witness."[24]

Within the monasteries, the reform followed the patterns established on the continent. Monks were to adhere to the cloister and "observe what were clearly regarded as the three necessities, chastity, the monastic rule, and the Lord's service, by means of a pledge to the bishop." In addition to celibacy and obedience, great emphasis was placed upon the correct and regular performance of the liturgy, which was enlarged and elaborated beyond Carolingian practice. "Even as the Capitula of Benedict of Aniane at the Council of Aachen had gone far in stressing a multiplication of rites and observances beyond those specified in the Rule, so also the Regularis concordia outstripped the Capitula in the proliferation of offices and the specification of additional rites." Here, as in Carolingian times, the prayers and psalms were performed primarily for the king. "The Anglo-Saxon offices prescribed by the *Regularis Concordia* included set psalms and prayers for the royal house, . . . which probably reflects the close connection of King Edgar with the reformers." "Peculiar to the English revival," David Parsons has noted, "are the prayers said daily for the King, Queen, and benefactors: a total of eighteen psalms, twenty-three collects, and usually the morrow (or early) Mass." Peter Levi likewise observed that the English reform liturgy was character-ized by "numerous and repeated prayers for the royal family." True to its Carolingian lineage, moreover, the liturgy for the king took on the military significance of spiritual warfare. This is made explicit in King Edgar's 966 foundation charter for the monk-bishop Ethelwold's New Minster monastic cathedral in Winchester. "The abbot is armed with spiritual weapons and supported by a troop of monks anointed with the dew of heavenly graces. They fight together in the strength of Christ with the sword of the spirit against the aery wiles of the devils. They defend the king and clergy of the realm from the on-slaughts of their invisible enemies."[25]

Women, not recognized as warriors, played no more a part in the English reform than they had on the continent. Inspired by Bede, King Alfred had longed to revive the lost greatness of English monasti-cism. But he and his successors paid no heed to the prominent role of women in that past glory, a role that had been duly acknowledged by Bede. Although Dunstan and Ethelwold enjoyed the adulation and support of royal and aristocratic women, their monastic reform movement, in keeping with the masculine spirit of this new age, largely ignored women—except for the hostile attention accorded clerical wives. Like the majority of male houses, the distinguished double monasteries and nunneries of the eighth century which had helped to fuel and sustain the continental revival had been destroyed in the Viking advance. But the tenth-century reform movement, which restored so many monasteries to their prior splendor, made little effort to restore the nunneries and no effort whatsoever to restore the great double monasteries of old. A century after the reforms began, there were only nine nunneries in the realm, compared with thirty-five monasteries.[26]

Those nunneries which were restored, in the name of the queen, were placed under strict episcopal supervision; "at the house of nuns at Winchester, the Nunnaminster [established by King Alfred's grand-daughter Eadburg], Ethelwold imposed the same tightening disci-pline" as he imposed upon his monks. Nuns and abbesses, moreover, were segregated from the monastic mainstream (including education) and strictly cloistered. Presumably in penance for his own dalliance with a nun (according to Goscelin's *Life of Wulfhilda*), King Edgar insisted, in the name of chastity, on the complete separation of nuns and monks.[27]

Restored abbeys that had once housed double monastic communities were now reconstructed as monasteries for monks only. A century after its destruction by the Danes, the great abbey of Ely, "where Ethelreda had ruled her monks and nuns," was refounded by Bishop Ethelwold and his monks of Abingdon. Thus, "by 970 monks were once more chanting the hours in Ely's choir," under the careful supervision of Ethelwold's reform protégé, Abbot Brihtnoth. But the women, the abbesses and nuns, were gone.[28]

On the continent, Aelfthryth, the English-born widow of Baldwin II, "stoutly refused that he be laid to rest in the chief cloister of his inheritance, that of St. Bertin . . . 'because she wanted to lie beside him, and no woman might cross the threshold of St. Bertin,' " even in death. Not long after the restoration of their abbey, "by a not very reputable ruse, [Abbot Brihtnoth] contrived to get the body of St. Ethelreda's sister Withburga away from Dereham and buried it beside the other three members of that royal family." As the legacy of a very different and distant age, here in England dead women at least might still be granted entry to a male monastery. Aside from that, it was strictly a world without women.[29]

After the death of Edgar and the subsequent passing of his monk-bishops, the momentum of the English monastic reform ebbed somewhat. Indeed, under Edward the Martyr, in the wake of a struggle for royal succession that bordered on civil war, there was even something of a popular antimonastic reaction; noble landholders and secular canons sought to retrieve their lost domains and ecclesiastical standing through a lay redistribution of church property. As D. J. V. Fisher observed, "all social classes had been affected adversely by the king's favours to the monks." But thereafter the reform patterns again took hold, even in the face of renewed Danish invasions and the Norman Conquest. Although the Normans swept away much of what the Anglo-Saxons had wrought, they also brought a revival of continental, and now papal, reform influence. Thus, as Duckett concluded, "in England, Dunstan's work of renewing was renewed by Lanfranc," King William's Benedictine archbishop of Canterbury. Under the Normans too, "monastic discipline was tightened up . . . [and] the canons of cathedrals were made to observe celibacy." And, as Cecily Clark has now demonstrated, the lot of women did not improve but was actually eroded further under the militaristic Norman regime. Indeed, as D. H. Farmer wrote, in its essence "the way of life, begun at the reform, was to survive the Norman Conquest for nearly five hundred years more, through varying changes of fortune, but in a form which was recognizably the same as that of 970," the time of the Council of Winchester. The English reform thus carried forth the legacy of the medieval wedding of monasticism and monarchy begun by the Anglo-Saxon Boniface under the Carolingians. In Europe as a whole, meanwhile, that legacy would now assume a new, or, rather, its original, Roman dimension, as emperors and kings were forced to give way to a revived papacy.[30]

If war is politics by other means, so oftentimes is religion. Certainly this was the case in the eleventh century, when, from the "outer darkness" of isolation, impotence, and dependency, the papacy arose to defy kings. But if temporal power for the pope was the immediate end of religious rhetoric, genuine religious ideals remained at the core of the papal revival. Just as the reforming popes of the eleventh century sought to recapture the original authority of imperial Rome, they also strove to refire and fulfill the clerical ascetic ambitions of the early church, the dreams of Damasus, Siricius, and fourth-century male monasticism.

As Southern suggested, the popes were the ultimate beneficiaries of the breakup of the Carolingian order, but it took several centuries for the papacy to reap the harvest of social disorder. After playing at least a secondary role in the Carolingian Empire, the papacy thereafter became but an aristocratic fiefdom, the mere plaything of central-Italian barons. Certainly the Carolingians' solicitation of the pope's blessing for their ill-gotten empire had been a tacit acknowledgment of papal suzerainty. Moreover, the ninth-century False Decretals claimed Constantine as guarantor of the church's imperial inheritance while the Roman see remained the repository of the tomb of St. Peter and hence the site of holy pilgrimage and the universally recognized font of apostolic prestige. But there was in the ninth and tenth centuries, in Workman's view, "no way of turning the Papal prestige into actual power." In the abject dependence of bishops and the pope upon aristocratic and royal power, their authority even within the church had become utterly derivative; thus, as Ephraim Emerton observed, "by the eleventh century . . . the line between the religious and the secular had become obscured almost to the vanishing point."[31]

Ironically, secular authority was crucial to papal ascendancy, even in the midst of unprecedented clamor for ecclesiastical autonomy and titanic struggle between popes and kings. The renewed power of the reforming popes rested not only upon their classical conception of imperial resurrection but also upon their political connections with secular power: the imperial protection afforded the holy see of St. Peter by Otto I, the timely papal association with Norman military might in Italy, an array of opportunistic church alliances among the myriad landed nobility and petty princes of Europe, and a new web of ecclesiastical affinity with the emergent urban merchant and financial "bourgeoisie" of Rome and Italy. If the so-called Reforming Party aimed at the restoration of a supposed ancient church discipline, in their reform campaigns they relied heavily upon the distinctly secular mechanisms of medieval discipline. At the same time, they derived their overriding spirit and their most assiduous agents and allies from the monasteries.[32]

The rise of the papacy in Europe reflected the fulfillment, within the church, of the dream of the church fathers to "turn the world into a hermitage." In the zeal of the reforming papacy, with its fanatical and final imposition of sacerdotal celibacy, the "rising tide of monasticism . . . submerged the whole Church hierarchy." In Workman's description, "for a while the world lay at the feet of the monastic ideal; no longer an ideal outside the Church, but dominating the Church itself"—as it had only barely begun to at the close of the fourth century. "The reforming spirit of the monasteries reached the papacy in the early eleventh century," and was reflected in the papal and conciliar legislation during the pontificate of Popes Benedict VIII and John XIX, which penalized the children of priests and punished married priests who continued to live with their wives.[33]

The monasticization of the church commenced in earnest, however, with the coronation of King Henry III's cousin, Bishop Bruno of Toul, as Pope Leo IX in 1049. "A keen supporter of the Cluniac monastic reform, [Leo] at once began to reform the Church"; immediately after his ascension, at the Easter Synod of 1049, "celibacy was enforced on all the clergy," followed by decrees against simony. Thereafter, "the principles of the reform campaign of Leo IX were reasserted by his successors" Nicholas II and Alexander II.[34]

This continuity owed most to the tireless efforts of the men whom Leo IX had recruited to promote his reform campaign; "they were all four monks": Frederick of Lorraine, abbot of Monte Cassino and later Pope Stephen IX; the theologian Humbert, legate and later cardinal bishop of Silva Candida; the zealous ascetic Peter Damian; and Hildebrand, monk of Cologne, who, upon his election as pope, took the name of Gregory VII in honor of that earlier champion of papal imperialism, Gregory I. (The entire reform movement would later be called the "Gregorian reform" after Gregory VII, who was perhaps its greatest, and certainly its most controversial, exponent.) If, as Frazee suggests, "the enthusiasm of the early church was reborn in the reform movements of the late tenth and eleventh centuries," it was owing primarily to these great champions of the clerical ascetic ideal; it was through them that "monastic ideals, especially the celibate life, came to influence the whole of Christendom once more." These monks formed the "nucleus for the reform of the Church."[35]

Outside Rome too, in the struggle to monasticize the church through the imposition of total clerical celibacy, "the monks everywhere were the pope's allies, stirring up the people against the seculars." Little wonder, then, that in the ensuing centuries "it was to monasteries, and later to religious orders as a whole [i.e., friars and orders of knights] that the pope [would] grant the most extensive privileges." And if the monastic imprint on the reform was indelible so was that of its now close cousin, the military.[36]

As Philippe Cantamine has suggested, just as the monasteries turned their attention increasingly to spiritual warfare, the church hierarchy had in troubled times adopted the habits and values of the secular warrior culture, "a movement which was especially visible at the level of the papacy." Thus the initiator of the papal reform movement, Leo IX, had himself been a warrior-bishop and continued to lead military campaigns as pope. A similar pattern is evident in the case of Hildebrand. Christopher Brooke noted that, whereas "St Ignatius Loyola [founder of the Jesuits] was a soldier before he was a churchman, in Gregory the roles seem almost to be reversed—he was a man of God turned soldier, but his soldiering always remained a matter for his dreams." Gregory was a reform warrior; "his letters are full of military metaphors, and also of the fury and exaltation of enthusiasm." It was actually Gregory who first came up with the idea of a holy military crusade. "Twenty years before the First Crusade," Southern points out, "Pope Gregory VII had suggested a way in which knighthood could be rescued from the radical defects attaching to its human and sinful origin, by dedication to the service of St. Peter." This idea signaled the final collapse of the distinction between the monastery and the military, and it would very soon place the monasticized church squarely at the center of the European warrior society; the First Crusade against Islam was proclaimed by Gregory's immediate successor, the ardent reformer—and Cluniac monk—Pope Urban II.[37]

Despite the profound worldliness of the reformers' habits and connections, they pursued ecclesiastical autonomy and papal power by preaching an otherworldly gospel against the sins of this world— epitomized by Peter Damian's shrill denunciations of the human race in general and of the secular clergy in particular. Above all, the reformers condemned what they believed to be the two ways in which the world maintained its grip on the clergy: "the influence of money and of the other sex." Their incessant attacks on simony, the buying and selling of church lands and offices (including the practice of lay investiture of abbots and bishops), were aimed at the first of these links; the campaign for clerical celibacy was directed against the second. Both efforts, in different but related ways, served the purpose not only of maintaining the integrity of ecclesiastical property but of achieving clerical autonomy from, and thereby church supremacy over, lay society.[38]

Like all church reformers before them, the papal reformers of the eleventh century sought to overcome the dangers of the medieval proprietary church primarily by condemning the lay entanglements of the clergy—now called the sin or even the heresy of simony. For some, like the piously self-righteous Damian, the elimination of lay influence over church property, appointments, and services was the means to a purified clergy. (Damian and Humbert were also concerned that simoniac practices gained influence in the church for ignoble and illiterate men, and, worse still, for women.) For others, like Hildebrand, a purified clergy was, rather, the means to enhanced hierarchical authority within the church and more legitimate (because uncompromised) and more potent (because economically stronger) authority outside it. But, whichever way ends and means were related, the practical measures taken were the same. As R. I. Moore notes, in the wake of the papal attack, "the most explosive of the questions that rent the church in the 1050's and 60's was whether the sacrifice of the Mass could be performed by a simoniac priest." And, however much the means might seem at times to have contradicted the ends (as in the case of Gregory's contest with Henry IV over lay investiture, in which he relied upon the lay power of the Germanic princes in order effectively to challenge the lay authority of the king), the results were impressive.[39]

The unrelenting papal attack upon the simoniac clergy in the end yielded the "recovery and stabilization of the Church's landed endowment," as David Herlihy has observed, and this in turn "worked a revolution in [the church's] relationship with the lay world." No longer, for example, could the landed aristocracy and nobility depend upon the relative "fluidity" between lay and ecclesiastical property when they had to provide for new heirs. What belonged to the church no longer belonged to them; they had to devise other means of preserving the aristocratic and royal patrimony—namely, a new narrow emphasis upon paternal lineage and a still narrower mode of inheritance, primogeniture. Lay society thus strove to prevent the dissipation of its property through primogeniture while the church sought to prevent the alienation of its own through its campaign against simony. In this regard, the reinvigorated crusade against clerical marriage was viewed as an aspect of the campaign against simony. If the elimination of clerical simony would prevent the loss of church property to lay families, the elimination of clerical marriage would eliminate the loss of church property to clerical families. It would also, of course, diminish clerical ties, through marriage, to lay feudal society. But the campaign for clerical celibacy had more ancient roots and deeper meanings.[40]

In its attack upon clerical marriage, the Gregorian Reform was a continuation, and culmination, of the clerical ascetic movement of the early church. As such, it reflected the deep-seated male monastic anxieties, not merely about the alienation of church property or the loss of ecclesiastical prerogatives, but about the corruption of the world, concupiscence, heterosexuality, and women. Though disdain for clerical marriage was certainly an aspect of papal concern about simony, clerical celibacy was also an end in itself, and the more essential priority. The Gregorian Reform movement, David Herlihy noted, "took as its supreme goal the restoration of celibacy as the fundamental rule of clerical living." That celibacy took precedence over simony in the minds of the reformers is easily seen in the readiness with which they sacrificed the latter goal in pursuit of the former.[41]

Frustrated in his zealous efforts to force clerical wives to leave their husbands, Damian appealed to the secular authorities of Savoy and Piedmont to intercede on behalf of the reformers. As Henry Lea wrote, "that so strict a churchman as Damian should not only tolerate but advise the exercise of temporal authority over ecclesiastics, and this, too, in a matter completely ecclesiastical, shows how completely the one idea had become dominant in his mind, since he was willing to sacrifice to it the privileges and immunities for which the church had been struggling . . . for six centuries." For their part, of course, the lay authorities were more than ready to acquiesce to papal demands, in that it gave them the opportunity to seize upon the church properties abandoned by the forcibly dissolved clerical families. Pope Gregory VII, that mighty foe of simony and lay investiture, was likewise ready to sacrifice such concerns in the interest of celibacy. As Lea wrote in his study of sacerdotal celibacy,

> to Gregory . . . was generally attributed, by his immediate successors, the honor of introducing, or of enforcing, the absolute chastity of the ministers of the altar. When Gregory took the reins into his vigorous grasp, the change at once became manifest, and the zeal of his predecessors appears lukewarm by comparison. He had had ample leisure to note how powerless was the ordinary machinery to accomplish the result, and he hesitated not to call to his assistance external powers; to give to the secular princes authority over ecclesiastics at which enthusiastic churchmen stood aghast, and to risk apparently the most precious immunities of the church to secure the result.[42]

Gregory was convinced by the inaction or resistance of the hierarchy that, "if the church was to be purified, it must be purified from without, and not from within." Thus, but a year into his papacy, and "to the unutterable horror of those strict churchmen who regarded the immunity from all temporal supervision or jurisdiction as one of the most precious of ecclesiastical privileges," Gregory took "the decided and unprecedented step of authorizing the laity to withdraw their obedience from all prelates and priests who disregarded the canons of the Holy See on the subjects of simony and incontinence." The princes of Germany did not quibble about the contradictions, but "were delighted to seize the opportunity of at once obliging the pope, creating disturbance at home, and profiting by the church property which they could manage to get into their hands by ejecting the unfortunate married priests."[43]

In the minds of the reformers, celibacy was clearly not just a means of preventing the loss of church property, through clerical inheritance, or the erosion of church autonomy, through clerical-lay relations. Nor was it simply a way of securing for the papacy the unalloyed obedience and loyalty of the clergy. Certainly celibacy was a way of divorcing the clergy from the interests, distractions, and corruptions of the world, a means of creating a holy corporate caste, and papal cadre, apart from and above the laity. But this campaign entailed more than immediately practical and political purposes. The platform of the reformers called for, in Brooke's phrase, a "devastating social revolution," or, rather, in Lea's more apt description, "a dissolution of society." If it demanded a clerical divorce from the world on an economic and political plane, it did so also on a more fundamental— the most fundamental—level. Clerics were henceforth expected to live in a religious realm purified of sex and family, unsullied by the basic unit of society itself—the relation between men and women, or, in Gregory's words, "the foul plague of carnal contagion."[44]

In essentially declaring war upon society itself, the papal reformers were bound to cause great pain and hardship and provoke serious opposition. "If we may admire the high idealism of Leo IX, Humbert, Hildebrand, and Peter Damian," Christopher Brooke surmised, "we must also conclude that their work had many victims. The legislation of the eleventh century popes on clerical marriage must have produced . . . many broken homes and personal tragedies." A member of the clergy was "forced to separate from his wife and children, or may have suffered severe penalties for refusing to do so: loss of his benefice and salary, loss of his priestly ordination, being fined, publicly ridiculed, imprisoned, even physically harassed, his children disinherited and declared illegitimate." According to Lea, "the clergy suffered horribly: reduced to poverty, homeless, exiled, others mutilated, tortured, murdered."[45]

In the face of such a campaign, the married clergy fought back. "It cannot be a matter of surprise," Lea observed, "if men who were thus threatened with almost every earthly evil should seek to defend themselves by means as violent as those employed by their persecutors." The vigorous but isolated resistance to the papal reform eventually coalesced into a "united body who boldly proclaimed the correctness of their course and defended themselves by argument as well as by political intrigues and military operations." The result was a schism within the church hierarchy itself, and civil war outside it. As the reformers allied themselves with secular powers such as the Normans, so the married clergy allied themselves with northern-Italian princes and nobility, centered especially in Milan. When the reformers selected their pope, Alexander II, the married clergy and their supporters chose a rival pope, Cedalus of Parma, or Honorius II. When champions of celibacy like Damian and Hildebrand echoed Augustine and Gregory, defenders like the Anonymous of York echoed Jovinian and Helvetius. "Cruel persecution" was met with defiant and unified resistance, violence with violence.[46]

For nearly a century, the issue divided the church. The German bishops condemned Hildebrand's "profane innovations"; a church council in Paris nullified the pope's decrees as "unbearable and therefore irrational." When Damian went on a reform mission to Milan, the site of near civil war over the issue of celibacy, "he barely escaped with his life"; on a similar mission to Lodi, "his saintly dignity came near being enhanced by the honors of martyrdom." The struggle in Milan was by no means unique. In Lucca, the clergy, "being condemned and excommunicated, resisted by force of arms, excited a rebellion in the city," and drove out the reforming Bishop Anselmo. Similar events occurred in Piacenza, Parma, Modena, Reggio, and Pistoia. Hildebrand was denounced as a "madman and a heretic [who] expected men to live like angels." Often "the clerks openly refused obedience," Lea noted, "and defended themselves by immemorial custom, and by the fact that none of their predecessors had been called upon to endure so severe and unnatural a regulation." At Mainz, the Thuringian clergy "raised a tumult [and] flew to arms."[47]

In the end, the reformers prevailed, owing to a superior force of arms, the enlarged resources of the papacy, and the expanding ideological hegemony of asceticism, reflected in the fact that secular rulers who tacitly supported the married clergy rarely did so openly. Whereas eleventh-century legislation against clerical concubinage and marriage prohibited the faithful from attending Masses performed by incontinent priests, the twelfth-century legislation put an end to clerical marriage once and for all. In 1123, the First Lateran Council actually annulled existing clerical marriages; the Second Lateran Council, of 1139, not only forbade the ordination of married men but decreed that ordination automatically invalidates the marriage bond. Perhaps more important than legislation, by this time the church had begun to institutionalize the intellectual and legal apparatus whereby such order would henceforth be maintained.[48]

Brooke wrote, in trying to account for the success of the papal reform movement,

The formal campaign is the first and most obvious cause, but I doubt if it was directly the most important. Celibacy had been the law of the Church since the fourth century, and it is far from clear why the mere reiteration of the law, however powerfully supported, should have been so startlingly successful. . . . Rather we must look at the situation of Western Europe as a whole in the early twelfth century. The revival of learning and all that went with it—the movement we call the twelfth-century renaissance—owed much to the stimulus of the papal reformers; but even more conspicuously, it was the papacy's most potent ally. . . . The revival in the study and technique of law enabled the papacy for the first time to operate through a network of courts enforcing a highly wrought and sophisticated legal system . . . [and] the generation which witnessed its appearance had been brought up to accept the standards of their schools, where they learnt to know and respect the law of the Church, and so the law of celibacy.

The revival of learning in the cathedral schools of Europe, which spawned the medieval university, was itself an instrument of the reform movement. Indeed, it was no accident that the new universities emerged at the very moment when the clergy was finally forced to become celibate, when the ecclesiastical world without women had at last been secured. As Heloise well understood, marriage to her lover, Abelard, the legendary father of the University of Paris, would undoubtedly mean the end of his career. Thus, by the mid-twelfth century, in the wake of the papal reform, "clerical marriage found few defenders"; ambitious clerics, including the lawyers and scholars, had come to find the charms of women far less seductive than the privileges and power of the papacy. It is hardly a wonder, then, that, as Frazee has pointed out, "the legislation of the Latin church remained unchanged from the twelfth century to the twentieth." Thus was created the most powerful and enduring men's club in history.[49]

Like all of the clerical ascetic campaigns that preceded and inspired it, the papal reform effort of the eleventh and twelfth centuries was driven by a vision of a world without women. For, in the eyes of the reformers, women were not just the unwelcome avenue for worldly cares and interests; they were the "devil's gateway." "Almost all medieval reformers inherited from St. Jerome the notion that the petticoat was the supreme symbol of the snares of the world," Brooke observed. But, in addition, insofar as the eradication of simony and clerical marriage was viewed as a means of clerical purification, the perceived pollutant was woman. "In the pollution of the priest," Moore suggests, "incontinence and simony were complementary in principle as they were in practice"; it was common, for example, for the reformers to use sexual imagery in denouncing simony as well as marriage. A reinvigorated clerical misogyny early appeared as a prominent, and apparently effective, theme in the reform campaign; the monastic reformers of the church regularly "equated women with insatiable sexuality, irrationality, and demonic temptation" and displayed a growing "tendency to regard women as the 'other.' " As Michael Kaufman suggests, "the systematic defilement of women was intended to win the clergy back to celibacy."[50]

The monk-cardinal Peter Damian, the leader of the celibacy campaign, was perhaps the strongest misogynist among the reformers. His monastic alarm and "hysterical virulence" about the polluting danger of women pervade the reformist tracts he wrote for Nicholas II, the *Book of Gomorrah* and *Concerning the Celibacy of the Clergy*. Women, Damian wrote, are "Satan's bait, poison for men's souls, the delight of greasy pigs, inns where unclean souls turn in." "Peter's obsession with women," Frazee writes, "brought him to caution an inquirer: 'Certainly I who am already an old man can safely and legitimately look upon an older woman whose face is lined with wrinkles. . . . But I guard my eyes at the sight of more beautiful and attractive faces, as I would children from fire.' " In this regard, Lea cites the case of the reforming Bishop Hugh of Grenoble, a contemporary of Hildebrand's, who, "during fifty-three years spent in the active duties of his calling, never saw the face of a woman, except that of one aged mendicant." In Damian and his fellow reformers, the monks of the desert had come alive to walk the lengthening corridors of papal power.[51]

Given the monastic fear and hatred of women fueling the fantasies and handiwork of the reformers, it is hardly surprising that women suffered the most from their efforts. "With regard to the status of women," Susan Stuard wrote, "the Middle Ages can appropriately be bisected by the Gregorian Reform of the late eleventh century. . . . The great medieval churchwomen all belong to the earlier period." First, the campaign against simony reflected not only a concern about lay influence upon the Church but about female lay influence in particular. "Cardinal Humbert, for example, felt that simony was the vehicle through which women 'to whom it is permitted neither to speak in church nor to rule over men' were enabled to play a role—

and sometimes a powerful role in church appointments and affairs." The elimination of lay influence meant also the elimination of female influence. As we have seen, "the aristocratic women of the earlier age had shared with the men of their class in the disposition and protection of ecclesiastical positions. With the destruction of this patronage, they lost that influence." Moreover, as David Herlihy has argued, the condemnation of simony and the subsequent consolidation and stabilization of church holdings, put an end to the previously prevailing "fluidity" of land tenures between lay and ecclesiastical ownership. Henceforth aristocratic families could no longer simply repossess church property to provide for their heirs, and had instead to invent new means of preserving their patrimony. "One tactic they adopted," Herlihy points out, "was to exclude some offspring—typically daughters and younger sons—from a full share in the inheritance." (This explains, in part, the swelling of monastic ranks during this period.) If the adoption of the principle of primogeniture was, in part, a consequence of the successful church condemnation of simony, a consequence of the adoption of primogeniture was that "daughters were pushed to the margins." The campaign against simony thus considerably diminished female lay influence on the church, not only at the time but for centuries to come.[52]

Women likewise bore the brunt of the papal campaign for celibacy. As the former monk Peter Levi observed, "the low status of women is of course exaggerated by men self-bound to chastity." The clergy were abused and deposed, but their wives were destroyed. Abandoned by the church to utter destitution, they and their children confronted the horrors of starvation, prostitution, servitude, murder, and suicide. And if Hildebrand's measures had been harsh with regard to the fate of clerical wives, those of his successor, the Cluniac monk Urban II, were worse. "Where Gregory had been content with ejecting husbands and wives, and with empowering secular rulers to enforce the edict on recalcitrants," Lea wrote, "Urban, with a refinement of cruelty, reduced the unfortunate women to slavery, and offered their servitude as a bribe to the nobles who should aid in thus purifying the church."[53]

The papal purification of the church through the elimination of clerical simony and marriage meant, at its most fundamental level, the purification of men through the elimination of women. Thus an ancient theme of clerical asceticism, revived again and again by monastic, ecclesiastical, and imperial reformers over the course of nearly a millennium, had at last taken hold of the Western Church. Now the entire hierarchy of the church, rather than just the monastics, inhabited a world without women. And this new homosocial ethos was reflected also in the efflorescence of what Natalie Davis described as a "remarkable degree of homoerotic expressiveness found in the writings and behavior of monks and priests." The strictures against homoeroticism in the penitential literature, monastic rules, and reform legislation had long attested to its pervasiveness among single-sex clerical communities; in the eleventh and twelfth centuries, at the height of the papal campaign against clerical marriage, this heretofore proscribed homoeroticism was officially tolerated and even celebrated.[54]

One of the greatest churchmen of the era, for example, the theologian and reformer Anselm, monk of Bec and archbishop of Canterbury, had "one of the most significant love relationships in the medieval period about which we know anything at all," with his young disciple Osbern; "Anselm sought friendship and love only from men," and the intensity of his fraternal friendship burst forth in a new kind of literary offering: "my eyes eagerly long to see your face, most beloved; my arms stretch out to your embraces. My lips long for your kisses; whatever remains of my life desires your company, so that my soul's joy may be full in time to come." What Anselm was to the eleventh century, Abbot Ailred of Rievaulx was to the twelfth. The uncertainty, hesitancy, and sublimation that often characterized Anselm's homoeroticism, however, was replaced by a self-confidence and openness in the the writings of the great English Cistercian abbot "who gave love between those of the same gender its most profound and lasting expression in a Christian context." Throughout the period of papal reform and the twelfth-century renaissance, the homoerotic culture flourished, reflecting an official toleration of intimacy between men at precisely the moment that intimacy between men and women was being condemned most severely.[55]

David Greenberg has suggested that the homoeroticism of the clergy was a consequence of the monasticization of the church in that it stemmed largely from the pressures common to a "single-sex milieu." He argues that "the elimination of heterosexual outlets for priests could only have fostered the development of homoerotic feelings." Greenberg maintained that "the same pressures that gave rise to monastic homosexuality in the early Christian monasteries were generated again by the closing off of heterosexual relationships for the medieval clergy. The emotional consequences of this measure can be seen in the homophile poetry and letters of passionate male friendship and love written by twelfth-century clergy to one another."[56]

The striking contrast between official church tolerance of homoerotic practice, on the one hand, and official church condemnation of heterosexual relations, on the other, did not escape contemporary notice. "The apparent indifference to homosexual behavior of the institutional church during this century [between the mid-eleventh and mid-twelfth] is all the more remarkable," John Boswell pointed out, "because it was precisely during this time that the most strenuous efforts were made to enforce clerical celibacy." Church leaders such as Leo IX, Alexander II, Urban II, and Anselm, who vigorously condemned erotic relationships between the clergy and women, were noticeably reluctant to condemn such relationships between men. "It might be argued," Boswell suggests, "that there was more than a coincidental relation between gay sexuality and some of the reforms effected during this century. Contemporaries, at least, were quick to note that gay priests would be more willing than heterosexual ones to enforce prohibitions against clerical marriage." Indeed, "there is some evidence of a power struggle between gay and married clergy over whose predilections would be stigmatized." "Leave us alone and chastise yourself, sodomite!" one married priest angrily responded to the reformers. Another rejoinder to a reforming bishop reflected the same sentiment: "The man who occupies this [episcopal] seat is Ganymedier than Ganymede, Consider why he excludes the married from the clergy, He does not care for the pleasures of a wife."[57]

Boswell notes that "some justification for these suspicions is eloquently provided by the astounding amount of gay literature which issued from the pens of clerics during this period. . . . Almost all were composed by priests and bishops in good standing. . . . Almost all [of these men] were intellectually influential, and some were among the major Christian thinkers of the day." Although Boswell acknowledges the coincidence between the homoerotic ethos of the reforming church and the drive for clerical celibacy, he ignores the equally obvious coincidence of both with the emergence of a virulent clerical misogyny. As E. Ann Matter points out, Boswell's sources betray just such a "misogynism"; although the church leaders displayed for a time an unusual tolerance with regard to homoerotic experience, they displayed no such tolerance toward either heterosexual experience or female homoeroticism. Rather, they "had very little tolerance for the most obvious differentiation between human beings"; "the 'gay' voices speak of an all-male world of sexual freedom in which women clearly had no place."[58]

The twelfth century, a period of papal reform and intellectual renaissance, witnessed also a spiritual revival that matched in intensity and reach that of early Christianity. Throughout Europe, new ascetic orders sprang up to challenge the worldliness of the church and monasteries. But the revival, for all its iconoclastic fervor, remained safely within the bounds of the new male order. The Cistercians, successors to the Cluniacs in papal favor and worldly success, resolutely excluded women, as did most of the other new religious orders—including, of course, the military orders. Later, the friars too, the military-minded Franciscans and Dominicans, though they roamed the world, kept their distance from women. (Francis of Assisi traveled afar while Clare remained confined to her cell.) Women, however, were drawn in droves to the new religious movement, much as they had been at the dawn of Christianity, and their enthusiasm and piety demanded attention. The new order of Prémontré was, in large measure, built upon the recruitment of such women. But in the oppressively masculine and misogynist ethos of the day, the novel experiment was short-lived. The spirit of the period is thus perhaps best summed up in the words of the Premonstratensian Abbot Conrad of Marchtal in announcing, at the close of the twelfth century, the belated decision to exclude women from the Order.

> Recognizing that the wickedness of women is greater than all the other wickedness of the world, and that there is no anger like that of women, and that the poison of asps and dragons is more curable and less dangerous to men than the familiarity of women, [we] have unanimously decreed for the safety of our souls, no less than for that of our bodies and goods, that we will on no account receive any more sisters to the increase of our perdition, but will avoid them like poisonous animals.[59]

It was within such social soil that the seeds of the modern Western intellectual tradition first took root. In their new celibate culture of learning, the cathedral schools and universities well reflected the fully monasticized ethos of the church—a world without women. Heloise's poignant allusion, in her letters to Abelard, to the intellectual and spiritual companionship of Jerome and Marcella, is a reminder of the distance in gender relations that had been traveled since the fourth century, a distance that rendered their own creative coupling so tragically impossible. Having expunged the female element from the life of the church, moreover, papal energies now turned outward, in combat against heathens and heretics (who, again, so often assumed female form). In the sweeping ecclesiastical reforms of the eleventh and twelfth centuries, R. I. Moore has discerned the "formation of a persecuting society," an "indispensable characteristic" of which was "a very much deeper and more pervasive penetration of society by the culture and institution of the literate minority." As the thirteenth century dawned, Pope Innocent III launched his genocidal Albigensian Crusade against the heretical anticlerical Cathars in southern France, who bore striking resemblance to the men and women of the early church. Seven years later, he conferred the official statutes on the University of Paris.[60]

Seven · *Bachelors:*
The Scholastic Cloister

B
Y THE END OF THE TWELFTH CENTURY, the papal-sup-
ported clerical ascetic reform movement against simony, clerical marriage, and the heretical vestiges of androgynous
asceticism had all but swept away the material and ideological supports
of future female participation in the mainstream (i.e., ecclesiastical)
world of learning. As never before, educated women were on the outside looking in. "Cast spiritually and intellectually adrift," as
Friedrich Heer described their plight, "women were confronted with
the closed ranks of a masculine society, governed by a thoroughly masculine theology and by a morality made by men for men." From the
thirteenth century onward, "there was no suitable outlet for their great
abilities and no satisfaction for their spiritual and intellectual
yearnings."[1]

The Gregorian campaigns of the eleventh century had been undertaken in order to consolidate the church's autonomy and authority,
and this overarching agenda had included also an effort to foster a
new, more worldly, ecclesiastical education for churchmen. In 1078,
Gregory VII adapted earlier Carolingian educational reforms to papal
purposes, ordering that "all bishops were to have the arts of letters
taught in their churches," a combination of both secular and "divine
learning." The remarkable growth and fame of the episcopal schools
in the eleventh and twelfth centuries marked the beginning of a new
educational era, with the shift of the chief locus of medieval learning
from male monastic schools like Bec to the cathedral schools (Tours,
Orléans, Chartres, Rheims, Paris, Liège, etc.), seedbeds of the Western universities. But, as Hastings Rashdall noted, "the cathedral
schools were of course as ecclesiastical in their character and aims as
the monastic"; devoted to clerical education, the new episcopal centers of learning were restricted to men.[2]

In the twelfth century, the First and Second Lateran Councils of
1123 and 1139 finally annulled clerical marriages and forbade the

ordination of married men, thereby creating once and for all a clerical world without women. The Third and Fourth Lateran Councils, of 1179 and 1215, mandated that "every cathedral church shall maintain a master to give free instruction to clerics in the church and to needy scholars" and prohibited the exacting of any remuneration from worthy applicants in exchange for licenses to teach. The papacy was seeking to ensure that access to the robust cathedral schools would not be controlled by local interests but would be available to a broad spectrum of students and masters, regardless of national origin or class background—as long as they were male. "This ecclesiastical character of the pre-University education should be remembered," Rashdall insisted, "as the first of the conditions which determined . . . the form of the intellectual movement out of which the universities grew and the shape of the university-system itself." Thus the monastic ideals that had engulfed the church and its cathedral schools had come to characterize as well the new European culture of learning.[3]

For a brief moment, however, the social, religious, and cultural ferment of the twelfth century held out the faint promise of other possibilities. Marked by a moderating climate, agricultural improvements, a new European expansionism (via the Crusades), the widening use of money, and the elaboration of institutions, the twelfth century was a relatively "open age" of urban growth, economic development, extended social mobility, broadened horizons, and intellectual and spiritual adventure. It was, in Heer's words, "a germinal time, pregnant with a thousand possibilities." Increasingly blocked from responsible positions within, influence over, or advancement through the church, aristocratic women nevertheless exercised considerable power by means of their courtly influence and control over property, which increased in the absence of their crusading husbands. This was nowhere more true than in Spain and southern France, where women took part in municipal politics and vast regions were governed by such powerful women as Eleanor of Aquitaine, Alix of Vergy in Burgundy, the countesses Marie and Blanche in Champagne and Ermengarde of Narbonne, and, later, Blanche of Castile. Flanders, the great center of economic activity in northwestern Europe, was ruled by women, the sisters Joanna and Margaret, for sixty-five years. Such ruling women became patrons, not only of economic activity and urban settlement, but also of the vernacular language, the poetry of male and female troubadors, and devotees of the new learning.[4]

Many other women meanwhile became active in the myriad economic activities of the burgeoning towns of Europe. In George Ovitt's survey,

> townswomen often worked for their craftsmen-husbands or as independent craftswomen in various parts of the textile industry but also in brewing, baking, small-scale metalwork . . . , net making, shoemaking, bookbinding, goldsmithing, butchering, candlemaking and, occasionally, as merchants, copyists, and moneylenders. While women were generally excluded from certain occupations, especially the highly skilled building crafts and some of the specialized textile crafts, overall they were well represented in the craft guilds.

But female participation in the twelfth-century "awakening" was perhaps most dramatically seen in the far-reaching religious revival of the period, which gave rise alike to powerful new monastic orders and heretical movements.[5]

As in the first four Christian centuries and again during the monastic resurgence of the seventh and eighth centuries, the evangelical fervor of the religious revivals of the late eleventh and early twelfth centuries drew in large measure upon the energies and enthusiasm of women. This latest religious awakening was prompted by a revulsion at the pretensions of an ever-worldly church and by a pious anxiety over the avarice and ambition which increasingly polluted society and church alike. And, as in the earlier episodes, the renewed movement, in challenging the corruption and constraints of the established order, gave rise to a veritable "surge" of female religious activity. Historians Penny Schine Gold and Sharon K. Elkins have amply documented this phenomenon in twelfth-century France and England. "Despite the male opposition to female participation," Gold noted, "women persisted in joining religious communities and in somehow finding the support they needed."[6]

In large numbers and throughout Europe, women were supported by lay founders and their families, as well as for a time by the pope, in a determined and temporarily successful effort to participate in the new Cistercian and Premonstratensian orders, despite increasing official strictures against them. The Cistercians initially tried to ignore "the large and rapidly growing number of women who adhered to its customs without being subject to its organization or control," and thereafter engaged in "a long struggle to discipline the women." Nevertheless, as Southern pointed out, the attempt to prevent new foundations of Cistercian nunneries was a complete failure. In several parts of Europe, especially in the areas of most rapid settlement—in Germany, Belgium, Holland, Portugal, and also in Switzerland—the number of Cistercian nunneries came in the course of the thirteenth century greatly to exceed the number of foundations for Cistercian monks. Over the Order as a whole, the number of nunneries—though not their wealth—was not far behind that of the male monasteries.

Women of course also played a defining role in the Gilbertine Order and the remarkably woman-centered Order of Fontrevault. Meanwhile, the royal nunneries of Saxony, which had continued the monastic traditions begun in the eighth century, produced in the twelfth century perhaps "the last nonmystical literary composition by a nun," the *Hortus Deliciarum* of Herrad of Heidenheim, and the most famous female religious of the era, Hildegard of Bingen. It is important to note, however, that Hildegard's remarkable reputation rested largely upon the evangelical standards of early Christianity, revived during the monastic reawakening, rather than upon the new intellectual criteria of the dawning High Middle Ages. Despite her mastery of Scripture and theological and philosophical works, Hildegard had had a rather rudimentary schooling, her command of Latin remained "uncertain," and she had "no specialist training in philosophy or theology." Her extraordinary influence rested not upon her scholarly abilities but upon her reputation as a mystic and papally sanctioned prophetess. (The recurring female recourse to mysticism, as the locus of intellectual life shifted from the monasteries to the male-only cathedral schools and universities, is seen later also in the lives of the nuns of Helfta, the two Mechtilds and Gertrude, Julain of Norwich, Margery Kemp, and Catherine of Siena). "As prophet," Peter Dronke has noted, "Hildegard assumed without serious opposition many high sacerdotal functions which in general the Church had seen, and continued to see, as male prerogatives. Always she distinguishes between herself in her own right, 'the poor little womanly figure . . . ,' and what the divine voice, or the living light, expresses through her. When she admonishes, warns, or castigates, it is always in the name of that light and that voice, not in her own."[7]

Before long, the mounting male resistance to this female religious upsurge drove many women outside the church. As Gold has noted, "some women, rather than squeezing themselves into the strictures of these orders, sought out less orthodox movements that willingly accepted them. In the twelfth century women were active in heretical movements, notably with the Albigensians and Waldensians." According to Heer, "heterodox and heretical groups offered women much greater freedom and a wider field of activity," as did mysticism. Throughout the twelfth century, the Cathars of southern France offered a religious haven for women in great numbers until they were exterminated in the Albigensian Crusade of the thirteenth century. In the thirteenth century, many women in Flanders, France, and Germany formed the Beguine movement, named disparagingly after the Albigensians. In Southern's view, "the beguines presented a new front to the ecclesiastical hierarchy." "It was basically a women's movement, not simply a feminine appendix to a movement which owed its impetus, direction, and main support to men." In its practices, it departed dramatically from the male monastic norms which had taken hold in the church. "It had no definite Rule of life; it claimed the authority of no saintly founder; it sought no authorization from the Holy See; it had no organization or constitution; it promised no benefits and sought no patrons; its vows were a statement of intention, not an irreversible commitment to a discipline enforced by authority; and its adherents could continue their ordinary work in the world." Moreover, "they had no quarrel with orthodoxy; they had no distinctive theological ideas at all; they were not perfectionists or Manicheans; they had no new revelation, only a desire to live 'religiously.' " Although in some respects they resembled the early friars, the Beguines in reality constituted the antithesis of the dominant male medieval religious institutions. Although their number swelled in the thirteenth century—by the middle of the century there were two thousand Beguines in Cologne alone—the movement was condemned in the beginning of the fourteenth, and its members were gradually either dispersed or absorbed into approved orders.[8]

Although they were denied entry to the new ecclesiastical educational centers, the cathedral schools, and later the universities, both lay and religious women were able to gain an education through the courts and the nunneries. In his survey of the literacy of the laity in this period, James Westphal Thompson noted the considerable degree of learning attained by such lay women as Countess Mathilda of Tuscany, Adelaide of Lorraine, Adelaide of Poitiers, Queen Mathilda (wife of William the Conqueror), Queen Edith Mathilda (wife of Henry I), her mother, Margaret, and, later, Henry II's wife, Eleanor of Aquitaine and her three daughters. Most accomplished lay women had received their early education, in languages and both secular and religious learning, in nunneries, even though they were not themselves destined to take the veil. One such lay woman was Heloise, later lover and wife of Abelard, cathedral-school master and father of the University of Paris. The relationship between Heloise and Abelard put in full Gothic relief the promise and limits of the new culture of learning.[9]

Peter Abelard was a noble youth from Brittany who forsook his birthright and knightly calling for intellectual combat, to become one of the legendary wandering scholars of the age. Before long, his gifts as teacher and dialectician brought him to Paris and eventually made this royal city the robust center of twelfth-century European intellectual life. Through his pioneering works on logic, ethics, and theology, he became the founder of medieval scholasticism, and, as a Parisian cathedral-school master, the progenitor of the University of Paris. He was also renowned for his poetry and love songs. If any single person embodied the medieval dawning of Western learning, spiritually as well as institutionally, it was Peter Abelard. At the same time, he was also the male half of perhaps the most tragic, certainly the most famous and revealing, of medieval love stories; if his experience as a master and a scholar mirrored the evolving cultural contours of Western learning, so too did his ill-fated romance with Heloise, whose career was also emblematic of the age.

Heloise was the brilliant and erudite niece of Fulbert, one of the canons of Notre Dame; her parentage is unknown. Although not committed to a religious life, she was raised and educated at the convent of Argenteuil, near Paris, and, according to Abelard, had already earned a reputation for learning by the time she arrived in Paris. Her ambitious uncle brought her to Notre Dame, presumably to arrange for an advantageous marriage, and privately provided for her continued education by retaining the already famous Abelard as her tutor. As Abelard tells it fifteen years later, he had had designs of his own; having been attracted by the girl's talents and grown reckless in the egotism of his fame, he had all but resolved to put his honored chastity to the flame of lust. In short order, dalliance overtook their studies, and then love their dalliance. Before too long, the lovers were found out, and soon they discovered that they had conceived more than ideas. Abelard arranged for Heloise's furtive flight from Paris to his family's compound in Brittany, and there she gave birth to their son, Astrolabe, whom they named after the astronomical instrument that symbolized the expansive new learning of Europe.

In a vain effort to appease Heloise's enraged uncle, but without thereby foreclosing his own ecclesiastical future (celibacy was by this time expected of cathedral masters), Abelard arranged for the couple to be secretly married, despite Heloise's grave reservations and great reluctance. Heloise thereafter returned to Paris, leaving her son in the care of Abelard's sister (nothing more is known of him), only to find that her uncle had vengefully broadcast the news of their marriage—which she was now compelled to deny for Abelard's sake. Faced with the prospect of continued harassment, Abelard had Heloise secreted out of her uncle's house in a nun's habit and sent to the relative safety of the convent at Argenteuil. But Abelard returned to his quarters in Paris at his own peril. The canon Fulbert was now further outraged by what appeared to be Abelard's abandonment of his niece. While Abelard lay sleeping one night, he was violently assaulted by men hired by the canon and castrated. If his romance with Heloise had been the scandal of Paris, Abelard's mutilation was a horrific sensation. In shame and despair, he became a monk and retreated to the Carolingian cloister of St.-Denis, after persuading Heloise, once again against her wishes, likewise to don a nun's habit permanently.

The tragedy of Heloise and Abelard, recounted in detail fifteen years later by Abelard in his *Historia Calamitatum* (the story of his misfortunes), and, perhaps more poignantly, by Heloise in her subsequent letters to Abelard, crystallized the fatal confrontation between the latent promise and the harsh reality of the twelfth-century awakening. Abelard's persistent persecutor, the influential Cistercian abbot Bernard of Clairvaux, epitomized the masculine ethos and eros of the clerical ascetic ecclesiastical culture; Bernard condemned Abelard as "an abbot without discipline who argues with boys and consorts with women." In contrast, Abelard and Heloise embodied the spirit of a new age of love and learning as well as the revival of an earlier Christian ideal of spiritual and intellectual companionship between men and women. As Friedrich Heer has suggested, for example, Abelard, in his relationship with Heloise, "presented his monastic and masculine contemporaries . . . with the idea that the type of the new Man was to be found in Woman." By his example as well as his new ethics of intention, Abelard encouraged the young men and women of Europe "to think boldly and to dare to love with passion."

As James Brundage has recently pointed out, "among the philosophers and theologians of the period, . . . Peter Abelard was almost alone in denying the intrinsic sinfulness of sexual relations and in maintaining that sexual intercourse is both natural and beneficial," as his notably un-Augustinian ethics makes plain. That Heloise shared such views, and much more ardently, is equally clear from her letters. Moreover, after they ceased being lovers, they patterned their belatedly chaste relationship after that of Jerome and his female patrons, disciples, and companions. "Such ideas," Heer noted, "could not fail to startle and enrage the 'monkish schoolmasters' for whom God was above all man incarnate, and for whom mind and thought were things not to be tampered with by impure womankind."[10]

Abelard's castration, then, and the couple's tragic lifelong separation, dramatically delineated the boundaries of the new ecclesiastical culture of learning. The message could not have been clearer for those wayward clerics who dared to associate with women, and it was a lesson well learned by future schoolmen. In the course of his relationship, Abelard had violated three taboos of the clerical culture: against sexual intercourse, against marriage, and against even chaste companionship with women. In the view of both Heloise and Abelard, it was their marriage more than their lovemaking that had undone them, caught up as they were in the Gregorian campaigns for clerical celibacy. "The punishment you suffered would have been proper vengeance for men caught in open adultery," Heloise wrote in her second letter to Abelard. "But what others deserve for adultery came upon you through a marriage which you believed had made amends for all previous wrong doing; what adulterous women have brought upon their lovers, your own wife brought on you." Even after they had been separately cloistered for ten years, according to Abelard, their chaste association continued to arouse the suspicions and disapproval of ecclesiastical authorities.[11]

But if Abelard suffered for his transgression of clerical norms, it was really Heloise—and, by extension, all women—who endured the burden of the new culture of learning. Certainly Abelard endured great hardship and ultimately suffered condemnation at the insistence of Bernard of Clairvaux. (Although he was condemned on theological grounds, the real reasons may well have been the cultural differences between the men; after all, Abelard's teachings soon became the established orthodoxy of the church through the work of his pupil Peter Lombard, author of *Sentences* and bishop of Paris.) Nevertheless,

Abelard the monk, his chastity now guaranteed, was able to resume his teaching and writing and even to return to teach in Paris. Indeed, to his later mind, recalling the self-castration of Origen, the injury done to him was more a blessing than a curse: it symbolized not merely his punishment but his perfection, enabling him, now beyond desire and above suspicion, better to pursue his pious purpose. He became an ardent champion of celibacy himself, and his letters to Heloise resound with belated monastic conviction.

Heloise, meanwhile, by all accounts his intellectual equal (and as abbess of the Paraclete apparently a more able administrator), was condemned to the relative isolation of the convent. Now denied even backdoor access, through Abelard, to the male-only centers of learning, she was unwillingly separated from her lover, husband, and teacher, from her child (male children were no longer permitted in female houses), and even from her own sexuality. As her letters poignantly testify, she did not don the veil by choice but out of deference to Abelard; with breathtaking sincerity and unbroken passion, she continued to maintain a dignified defiance of his sterile piety. One can only wonder what might have been had Abelard remained under this remarkable woman's influence. Could their conjugally conjoined brilliance have given the emergent culture of learning a different tone? But the dominant culture of celibacy to which Abelard was now so well suited offered her nothing but marginality and perpetual torment. The real burden of the calamity thus fell upon her. Whereas he had merely been, in effect, cut to fashion, she had been cast utterly adrift and aside. In an illuminated thirteenth-century manuscript of Abelard's *Historia Calamitatum*, which belonged to Petrarch, a portrait of the ill-fated couple was drawn in the illuminated initial first of the text, providing the only medieval representation of Abelard. The face of Heloise has been scratched out.[12]

In the wake of the Gregorian reforms, the new European centers of learning were finally formed in the male monastic mold, despite a brief early promise of something different, and certainly not for lack of abundant available female talent. The new academic culture, like the clerical culture of which it was a part, thus became a world without women. Generations of scholars were henceforth "brought up to accept the standards of their schools, where they learnt to know and respect the law of the Church, and so the law of celibacy."[13]

The social context of the new cathedral schools and universities was suggested in Achille Luchaire's able description of the schools of Paris, the pre-eminent medieval European center of education, which set the pattern for schools north of the Alps. (Italian schools, notably Salerno, Bologna, and later Padua and Florence, differed in having a larger percentage of lay masters—a consequence of the continuity of Italian lay education through the early Middle Ages—but these schools too came under ecclesiastical authority in issuing degrees and, according to Paul Oskar Kristeller, excluded women "from university studies and degrees and from the careers of university teaching and of the academic professions.") "One must picture a society," Luchaire writes, "in which there were no other educational institutions than these large and small seminaries where the clergy was molded and recruited. . . . Nearly all members of the higher clergy began as students; the schools were the nurseries of chapters and prelacies." In Paris, in addition to the abbey and cathedral schools attached to St.-Victor, Ste.-Genevieve, St.-Germain-des-Prés, and Notre Dame, there were private schools founded by clerics who had been granted licenses to teach. They "taught without restraint," notes Luchaire, "but always under the control of the bishop or the chancellor. . . . In short, it was the church which gave instruction, which created masters and conferred upon them the capacity of teaching. Bishops, chapters, and abbots had the supreme direction and control of teaching in the whole extent of their spiritual and feudal jurisdictions. No one could teach without their authorization." The corporate associations of masters and scholars which arose in the so-called university movement of the late twelfth and early thirteenth centuries, followed this pattern. In Luchaire's description,

> The university was a brotherhood almost entirely composed of clerics; masters and students had the tonsure; collectively they constituted a church institution. To say that the creation of universities was one of the characteristic signs of the emancipation of the mind in the religious domain, and that the "university movement" had as its principal object the replacing of the clerical schools of chapters and abbeys by corporations imbued with the lay spirit, is a gross error. Universities were ecclesiastical associations and were organized accordingly.

The seal of the University of Paris was composed of a cross and portraits of the Virgin Mary, the bishop of Paris, and a saint.[14]

Whereas in the eleventh and twelfth centuries the new schools had been established under local ecclesiastical auspices, "in the form of isolated and spontaneous creations," in the twelfth and thirteenth centuries the papacy "openly sought to complete, unify, and regulate this scholastic organization" so as to make of each school a "franchise from Rome." As Herbert Workman observed, "Rome saw that it would avail her nothing that she had crushed the independence of the bishops if the control of the new learning should pass into their hands." Though "it is true that the university was born of an effort for independence," this meant independence from local ecclesiastical power, which was gained at the price of exclusive submission to the authority and protection of the pope. As one historian of the University of Paris, Stephen C. Ferruolo, has explained, "for most scholars [in Paris], another city, Rome, and its ruler, the pope, mattered more. It was . . . to Rome and to the pope, not to their bishops or to the French king that the Paris masters and scholars turned at critical points in the university's development to protect their liberty or to gain recognition of their privileges." Innocent III issued the papal charter for the University of Paris to avoid having the masters swear their obedience to the bishop. Thus, as Luchaire insists,

> no more than the great schools of the preceding age did the universities cease to be ecclesiastical institutions; but they did cease to be diocesan institutions under the control of the bishop or his chancellor. They became an instrument of power in the hands of Rome, which meant a weakening of the episcopacy and a strengthening of the Holy See. It was the popes who created or developed these university corporations when they wished to take possession of the institutions of higher education. . . . The history of the origin of the French universities is, in this sense, nothing more than a phase of that larger evolution which from the beginning of the middle ages tended to exalt the papal monarchy above local ecclesiastical authorities.[15]

The "placelessness" or "abstraction" vis-à-vis their local environs that characterized the cosmopolitan universities, as well as their relative immunity from local authority, were thus the products of their concrete attachment to a higher—i.e., more powerful—temporal authority in Rome. This subordination to the pope was, in Luchaire's estimate, the "essential fact" of the University of Paris. King Philip Augustus' famous charter of 1200, exempting the university from civil and royal authority and placing it under exclusive church jurisdiction, assured "the independence, and consequently, the prosperity, of the great international corporation for centuries . . . guaranteeing the scholars almost complete impunity." At the same time, however, it gave the papacy unrivaled academic control. "The pope had full power over the professions and scholars, administrative and legislative power—power of direction, of control, and of correction; absolute power over the mind and over the body, over subjects to be taught as well as over the personnel teaching them."[16]

As a papal instrument, the university served the papacy as a cosmopolitan recruitment-and-training ground for the clergy, the church bureaucracy, and the church-dominated professions. At the same time, in a Christian world once again plagued by heresy and confronted by the challenge of Islam, the university became a bastion of orthodoxy, an intellectual arsenal of conformity. Like the Carolingian monasteries upon which they were modeled, the universities were, in this sense, military institutions, engaged in theological warfare on behalf of the church. In 1205, for example, the year after the Latin conquest of Constantinople in the Fourth Crusade, the scholars of Paris received an appeal from Pope Innocent III to relocate in Constantinople as a bulwark against Islam. "We pointedly ask and urge your university [that] many of you shall not hesitate to go out to a land . . . in order that to the honor and glory of Him, from whom is the gift of all science, you may be of profit there to Him and others." In 1229, a master of the newly founded University of Toulouse likewise appealed to the scholars of Paris to move to Languedoc following the Albigensian Crusade.

> Do ye well with us to prepare good will for the Lord which, when he finds prepared, he will lead on to holy works, so that where once swords cleaved a path for you, you shall fight with a sharp tongue; where war waged carnage, you shall militate with peaceful doctrine; where the forest of heretical depravity scattered thorns, the cedar of catholic faith shall be reared by you to the stars. You soldiers of philosophy may be able to fight the more safely with the art of Mercury, the weapons of Phoebus, the lance of Minerva. . . . So let each upright man put on the warlike mien of Achilles, . . . so that at least, the war finished, he may admire the zeal of the militant and the zeal of the philosophizing. The professors of Toulouse have cleared away for you the weeds of the rude populace.[17]

As was the case with the Cluniac monasteries, this military aspect of the university served the psychological needs of noble-born students to ritualize and thereby sublimate their knightly spirit—in intellectual rather than liturgical warfare. Abelard, himself the firstborn son of a feudal lord, described his own early academic career in distinctly military terms, in his *Historia Calamitatum*. He recalled that, as a youth, "I was so carried away by my love of learning that I renounced the glory of the soldier's life . . . , withdrew from the court of Mars in order to kneel at the feet of Minerva. I preferred the weapons of dialectic to all the other teachings of philosophy, and armed with these I chose the conflicts of disputation instead of the trophies of war." Recounting his early rivalry with William, archdeacon of Paris, Abelard recalled how he had established his school upon Mont Ste.-Genevieve—site of the later University of Paris—"in order to lay siege to my usurper," the master of Notre Dame who had been installed by William. William thereupon returned to Paris "to deliver from my siege the soldier whom he had abandoned." "Anyone who had watched warriors at work, or had read of them in epic," Alexander Murray observed, "knew that strength was an occasion for boasting. This rule transferred itself to the intellectual field." The ceremonial intellectual combat of the academic world, fully displayed in the agonistic rituals of dialectical disputation, was, as Walter J. Ong has suggested, "as inseparable from the universities as the universities were inseparable from scholasticism." It constituted the "deep structure in academia," which, on the one hand, fostered a particular form of rationality, and, on the other, "registered masculine needs."[18]

A century after Abelard, the students of Paris were still well known for their aggressive behavior, and not only in disputation. According to Ferruolo, "scholars often went about the city, armed with weapons which they, as the sons of feudal lords, well knew how to wield." One contemporary account "described the scholars, completely armed, coursing about the streets of Paris at night, breaking in the doors of the bourgeoisie and filling the courts with the bruits of their escapades." Divided into "nations," they regularly engaged in armed contests among themselves. "They are hardier and readier for battle than my knights," Philip Augustus is reputed to have said of the scholars of Paris. As it had in the imperial monastery, then, this military ethos, together with the clerical orientation, fostered an exclusive culture of masculinity in the papal university, a brotherhood. In addition to knightly spirits and clerical ambitions, this culture was sustained by its own distinctive puberty ritual, the cult of Latin.[19]

"Because they incorporate youth into the tribe rather than into the family," Walter J. Ong has noted, "puberty rites involve sexual segregation. The rites for boys are for boys alone." In the High Middle Ages, Ong wrote,

> the status of Latin encouraged in a special way the development of a puberty rite setting and puberty rite attitudes in the educational activity of the time. . . . For when Latin passed out of vernacular usage [and thus "was no longer a 'mother tongue' "], a sharp distinction was set up between those who knew it and those who did not. . . . The cleavage between the vernacular world and the Latin world did not coincide with the division between literacy and illiteracy but it did coincide . . . with a division between a world in which women had some say and an almost exclusively male world.

"Latin," Ong noted, had thus "become a sex-linked language, used only by males" and taught exclusively in the all-male schools. "Closed to girls and to women, the schools, including the universities . . . , were male rendezvous strongly reminiscent of male clubhouses in primitive societies. . . . This specially closed environment of the university was maintained by a long apprenticeship or bachelorship. . . . But in helping to maintain the closed male environment the psychological role of Latin should not be underestimated. It was the language of those on the 'inside,' and thus learning Latin . . . was the first step toward initiation into the closed world . . . , a secret language to nourish their esprit de corps." The typical contents of courses for Latin, "epics and histories full of violence and tales of valor," together with the argumentative methods of teaching and the physical punishment that regularly accompanied Latin instruction (reminiscent of monastic flagellation), further contributed to "male bonding." The exclusive possession of Latin thus provided a collective identity for this homosocial, celibate world of learning.[20]

As Marilyn French observed, the new institutions of learning "taught men what they were expected to be, how they were to approach life. It separated men from all women (for no women were permitted to enter the universities.)" The celibate ideal of the universities derived, of course, from their monastic and clerical heritage. In the view of the twelfth-century Benedictine abbot Philip of Harvengt, the school was just "another monastery." And by the thirteenth century, as Alexander Murray has shown, the name "cleric" was applied to scholars and clergy alike, the two meanings "confounded so deeply as to defy modern efforts to separate them." But the celibacy of the academy reflected also the spread of the celibate ideal beyond both cloister and church, in the wake of the religious awakening of the period. As several studies now demonstrate, the ideal had taken hold among the lay nobility of France, England, and Germany—the chief source of university masters and students—to an extent that defies any mere economic explanation. (The proportion of children opting for celibacy exceeded what might be expected from restrictions on inheritance, and often threatened dynastic survival.)[21]

Within the university, this celibate orientation was reflected in the widespread and persistent popularity, at both Paris and Oxford, of the famed twelfth-century antimatrimonial treatise of Walter Map, archdeacon of Oxford (and former student at Paris). Map wrote the treatise, under the name Valerius, in the form of a letter to Rufinus, in order to dissuade his friend from marrying. This eloquent attack on marriage, historian Robert Pratt has written, "seemed the perfect device for encouraging young men to hold to celibacy"; it was used to effect by generations of commentators to instruct their students about "woman and her evil wiles" and "the sensuous weaknesses of men." Even Chaucer made good use of it, in his prologue to "The Wife of Bath's Tale." "Women," wrote Valerius, "journey by widely different ways, but by whatever windings they may wander, and through however many trackless regions they may travel, there is only one outlet, one goal of all their trails, one crown and common ground of all their differences—wickedness." "No matter whether a young man went to Oxford under the auspices of the Franciscans or the Dominicans," Pratt noted, "he was evidently subjected to a thorough treatment of Valerius and his doctrine of celibacy and antifeminism." The attitudes expressed by the text were seconded by the anonymous commentators, compilers, and copyists who scribbled their misogynous thoughts into the margins of the medieval manuscripts, variously describing women as confused and tempestuous, insatiable beasts, scorpions, diabolical, infirm, an insane plague, or, as Abelard might have added, a calamity. The message was clear and insistent: marriage and women were perils to be avoided at all costs. It was a lesson well learned by future schoolmen.[22]

In his survey of the letters of medieval students, Charles Homer

Haskins offers the example of one medieval scholar called home to marry a lady of "many attractions." "He answers that he deems it foolish to desert the cause of learning for the sake of a woman." Lynn Thorndike cites the case of a divorced scholar at Paris who in 1290 was required to take an oath against any marital reconciliation in order to continue to teach. The official document reads like marriage counseling in reverse and well reflects the grave earnestness with which the strictures forbidding marriage were taken by the academic authorities.

> We make known that in our presence John, called Florie, a cleric and scholar of Paris, asserted on his oath in law before us with personal security from the same cleric, that a divorce was made between him on one side and his wife Simonia on the other by the venerable man and discreet official of the court of Rouen, as he said. And the same cleric promised by the said oath that, if the said divorce should be revoked in any way so that there should be a reconciliation between them, thereupon the said John would be deprived of the function of teaching at Paris in the faculty of arts.[23]

The academic emphasis upon celibacy was, if anything, reinforced in the thirteenth century under the influence of the mendicant Franciscan and Dominican orders, which produced such leading schoolmen of the age as Albertus Magnus, Aquinas, Bonaventure, Duns Scotus, and William of Ockham. The first chancellor of Oxford, Robert Grosseteste, taught in the Franciscan school. He is best known for his early work on optics and the courageous political stances he took while bishop of Lincoln, but he was also a staunch proponent of clerical ascetic reform. He was, according to Henry Lea, "perhaps the man to whom the church owed most for his energy and activity in promoting the cause of reform." As both chancellor and bishop, Grosseteste was "an inflexible enemy of clerical irregularities," insisting upon "strictest chastity," and "punishing transgressors with deprivation." Regarding his treatment of women religious, Lea remarks that "it is not easy to approve of his brutal expedient for testing the virtue of the inmates of the nunneries"; according to the contemporary account by Matthew Paris, the learned bishop regularly had his men squeeze the nuns' breasts for evidence of lactation, so that, "according to the natural philosophers, he could discover who was corrupt." That Grosseteste embodied the celibate ideal is attested also by his version of the six stages of man's life cycle: the recognition of free will, the pursuit of truth, the conquest of lust, good deeds, proper doctrine, and the contemplation of God. In this view family, children, and generational continuity have no place in man's life. Instead, conjugality and continuity took other, institutional and intellectual, forms.[24]

An educational treatise of the mid-fourteenth century which, according to Thorndike, "presents a very vivid picture of educational ideals and practice in the fourteenth century," clearly suggests how the celibate community of scholars appropriated, in appropriately ascetic form, such things as marriage and reproduction. "Those sleeping amid the clerics sleep the sleep of safety under the wings of the dove and arms of the spouse, the spouse, I say, of God, most beautiful of all women, whose clerics are the rulers and dispensers of her riches." The relationship of "master with disciples [is] as of fathers with heirs. . . . For in this divine house we do not have the association of man and wife as in the domestic house; nevertheless there is no master without mistress, nor poet without muse. For the lawful mate of the philosopher is the leading lady of all delights in this life, Philosophy herself, who the Lord ordering is mistress of all virtues. We assert that the true wife of each philosopher is his philosophy from which he begets books like himself according to the forms and cast of his mind, and his disciples are in a fashion his sons."[25]

As Marilyn French has suggested, this celibate-culture learning which took shape in the twelfth and thirteenth centuries "shaped European education for centuries to come," extending even beyond the reach of the Catholic Church itself. In 1561, in angry defiance of the Anglican rejection of clerical celibacy, Queen Elizabeth issued an order to the archbishops of Canterbury and York, insisting that academic celibacy be continued and commanding that no women be allowed into the universities on any pretext. "To these influences, perhaps," Henry Lea surmised, "we may attribute the last relic of clerical celibacy enforced among Protestants, that of the Fellows of the English universities." It was not until 1882, roughly eight hundred years after the birth of Abelard, that the Fellows of Oxford and Cambridge were allowed to marry. Thus, in trying to convey the peculiar characteristics of monastic life to a more secular twentieth-century world, Peter Levi was able to compare the eccentricities of celibate monks best to those "that Oxford dons used to exhibit before they were permitted to marry."[26]

As had been the case with the monasteries, the celibate communities of the new urban schools and universities were fertile ground for misogyny and homoeroticism, both of which flourished and, perhaps, reinforced each other. As Michael Goodich noted in his study of medieval homosexuality, the universities were "peopled by young, single, male clerics," whose youth and single status had been prolonged not only by ecclesiastical and academic strictures against marriage but also by feudal disinheritance following the widespread adoption of primogeniture. Like the monasteries and military orders (eg., the Templars) which also attracted such rootless youth, the exclusively male educational enclaves at Paris and Bologna became noted centers of homosexuality. And, as Heer noted, "the contemporary distaste for 'filthy womanhood' and 'filthy matter' had substantially contributed to making the burden of 'sodomy' an occupational disease of the European intellectual." The classical revival no doubt accentuated this tendency. As Thomas Stehling has observed,

> the great cultural renaissance during the twelfth century in Western Europe included a sudden flourishing of homosexual poetry. Just as men were laying the foundations for universities, reviving interest in law and science, developing the tools of scholastic philosophy, and learning again to appreciate classical literature, so too were men writing poems of love and seduction among men and between older men and boys, as well as poetic defenses and condemnations of homosexuality.

The lifelong relationship between Robert Grosseteste and his collaborator, Adam Marsh, is perhaps illustrative in this regard. In his authoritative study of Grosseteste's thought, James McEvoy indicates that Grosseteste found in the younger Franciscan scholar and fellow reformer "the other half of his soul," whom he always addressed as "dearly beloved," to whom he sent in his greetings "health and himself," and beside whom he would lie in eternal rest. As Stehling suggests, "for men in such communities, women always remained other," irrelevant, it seems, not only intellectually and socially but erotically as well. In the learned view of academics, only ignorant rustics, like beasts, should "filthy themselves with women."[27]

That misogyny would naturally flourish in this closed all-male world has already been indicated by the popularity of Walter Map's antimatrimonial treatise, which rested its case primarily upon the alleged evils of women. As was the case in the the early Christian centuries, the association of women with evil was reinforced by the association of women with heresy, in this case with the Albigensians. Women were thus viewed not simply with a lack of interest but with hostility. If university youth terrorized the town with their pent-up warrior spirit, their victims were more often than not women. Against other men the violence of noble scholars remained largely ceremonial and ritualized, but against women it was quite real. In 1269, a Paris court proclaimed against such scholars and clerics that "they atrociously wound or kill many persons, rape women, oppress virgins, break into inns. . . ." Luchaire cites a contemporary report that "every day public women . . . come to dispose against them, complaining of having been beaten, of having had their garments cut into shreds, or their hair cut off." Ferruolo also notes that university students in Paris were known for their "violent attacks on the city's prostitutes" and suggests that "a vicious attack on a woman by a group of armed scholars was probably one of the major precipitants of the bitter dispute between the university and the bishop of 1218–19."[28]

It was perhaps no mere coincidence, therefore, that the only outright retaliatory attack on the university ever undertaken by the civil authorities was made, in 1229, on the orders of a woman, the regent Blanche of Castile. This bold act, in response to a veritable town-gown war triggered by a tavern brawl, resulted in the famous, and ultimately successful, strike by the Parisian masters, who temporarily closed down the university in self-righteous protest. In his account of the controversy, the monk-chronicler Matthew Paris well reflected the prejudices of the age and his calling, blaming the crisis on the queen's "female impudence and impetuosity." The episode neatly symbolized the embattled spirit of the new academic culture, as it viewed itself, a fortress of pious learning pitted against female danger and assault. During the following century, the peasant revolts in France and England were often marked by female hostility against academics. In one such episode, in 1381, the privileges of Cambridge University were publicly burned; "at the bonfire an old woman is said to have cried, 'Away with the learning of the clerks, away with it.' " A half-century later, the tables were turned, in a bonfire of a different sort. At the instigation of the University of Paris and under the direct supervision of its rector, the academics engaged in their most vigorous prosecution of heresy to date, against "the one type most conspicuously foreign to university sympathy: an illiterate girl, Joan of Arc."[29]

By the thirteenth century, the celibate culture of the new learning was firmly established in the medieval university, the legacy of a millennium of clerical ascetic development. Only now, with the European rediscovery, via the Arabs, of the entire corpus of Aristotle (Plato's *Symposium* did not became available until the fifteenth century), did the misogyny of this essentially monastic culture gain the classical, naturalistic, seemingly scientific legitimacy that would perpetuate it for centuries to come. In his work on *Generation of Animals*, translated in the thirteenth century at the request of Aquinas, Aristotle had asserted that women "were weaker and colder by nature" than men and that "we should look upon the female state as being as it were a deformity, though one which occurs in the ordinary course of nature." In the process of generation, women provided merely the matter, men the all-important form. Although he differed from Aristotle on the actual role women play in procreation, Galen reinforced the idea of women's natural biological inferiority, based also upon the theory of humors. Such works profoundly influenced the great Parisian master Albertus Magnus, who argued that women enjoyed and sought sexual relations more than men because, being imperfect beings, they desired conjunction with those who were perfect, namely men. Albert's pupil Thomas Aquinas thereafter incorporated these classical views of women in his *Summa Theologica*, the authoritative scholastic summation of Catholic orthodoxy. Following Aristotle, he argued that, since the male seed produces a "perfect likeness"—that is, a boy child—a girl child results only from a defective seed. Women are "deficient and misbegotten," wrote Aquinas, inferior to men by nature except for purposes of procreation, and naturally subordinate to men because of their more limited capacity for reason. Thus "it was not only . . . the unsupported prejudices of the medieval clergy which led to medieval (and modern) misogynism but also the medical and scientific assumptions of the ancient world that were incorporated into medieval thinking with but little challenge."[30]

There is some irony in this ready medieval appropriation of classical, especially Aristotelian, misogyny; Ibn-Rushd, or Averroës, the great twelfth-century philosopher of Cordova and foremost Arab commentator on Aristotle, from whom European scholastics like Albert and Aquinas learned their Aristotle, was himself a strong believer in the natural similarity, and hence social equality, of men and women. In marked contrast to Aristotle and Muslim practice alike, but in keeping with what he believed to be the true Koranic teaching, Averroës accepted Plato's "argument for the equality of women in respect of full citizen-rights and duties." In his commentary on Plato's *Republic*, Averroës argued that "the nature of women and men" is of "one kind," differing only in degree; while he allowed that women might be weaker than men at some activities, he suggested that women are superior to men in others. He also maintained that, "since some women are formed to have a distinction and a praiseworthy disposition, it is not impossible that there may be among them philosophers and rulers."[31]

Although unacceptable to orthodox intellectuals, Averroës' views of women were perhaps carried forward for a time, culminating in the bold proposals of Pierre Dubois, a student of the Averroist Siger of Brabant, for the equal education of women. Dubois, an early-fourteenth-century antipapal propagandist for the king of France, offered his unique proposals as part of a grand scheme for French hegemony in both East and West, the Christian maintenance of Constantinople, and the reconquest of the Holy Land. The education of women was essential for the adequate preparation of female missionaries to the East, and all the more important because such women could ultimately become the wives of Byzantine clergy, who were not required to be celibate, or Muslim nobility, and thereby wield considerable influence. He proposed that special missionary-training schools for both young men and women be established in all French provinces. Like the boys, the girls would receive instruction in Latin grammar, Catholic fundamentals, and surgery; the more talented pupils, girls as well as boys, would also study logic, the foundations of the natural sciences, medicine, and a foreign language. Although Dubois was not interested in female education as a worthy end in itself, his missionary scheme, which was never acted upon, nevertheless reflected a firm belief in women's intellectual capability—"the first, perhaps, to venture so far," in C. G. Coulton's estimate, "since the Arab Averroës of 150 years earlier."[32]

If Averroës, through his commentaries, tutored Europe in Aristotle, it was not very long before his own work was repudiated as heretical and officially condemned. Though scholastic attacks against "Averroism" were expressed in theological terms—the status of the soul, the unity or duality of truth—the antagonism, as with Abelard, may well have been social as well, reflecting a discomfort with his unorthodox ideas about women and sexuality. According to several scholars,

there were some sexual connotations in the debate, and charges of sexual deviation were made. The Averroist commentators on Aristotle were, in fact, charged with teaching that continence was not a virtue, that perfect abstinence from sexual activity corrupted virtue, and that a delight in the act of sex in no way impeded intellectual progress. It was even alleged that some Averroists stated that simple fornication between two unmarried people was not sinful,

a view that was officially condemned as heresy in 1277, during the controversy over Averroism at the University of Paris. Subsequently, Siger of Brabant, teacher of Peter Dubois, was condemned as an Averroist and officially charged with heresy by the Inquisition.[33]

With the condemnation of Averroës and the Averroists, the misogynous classics were shorn of their heterodox Arab commentary, and henceforth unambiguously provided belated scientific fortification for the established European world without women. Early in the fourteenth century, one bold but as yet anonymous woman surreptitiously gained entry into this alien world of scholars, and her somber experience vividly reflects how the universities had come to symbolize the total divorce between women and learning. Having received her inheritance upon the death of her parents, a young woman of Krakow entered the university there, disguised as a man. In male dress she succeeded in actually attending the university for two years and even came close to receiving the baccalaureate degree. Her ruse was rudely uncovered in an assault by a soldier, however, and, taken before the judge she was summarily sent to a convent. When asked by the judge why she had so disguised her sex, she answered simply "for love of learning."[34]

It was also for love of learning that the writer Christine de Pisan similarly wished that she had been born a man and, later, as an isolated, if successful, woman of letters, suffered a life of "painful estrangement from society." Christine was tutored at home by her Italian-humanist father, a court physician who had studied at the University of Bologna, but was denied a formal education. What learning she did obtain, moreover, consisted of works by men that disparaged women as "abominable," "the vessel, as the men say, of all evil and of all vices." Thus her rudimentary education only left her "despising [herself] and all womankind," assailing God for not having been "born into this world . . . masculine." Christine emerged from this early despair, however, by recognizing that it was neither nature nor justice but merely, and profoundly, a misogynous male culture that so condemned her and her sex.[35]

"Since I was born a girl . . . ," she wrote in 1400, "I could not inherit that which others take from the precious spring [of knowledge], more by custom than by right. If justice were king, neither female nor male would lose, but mostly, I am certain, custom reigns, rather than justice, and for that reason, in every way I have been unable by lack of learning, to gather any of this most precious treasure, concerning which custom I am displeased, since if things were otherwise I presume I should be rich, full to the brim of treasure taken at the fountain. . . ." Armed with this understanding, she resolved to explore and expose, the better to oppose, "what might be the cause . . . that so many different men, clerics and others, . . . think and write so much slander and such blame of women and their condition." "I began to examine myself and my condition as a woman," Christine wrote in *The Book of the City of Ladies*, urging other women likewise critically to compare what they read about women with the reality of their own female experience. "Although you have seen such things in writing," she pointed out, "you have not seen them with your eyes [and hence ought not believe] that which thou feelest not, nor see not, nor know other than by a plurality of strange opinions." "The books that so sayeth," she reminded them, "women made them not."[36]

Part Three

SCIENCE

Eight · *Revelation in Nature*

HOWEVER SOME HISTORIANS might retrospectively characterize Western science as a secular enterprise, it was always in essence a religious calling, more a continuation of than a departure from Christian tradition. Whether as a clerical expression of the established church or a vehicle of lay rebellion, science remained above all a medium of Christian devotion. To their own minds, the early devotees of science were not precursors of a secular future but heirs to the Christian past, with which they were obsessed. They reasoned in religious categories and were thoroughly and earnestly embroiled in an epochal contest between religious enthusiasm, revelation, and heresy, on the one hand, and shifting Catholic, and later Protestant, orthodoxy, on the other. Thus, over the course of its evolution as a religious activity, science was marked by already familiar tendencies toward iconoclastic revivalism and clerical consolidation, patterns that reflected and influenced, among other things, the relations between devout men and women.

At the outset, of course, the culture of science was the culture of the ecclesiastical academy and, hence, a world without women. "Early modern science," historian Frederick B. Artz noted, "was, to a great extent, the creation of the universities." Historians Pearl Kibre and Nancy G. Siraisi have likewise observed that "from the close of the twelfth century onward, science found its chief institutional home in the universities"—first at Paris and Oxford, later at Bologna and Padua—which became "the nuclei and breeding ground for the creative and dynamic forces that were to coalesce and produce the subsequent scientific achievements of Western culture." Western science thus first took root in an exclusively male—and celibate, homosocial, and misogynous—culture, all the more so because a great many of its early practitioners belonged also to the ascetic mendicant orders.[1]

The Northern universities were home to these first "monkish scientists," as Friedrich Heer aptly described them. Intoxicated by the flood of Arab and Greek writings which coursed through Europe in the twelfth and thirteenth centuries, the intellectually adventuresome clerics at Paris and Oxford—"medieval theologian–natural philosophers," in Edward Grant's tellingly hyphenated terminology—saw in Aristotelian natural philosophy a useful aid to theological speculation and scriptural interpretation, a guide to knowledge about God which supplemented rather than supplanted faith. "Science and theology were never more closely interrelated than during the Latin Middle Ages in Western Europe," Grant observed, and "theology was clearly the dominant partner." Natural philosophy offered a new "methodology of theology" with the application of Aristotelian concepts and techniques to theological speculation, but "the medieval theologian–natural philosopher knew how to subordinate the one discipline to the other"; "the glorification of God was the ultimate goal of scientific study."[2]

Among the earliest to appropriate Aristotelian natural philosophy was Robert Grosseteste, master of the Franciscan school at Oxford, Oxford's first chancellor, and later bishop of Lincoln. Grosseteste epitomized the high-medieval culture of learning, as both an ardent champion of ecclesiastical reform and a pious devotee of the new learning. Best known to historians of science for his Neoplatonic "metaphysics of light," with its emphasis upon mathematics (geometric optics) as a guide to understanding, Grosseteste also pioneered, as teacher, translator, and author, in bringing Aristotle's work, including his philosophy of nature, into respectable fashion. Grosseteste's contribution was carried forth by the Oxford Franciscans, notably the friars Roger Bacon and John Pecham. Bacon, a spiritual Franciscan, has often been mistakenly identified as a rationalist critic of scholasticism and ecclesiastical dogma and a prophet of modern scientific technology. In reality, as historian David C. Lindberg has argued, Bacon was less a harbinger of modernity than an ascetic reactionary, conservative even by thirteenth-century standards. Although he explored astronomy, astrology, optics, and medicine, emphasized the value of mathematics, and had visions of automata, powered ships, airplanes, and cars, Bacon looked not to the future but to the past, hoping to claim the new learning for an essentially Augustinian pursuit of salvation through faith. He insisted upon the importance of experience as a guide to truth, yet such experience included at its core divine illumination. Bacon opposed the suppression of natural philosophy but insisted upon its "sacred usefulness" to biblical exegesis and the conversion of unbelievers. For him philosophy was "but the unfolding of Divine wisdom." In the same spirit, John Pecham, who became archbishop of Canterbury and was noted also for his zeal for ecclesiastical discipline, embraced the new learning in order more ably to defend the Augustinian position against an Aristotelian challenge. His work on mathematics and optics stimulated the development of physics at Merton College in the fourteenth century.[3]

The Franciscans at the University of Paris, notably Alexander of Hales and Bonaventure, though acquainted with Aristotle's work, were less receptive to the new learning than their brethren at Oxford. They preferred to perpetuate the Augustinian theological tradition without the aid of natural philosophy and appeal to experience. The other mendicant order at Paris, however, the Dominicans, took a different tack. They embraced Aristotelian natural philosophy as a separate realm of inquiry, handmaid to theology, elevating it to near equality with revelation. Here the major figures were Albertus Magnus and his pupil Thomas Aquinas. These academic friars too exemplified their clerical culture; their disdain for women was matched by their zeal for learning.

Albert taught at Cologne and Paris and served for a time as bishop of Ratisbon (Regensburg). According to William A. Wallace, he was apparently "the first to realize how Greco-Arabic science could best serve Christian faith by granting it proper autonomy in its own sphere"; thus he urged reliance upon Augustine in matters of faith but upon Galen or Hippocrates in medicine and Aristotle in physics. He was encyclopedic in his learning and an "indefatigable observer and cataloguer of nature." The great theologian Aquinas, a student of Albert's at Cologne, had been inspired by his teacher to "christianize Aristotle" but, in Wallace's view, ended up with an "aristotelianization of Christianity." For him, as for Albert, Aristotle's physics provided not only a firm foundation for theology and metaphysics but also a reliable guide for the independent study of nature based upon experience. Nevertheless, such study was always a means to religious ends, an effort whereby God "revealed the details of his inner being to all who accepted on faith his divine revelation." For Aquinas, Wallace points out, "not only did Aristotle's principles open up the possibility of rendering intelligible all of nature's operations, but they could even lead one to a knowledge of the Author of nature by purely rational means. . . . They made available reasonable proofs for the existence of a mover that was incorporeal, immaterial, of infinite power, and eternal in duration, who could be identified with the God of revelation."[4]

With their Greek learning "buttressed by Catholic faith," and vice versa, the schoolmen of the thirteenth century began to explore "the subject matter that would later become modern science." In time, the Oxford legacy of the importance of mathematics as a guide to comprehending nature was combined with the Parisian reliance upon empirical observation and the conviction that natural philosophy was worthy of study as an independent source of knowledge about God's universe. In the short run, however, the last element of this incipient science provoked legendary controversy and an energetic ecclesiastical insistence upon the priority of faith over reason. In defense of faith, and hence of ecclesiastical doctrine and clerical authority, the church mounted an assault upon Aristotelian natural philosophy, especially as interpreted by Averroës (and his Latin disciples, notably Siger of Brabant), which culminated in the papal condemnation of 1277. The target of the attack has been variously labeled "philosophical naturalism," "naturalistic rationalism," "heterodox Aristotelianism," or "Latin Averroism," all referring to works that seemed to imply, in the eyes of the church, a "double truth." Although he had himself upheld some of the principles later condemned, Aquinas joined in the attack against the Averroists, thereafter withdrawing into mysticism, laying down his pen at the age of forty-seven, and discounting his prodigious Aristotelian efforts as just so much "straw."[5]

Although the papal condemnation of Aristotelian principles resulted in a prohibition against the introduction of theological concerns into the studies and teaching of masters of arts, theologians remained free to study natural philosophy—albeit in a more circumspect manner. The result was a skepticism about the supposed truths of natural philosophy, doubts about the certainty of scientific knowledge—epitomized in the work of the Franciscans Duns Scotus and William of Ockham, and Nicholas of Autrecourt (a "medieval Hume"). Thus, as Edward Grant has argued, the condemnation prompted a more critical and far-reaching examination of Aristotle, and thus "beneficially stimulated speculation outside the bounds of Aristotelian natural philosophy. . . . From such analysis intelligible and plausible alternatives to Aristotelian physics and cosmology emerged," as well as a greater appreciation for contingency (interpreted as divine omnipotence) in nature. By the mid-fourteenth century, therefore, ecclesiastical censure and theological skepticism had together begun to move Western scientific thinking beyond its Aristotelian heritage.[6]

The new thinking took root at Oxford's Merton College, which had inherited the intellectual legacy of Grosseteste. Here the emphasis upon mathematics was combined with new kinematical and dynamical concepts to produce a science of the mechanics of motion, as in the work of Merton fellows Thomas Bradwardine, Walter Burley, and William of Heytesbury. Bradwardine became archbishop of Canterbury, Burley became a priest and canon at York, and William of Heytesbury, also ordained as a priest, became chancellor of Oxford. In Paris, this work was carried on by the "Parisian precursors of Galileo," as Pierre Duhem called them: Jean Buridan, rector of the university, and his pupils Albert of Saxony, later bishop of Halberstadt, and Nichole Oresme, later bishop of Lisieux. All, as William Wallace has shown, had a direct influence upon Galileo's thought. By the end of the fourteenth century, a significant new body of knowledge had emerged, basically Aristotelian but "enriched by mathematical and dynamical concepts showing considerable affinity with those of modern science." It was a body of knowledge produced by men who had forsaken the body, celibate clerics in a world without women.[7]

By the end of the fourteenth century, the locus of natural philosophy had begun to move southward, to Bologna and Padua, the intellectual centers of Italy. The Italian schools differed from their counterparts north of the Alps in several important respects. First, they had become a refuge of sorts for the radical Averroist Aristotelianism purged from Paris. Second, here the faculty of arts was associated not with theology (which was left to the regular clergy, especially the mendicant orders) but with medicine, and the orientation was more practical than contemplative. Thus "at Bologna and Padua the study of mathematics and physical science was more likely to be undertaken with a vocational purpose than was true for Oxford or Paris." Third, the uninterrupted lay educational tradition of Italy, together with this more professional orientation of learning, gave these centers, to use William Wallace's phrase, a "more secularized atmosphere."[8]

Whereas the natural philosophers of the North were almost all clerics supported by ecclesiastical resources, here they included professional practitioners supported by lay economic and social arrangements. As a result, Italian university faculty included lay masters and even some married lay masters. Indeed, Rashdall observed that "from about the middle of the thirteenth century the professoriate of Bologna became largely hereditary" as fathers passed faculty positions to sons or nephews, giving rise to professional dynasties in medicine and astrology (e.g., the del Garbo, Santa Sofia, and de Dondi families). This is not to say, however, that the Italian universities were free of ecclesiastical influence. In 1219, Pope Honorius III, former archdeacon of Bologna, ordered that all promotions to the doctorate at the University of Bologna required the consent of the archdeacon of Bologna. "By that Bull and the imitation of its provisions in favor of other schools," Hastings Rashdall explained, "the Universities were, so to speak, brought within the ecclesiastical system. . . . The gulf which had hitherto separated the free lay system of education in Italy from the ecclesiastical system of Northern Europe was to some extent . . . bridged over." Moreover, according to Rashdall, "ecclesiastics attended the universities as much in Italy as in France." Thus, although lay educational traditions and a lay professional orientation created space within the academy for lay teachers and even marriage (and hence for the presence of women at its margins), here too the universities themselves remained worlds without women.[9]

The lay influence in Italian universities did apparently allow for some female participation in higher learning, especially on the part of wives and daughters of lay medical masters (Christine de Pisan, for example, was the daughter of a physician and astrologer from Bologna). The extent and significance of this participation remains unclear, however. Apparently women held positions on the medical faculty at Salerno, the earliest Western center for medical education (superseded in the thirteenth century by Bologna). According to Rashdall, "at Salerno lady Doctors were a recognized institution." The legendary Trotula was presumed to have been the wife and mother of physicians and to have taught and written at Salerno. Although a treatise on gynecology bears her name, Paul Kristeller points out that there is no evidence of her professional status, family relations, or even historical existence. A number of women in southern Italy received royal medical licenses in the early fourteenth century, but there is no evidence of their having attended university courses. One woman known to have received a degree in medicine in the fifteenth century was Costanza Calenda, daughter of a medical professor at Naples. Alessandra Scala, daughter of the chancellor, might have attended the University of Florence but received no degree. Elena Cornaro, on the other hand, was known to have received a doctorate in philosophy at Padua in 1678, but there is no evidence of her having actually attended courses. In the eighteenth century, two other women, Laura Bassi and Maria Gaetana Agnesi, held faculty positions at Bologna, in philosophy and mathematics, respectively. In Kristeller's view, these examples of Italian academic women "are few in number, and they are illustrious exceptions, which confirm the rule that women were excluded from university studies and degrees and from the careers of university teaching and the academic professions" until the nineteenth and twentieth centuries.[10]

This separation of women from the Italian centers of learning was the result not only of Aristotelian prejudice and ecclesiastical—and now academic—tradition, but also of the rise of the Italian despotic state and a renewed Renaissance emphasis upon marriage. As Joan Kelly-Gadol observed, "the kind of economic and political power that supported the cultural activity of feudal noblewomen . . . had no counterpart in Renaissance Italy"; by the fourteenth century the landed nobility of northern Italy had been upstaged by despotic princes whose claim to power rested upon military force rather than heritage and whose courts became the new fulcrum of social authority and influence. "As the state came to organize Renaissance society," moreover, "a new division between personal and public life made itself felt . . . , the bourgeois sex-role system, placing man in the public sphere and the patrician woman in the home." Cultural and political power thus fell increasingly into the hands of men.[11]

Intent upon consolidating their patrimony and regulating entrance to the court-dependent aristocracy, the new elites placed increased emphasis upon legitimacy and purity of blood, and thus upon both marriage and chastity. As Lawrence Stone has noted, following Guido Ruggiero, fifteenth-century Italy witnessed a "new stress on marriage. . . . The protection and encouragement of marriage and the family had become a central concern of the Venetian state at least by 1450." In the process, the lives of aristocratic women—who were most likely to engage in intellectual and professional pursuits—were ever more restricted. (Judith C. Brown suggests that working women in Renaissance Tuscany actually experienced an expansion of economic power, but this did not include an opportunity for advanced learning.) As Patricia Labalme pointed out, the expectations for such women were, "in the Italian idiom, 'maritar o monacar,' marriage or the convent. Advanced learning was necessary for neither. Intellectual activity . . . was not appropriate for women."[12]

Those women who pursued learning, therefore, had ventured "be-

yond the expectations for their sex." Educated, for the most part, at
home by their fathers or other male relatives or tutors, they found no
respectable place in Italian society. "A young woman was free to be
studious," Margaret L. King explained, "but that freedom could not
last into adulthood. A young woman eventually confronted a choice
between two futures: marriage and full participation in social life on
the one hand, or abstention from marriage and withdrawal from the
world. For learned women, the choice was agonizing. To marry implied the abandonment of beloved studies. Not to marry implied the
abandonment of the world." "Shall I marry or devote my life to
study?" Alessandra Scala asked Cassandra Fedele, knowing the two
were mutually exclusive. Both women married and gave up their
studies, as did Costanza Varano and Ginevra Nogarola. Those few
who did pursue a life of learning were compelled to withdraw from
the world—Cecelia Gonzaga to a convent, Isotta Nogarola to self-
imposed solitude at home (some, like Laura Cereta, renewed their
studies as widows, but in solitude). Thus, as King notes, "the community of marriage . . . inhibited the learned women from pursuing
studious interests" and confined the unmarried or widowed who continued their studies to the isolation of their "book-lined cells." If the
latter were sometimes celebrated, they were nevertheless viewed as
anthropological oddities, chaste and "virile" females rather than real
women, belonging to neither the opposite nor their own sex. Learned
women were more likely to be vilified than celebrated by their male
counterparts, however, and, as a result, they tended to internalize
the male assumptions of their inferiority and betray a "fragile self-
confidence." Hesitating to distribute her writings, Isotta Nogarola
explained to her uncle that she worried about arousing the ire of those
men "who call learning in women a poison and public pest."[13]

The evolving social norms of Italian society thus converged with
academic and ecclesiastical expectations to ensure that the centers of
learning—and the new science—would remain worlds without
women. The University of Bologna had from its inception been the
ecclesiastical center for the study of civil and canon law and, under
the control of the Papal States, it long remained, in essence, a "papal
university." In the fourteenth century, however, the university became for a time the center of Averroist teaching, and its combined
faculty of arts and medicine came to the fore as a school of natural
philosophy. The study of medicine was intimately bound up with the
study of Aristotle as well as other Greek and Arab masters, and it also

entailed a thorough grounding in mathematics, because of its close practical relationship to astrology (the position of the celestial bodies was considered of great relevance to human ailments and health).[14]

The development of natural philosophy as an aspect of medical, and hence astrological and mathematical, studies reached its zenith at the University of Padua, which grew as a consequence of a succession of emigrations from Bologna. "Famed for its tolerance" (in Heer's words), the University of Padua was protected from ecclesiastical sanction and the Inquisition by the Republic of Venice and provided a haven for radical Aristotelian thought. In the late fourteenth century, Paul of Venice returned to Padua after study at Oxford and planted there the seeds of Mertonian mathematics and mechanics. It proved fertile soil indeed, and before long Padua had become the premier European center for the study of natural philosophy, whose faculty included the physician Gaitano de Thiens, mathematicians Geronimo Cardano, Niccolò Tartaglia, and Giovanni Battista Benedetti, and the famed astrologers and clockmakers of the de Dondi family. The University of Padua attracted scholars from throughout Europe, including Cardinal Nicholas of Cusa, the astronomers and mathematicians Georg von Purbach and Regiomontanus (Johannes Muller), and, of course, Nicolaus Copernicus, the celibate canon of Frauenburg and founder of modern astronomy.[15]

WESTERN SCIENCE first took shape within the male enclaves of the medieval universities and thus, at the outset, reflected the monastic culture of Latin Christendom which these institutions had come to embody. At the same time, the monastic orders themselves contributed to the new learning, as Paul Kristeller has shown, producing scholarly work not only in theology and Aristotelian philosophy but also in mathematics and the new humanistic studies—a clerical scientific tradition later epitomized by the Jesuits. But the universities (and monasteries) were not the only centers of Renaissance learning that gave rise to Western science. Beyond the walls of these medieval institutions, yet another revival of religious ferment had begun to take hold under the auspices of feudal fiefdoms, creating new social spaces for intellectual endeavor. This latest revival, which was to produce the Reformation, gave rise to the humanist movement and its new courtly centers of learning, the Neoplatonic Renaissance academies. Moreover, in its earnest revival of classical learning as an aid to religious revitalization, the humanist movement revived and renewed ancient alchemical and hermetic traditions which were to have great influence upon the subsequent evolution of Western science. Predictably perhaps, the new humanist scholars of the Renaissance betrayed an aversion to women not unlike that of their intellectual adversaries in the universities and monasteries; the humanist academies too remained worlds without women. On the other hand, the iconoclastic implications of humanist teaching constituted a serious challenge to the medieval monopoly of learning, opening anew intellectual possibilities for women.[16]

The male culture of the humanist academies reflected not only an evolving bourgeois family structure and established clerical and academic norms—the humanists were fervent Catholics and university-trained—but also the revival of a classical homosocial orientation to learning. James M. Saslow, in his study of Renaissance homosexuality, has observed that, though there was no "identifiable and self-defining homosocial subculture" in Renaissance Italy such as there apparently was in the eleventh and twelfth centuries, there was, among the humanists, "a generalized misogyny, which in turn served as one justification for male homosexuality." Witt Kowers has noted that, despite an official climate of repression against sodomy, a "tolerance toward homosexuality . . . arose among humanists aware of its sanction in Greek tradition." The bond between Pico della Mirandola and Gerolamo Benivieni, for example, was reminiscent of that of the earlier Neoplatonists Robert Grosseteste and Adam Marsh; they were "so closely bound in Platonic love," Saslow writes, "that they were buried together like husband and wife." Marsilio Ficino, who became an ordained priest, "paraphrased Plato in stating that homosexual relationships are superior to heterosexual ones both intellectually and spiritually." "Some men," wrote Ficino in his commentary on the *Symposium*, "are better equipped for offspring of the soul than for those of the body [and] . . . therefore, naturally love men more than women." Such a relationship between men is preferable, because men are "much stronger in mental keenness" and "its higher beauty is most essential to knowledge."[17]

The homosocial character of the Renaissance culture of learning was clearly reflected in the life of Leonardo da Vinci, who was twice anonymously accused of sodomy. Saslow observed that this and his "long-suffering toleration of his beautiful but unscrupulous assistant Gian Giacomo de' Caprotti suggest that Leonardo's emotional and erotic interests were principally directed toward men." At the same time, Leonardo's life indicates how the ascetic and celibate ideals of the church extended beyond strictly ecclesiastical and academic circles. In fact, "there is no evidence of any overt sexual activity on the part of this lifelong bachelor," Saslow points out; indeed, Leonardo betrayed, as Freud also noted, a "deep antipathy toward sexual passion" and "an atrophy of his sexual life." "Intellectual passion," Leonardo wrote, "drives out sensuality. Whoever does not curb lustful desire puts himself on a level with the beasts." Saslow suggests that Leonardo's erotic ideal was in essence hermaphroditic, recalling the primordial unity of humanity. Like the Gnostics of old and the new hermetic philosophers of the Renaissance, Leonardo viewed sexual division as a sign of disorder to be overcome in a resolution of opposites. His faith in the transcendence of desire, however, though perhaps reminiscent of the androgynous ascetic ideal, engendered more anxiety than freedom, in the still-thriving spirit of male monasticism.[18]

If, like the monastic culture, the humanist culture was homosocial in essence, it also contained another, opposite, tendency. In carrying forward the debate about women begun by Christine de Pisan, which had by this time become a recurring subject of academic disputations, the humanists fostered some positive reassessment of the relationship between women and learning. The humanist defense of women's intellectual abilities was grounded ideologically on a stress upon individual education as a vehicle of Christian virtue. Moreover, in its emphasis on original sources, including the Scriptures, over later commentary and interpretation, the humanistic movement fostered a faith in the Word which foreshadowed the Reformation. Such an implicitly anticlerical and revivalist thrust held great appeal for women. Materially, the humanistic defense of women reflected the immediate interests of the humanists themselves, many of whom were patronized by and served as tutors for royal and aristocratic women. In the Renaissance, Constance Jordan has pointed out, "women 'governors' became conspicuous," and this fostered serious and sustained reflection upon women's nature, powers, and place in society. Among the more avid humanist advocates of women's education were Juan Luis Vives, Thomas More, and Thomas Elyot, all of whom were, in Foster Watson's view, "under the spell of Catherine" of Aragon. Vives wrote his famous treatise on the education of women, at Catherine's request, for her daughter, Mary. The alchemist Cornelius Agrippa, who wrote a famous treatise on the superiority of women, likewise served, and sought the favor of, women of the court, in particular Margaret of Austria, to whom his treatise was dedicated.[19]

If humanist proposals for the education of women marked a departure from the virulent misogyny of the medieval academy, they were still in keeping with conventional religious and bourgeois notions about women's capacities and place. Vives, for example, in his treatise *Duties of Husbands*, insisted that women were created by the Lord "to know high matters and to come as well as men unto the beatitude, and therefore they ought and should be instructed and taught, as we men be." On the other hand, in his influential treatise on the instruction of Christian women, he stressed the physical and moral vulnerability of women, while otherwise acknowledging their equality with men, and formulated his proposals accordingly.

> Women should study for their own sake, or, in the best case, for the education of their children as long as they are very little. It is not proper for a woman to be in charge of schools, to socialize with strange men, to speak in public, or to teach at the risk of jeopardizing their own [virtue] and chastity. The honest woman stays at home, unknown to others. In public meetings she should keep her eyes down, be silent and modest, seen but not heard.

For Vives female education was restricted to domestic rather than public or professional concerns and excluded any "detailed knowledge of nature, deep theological questions, philosophical controversies . . . , grammar, dialectic, history, political science, and mathematics." Needless to say, though Vives urged that women be instructed in the home and the court, he never proposed they should have access to universities. Nor did his fellow humanist Thomas More, who carefully provided in his home for the education of his daughters but maintained with Aristotle that women were by nature intellectually inferior. It was for this reason that women should be laboriously instructed, "that the flaw of nature might be corrected by industry."[20]

However much the humanists belittled the labors of the scholastic "calculators" and natural philosophers, they themselves contributed immeasurably to the development of natural science through their revival of alchemy. Ficino and Pico recovered and translated ancient hermetical and cabalistic texts which they viewed as repositories of pre-Christian knowledge of enormous value to a revitalized Christianity. This body of learning (later identified as early Christian in origin), stimulated the subsequent efflorescence of alchemy and astrology.

Thus the celebrated magi of the sixteenth and seventeenth centuries—Agrippa, Paracelsus, and Fludd—were the direct heirs of Renaissance Neoplatonism. Predictably, the culture of this new hermetic movement resembled that of the humanistic movement which had spawned it; it was male in composition, ascetic in spirit, and masculine in purpose. Thus, although the alchemists, like the humanists, tirelessly railed against the outworn medieval world of the scholastics and clerics, they too inherited its homosocial culture. At the same time, however, as an essentially antischolastic, anticlerical intellectual and religious revival, the alchemical movement generated myriad temporary openings in the world without women.

Like the men of the Renaissance academies, and the monasteries, the new devotees of occult magic tended to gather in the closed all-male milieu of secret fraternal societies. "It was no accident," Keith Thomas observed, "that . . . many medieval alchemists had been monks and that the monasteries retained a reputation for occult learning." Likewise, in the manner of the Gnostic "perfecti" of early Christianity, the Renaissance magi believed that their esoteric knowledge had to be carefully guarded lest it fall into unworthy, unlearned hands. Agrippa, probably the most renowned and influential of the sixteenth-century magi, had early in his career formed "some kind of secret society," according to Charles G. Nauert, "a brotherhood with definite organization and secrets," coded communication, and oaths of induction. "The brotherhood was secret because ancient wisdom would be dangerous to society unless confined to the restricted circle of true lovers of learning. This 'gnostic' or 'occultist' attitude, the belief that certain kinds of knowledge might be safely studied by a tightly knit group of initiates, but must be kept from the view of the ignorant and depraved masses of humanity, was quite common in that age. . . . Magical, astrological, alchemical and cabalistic studies were almost always regarded as esoteric, that is, unsuited to public disclosure." In the case of Agrippa, "this brotherhood produced, in the form of Agrippa's own De Occulta Philosophia, one of the most important and influential pieces of Renaissance occultist literature."[21]

If the hermetic movement mirrored monastic culture in its closed fraternal cabals, it also did so in its fundamentally ascetic orientation. As Thomas noted, "alchemy was associated with asceticism and contempt for the world." "For the magicians themselves, the summoning of celestial beings was a religious rite, in which prayer played an essential part and where piety and purity of life were deemed essential." Such "purity of life" was achieved, in monkish fashion, through prayer, fasting, chastity, and spiritual discipline. Self-purification was the essential precondition of divine revelation, and hence alchemical wisdom. The great alchemist Paracelsus, who taught for a time at a Benedictine monastery, "sought eternal bliss in deeds of self-denial." For him, alchemical wisdom was "knowledge that enables the philosopher to ascend, to transcend, and to commune with the universe outside himself—a knowledge that liberates him from the fetters of passion and predestination." According to his apprentice, Paracelsus "was capable of the strictest self-discipline." "He forsook all things which could lead to worldly preferment," wrote one biographer, "and went out to seek wisdom with as little provision for his bodily comfort as the poverello of Assisi." Agrippa, though he battled the intolerance and hypocrisy of the monks throughout his life, characterized the mystical life of the magi, marked by poverty, chastity, and obedience, as "the true monastic life." "To the proud rationalism of the professional theologians, Agrippa and his friends contrasted the firm and humble faith of the true believer, who praises God for illuminating man by grace, and who prepares himself for enlightenment with vigils and fasts, and a life lived in imitation of Christ."[22]

As in the case of monasticism, the ascetic ideal of the alchemists often entailed sexual renunciation and voluntary celibacy. Paracelsus was the classic case. Some have suggested that he was a eunuch who was castrated as a child. Whether or not this was true, it is clear by all accounts that Paracelsus was a "natural celibate"; he remained chaste throughout his life and showed no erotic interest whatsoever in the opposite sex. In the view of his personal secretary, "he was not interested in women, and . . . had never had intercourse." Paracelsus' personal disposition toward sexuality was consistent with his ascetic religious calling. "Abstinence in acts is useless for spiritual development unless it is followed by abstinence in thought. Enforced celibacy does not make a priest; a true priest is a saint, and saints are persons who have outgrown their carnal desires." Robert Fludd, the seventeenth-century Paracelsian, likewise "took a vow of chastity and regarded the flesh as the root of all evil."[23]

Agrippa dismissed clerical celibacy as only a human rather than a divine imposition, condemned the hypocrisy of the clergy, wrote that men must marry to be saved, and was himself thrice married. However, much as he had written his treatise on the superiority of women to win the favor of his patroness Margaret of Austria, so he dedicated his defense of marriage to Marguerite d'Alençon, patroness of reforming churchmen, "in the hope of winning her sympathy and so regaining the favors of his own patron, Queen Mother Louise of Savoy." Moreover, he described his own wives as mere "well behaved" and "obedient" attendants and mothers, who played no apparent role in his intellectual and spiritual labors. Perhap most important, Agrippa explicitly exempted from marriage "those who for the love of God vowed perpetual chastity," among whom he included "the purified soul, the magus." "The enlightened soul, the soul which had attained a true understanding of God's revelation, would not only regain mastery of its own body but would also win power over all nature."[24]

Carl Jung suggested that, in its project of mastery of self and nature, alchemy emerged as the unconscious corrective to Christian consciousness, bringing back "the feminine, the image or memory of the fertility Mother Goddesses of prehistoric and neolithic religions discarded by the Christian trinity." The hermaphroditic paradigm of the alchemists, with its erotic emphasis upon the reconciliation of the masculine and feminine elements in nature, in theory restored the status of the feminine denied by Christian theology. Paracelsus, the alchemist par excellence, not only sought such a reconciliation in his medicinal theories and practice, but claimed himself to embody it. His self-mastery, his "natural celibacy," entailed a recovery of the feminine side of his being, rendering him, as a hermaphrodite, a regenerated being reminiscent of the ideal androgynous ascetic of early Christianity. Wrote Paracelsus,

Originally, man and woman were one and consequently their union could not have been more intimate than it actually was; but man having become separated from the woman in him, lost his true light. He now seeks for the woman outside of his true self, and wanders about among shadows, being misled by the will of the wisps of external illusions. Being fascinated by the charms of the terrestrial woman, he drinks of the cup of desires which she presents to him and sinks into a still deeper sleep and forgetfulness of the true celestial Eve, the immaculate virgin who once existed within himself. . . . God did not create souls in halves, nor can Adam find his Eve unless she grows within his heart. Man will never find his celestial bride unless he looks for her within his internal heaven,

within the Lord. Sexual cohabitation . . . is merely an animal function. . . . To the semi-animal man, it may be a school of education,
but the regenerated man requires no sexual relationship.[25]

But, however reminiscent of the androgynous restoration of perfection espoused by early Christians, the creed of the alchemists, in their
quest to become not angels but masters over nature, entailed less a
primordial reunification of the sexes than an appropriation of the one
by the other. The alchemists aimed, in their studies of nature, at the
"arrogation of the powers of the feminine," especially the powers of
procreation. "Despite the insistence on the balance of the two sexes,"
two recent scholars of alchemy have observed, "the writings of both
critics and adepts reveal, perhaps inadvertently, that the union is in
actuality not an equal one. In the Christian framework within which
Western alchemy developed, the feminine is relegated to the interior
realm of nature, in which the spirit is trapped." The passive feminine
quality of nature is released and fulfilled only in thrall to the masculine
spirit. In Jung's words, "thus the higher, the spiritual, the masculine,
inclines to the lower, the earthly, the feminine; and accordingly the
Mother who was anterior to the world of the father accommodates
herself to the masculine principle and with the aid of the human spirit
(alchemy or 'The Philosophy') produces a son. . . . Although he is
decidedly hermaphroditic he has a masculine name." In sum, "the
equality of masculine and feminine in the alchemical opus is created
in order to produce a masculine being, to right a masculine imbalance
in masculine terms." Thus, in the hermetic revival, another male
subculture had given rise to a new, yet still decidedly masculine,
project.[26]

At the same time, as was the case with humanism, there was much
in this new project of the alchemists that potentially challenged the
established homosocial culture. Like the humanists, the alchemists
traveled outside the academic and clerical circles, plying their trade
as astrologers, medical practitioners, and magicians at the Renaissance
courts, quite often at the behest and under the patronage of women.
In this institutional way, they catered to royal and aristocratic women's
interest in the new learning. More important, the substance of their
intellectual contributions broke the clerical monopoly on learning and
spiritual perfection. Above all, the hermetic movement was a vital
part of the new religious revival of the sixteenth and seventeenth
centuries, a revival that produced the humanistic reform movement

within the Roman Church, the emergence of rival Protestant churches, and the robust resurgence of radical religious sects.

Alchemy itself is best understood as a fundamentally revivalist phenomenon. In their fervent search for God's truth, the magi placed stress upon the primacy of revelation over reason, of Scripture (now including hermetic texts) over commentary, of the book of nature over the books of schoolmen, of the lessons of practice and experience over the formal education of the universities. In all of these ways, their teaching defied the established clerical and scholastic order, offering the unordained—including women—direct, unmediated means of spiritual enlightenment. For a time, moreover, their intellectual iconoclasm, which brought them into contact with the common people, lent a measure of elite respectability to those "below" who had already taken their spiritual affairs into their own hands. Indeed, it was the alchemists' relationship to, and identification with, such lower-class and revolutionary elements of society that in the end proved their undoing.

"The art of magic is the art of worshipping God," wrote Sir Walter Raleigh. The practice of magic was a "holy quest," a "search for knowledge, not by study and research but by revelation." It was precisely its pursuit of "direct divine inspiration," and thus its heterodox implications, that had led to the ecclesiastical suppression of magic during the Middle Ages. Whether received through mystical rapture, the study of Scripture, or the observation of nature, alchemical revelation flowed, above all, from divine grace. And grace followed faith, grounded in a pure and pious life, for only "religious perfection would bring magical power." As Paracelsus taught, "in matters eternal it is Belief that makes all works visible." Similarly, for the English Paracelsian Fludd "the use of observational evidence was consistently linked with [the] quest for truth in religion. . . . As his prime authority he chose to turn to God's two books of revelation: the Holy Scriptures and God's book of creation—nature. There was no question in Fludd's mind that the first of these was the more important." Fludd clearly "regarded all true natural science as rooted in revelation." Likewise, the Flemish Paracelsian Jan Baptista van Helmont "exalted the knowledge of illumination above that derived from 'carnal reason.' "[27]

Agrippa, the undisputed master of occult learning, aimed at "knowledge of God," through the study of nature and mosaic law but, above all, through "illumination." "Like the other humanists,"

Nauert explained, he "upheld the ideal of a return to the pure, unde-filed faith of the early church, in opposition to the contentious wran-gling of scholastic theology." He viewed his own studies of hermetic texts in "theological" terms, as a means of "regenerating Christian-ity," convinced that they "would provide the key to a profound and truly religious understanding of the truth revealed in the Christian Scriptures." However, he believed that any "esoteric revelation," whether received through the study of nature or the Word, ultimately rested not upon reason but upon faith. Like Nicholas of Cusa before him, Agrippa espoused a radical rejection of religious rationalism and the pretensions of scholastic natural philosophy. Throughout his work, and most forcefully in his celebrated indictment of the "uncertainty and vanity of the sciences," he insisted that "knowledge of God occurs only in the realm of grace, not in that of reason." "By the speculations of no science," he maintained, "by no urgent judgement of the senses, by no arguments of logical artifice, by no evident proof, by no demonstrating syllogism, and by no discourse of human reason can [truth] be seized upon, but only by faith."[28]

In consistently emphasizing the importance of unmediated faith and unadulterated Scripture in the quest for direct revelation, the alchemists diminished the significance of clerical and scholastic in-struction and, by implication, the role of the church in individual salvation. Their pursuit of divine illumination through the ecclesiasti-cally unaided study of the book of nature, especially by means of practical experience, had similar implications. Agrippa concentrated his energies on the acquisition of hermetic and cabalistic wisdom, which, together with pious humility, would afford access to the divine secrets of, and power over, nature. "The enlightened soul," he be-lieved, "the soul which had attained a true understanding of God's revelation, . . . would win power over all Nature." Knowledge of nature thus presupposed magical insight, but it also required careful attention to nature's divine signs. Just as the magus had to learn to read the books of magic, so he had to learn to read the book of nature, and this required "long experience" rather than mere "rational investigation"; "only long experience could teach man what were the real forces working in the universe and how they could be controlled." As a practicing physician and astrologer, Agrippa certainly confronted the vicissitudes of nature, but in this regard Paracelsus epitomized the true alchemist.[29]

Whereas in his own peripatetic career Agrippa remained within elite, albeit reform, society and communicated primarily with like-minded students of humanistic and occult learning, Paracelsus roamed far beyond these aristocratic and scholarly circles in his spiritual quest for enlightenment. "The universities do not teach all things," the young Paracelsus had discovered; "so a doctor must seek out old wives, gypsies, sorcerers, wandering tribes, old robbers, and such outlaws and take lessons from them. A doctor must be a traveller, because he must enquire of the world. Experiment is not sufficient. Experience must verify what can be accepted or not accepted." Paracelsus stood for "practicing rather than preaching Christianity." Son of a physician, he studied with the famed alchemist Johannes Trithemius, but gained his real education as an apprentice in the Fugger mines, studying the mysteries of metals as well as the special diseases that afflicted miners. His was "a practical and at the same time a contemplative—religious—mind, intent on discovering truth." At the age of fourteen, he began his prolonged peregrinations, which took him throughout Europe, Russia, and the Near East. In his life's wanderings, he was variously employed as an army surgeon, a municipal physician, and an itinerant teacher. Immersed in the practical world of artisans and healers, he relentlessly railed against the academic medical faculties; "there was much more for him to learn in daily life as it presented itself to a vagrant scholar-journeyman and above all in the mines."[30]

Paracelsus was, in his biographer Walter Pagel's view, "first and foremost a naturalist," with pantheistic leanings, who undertook a sustained "empirical search for the divine seals in nature" and in the process transformed the practice of medicine. "The work of nature," Paracelsus believed, "constitutes, however inadequately, a visible reflection of the invisible work of God. Nature provides signs by means of which God has graced us with glimpses into His secret wisdom." In his personal quest for religious enlightenment, Paracelsus spent his life accumulating practical knowledge about the wondrous workings of nature. What he did not actually experience himself, he gleaned from others, from people whose knowledge and salvation had little to do with the righteous world of scholars and clergy.[31]

Keith Thomas has shown that the new "intellectual magic" of the Neoplatonic alchemists evolved alongside, and in association with, independent and long-standing traditions of "popular magic." The practice of the village magician hardly reflected the new philosophical movement but, rather, had its roots in ancient oral traditions. As Thomas noted, "instead of the village sorcerers putting into practice the doctrines of Agrippa or Paracelsus, it was the intellectual magician who was stimulated by the activities of the cunning man into a search for the occult influences which he believed must have underlain them." As the experience of Paracelsus indicates, "the period saw a serious attempt to study long-established folk procedures with a view to discovering the principles on which they rested." The alchemists, then, appropriated a great deal of their knowledge from the healing, divining, and other practices of "cunning men and wise women."[32]

At the same time, the intellectual magicians, having striven to "purify" magic, to distinguish their good Christian magic from malevolent heretical magic, helped to make the study of magic more acceptable within established circles. "Agrippa's avowed aim in writing De occulta philosophia," Nauert notes, "was to distinguish the good and holy science of magic from scandalous and impious practices of black magic, and to restore its good name." As a result of such efforts, "the work of the practicing wizard [of popular magic] was sustained by the parallel activities of many contemporary intellectuals. Indeed the possibility of certain types of magic was a fundamental presupposition for most scientists and philosophers." The popular animistic view of nature thus gained new intellectual force in the hermetic system; throughout the sixteenth and much of the seventeenth centuries, "magical inquiry possessed some intellectual respectability," even among clergy and academics. According to Lynn Thorndike, "belief in astrology, witchcraft, alchemy, cabala . . . was well-nigh universal."[33]

Despite the occultist orientation of the hermetic movement, the alchemical association with popular magic—and especially its emphasis upon the study of nature through practical experience—helped to narrow the traditional gap between natural philosophy and artisan knowledge and culture. Fruitful interaction between the worlds of the craftsman and the scholar was already under way during the sixteenth century, as Paolo Rossi and Edgar Zilsel have shown, in the wake of developments in navigation, mining, metallurgy, and military technology. The teachings of such Renaissance reformers and magi as Juan Vives, Giordano Bruno, Tommaso Campanella, Rabelais, Giovanni Battista della Porta, Geronimo Cardano, Agrippa, Paracelsus, Johann Andrea, John Comenius, Samuel Hartlib, William Gilbert, John Dee, and Thomas Vaughan accelerated this process, lending a new intellectual dignity to the heretofore lowly arts. Paracelsus epitomized the alchemical orientation toward artisanal culture.[34]

Paracelsus was, as Brian Easlea observed, "a man of the people." "Without charge, he cured the poor—or did his best to cure the poor. He investigated diseases specific to working-class occupations, such as silicosis in the case of miners," and in other ways cast his lot with the common people and espoused their virtues. He did not merely try to appropriate the knowledge of those in the mines and workshops for a "higher" theoretical purpose, but labored beside and sought to serve them. What gave his life its "singular mark," Walter Pagel observed, was his "vacillation between the academic and artisan attitudes to life and medicine." At the University of Basle, where he briefly gained a position following his successful treatment of Erasmus' publisher, Johannes Frobenius, Paracelsus dramatically broke with tradition by lecturing in the vernacular rather than Latin and inviting the attendance of nonacademic barbers, surgeons, and apothecaries. His daring introduction of such "absolute novelty in academic life" no doubt contributed to the brevity of his professorial tenure.[35]

The utopian writers, educational reformers, and alchemists of the seventeenth century followed the example of Paracelsus. Campanella and Andrea placed great emphasis upon the practical arts in their visionary communitarian constructions, as did Comenius and Hartlib in their universalist efforts to transform European education. The English alchemist Thomas Vaughan, addressing those who seek knowledge, advised "to use their hands, not their fancies." The Paracelsian surgeon John Webster, in like fashion, maintained that "youth may not be idly trained up in notions, speculations and verbal disputes, but may learn to inure their hands to labor, and put their fingers to the furnaces . . . that they may not grow proud with the brood of their own brains, but truly taught by manual operation. . . ." But if the practical intellectual orientation of the reformers tended to bring them into alliance with the lower classes, it was principally their revivalist religious spirit that inspired, sustained, and defined the relationship.[36]

The sixteenth and seventeenth centuries witnessed what has been called "a general spirit of cultural revolt," centered upon the social upheaval of the Protestant Reformation. The alchemical movement emerged within and was in fact a part of that revolt. The magi believed that the pious study of the ancient hermetic texts offered Christians a new means of divine illumination and hence contributed immeasurably to a religious rebirth, a revival of authentic Christianity. "Such interests in ancient esoteric lore," Nauert notes, "were often . . . combined with tendencies toward fanatical religious enthusiasm." Agrippa believed, for example, that "the cabalistic, Hermetic and other supposedly ancient sources would restore knowledge of God's original revelation and so would assist the work of religious regeneration." Although, like many other humanists, he remained a Catholic, Agrippa associated closely with participants in the reform movement, and became himself "in each of the many places where he . . . resided, the center of a small group of bold spirits who sought to use occult truth . . . for the purification and reform of their present world." He played a "prominent role" in the intellectual life of Lyons, for example, a principal center of the new spiritual movements. While he maintained an ambiguous relationship to Protestantism proper, the "violently anticlerical" tone of his writings betrayed a profound "religious discontent" and gained him a "reputation for religious radicalism."[37]

The social and religious reform leanings of Paracelsus were less ambiguous. Like Agrippa, he "was known for his long record of friendship with progressive circles and the Reformation," but his religious zeal and identification with the lower classes carried him somewhat further. Although he was inspired by Luther, he condemned Luther's church for its complicity in the suppression of the rebellious poor, dissenters, and enthusiasts, such as the baptists, and assumed a more radical religious stance, associating with the pantheistic millenarian sects that re-emerged during the sixteenth century. As Pagel observed,

> the Reformation carried theology and the gospel to the people, thus legitimizing and paving the way for the secret heretical doctrines of the Middle Ages. Paracelsus' life and work offer many contacts with these. . . . Certain traits exhibited in [his] life and behavior as an individual are reminiscent of those displayed by the groups of heretics which emerged in the "autumn of the Middle Ages," notably the Beghards and the Beguines.

"Paracelsus," Pagel has stressed, "was passionately moved by the misery of the poor. . . . His religious and social ethical speculations are in line with those of the Brethren of the Spirit, the Anabaptists and the exponents of 'popular pantheism'. . . . That he should be found in the ranks of the rebellious peasants was a foregone conclusion." Little wonder, then, that Paracelsus should make enemies among the new Protestant establishment. The sixteenth-century Swiss physician, academic, and Protestant theologian Thomas Liebler (Erastus), for example, denounced natural magic altogether and insisted that Paracelsus, in league with the devil, had "vexed" the people. In his vigorous attack on alchemy, Erastus condemned Paracelsus for resurrecting ancient Gnostic heresies and hysterically identified him with the Valentinians and Marcionites of early Christianity.[38]

Despite the official Protestant condemnation of magic (including especially the clerical magic of the Catholic Church), the connection between hermetic natural magic and religious radicalism intensified during the seventeenth century. Indeed, the period witnessed a veritable explosion of sectarian religious enthusiasm, strikingly similar in many respects to that of both early-Christian heresies and the alchemical revival. Primarily lower-class and artisan-based, these were millenarian movements marked by a deep-seated anticlericalism and a social-revolutionary spirit. Enjoying a widespread popular following among the underclass, especially in England during the Civil War, the sects held out the promise of eschatological deliverance through direct divine illumination—gained with the aid of prophecy, scriptural exegesis, and natural magic.

"For all its hostility to magic," Christopher Hill noted, the Reformation "had stimulated the spirit of prophecy. The abolition of mediators, the stress on the individual conscience, left God speaking direct to his elect." Thus, by the seventeenth century, "eschatological prophecy became a major part of Protestant controversial literature, aided especially by the invention of printing" and, of course, the vernacular Bible. In England, especially with the breakdown of censorship during the Interregnum, there was, in the view of Keith Thomas, "no precedent for the scale of enthusiastic activity." Along the lines of the Brethren of the Free Spirit and the Anabaptists, new religious sects emerged—Ranters, Diggers, Levellers, Seekers, Familists, Antinomians, Muggletonians, Fifth Monarchists. "The new religious groups expressed the social and political aspirations of the poorer members of society for whom the Anglican Church had never really catered. But one should also recognize the importance of the claim made by many sectarians to provide that supernatural solution to earthly problems which the makers of the Protestant Reformation had so sternly rejected. The sects revived the miracle-working aspect of medieval [magic]." "It is difficult to exaggerate the extent and strength of millenarian expectations among ordinary people in the 1640's and 50's," Hill has emphasized, an observation seconded by Thomas, who noted the "widespread belief that the Kingdom of God was at hand."[39]

As had been the case during earlier revivals, the new religious impulse lent momentum to social and political radicalism. Most sects were drawn from the ranks of artisans and petty tradesmen; indeed, the Civil War period became, in Hill's description, "the great age of the mechanic preachers." "The association between religious enthusiasm and social radicalism, always close, was strengthened during the Interregnum," Thomas also noted; "religious prophecy provided an admirable vehicle for radical propaganda," and the period resounded in pious attacks upon the established authority of church, crown, and universities alike. "The overwhelming majority of those who claimed divine authority for their utterances were seeking authority for a political and social programme," aimed at democratizing both religion and society. Among other things, as Hill has shown, the sectarians "attacked the monopolization of knowledge within the privileged professions, divinity, law, medicine." In an egalitarian spirit, "they criticized the existing educational structure, especially the universities, and proposed a vast expansion of educational opportunity," to women as well as men. And in all of their combined religious, political, and intellectual efforts, they drew heavily upon the hermetic, and especially the Paracelsian, legacy.[40]

"There were a number of features of the Paracelsian teaching which struck a responsive chord in the 1640's and 1650's," P. M. Rattansi observed. "One of these was the mystical, anti-rational aspect of Paracelsus, which is also prominent in [van] Helmont. In a time of crisis, when men sought in supernatural 'illumination' an ideological sanction for acts which overthrew the established order in State and Church, that side of Paracelsian and Helmontian doctrine which exalted the knowledge of illumination above that derived from 'carnal reason' had a particular attraction for reformers and revolutionaries." Thus, at the time, as Thomas noted, pantheistic "alchemy was closely linked with religious enthusiasm," and through it with social radicalism. "To know the secrets of nature is to know the works of God," wrote Gerrard Winstanley, organizer of the revolutionary Diggers.[41]

The Civil War period witnessed what Thomas described as "the democratization" of the Renaissance magical tradition, with the unprecedented publication and translation of standard hermetic and Rosicrucian texts and the works of Agrippa, della Porta, Paracelsus, Fludd, Dee, Vaughan, van Helmont, and others. More such books were published in England between 1650 and 1680 "than before or afterwards," according to Thomas, as "magic gained new converts among the radical sects." "For Familists and Behmenists, so influential on Ranters and Quakers," Hill found, "alchemy was an outward symbol of internal regeneration." In addition to their own practices, the members of these sects consistently "pressed for the introduction of the occult sciences into the educational curriculum"; as Rattansi noted, Paracelsian ideas "had a particular attraction for those who wished to introduce thoroughgoing reforms in the curriculum of the universities." The Polish émigré Samuel Hartlib, for example, follower of Comenius and probably the greatest educational reformer of his day, "was at the center of a flourishing hermetical movement." Hence, immeasurably, as Hill concluded, "astrology, alchemy and natural magic contributed, together with Biblical prophecy, to the radical outlook" of the early and mid-seventeenth century.[42]

The hermetic intellectual tradition, in its break with the cloistered clerical academy, had thus created a new, enlarged social space for religious and philosophical inquiry. Moreover, to the extent that it had become connected with popular magic and the radical religious revival, it had also become identified, by association, with women. For women played a prominent, perhaps even defining, role in both. At the same time, in their avid pantheistic pursuit of alchemical wisdom, some radical religious women gained a momentary means of entry into the heretofore closed world of natural philosophy.

If the village practitioners of popular magic were sometimes called "cunning men," they were more often than not "wise women." Many women of the village, as Thomas has shown, were invariably steeped in animistic pagan and Christian magic and herbal lore, passed on orally from generation to generation, by means of which they addressed their trials and sorrows and attended to the pain and suffering of their families and neighbors. And, with physicians geographically and financially beyond their reach, villagers of necessity relied upon the services of local healers, surgeons, barbers, midwives, many of whom were (usually older, and widowed) women. In addition to their store of amulets and charms, "they had effective painkillers, digestive aids, and anti-inflammatory agents" and other practical remedies unmatched by university-trained physicians. Paracelsus himself apparently acknowledged that, in his seemingly pedestrian peregrinations, he "had learned from the Sorceress all he knew" about pharmaceutical lore. Beyond such practical medicine, these "wise women" appealed to the stars and the spirits of nature to divine the sources of mischief and misfortune, distinguish the innocent from the guilty, and prophesy peril and promise. In short, in addition to her midwifery and medical remedies, for many people of Reformation Europe the inherited time-honored wisdom of the "wise woman" offered the soundest guide to the health of soil and soul, the most reliable respite from disaster, dispute, and despair.[43]

The preponderantly female personification of popular magic, amply reflected in the marked predominance of women defendants in witchcraft trials, was clearly evoked by one early-seventeenth-century English observer, in a book entitled *The Wise-Woman of Hogsdon*.

> You have heard of Mother Nottingham, who for her time was prettily well skilled in casting of waters, and after her, Mother Bomby; and then there is one Hatfield in Pepper Alley, she doth pretty well for a thing that's lost. There's another in Coleharbour that's skilled in the planets. Mother Sturton in Golden Lane is for fore-speaking; Mother Phillips, of the Bankside, for the weakness of the back; and then there's a very reverend matron on Clerkenwell Green good at many things. Mistress Mary on the Bankside is for erecting a figure; and one (what do you call her?) in Westminster, that practiseth the book and the key, and the sieve and the shears; and all do well according to their talent.

"Empirics and old wives," wrote Francis Bacon, "were more happy in their cures than learned physicians." Thomas Hobbes agreed, declaring that, in comparison with the university-trained, he would "rather have the advice or take physic from an experienced old woman."[44]

Like the practitioners of popular magic, the most fervent proponents of religious revival also tended to be women. "From the Montanist movement onwards," the historian R. A. Knox declared, albeit somewhat hyperbolically, "the history of enthusiasm is largely a history of female emancipation." The reform movements of the sixteenth and seventeenth centuries were no exceptions in this regard. The Protestant attack on clerical celibacy directly challenged the homosocial culture of the church. The male leaders of the Reformation, many of them former monks (such as Martin Luther, Ulrich Zwingli, Martin Bucer, and Matthew Zell), nevertheless sought to replace the clerical monopoly on religious discipline with that of the patriarchal family. At a time of diminishing economic opportunity for women, which increasingly restricted them to the domestic sphere, the reform leadership insisted upon the subordination of wives to the authority of their husbands (now including pastors of the reform church). But the explosive enthusiasm of the reform movement, especially on the part of women themselves, initially defied so limited a vision. The upheavals of the Reformation era allowed "women's roles to be less sharply defined or to be defined under the rubric of religious or political action rather than women's roles themselves," Sherrin Marshall explained. Thus "the scope of women's activities was temporarily broadened." In Germany, as Merry Wiesner has insisted, "women were not simply passive recipients of the Reformation and the ideas and changes it brought about but indeed responded actively to them. Swept up by the enthusiasm of the first years of the Reformation, single and married women often stepped beyond what were considered acceptable roles for women." Just as, at the dawn of the Christian era, women had responded enthusiastically to the Pauline injunction that in Christ there was neither male nor female, so here too, "taking literally Luther's idea of a priesthood of all believers, women as well as uneducated men began to preach and challenge religious authorities."[45]

"One of the most dramatic changes brought about by the Protestant Reformation," Wiesner observed, "was the replacement of celibate priests by married pastors with wives and families." As had been the case during Christianity's first millennium, the wives of God's ministers could now again participate directly in the affairs of the church, albeit in a subordinate role. Notable examples include Luther's wife, Katherine von Bora, a former nun; and Katherine Zell and Wibrandis Rosenblatt, wives of reform leaders Zell and Bucer. Indeed, as Marshall maintains, "within the limits of supportive, traditional lifestyles, a wide range of extraordinary and independent behavior was encompassed and made acceptable through identification with the church." The more radical reform movements, however, held out far greater opportunities for women, as had been the case with the early-Christian sects, the Cathars and, more recently, the Lollards. "The Radical Reformation's insistence on freedom of conscience for all adult believers," Marshall explained, "eliminated distinctions based on sex, and the doctrine of baptism or rebaptism for all believers became an equalizing covenant."[46]

Forerunners of the Reformation, the Lollards, followers of the fourteenth-century reformer John Wycliffe, had sought a "personal, nonhierarchic, lay dominated religion that looked to Scripture for its authority." Lollardy thus "presaged the Reformation" in numerous ways, including its treatment of women. "Lollardy appealed to women," Marshall noted, "who often comprised up to one-third of the membership. Many Lollard women participated in the movement for lengthy periods of time and helped its growth in the same ways as did men." According to Thomas, the Lollards "encouraged women to read the Bible and to recite the Scriptures at their meetings; several deposed on examination that perfect women were capable of the priesthood and there is some evidence of actual preaching by Lollard women." In the sixteenth century, the Anabaptists, a number of different radical reforming sects identified by their insistence on adult baptism, revived some of these ideals.[47]

Lower-class in membership, as opposed to the middle-class Lutherans and Calvinists, "they advocated wide-ranging social and religious changes, such as communal property holding, and were thus considered a threat to the established order and persecuted almost everywhere"—by Protestants and Catholics alike. As had so many of their forebears in the early centuries of Christianity, the Anabaptists sought "to establish the Kingdom of Christ on earth, not in heaven, and to confine the church to the minority of true believers," the saved, the perfecti, the elect, the earthly angels. Following the earlier sectarian experience, some of these radical Christians withdrew from the corruption of the world into isolated communities; others became active millenarians, even violent revolutionaries. Whereas some of the more actively revolutionary groups took on an increasingly militaristic and patriarchal cast hostile to women, the more pacific Anabaptists remained open to the "equalizing covenant" of radical reform. Thus "the Anabaptist priesthood included all members of the laity, both men and women."[48]

Some Anabaptist women, moreover, such as Ursula Jost and Barbara Rebstock in Strasbourg, "attracted followings as prophets"—again in the spirit of early Christianity. "Female prophecy was accepted in most radical sects," Wiesner noted, "for they emphasized direct revelation and downplayed theological training." Of course, as she also points out, "female prophets were much less threatening than female preachers," given their biblical sanction and lack of official function.

Nevertheless, it was noteworthy enough that, in the period of radical reform, "female prophets were taken no less seriously than their male counterparts." And if radical religious women made their mark as preachers and prophets, they also did so as martyrs, for, like their early Christian counterparts, they often faced death for their beliefs. In Germany, where the Reformation began, most of the female martyrs were Anabaptists, and the record of their interrogations offers "a good indication of the high degree of religious understanding among many Anabaptist women." The prowess of one such woman was acknowledged by her inquisitors, who told her: "your condemnation will be greater than your husband's because you can read and have misled him." Such martyred women died much as they had lived their eschatological lives, no different from men. Likewise in the Netherlands, another center of Anabaptist revival, where "religious changes created a milieu in which women could emerge in strong and independent positions, . . . women were executed for their beliefs as were men." As the Christian martyr Perpetua, on the eve of her martyrdom a millennium and a half earlier, had abandoned her children and dreamed that she had become a "man," so the condemned Antwerp Anabaptist Elisabeth Munstdorp wrote to her infant daughter, on the eve of her own execution, that she was, like her husband before her, going the way of the "prophets and the apostles."[49]

Anabaptist circles never were established in France as they were in Germany and the Netherlands, but here too women played a major role in the reform movement. "Noblewomen in particular played a vital role in the formation of Calvinist policy in France," Marshall noted, especially Jeanne d'Albret, daughter of Marguerite of Navarre and one of the leaders of the French Calvinists, the Huguenots. In a decidedly hostile environment, "noble ladies could often protect not only the preachers themselves but many of their less prominent converts." After the massacre of the Huguenots in 1572, many of these women fled to the Netherlands or Germany. The Bordeaux jurist Florimond de Raemond, himself a former Huguenot, later recalled the Calvinist movement as having been particularly marked by the involvement of women, noting derisively "how much easier it was to entrap women into heresies than men."[50]

Protestant women, literate and illiterate alike, "belonged mostly to the families of craftsmen, merchants, and professional men," historian Natalie Davis found.

Into a pre-Reformation situation in which urban women were es-
tranged from priests or in tension with them over the matter of their
theological curiosity, the Protestant movement offered a new option:
relations with the priestly order could be broken, and women, like
their husbands (indeed with their husbands), could be engaged
in the pure and serious enterprise of reading and talking about
Scripture. . . . Women already independent in the street and market
now ventured into the male preserve of theology.

Some, like the expelled abbess Marie Dentière, went even further,
becoming lay preachers, prophets, and authors of religious works. "If
God has done the grace to some poor women to reveal to them by His
Holy Scriptures some good and holy thing," Dentière wrote in her
Defense for Women, "dare not they write about it, speak about it, and
declare it, one to the other?"[51]

Some of the more erudite and earnest female participants in the
movement for spiritual renewal in France were not Protestants but
aristocratic Jansenists. The Jansenists were reform Catholics, Augustinian theologically and Gallican politically; their morally rigorous
views on divine grace and freedom of the will, and their defense of
the French Church vis-à-vis Rome, aroused the bitter enmity of the
Jesuits, and the movement was ultimately condemned as heretical by
Pope Innocent X, in 1653. From the start, women as well as men
embodied the "erudite spirituality" of the Jansenist reforms. The
male Jansenist leaders Jean Duvergier de Hauranne (the abbé de
Saint-Cyran) and the theologian Antoine Arnauld were successively
spiritual directors of the Cistercian convent of Port-Royal, headed by
Arnauld's sister, the reform abbess Angélique Arnauld. The abbess
was herself a leader of the movement, and her convent became its
intellectual and spiritual center, home to Pierre Nicole, her brother
Antoine, and Jacqueline, Gilberte, and Blaise Pascal. According to
one student of the movement, the Jansenists "defended the right of
the laity, including women, to participate in the offices of the Church
and have access to Scripture and liturgical texts through translations.
The nuns of Port-Royal were part of the Jansenist movement of spiritual renewal from the beginning, and lay women were drawn into the
movement and became prominent in its later stages." Education was
a central concern of Jansenist women, many of whom devoted their
lives to teaching; when the movement was forced underground, such
women readily became preachers at Jansenist prayer gatherings. "Jan-

senism promoted a vision of the Church which was less hierarchical than the prevailing view," F. Ellen Weaver has noted, "where the treasures of liturgy and scholarship were available to all, laity as well as clerics, women as well as men."[52]

In England, a "continuous tradition linked female reformers and sectarians throughout the sixteenth and seventeenth centuries," historian Diane Willen wrote. Aristocratic women had always played a significant role in the English Reformation, "through their patronage, their pen, and their example." Among these were Catherine Parr, Mary Fitzroy, Anne Seymour, Jane Seymour, Anne Boleyn, Elizabeth Tudor, the Cooke sisters, Catherine Brandon, and Mary Sidbey Herbert. In 1539, Henry VIII mandated the publication and wide availability of the vernacular Bible, thereby fostering religious development throughout the realm, including among women of the middle and lower classes. Apparently the effects of this reform quickly extended "far beyond the king's intentions," and four years later an Act of Parliament formally restricted access to the Scriptures along class and gender lines. Aristocratic men and women were still allowed to read the Bible in private, but only men were permitted to read from it aloud to the assembled household. Men of the merchant class remained free to read the Scriptures in private, but their wives and daughters could no longer share that privilege. Among the lower ranks of society, both men and women alike were denied the right to read the Bible. Such restrictive legislation was difficult to enforce, however, especially at a time of mounting religious enthusiasm. The principal obstacle to firsthand knowledge of the Bible remained not law but illiteracy.[53]

For women, illiteracy was a major hurdle, since they "did not participate in full literacy or in the so-called educational revolution of the Elizabethan and Jacobean period, which rested on the expansion of grammar schools and increased admissions to the university." But "for devout Protestant women, the importance of Scriptures and, therefore, of the necessity of literacy, was central." Thus, by all means at their disposal—transient "petty and dame schools," instruction by parents, siblings, or employers, or resolute self-education—many such women learned to read. Willen has suggested that perhaps the greatest effect of such female learning, in both the short and the long term, was felt within the "spiritualized household" of the Protestant family; here, despite patriarchal pressures, women came to exercise considerable influence over religious matters, especially in the rearing of their children. But the renewed religious education and enthusiasm of women reverberated beyond the household as well. Among the Puritans, for example, women wrote and distributed literature and even served as printers. Outside of marriage, as was the case during the early centuries of Christianity, women became the spiritual companions of Puritan clergymen. "For all of them, friendship with a cleric advisor was the only legitimate relationship permissible between a male companion and a respectable married woman." Elizabeth Bowes, for example, established a "spiritual and ideological relationship" with the reformer John Knox, who later became her son-in-law; eventually, she abandoned her husband to join Knox and her daughter in exile, a latter-day Paula to her Eustochium and Jerome.[54]

By the seventeenth century, the role of women in reform became more apparent, with the increasing visibility of the radical religious sects. "The prototype for much of women's subsequent participation in radical Protestantism was their involvement in late medieval Lollardy . . . which survived and merged with" the later radical reform movement. As Christopher Hill noted, "women had played a prominent role in the heretical sects of the Middle Ages and this tradition came to the surface again in revolutionary England. Sects allowed women to participate in church government, sometimes even to preach." Reminiscent of the early enthusiasts of the third century castigated by Tertullian for their boldness, the Puritan reformers were readily identifiable by their denunciation of the Catholic veiling and "churching of women," both of which practices implied that women were unclean and hence unworthy by nature. With the surfacing of the more radical sects, moreover, there emerged "open and widespread advocacy of religious equality for women, and public attacks by women themselves on their limited educational opportunities, their confinement to domestic duties, their subjection to their husbands, and the injustices of a commercial marriage market." As earlier sects, "from the Manicheans to the Waldenses, the Donatists to the Cathars," had welcomed women as patronesses and "active members on a basis of practical equality," so here too, Keith Thomas points out, the sects of Civil War England "allowed women self-expression, wider spheres of influence, an asceticism which could emancipate them from the ties of family life."[55]

The sectarians were the successors to the Elizabethan separatists who had emigrated to Holland or America or had remained underground in England. They surfaced during the period of religious tolerance, and relative absence of censorship, ushered in by the Long Parliament. Brownists, Independents, Baptists, Familists, Quakers, Seekers, and Ranters, they were drawn primarily from the lower classes and held a "wide diversity of theological opinion." What they had in common was not just their identity as sects but also their treatment of, and indeed public identification with, women. "From the very beginning," Thomas has shown, "the separatists laid great emphasis upon the spiritual equality of the two sexes." Membership in the sect was predicated primarily upon evidence of "individual regeneration," Thomas wrote, "and once admitted to the sect women had an equal share in church government." Independent congregations, for example, allowed "all their members to debate, vote and, if not preach, then usually at least to prophesy, which often came to much the same thing." Perhaps best known of the Independent women preachers was Catherine Chidley, whose militant pamphlets aroused much hostile debate. If, as Thomas suggests, it was with the Quakers that the religious rights of women "reached their apogee," it was as Brownists and Baptists that, after a lapse of eight hundred years, women once again preached in Ely.[56]

As in previous periods of evangelical Christian ferment and fervor, such as those that created not just the abbey of Ely but the church itself, in the Interregnum years the revival spirit generated an "apocalyptic atmosphere" in which all things suddenly became possible. Fundamentalist exultation in the power of direct revelation, and the correspondingly confident belief in the imminence of the Kingdom of God, swept aside all merely earthly authority, of church, of state, of family. "The women who walked under the Spirit were not under the law"; in the light of such belief, "women were priests as much as men." "We will not be wives, And tie up our lives, To villainous slavery," went the chorus of a ribald skit, "a form of literature which had great vogue at this time." If, in later, more secular times, such claims to female equality might be made in terms of natural rights and physical endowments, in religious times they were invariably grounded upon the "spiritual equality between the sexes." "The soul knows no difference of sex," the Puritan divine Samuel Torshell wrote in 1645. "May not the spirit of Christ speak in the female as well as the male?" asked Quaker founder George Fox. The "Inner Light knew no barriers of sex because, with the redemption of humanity by Christ's sacrifice, men and women had regained their equal state prior to the Fall."[57]

Once again, as in earlier eras, such belief in the spiritual parity between the sexes might be bound to the ideal of androgynous asceticism and lead in the direction of chaste companionship between men and women. "Christ was one in male and female alike," Fox maintained, echoing the ancient ideal. According to Christopher Hill, among the Familists, for example, it seems to have been "perfectly simple for any couple to team up together and wander round the country, preaching and presumably depending on the hospitality of their co-religionists." William Franklin and Mary Godbury were such a couple. "Sin, Mary assured an enquiring clergyman, is taken away when men and women come to be in Christ"; later she similarly assured a court that "she companied not with him in an uncivil way, but as a fellow-feeler of her misery." The Ranters and Quakers came to practice an intense asceticism. The Quakers, believing "that they had been brought into the condition in which Adam and Eve were before the Fall," maintained, like so many desert heretics before them, that (in Fox's words) "the saints' bodies are the members of Christ and the temples of the living God." Defiant of decorum and convention, they believed themselves to be already like the angels, in God's Kingdom come to earth.[58]

The existence of the radical sects, historian Moira Ferguson has written, "evinced a growing sense of female independence, bred by unconventional and changing times. Ecstatic women prophets, world travelers spreading God's word, itinerant preachers . . . and a plethora of writers on unorthodox beliefs bespoke a personal and collective style of female independence." Before the Civil War, women had to resort almost exclusively to prophecy to be heard, whereas the Interregnum offered them new means of expression. Lady Eleanor Davis, for example, perhaps the best-known prophetess of the pre–Civil War period, published some thirty-seven tracts between 1641 and 1652. Literally hundreds of women wrote publicly for the first time during this euphoric but brief period. One was Mary Cary, a self-described "minister" who viewed the onset of the Civil War as the emancipatory and leveling Second Coming of Christ. "The time is coming," she wrote in 1647, when "not only men but women shall prophesy, not only aged men but young men, not only superiors but inferiors, not only those who have university learning but those who have it not, even servants and handmaids."[59]

Given the prominence and unprecedented visibility of sectarian women, it is hardly surprising that the movement itself assumed, in the eyes of many contemporaries, a decidedly female appearance. "Women were numerically extremely prominent among the separatists," Thomas observed, and played a "disproportionate role." "During the Civil War period," he wrote, "it was a favourite gibe against the sectaries that their audience consisted chiefly of the weaker sex. Information extant about individual congregations suggests that it was quite usual for women to preponderate." Because "the female sex played so large a part among the Quakers," Thomas added, "it was rumoured at first that the sect was confined to them alone." Documents from the reign of Charles II indicate that, after the Restoration, sectarians, otherwise so diverse in opinion and behavior, were routinely characterized by their common feature: "chiefly women," "more women than men," "most silly women." As had been the case during the clerical ascendancy of the third and fourth centuries, and repeatedly thereafter in defense of orthodoxy, rebellious religious revival came to be identified by its most apparent, and for some most disturbing, feature: the presence of women.[60]

IN THE WAKE OF the hermetic and humanist movements and the larger religious revival of which they were a part, the current of new naturalistic learning had begun to flow outside the confines of the church and the academy, challenging at every turn the inherited conventions of clerical culture. And it was within this energetic flood of pious and practical enthusiasm so marked by the presence of women that some of them were able once again to re-enter the mainstream of Western thought. As in the ferment of early-fourth-century monasticism, the ascetic revival of the seventh century, and the promising predawn of the twelfth-century awakening, women were now able for a moment to share in the birth of a new intellectual epoch. As Londa Schiebinger has shown, this "momentary rapprochement" between women and early modern intellectual culture took place not within the established institutions of culture but within the less formal circles of salon, court, and craft. "Modern science emerged from a variety of social locations," Schiebinger observed, "including the workshops of artisans, informal salons, and the king's academies." Following the lead of Christine de Pisan, seventeenth-century women such as Anna Maria von Schurman, Hannah Wooley, Bathsua Makin, and Mary Astell continued forcefully, if unsuccessfully, to demand access for women to the mainstream male educational institutions, now more vital than ever after the Protestant dissolution of convents. Meanwhile, here in the "looser" organizational milieu of early science, artisan, noble, and royal women readily found a prominent place among their male counterparts.[61]

Royal women were of course superbly situated to gain entry into the emergent scientific circles. Like the privileged patrons of Renaissance humanism, they were among the earliest and most ardent students and proponents of new learning. "With family alliances connecting European courts," Schiebinger pointed out, "queens served as ambassadors preparing the way for both cultural and philosophical exchange." Sophia, electress of Hanover, was perhaps G. W. Leibniz's "closest associate," and she also conducted an extensive correspondence with the hermetic philosopher Francis Mercury van Helmont (son of Jan Baptista van Helmont). Her daughter, Sophia Charlotte, studied with Leibniz as well and later persuaded her husband, Frederick I of Prussia, to establish the Berlin Academy, with Leibniz as its perpetual president. Sophia Charlotte's ward Princess Caroline of Ansbach was yet another pupil of Leibniz. As princess of Wales and then queen of England, she became a major patron of science. In her capacity as mediator of the famous dispute between Leibniz and Newton, she "debated the question of the nature of the soul" with Newton's advocate Samuel Clarke. In like spirit, Elizabeth of Bohemia, patron of Descartes, found in him "a physician of the soul," as did, presumably, his last patron, Queen Christina of Sweden.[62]

In exchange for their patronage, male scholars of the seventeenth century became deferential tutors, correspondents, and courtiers to royal women, dedicating their work to them and, like Agrippa before them, defending the dignity of female learning. Much like their royal sisters, "noblewomen were often able to exchange social prestige for access to scientific knowledge," holding their court in the informal milieu of the salon. In France, for example, according to Schiebinger, noblewomen "sought refuge from hostile academics in the salons of Paris"; in the course of the seventeenth and eighteenth centuries, "the number of women attending informal academies and salons proliferated." Noblewomen "gathered among the curious" every Monday at the home of Théophraste Renaudot and every Wednesday at the home of Jacques Rohault to watch experiments and discuss philosophy. In addition, Schiebinger notes, "the grand salons of Paris offer unique examples of intellectual institutions run exclusively by women." The first of these, the Hôtel de Rambouillet, was modeled by the Italian-born marquise de Rambouillet after Elizabeth Gonzaga's Renaissance court in Urbino. Other French salons were presided over by Mesdames Geoffrin, Tencin, Lespinasse, Helvetius, Rochefoucauld, Lavoisier, and Lambert.[63]

It was this kind of extra-academic culture that later produced perhaps the foremost female French intellectual of the eighteenth century, the Marquise Emilie du Châtelet. Mathematician, physicist and philosopher, du Châtelet was (like her celebrated Italian contemporary Maria Gaetana Agnesi of Bologna) an influential and creative commentator on the philosophy of both Leibniz and Newton, producing the first and only French translation (from the Latin) of Newton's monumental *Principia* (published by Chez Lambert). "Never was woman so learned as she," wrote her longtime companion Voltaire. "She was a great man whose only fault was in being a woman. A woman who translated and explained Newton . . . in one word, a very great man." For her own self-esteem, du Châtelet, who died in childbirth, had no such need to masculinize herself. "Do not look upon me as a mere appendage," she wrote Frederick of Prussia; "I am in my own right a whole person, responsible to myself alone for all that I am, all that I say, all that I do."[64]

As in France, informal "noble networks" in seventeenth-century England coalesced in elite centers of philosophical discussion frequented equally by men and women. Here the hermetic tradition merged with religious enthusiasm in the formation of a new science of nature. One such center was the Dorset estate of the Boyles, Robert and his two sisters, Mary Boyle, later Lady Warwick, and Lady Ranelagh. Boyle himself, the so-called father of modern chemistry, indulged in both religious enthusiasm (see chapter nine) and alchemy. His sisters collaborated on a book of medical remedies which included a description of herbs and their uses and an index of chemical and astronomical symbols. Another such center was Ragley Hall in Warwickshire, home of Anne Finch, the Lady Conway. Perhaps more than any other philosophical figure of the period, Conway embodied the merger of the hermetic and religious revivals.[65]

Anne Conway early became a disciple of the Cambridge Platonist Henry More, through the mediation of her brother John, a student of More's at Cambridge. Through More, she also became a longtime companion of Francis Mercury van Helmont, editor of the largest collection of Latin cabalistic treatises. Steeped in ancient alchemical lore, Conway developed an animistic (vitalistic) and monistic natural philosophy—opposed both to Cartesian mechanism and dualism—in which body and spirit were united in the hermaphroditic unity of feminine (body) and masculine (spirit) principles. This philosophy, formulated in her posthumously published *Principles of the Most Ancient and Modern Philosophy* (often mistakenly attributed to van Helmont), influenced both Leibniz and du Châtelet. Under her auspices, Ragley Hall became an intellectual meeting place for such philosophical figures as More, van Helmont, Joseph Glanvill, and Ralph Cudworth. Believing that all spirits were "in kind of fellowship with God," Conway studied the beliefs of such enthusiasts as the Behminists, Seekers, Familists, and Quakers—whose sect she considered a "spiritual refuge friendly to women." Ultimately, both she and van Helmont joined the Quakers, to More's consternation, and Ragley Hall became a center of Quakerism—visited frequently by such Quaker leaders as George Fox, George Keith, and William Penn—as well as natural philosophy.[66]

The Newcastle circle, which at one time or another included such luminaries as Thomas Hobbes, Marin Mersenne, Pierre Gassendi, and Descartes, was presided over by the exiled English royalists William and Margaret Cavendish, the duke and duchess of Newcastle. It was her marriage to Cavendish and her entrée to this circle, as well as her association with her brother John, who was one of the original fellows of the Royal Society, that prompted Margaret Lucas' interest in the new learning. Over the years she "participated in discussions central to her life and times, taking up debates about matter and motion, the existence of the vacuum, the nature of magnetism, life and generation, color and fire, perception and knowledge, free will and God." Cavendish railed against the unfair exclusion of women from the universities, "where Nature is best known," and often despaired about her lack of formal education. In a 1655 letter "To the Two Most Famous Universities of England," she declared that, "ordained and Created by Nature, and wanting the Experience of Nature, we must needs want the Understanding and Knowledge, and so consequently Prudence, and Invention of Men." "The upheaval of the Civil War, bringing with it a certain tolerance for public voices for women, may have influenced Cavendish in her youth," Schiebinger concluded, but "without the private philosophical network, Margaret Lucas Cavendish could not have become a natural philosopher."[67]

Exiled in Paris and Antwerp during most of the Civil War, Cavendish produced many philosophical tracts, including *Philosophical and Physical Opinions, Observations upon Experimental Philosophy*, and the *Grounds of Natural Philosophy*. Of fiercely independent mind, she echoed Anne Conway in her own monistic and animistic critique of Cartesian mechanism and dualism. For her too there was a "fundamental unity pervading the world"; nature was composed of "one material yet 'self-moving' and 'self-knowing' body." Moreover, she wrote, "there is not any Creature or part of Nature without . . . Life and Soul. . . . All parts of Nature, even the inanimate, have an innate and fixt self-knowledge; it is probable that they may also have an interior self-knowledge of the existence of the Eternal and Omnipotent God, as the Author of Nature." Like Agrippa before her, Cavendish also attacked the "vanities and uncertainties" of scientific experimentalism and rationalism. In marked contrast to the leading lights of the Newcastle circle and the emergent Royal Society, she steadfastly insisted upon the ultimate unreliability of both the human senses and reason when it comes to understanding "the interior natural motions of any part or creature of Nature."[68]

If the royal courts and aristocratic salons of seventeenth century Europe afforded women a role in the emergent scientific culture, so did the more customary women's arts and established craft traditions, especially after having been brought into closer touch with philosophical discourse. In medicine especially the seventeenth century was a time of transition for the wise women of Europe, as the theory and practice of surgery, midwifery, and medical cookery underwent significant changes. During this temporary transitional period, women contributed to the convergence of popular and learned traditions. Marguerite du Tertre de la Marche, head midwife at the Hôtel Dieu in Paris, recorded her experiments on amniotic fluid and blood serum in an influential obstetrics text, first published in 1677. In Germany, which was renowned for educated (privately tutored) women surgeons and midwives, Justine Dittrichin Siegemundin of Brandenburg, midwife to the Prussian royal family, published her learned remedies and observations in 1689.[69]

Between the sixteenth and eighteenth centuries, the ancient lore of medical cookery, the essential production of drugs and medicines, underwent its transformation into the academic fields of nutrition, pharmacy, and botany. In the process, the practice became wedded to Paracelsian alchemy, and "women physicians and herbalists added alchemy to their repertoires." A late-sixteenth-century medical treatise by Isabella Cortese, for example, contained alchemical recipes, as did that of the Spanish medical woman Oliva des Nantes Barrera. In seventeenth-century England, alchemical learning informed the work of Elisabeth Grey, whose manual "of rare and select secrets in Physick and Chirurgerie" went through nineteen editions, and the book on medical practice prepared by Mary Boyle and her sister, Lady Ranelagh. Probably the most famous seventeenth-century treatise on medical cookery was Marie Meurdrac's *La Chymie charitable et facile, en faveur des dames*, published in Paris in 1666. This elaborate six-part work—with extended discussions of chemical-laboratory procedures and equipment, the properties of the basic elements (the Paracelsian salt, sulfur, and mercury), the chemical use of metals and minerals, and medical and cosmetic remedies—well reflected the alchemical influence on traditional medical practice. In addition to its table of weights, it listed 106 alchemical symbols. In defense of such a publication by a woman, Meurdrac declared to her readers that "minds have no sex."[70]

Like the traditional arts, the household-craft tradition afforded women a role in the new learning. "Of the various institutional homes of the sciences," Schiebinger observed, "only the artisanal workshop welcomed women. . . . In the workshop, women's (like men's) contributions depended less on book learning and more on practical innovations in illustrating, calculating, or observing." In Germany especially, where household-craft traditions persisted beyond those in other European countries, women participated in family-run workshops as daughters and apprentices, wives and assistants, independent artisans, and widows carrying on the work of their late husbands. As illustrations of this tradition, Schiebinger has described the work of women in the seventeenth-century German household-artisan fields of astronomy and entomology. "The German astronomer of the late seventeenth century," she notes, "bore a close resemblance to the guild master or apprentice, and the craft organization of astronomy gave women a prominence in the field." Thus "between 1650 and 1710 a surprisingly large number of women . . . worked in German astronomy," among them Maria Cunitz, Elisabetha Hevelius, Maria Eimmart, Maria Winkelmann, and her daughters Christine and Margaretha Kirch. All of these women were privately educated by their families and pursued their astronomical labors in family observatories. Like clerical wives of old, and the wives of royalty and nobility in their own day, these guild wives gained informal access to the mainstream of European intellectual and scientific life.[71]

Maria Cunitz was tutored by her father in languages as well as history, medicine, and mathematics, and, together with her husband, a physician and amateur astronomer, prepared astronomical tables that were published in 1650. Maria Eimmart was educated by and then apprenticed to her father, and in that capacity prepared drawings of the sun and moon from careful and sustained observations. Through her, her husband, a physics teacher, inherited her father's observatory, and she continued her astronomical investigations until her death in childbirth in 1707. Elisabetha Koopman became the second wife and, for twenty-two years, chief assistant of the astronomer Johannes Hevelius. When her husband died, she edited and published their joint work, an unprecedented catalogue of 1,888 stars. Maria Winkelmann was educated by her father, a Lutheran minister, and later married Gottfried Kirch, Germany's leading astronomer, a student of Hevelius and future director of the new Royal Observatory. Collaborating with her husband, Winkelmann made a number of important astronomical observations, among them the comet of 1702 (for which her husband was mistakenly credited), the aurora borealis (1707), and the 1709 conjunction of the sun, Saturn, and Venus. She also corresponded with Leibniz about her observations and was the author of three astrological pamphlets. "I am not sure what nature is trying to tell us," she wrote to Leibniz. After the death of her husband, she attempted unsuccessfully to succeed him as director of calendar preparation for the Royal Observatory. Citing biblical authority, she argued that the "female sex as well as the male possesses talents of mind and spirit"; with education and experience, a woman could prove "as skilled as a man at observing and understanding the skies." The sentiment was shared by the seventeenth-century French astronomer Jeanne Dumée, whose treatises on the motion of the earth, based on observations of Venus and the moons of Jupiter, confirmed the validity of Copernican and Galilean theories. "Between the brain of a woman and that of a man," she wrote, "there is no difference."[72]

Like that of the heavens, the observation of terrestrial nature also remained open to women of the seventeenth century. The French baroness de Beausoleil, for example, spent thirty years studying mineralogy, chemistry, and mechanics and in 1640 produced an influential report on the mines and ore deposits of France which included discussions of mining, assaying, smelting, and metallurgy. The German illustrator Maria Sibylla Merian made major contributions to natural history, enlarging "significantly the empirical base of European entomology." The daughter of the well-known artist and engraver Matthäus Merian, who died when she was three years old, Maria received her artistic training from her painter stepfather and his apprentices in the family workshop. She thus became an accomplished naturalist-illustrator at a time when scientific investigation depended upon exact observation and meticulous illustration. She married one of her stepfather's apprentices, Johanne Graff, and eventually developed her own trade, selling flower-painted silks, satins, and linens. At the same time, she experimented with media and techniques and, attuned to the needs of the silk business, studied the life cycle of silkworms. Following an unsuccessful search for fine thread-producing worms, she published an illustrated volume on the metamorphosis of caterpillars. By this time, she had taken on female apprentices.[73]

After seventeen years of marriage, Merian left her husband, assumed her maiden name, and with her two daughters joined the Labadist ascetic religious community, forerunners of the German Pietists. Like the Quakers, "the Labadists were sympathetic to independent and accomplished women"; indeed, Anna von Schurman, one of the foremost advocates of women's education, was a founder of the Labadist community. At the age of fifty-two, Maria, with her daughter Dorothea, left Europe for the South American Labadist mission in Surinam. Here she avidly pursued her naturalist observations and illustrations. Upon her return to Europe, she published her major scientific work, a large illustrated volume on the life cycle of the caterpillars, worms, moths, butterflies, beetles, bees, and flies found in Surinam (it included as well sympathetic descriptions of the folk remedies and popular magic of the indigenous peoples). This remarkable volume made Merian famous among leading naturalists, and copies soon graced natural-history cabinets throughout Europe. In honor of her contributions, six plants, nine butterflies, and two beetles are named after her. But this tribute was perhaps misplaced. As a woman who truly embodied the seventeenth-century convergence of scientific inquiry and religious enthusiasm, Merian herself devoutly insisted that she published "not for my own glory, but for the glory of God alone, who created such wonders."[74]

Nine · *The Scientific Restoration*

THE CONVERGENCE of revivalist iconoclasm and natural philosophy reached its apogee at the dawn of the scientific revolution. Fueled and fostered by humanistic and Protestant reform, hermetic teachings, royal patronage, informal elite networks, sectarian enthusiasm, social radicalism, artisan culture, and popular magic, this fortuitous coupling had temporarily diverted the flow of mainstream European culture beyond the walls of established ecclesiastical and academic institutions, thereby opening it to women. This challenge, however, had merely circumvented rather than transcended clerical authority, offering women only temporary entry. For by this time too the guardians of the established order had begun anew to behold the specter of heresy in the image of woman. Few reformers, of course, for all their iconoclasm, viewed themselves as part of a heretical, much less a women's movement. However, given their associations with popular magic and religious revival, both of which involved pronounced and visible female participation, they inescapably became identified with women. Women, meanwhile, in the wake of the Catholic Counter-Reformation and the consolidation of the Protestant churches, were increasingly being identified with heresy, as witches and enthusiasts (even while some women were gaining momentary entry into the cultural mainstream). Thus, as so often in the near and distant Christian past, the ready identification of diverse social and intellectual movements with women offered the orthodox a sure and time-honored sign of heresy. From those anxious savants who sought legitimacy and refuge in religious respectability, therefore—especially those who had been caught up in the enthusiasm themselves—the times had begun to demand, yet again, a reliably masculine identity. The challenge that had confronted the clerical ascetic authors of Christian orthodoxy now arose once more for the men of modern science.

Women are "the Devil's gateway," Tertullian had declared in the third century, describing the "bold" female sectarians of Carthage.

Thirteen hundred years later, in the wake of the Reformation, alarmed defenders of orthodoxy responded in like fashion to the bold women in their midst. "Everywhere in Catholic Europe, churchmen attempted to enforce claustration on often unwilling nuns and monastic vows on third-order communities," Sherrill Cohen noted. In Catholic Italy, "the counter reformers . . . resisted the Protestant challenge to the monastic ideal and instead reiterated that ideal and aimed to enforce it in reality." The church, focusing its attention especially on women, exhibited a "desire to bring all institutions . . . into closer conformity with the esteemed monastic ethos." Thus it "attempted to cleanse the convents of long-time abuses" by imposing rigid discipline and strict cloistering of nuns, while, at the same time, institutionalizing "surplus" unwed women to protect them from temptation.[1]

In Catholic France, the jurist Florimond de Raemond, a former Huguenot, wrote a treatise on "the history of the birth, progress and decadence of the heresy of this century," and noted the special affinity women had for heresy. As Natalie Davis observed, "he was not the only Catholic male to try to discredit the Protestant cause by associating it with the weak will and feeble intellect of the female." In Protestant Germany, the boldness of religious women was "viewed with alarm by civic authorities, who even objected to women's getting together to discuss religion." No German government legally prevented women from reading the Bible, as the regime of Henry VIII did in England, but the authorities "did attempt to prevent them from discussing it publicly." The city council of Memmingen went so far as to formally forbid women "to discuss religion while drawing water at neighborhood wells." To their contemporaries in England, the appearance of female enthusiasts represented "nothing more than Satan working through his usual channels." Women's "discontent," noted John Brinsley, "layeth them open to Satan's delusions, who readily worketh upon such an advantage." "When women preach and cobblers pray, the fiends in hell make holiday," wrote a Civil War pamphleteer.[2]

Women had long been linked to witchcraft, because of their prominent role in popular magic. But their practice of "maleficium" or harmful witchcraft had been condemned because it was antisocial, not necessarily because it was heretical. The sixteenth- and seventeenth-century connection between witchcraft and heresy, which fueled the period's unprecedented witch-craze, drew its inspiration from the earlier association between women and heresy. The late-medieval notion of witchcraft as heresy had its roots in the Catholic crusade against the Cathars and was thus from the start linked both to heresy and to women (who played a visible role among the Cathars). "The main agency responsible for the introduction of this new concept," Keith Thomas explained, "was the Roman Catholic Church." According to this clerical construct, "the essence of witchcraft was not the damage it did to other persons, but its heretical character." The witch "owed her powers to having made a deliberate pact with the Devil." Thus "witchcraft had become a Christian heresy . . . because it involved the renunciation of God and deliberate adherence to his greatest enemy"; it was a "false religion." This Catholic demonization of witchcraft was formalized in a 1484 papal bull of Pope Innocent VIII, which extended the power of the Inquisition to hunt witches throughout southern Germany. Two years later, the German Dominican inquisitors Jacob Sprenger and Heinrich Kramer published what became the major witch-hunters' manual for two centuries, the *Malleus Maleficarum*, or *Hammer of the Witches*.[3]

According to the church concept of witchcraft, witches were women. Throughout Europe, "witch" was defined in female terms; the *Malleus Maleficarum*, for example, used the feminine noun for "witch," as did most other manuals. "When a woman thinks alone," Sprenger and Kramer wrote, "she thinks evil." Most witches are women, because women "are more impressionable than men and more ready to receive the influence of the disembodied spirit. . . . Since they are weak they find an easy and secret manner of vindicating themselves in witchcraft." Woman "is a liar by nature," they warned, "a wheedling and secret enemy." As Rosemary Reuther pointed out, "this misogynist pattern was not peculiar to the Dominicans' work. . . . It was standard to refer to witches as women in the witch-hunters' treatises and to include a section showing, from the 'nature' of women, why witches are female." Keith Thomas observed that "learned authorities never had any doubt that the weaker sex was more vulnerable to the temptations of Satan." This feminization of witchcraft was but the reverse side of the demonization of women by the clerical world without women. Women, in that view, were by definition sexually insatiable and thus quite likely to be copulating with the devil. "Undoubtedly there was a strong anti-feminist streak about such monkish fantasies as the Malleus Maleficarum," Thomas pointed out. It is striking to note, in this regard, that the only place in Europe in which a masculine word was used for "witchcraft" was Iceland, the one country where clerical celibacy had never been accepted, even among the higher clergy.[4]

Practice followed theory. With their primary focus upon women, witchcraft accusations, persecutions, and executions increased throughout the sixteenth century, reaching their "greatest extent and ferocity" in the seventeenth—precisely the time when women had begun to make some gains. A trans-European exercise in exorcism, the witch-hunt also offered authorities convenient means of expropriating land, property, and knowledge from vulnerable widows, healers, and midwives. In 1580, the French witch-hunter Jean Bodin estimated that female witches outnumbered males fifty to one. In England, the notoriously misogynous King James I suggested in his *Daemonologie* that the ratio was closer to twenty to one, while his countryman Alexander Roberts put it at one hundred to one. In Germany, the medical professor and witchcraft prosecutor Thomas Erastus also emphasized the preponderance of female witches. Statistics from several European countries indicate that women constituted nearly 85 percent of witch-hunt victims. Only in Iceland did male witches outnumber females.[5]

Some estimates place the total number of witch-hunt victims, including those who died in prison, in the millions. Throughout the fifteenth and sixteenth centuries, Germany and Italy witnessed thousands of executions of women. In some German cities, executions averaged two a day; nine hundred women were killed in a single year in Würzburg, and over a thousand around Como. In the late sixteenth century, this wave of gender-bound genocide swept through France. In Trier, two villages were left with only one woman each; in Toulouse, the old Cathar stronghold, four hundred women were murdered in one day. By this time too the deadly notions of witchcraft had begun to be disseminated in England—as Thomas noted, "mostly by clergymen." "It was only when continental ideas poured into sixteenth century England . . . that witchcraft stood revealed as the greatest crime of all. As soon as witches were seen as heretics and the sworn enemies of God, a campaign was launched to root them out of the land. Hence the subsequent trials and executions." Here, in the wake of the enclosure movement and the breakup of the manorial system of land tenancy, "the judicial records reveal two essential facts about accused witches: they were poor, and they were usually women."[6]

In the person of the witch, the female practitioner of popular magic, like the female religious enthusiast, became identified with heresy, and now, as heretics, the witch and the enthusiast became practically indistinguishable. As Edward Peters observed, "heresy, idolatry, and superstition indiscriminately merged in the person of the heretic, and the heretic merged into the witch." "The Counter-Revolution, which proceeded strongly against magic, sometimes explicitly associated sorcery with the rise of Protestantism," Thomas wrote. This collapse of careful distinctions between magic, witchcraft, enthusiasm, and heresy was plain as well in Protestant England. "At this day," Reginald Scot observed in 1584, "it is indifferent to say in the English tongue, 'she is a witch,' or 'she is a wise woman.' " As Thomas has shown, "with the proliferation of the sects under the Interregnum cases of alleged diabolical possession multiplied [since] its symptoms were scarcely capable of being differentiated from those of religious ecstasy. Sectaries who engaged in marathon acts of fasting or gave vent to religious prophecy were often said by enemies to have been bewitched, or even to be witches themselves." Of course, the sectarians had done much to fuse magic and religion, having "brought back much of the magic which their early Tudor predecessors had so energetically cast out." "During the Interregnum they exploited the possibilities of religion for healing and prophesying [such that] the practical attractions of enthusiastic religion during these years closely matched those of magic arts." Thus "the lectures of Fifth Monarchy men resembled astrology," and "Quaker revelation resembled sibylline prophecy." "To the unsophisticated there was little to choose . . . between a witch and a godly divine." Such had been the case with Anne Bodenham, the wise woman of Wiltshire who was executed in 1653. According to Thomas, "it is not surprising that one contemporary, after seeing the cunning woman Anne Bodenham at work, should have concluded that she was 'either a witch or a woman of God.' " There was no mistaking, however, that she was a woman.[7]

Alchemists and hermetic philosophers readily fell prey to the same sorts of confusion. Agrippa and Paracelsus, like Ficino and Pico before them, had insisted that there were two kinds of magic, angelic and demonic, and that they strove to purify the former of the latter, thereby rendering magic an aid to human welfare and salvation. Magicians, they maintained, were not witches. But, as Edward Peters pointed out, these "attempts of learned magicians and some philosophers to separate 'good' and 'bad' magic, 'learned' and 'unlearned'

magic, 'philosophical' from 'bestial' magic, never wholly succeeded."
From the late fifteenth century on, theologians and inquisitors "associated the learned magicians with the unlearned witches." Indeed, Peters notes, "many of the elements of sixteenth century witchcraft were first brought to light in charges against magicians." Thus, in the view of contemporary inquisitors, "the figure of the learned magician and the type of the sixteenth century witch [were] not as far apart as some excessively schematized histories of witchcraft usually suggest." "Whether it pleased him or not, a magician like Agrippa . . . was closer to the victims of witch-trials than he knew, or cared to acknowledge."[8]

Agrippa had in his own lifetime been accused of religious extremism, if not heresy; he had also been associated with witchcraft because of his celebrated role in successfully defending an old woman of the charge (he accused her Dominican persecutor of trying to confiscate her property). Paracelsus, another associate of wise women, had likewise been attacked, by the sixteenth-century Heidelberg medical professor Erastus, as a latter-day Marcion, one who associated with the devil, vexed the people, and revived ancient Gnostic heresies. (Physicians played a prominent role in the witchcraft persecutions and the attack on the alchemists, perhaps in order to eliminate competition from lay healers and midwives.) In the seventeenth century, such attacks upon the hermetic philosophers increased in intensity. The Paracelsian Robert Fludd was accused of being a heretical Rosicrucian by Pierre Gassendi and René Descartes and an "evil magician" by Marin Mersenne. Richard Baxter in 1655 "cited Paraselsus as proof of the fact that there was a devil, and that he raised heresies."[9]

Perhaps the most revealing attack on the alchemists came from Henry More, the Cambridge Platonist. After the Restoration in England, this former mentor and friend of Anne Conway and Francis van Helmont (before they became Quakers) joined forces with his Royal Society colleague Joseph Glanvill in a celebrated debate against John Webster on the existence of witches. Webster was a radical Puritan and hermetic physician who had urged the universities to incorporate Paracelsian learning into their curriculum. Alarmed at the repressive consequences of the witchcraft persecutions, much as Agrippa had been, Webster denied the reality of witchcraft. More and Glanvill defended it. Calling Webster a "Gallant of Witches," More focused his attention upon Webster's associations with women, insisting that Webster's philosophical stance was just a way of concealing his own association with "old Wives" and the devil. "But what will this profane Shuffler stick to do in a dear regard to his beloved Hags, of whom he is a sworn advocate and resolved Patron . . . ?" More asked. "Take notice how weak and childish, or wild and impudent, Mr. Webster has been . . . in the behalf of his Sage Dames."[10]

In so harshly focusing upon Webster's female affinities, much like his own, at an earlier time, More well reflected the response of men of science to the new demands of the day. In their flight from heresy, they took flight from women. They identified female witchcraft in order better to distance themselves from it, and condemned the magi and alchemists for the same reason. They discarded the animism of popular magic and ridiculed the hermetic philosophers' alchemical resolution of body and spirit. They denied the possibility that nature might be, like Scripture, a medium of revelation through which regenerated men and women could become again as one before God. In the place of such revivalist notions, they substituted mechanism and dualism, purging the natural world once and for all of its unseen sympathies and irrevocably divorcing spirit from earth, mind from body, subject from object, male from female. They withdrew from the disorders of enthusiasm and experience to the abstract certainties of mathematics. In league with papal and secular rulers, and a reinvigorated state, these new Augustines, Benedicts, and Dunstans sought a restoration of spiritual and intellectual order to match the restoration of political order. And like their glorious forebears, they found such order, and a lasting refuge, in a world without women.[11]

Counter-Reformation Italy offered just such a refuge for the Dutch physician Johannes Heckius, initiator of the pioneering Italian scientific society, the Accademia dei Lincei. A devout Catholic, Heckius met the dawn of the seventeenth century by fleeing the blasphemous Protestant environment of his native Deventer in the Netherlands for the reliable retreat of Catholic Italy. From papal Rome he issued his scathing anti-Protestant treatise against heresy, secure that he was among friends. Indeed, papal Italy offered intellectuals like Heckius an almost medieval religious environment. Counter-Reformation Italy, historian William R. Shea observed, "is notorious for its return to the rigor of an earlier age." The military and political turbulence of the sixteenth century had resulted in an increasing consolidation of authority by princes and papacy alike, the latter almost akin to a second Gregorian reform. This "reassertion of pontifical authority," moreover, well served the Council of Trent's commitment to a rigorous reinforcement of church discipline and a vigorous counteroffensive against the Protestant heresy. "Supported by powerful new religious orders, such as the Jesuits, and a reorganized and efficient bureaucracy, the papacy mounted a systematic campaign against the dangerous political and philosophical ideas of the Renaissance and the Reformation." The church was also armed with formidable new means of imposing its ideological authority, including the Inquisition, which was employed to great and well-known effect. Among those who came readily under its often fatal purview were not only people who preached the priesthood of all believers, but also the practitioners of rival magic, alchemists, and hermetic philosophers of nature such as Bernadino Telesio, Tommaso Campanella, Giordano Bruno, and the Paracelsian Jan Baptista van Helmont.[12]

The hostility of the church to hermetic natural philosophy, however, did not by any means extend automatically to the newly emergent mechanistic and mathematical approach to nature. Quite the contrary. While it denounced alchemical heresies at every turn, the church, and especially the regular monastic orders, avidly supported what they considered doctrinally sound scientific inquiry. "The number of scientists within Catholic religious orders is impressive, as is the quality," noted the historian of science William B. Ashworth. The one order that far surpassed all the others in this regard was the Society of Jesus, the Jesuits. First and foremost inquisitors and missionaries, the Jesuits also included dedicated scientists, among them Christoph Scheiner, Giambattista Riccioli, Francesco Grimaldi, Francesco Lana Terzi, Honoré Fabri, Niccol Cabeo, Gaspar Schott, and Athanasius Kircher.[13]

"The Jesuits had a particular zest for experimental science," Ashworth has written. "They were interested in every newly discovered phenomenon, from electrostatic attraction to the barometer to the magic lantern, and Jesuits played a major role in discovering many new effects on their own, such as diffraction and electrical repulsion." John Heilbron credited the Jesuits with being the greatest single contributor to seventeenth-century experimental physics, and in optics, according to Ashworth, "virtually all the important treatises of the period were written by Jesuits." "It is instructive to remember," Ashworth has pointed out, "that it was Riccioli—not Galileo, and not Mersenne, and certainly not Descartes—who first accurately determined the rate of acceleration for a freely falling body." Finally, the Jesuits pioneered in scientific collaboration. Under the supervision of Kircher, the "impresario in Rome," they collected and disseminated scientific knowledge on a "wide scale." Indeed, as Ashworth has suggested, the Jesuits were perhaps really "the first true scientific society." If so, the order established a clear cultural pattern for such scientific organizations, one already well reflected in all clerical and academic institutions: the Society of Jesus was a world without women. By a strange but compelling coincidence, Kircher, the guiding figure in this new celibate scientific community, was named Athanasius, after the man who first introduced monasticism to the West.[14]

The scientific society inspired by Johannes Heckius in 1603, like all those to follow, also mirrored faithfully this inherited monastic culture. After studying medicine at Perugia and establishing contacts with Italian Counter-Reformation circles, the charismatic Heckius moved to Rome and there made the acquaintance of a young nobleman ten years his junior, Frederico Cesi, whose family had extensive and influential connections to the church hierarchy. Indeed, as Richard Westfall described it, "The Cesi family rode to prominence on the back of the church." The young Cesi himself was the son of the duke of Acquasparta, the nephew of a cardinal, an abbot, and a bishop, and the brother of a priest and later bishop. In time, he himself would become an intimate of the highest church officials. Heckius, it seems, charmed the eighteen-year-old Cesi with his brilliance and, playing upon the aristocrat's youthful idealism and sense of self-importance, convinced him to establish the Accademia dei Lincei (Academy of the Lynx-Eyed), with Cesi as its prince. According to Westfall, there was also "more than a modest hint of a homosexual relation between young Cesi and [Heckius]."[15]

With Heckius as its spiritual guide and Cesi as its prince, the new academy, which also included two of Cesi's retainers, Francesco Stelluti and Anastasio Filiis, became, in A. Rupert Hall's account, the "first of such groups to be almost wholly concerned with scientific matters." (Cesi himself had a deep and sustained interest in botany and natural history.) The group met regularly at Cesi's house to discuss scientific matters. Eventually, owing perhaps to Heckius' dramatic personality or the secrecy of the proceedings (like those in the Renaissance academies, the members communicated in cipher), the academy came under suspicion and was forced to disband. (Westfall suggests this might also have had something to do with the duke of Acquasparta's concern about the intimate relationship between Heckius and his son). The academy was revived seven years later, in 1610; by this time, Cesi had inherited his estate and was prepared to proceed more boldly. He and his colleagues had good reason to be optimistic. As Pietro Redondi observed, "in papal Rome, . . . as under any dictatorship, their privileged personal relations with the ecclesiastical powers had a significance and political value which rendered their aspirations realistic."[16]

Under Cesi's authority, the renewed Accademia dei Lincei recruited more members, among them the prominent natural philosopher Giovanni Battista della Porta, Johannes Faber, Johannes Shreck, Theophilus Muller, Marc Welser, and Filippo Salviati. Cesi formulated the goals and statutes for the academy, and rules of behavior for its members (centering upon fealty to him). The academy had already adopted for itself a name and a chivalric emblem, which portrayed a sharp-eyed lynx gazing upward to God while beating down upon Cerberus, symbol of ignorance and vice. To their own minds, the new academy was akin to an order, a military order; as Carolingian monks had become under Benedict of Aniane spiritual warriors on behalf of the empire, so the Lynceans would be intellectual knights at the service of both secular and clerical authority. In addition to its obvious connections to the powerful aristocracy, as Redondi points out, "the alliance between the Academy [and papal power was] not merely symbolic." The academy originally excluded priests, but this rule was later suspended with the inclusion of Father Benedetto Castelli. By 1620, the Roman "nucleus" of the academy included men who enjoyed "the closest personal relationship with top figures in the Church," the priest Giovanni Ciampoli, canon of St. Peter's and "gray eminence of the Secretariat of Briefs," Virginio Cesarini, master of the pontifical chamber (lord chamberlain to Pope Urban VIII), and the layman Cassiano dal Pozzo, secretary to the pope's nephew, Cardinal Francesco Barberini, "the most powerful man in Rome." Finally, Frederico's uncle Cardinal Cesi was a friend of Cardinal Robert Bellarmino, papal theologian and counselor to the Inquisition.[17]

If the Lynceans resembled their archrivals the Jesuits in their links with papal power, they did so even more in what Marie Boas termed their "quasi-monastic" orientation. The original plan for the academy called for the missionary establishment throughout the world of likeminded "scientific, non-monastic monasteries." As Redondi described it, the Accademia dei Lincei "competed with Jesuit culture, imitating its very techniques of success: the discipline and solidarity of the Society's members, the absolute dedication to the aims of research—even to the presumed Lyncean celibacy—the pronounced international vocation, the will for proselytism and decentralization." Just as a Jesuit priest could not publish a book unless it had been reviewed by at least three theologians of the Society, so a Lyncean had to submit to the reading of several members of the Academy any book that he hoped to publish under its aegis and collective approval. The celebrated opposition between the Lynceans and the Jesuits has obscured the fact that "these two cultural organizations [had] such similar methods." Among these was an early commitment to celibacy, no doubt at the insistence of the devout Heckius. "As is well known," Ada Alessandrini noted, "the Lynceans had explicitly expressed a negative position toward marriage with regard to their members, who had decided to organize the academy in order to conduct together a communal cultural activity. Marriage was for them a 'trap,' a 'feminine bond' which deterred scientific activity and limited the liberty of the studious." The indelible monastic imprint of a world without women, having been passed outward from the monasteries to the church, and then later from the cathedral schools to the universities, now manifested itself yet again in the nascent institutions of modern science.[18]

The significance of the Accademia dei Lincei might perhaps have been overshadowed and obscured by later developments had it not been for the prominence of its most illustrious member, Galileo Galilei. Born the year after the Council of Trent ended, Galileo lived his entire life in the Italian Counter-Reformation environment. His legendary misfortunes, the result of his having gotten caught up in the political intrigues of the church and the Holy Office (the Inquisition), have obscured the fact that Galileo was a devout Catholic to the day he died. "The popular conception of Galileo as a martyr for freedom of thought is an oversimplification," William Shea has suggested. If he replaced Aristotelian dogma with "his equally dogmatic faith in the validity of a mathematical interpretation of nature," he did so strictly within what he felt to be the bounds of orthodox belief. In his work, for example, he "was inclined to describe his own point of view as 'divinely inspired' and to brand that of his opponents as 'contrary to Scripture.' " Galileo always had good relations both with the priesthood, some of whom were among his closest colleagues and students (including his favorite pupil, the Benedictine priest Benedetto Castelli), and with the church hierarchy. In 1623, for example, he had no fewer than six audiences with the Florentine Pope Urban VIII (Maffeo Barberini), from whom he received gifts and the promise of a pension for his son. Thus, during most of his career, Galileo "no doubt cherished the hope that the church would endorse his opinions. Along with many of his contemporaries he looked to an enlightened papacy as an effective instrument of scientific progress." Indeed, even at the height of his persecution by the Inquisition he rejected possible avenues of escape. "Had Galileo been less devout," Shea points out, "he could have refused to go to Rome [to face the Inquisition]; Venice offered him asylum." It is noteworthy also that, however serious his crime (and exactly what that was is still a matter of scholarly debate), his penalty, in these "burning times," was not so severe; he was never formally incarcerated, much less tortured or executed, but was permitted to return to Florence, where he was merely confined to his country estate, and allowed to continue his work, albeit having had to acknowledge papal authority over it.[19]

Galileo was born in Pisa. As a youth, he was an inmate of the Benedictine monastery of Vallombrosa, where he received his early training in logic. Before he took his vows, his father withdrew him from the monastery and sent him to the University of Pisa to study medicine. Galileo soon dropped out of his medical studies and never took his degree, but his reputation as a mathematical prodigy gained him a teaching position, first at Pisa and then at Padua. In 1599, seven years after his arrival in Padua, Galileo began a relationship with his mistress, Marina Gamba, who bore him three children (two daughters and a son). Galileo never married Marina Gamba—who came from a lower class—nor did she ever share his home, which was occupied instead by students from the university. In 1610, the same year Frederico Cesi had revived the Accademia dei Lincei, Galileo decided to improve his fortunes by moving back to his native Tuscany, to the court of Cosimo de' Medici in Florence. In a letter to a Florentine correspondent, he made it clear that he had wearied of the demands of democracy in the Venetian Republic and "longed for the haven of a princely court," for the freedom that could be granted only "by an absolute ruler."[20]

The freedom Galileo sought was not just from teaching. "Galileo's move from Padua," writes one biographer, "marked his lasting separation from the mother of his children. He desired to solve all his practical and domestic affairs as quickly as possible, that he might dedicate himself completely to the great scientific questions that were opening before him." Like Augustine in the fourth century, the father of modern science abandoned his mistress in pursuit of a higher calling, in a world of men. The year he left Padua, he published his celebrated *Sidereal Messenger*, which was an "instant success," especially when his discoveries were publicly confirmed by the Jesuits. The following year, flushed with his new fame, Galileo visited Rome, where Frederico Cesi invited him to become a member of the Accademia dei Lincei. Galileo's timing could not have been more perfect; a year earlier, he would probably have had to decline the invitation, handicapped as he was by his "feminine bond."[21]

Having rid himself of his mistress, Galileo still had his children to worry about. His four-year-old son, Vicenzo, remained with his mother; later, Galileo would arrange to have him made "legitimate" through the good offices of Cosimo de' Medici, and Vicenzo would eventually go on to marry and lead a normal life. With regard to his daughters, Virginia and Livia, Galileo decided upon a different solution. Having had responsibility for his sister after the death of his father, Galileo well understood the difficulties and costs of raising and marrying off daughters, especially as dowry prices were still on the rise. To make matters worse, his daughters had been born out of wedlock to a woman of lower station. Before leaving Padua, Galileo had intended to place his elder daughter, Virginia, in a convent, but this plan was for some reason never carried out. In Florence he redoubled his efforts to place both of his daughters, aged eleven and twelve, in a convent, but he faced two difficulties. Counter-Reformation reform legislation had prohibited sisters from taking the veil in the same convent and had prevented parents from forcing their daughters to take the veil before the canonical age of sixteen.[22]

Galileo was able to get the Florentine Cardinal Del Monte to waive the first obstacle, but he had to appeal to another official, his friend Cardinal Bandini, to get special dispensation from the second. A letter from Cardinal Del Monte at the time reveals "how strongly Galileo desired to place his daughters in a convent." "Beneath it all," Ludovico Geymonat concluded, "lay Galileo's desire to find for them a mode of life which would not entail new responsibilities for him in the future, and would relieve him of all worry on the subject forever." And that it did. In the wake of the Counter-Reformation's reinforcement of strict enclosure rules, the two girls entered the Franciscan convent of San Matteo at Arcetri in 1613 and never left. Livia apparently suffered a permanent breakdown. The celebrated Virginia, later described by her father as "a woman of exquisite mind," is remembered for her selfless piety, for her own stillborn scientific pursuits, and for the comfort she later provided her aged, ailing, and persecuted father. What is rarely remembered is that she and her sister were, in effect, "innocent little victims of science." Against her will, Virginia had been imprisoned for life by an ambition that excluded the presence of women. Despite Galileo's praise for his beloved daughter, expressed most fervently after her premature death, Virginia never saw him save when he visited the convent. In her poignantly pathetic letters to him, echoes of Heloise, she confided that her fondest dream was not so much to fathom the heavens but to step foot just once inside her father's house.[23]

With the death of Cesi and the condemnation and death of Galileo in 1642, the Accademia dei Lincei lost momentum and eventually ceased to exist. For a time, its mechanistic scientific labors, and its clerical cultural orientation, were sustained by its successor, the Accademia del Cimento, under the patronage of Galileo's pupil Grand Duke Leopold of Tuscany and the leadership of Galileo's disciples Vincenzio Viviani and Evangelista Torricelli. In Catholic France, meanwhile, a parallel effort to restore intellectual and religious order by means of a more mechanistic conception of nature was under way. From his monastic cell in Paris, the latter-day warrior-monk Marin Mersenne, "inspirer of the French Academy of Sciences," was conducting another philosophical campaign against heresy. In this he was joined by René Descartes, who had been a fellow student at the Jesuit College of La Flèche, and by the priest Pierre Gassendi.[24]

In 1611, the same year Galileo joined the celibate Accademia dei Lincei, Marin Mersenne joined the regular religious order of Minims. He was later ordained a priest and ultimately became a brother and then "corrector" (abbot) of the Minim convent in Paris. The mendicant order of Minims, founded by St. Francis of Paola in 1435 upon the twin models of St. Anthony and St. Francis of Assisi, was "one of the most ascetic orders in all of France." The Minim rule required obedience to the church, chastity, humility, and perpetual Lenten fasting. The first three rules were, of course, common to all monastic orders, but the last was unique to the Minims, requiring total abstinence from, among other things, meat, eggs, milk, cheese, and butter. In its emphasis upon "cloistered virtue," the order was known for "the severity of the rules imposed upon bodily perfection." It also maintained "strict rules governing the observance of ritual," enforced by "correctors" who "castigated all lapses." The members vowed to commit themselves to a rigorous regimen of "monastic perfection," including long hours of contemplation and meditative prayer and "harsh discipline based on firm liturgical principles by which the Order escaped from the odium of enthusiasm." Like the reformed Benedictine Order established on the same soil a millennium earlier by the Carolingians, the Minims were tied closely to royalty. Intensely patriotic, the order claimed Louis XIV as its child (on the grounds that his mother, Anne of Austria, had often prayed at a Minim church), and its monks "wrote long eulogistic works on the kings and queens of France." Such was the august and austere setting that became under Mersenne's inspiration "the virtual nerve center of European science."[25]

In his definitive study of Mersenne and the birth of mechanism, Robert Lenoble described Mersenne as striving to construct "an approach to natural philosophy that was tailored to support social stability and to combat religious division, through apologetic defense of orthodox Catholic positions on the relationship of God to his creation." As Peter Dear has pointed out, "the religious significance of his work was never submerged, always remaining a central motivation." Mersenne's defense of religious orthodoxy was marked by vituperative attacks against heresy and enthusiasm, whether on the part of the Protestant Huguenots or the Catholic Quietists and Jansenists. Alarmed by the rumored arrival in Paris of the elusive occultist Rosicrucians, whom the Jesuit father François Garasse had condemned as "evil magicians," Mersenne "declared war not only on heterodoxy but on all occult philosophies, such as hermeticism, alchemy, and natural magic." Joined by his two Minim brothers François de la None and Jean Durée and later by his friend Gassendi, Mersenne launched his famous attack against the Paracelsian Robert Fludd, accusing him of heresy. For Mersenne, the mechanistic philosophy, which purged nature of its own spirits and hence any imminent meaning, made possible the orthodox reappropriation of nature. Nature would become a divinely ordered domain, fixed in its behavior by externally imposed natural laws to be discerned only by the proper authorities. The idea held similar appeal for Mersenne's friend and former Jesuit schoolmate Descartes.[26]

After completing his schooling, Descartes took a rather different path from Mersenne, although he too remained a lifelong Catholic. Leaving his native France, he became, like Agrippa, a wanderer, traveling with armies through Europe. Moreover, like Galileo, he at least once had a mistress, the domestic servant Helena Jans, and a daughter, Francine, who died at age five. Descartes considered his daughter's death the greatest sorrow of his life (excluding his mother's death, in childbirth, when he was one year old). Perhaps as a refuge from such grief, Descartes turned to the certainties of mathematics and a mechanical universe. When he returned to Paris in 1623, he was rumored to be associated with the Rosicrucians, and, perhaps to dispel such slander, re-established contact with Mersenne, in whose circle he traveled until he left France again for Holland. It was here that Descartes embarked upon the life's work which established him as the mechanical philosopher par excellence. "We do no injustice to Descartes if we see him as a second Aquinas," Hugh Kearney has written, "creating a synthesis of all knowledge and bringing Christian revelation and new learning in a fresh whole. . . . In the history of science, his significance lies in the fact that he was the first to construct a scientific system" of the mechanical philosophy, rendering "explicit the mechanical assumptions that were merely implicit in Galileo and Mersenne." The supreme antianimist, Descartes aimed at the reconceptualization of the universe as a grand divine mechanism whereby all spirits would be effectively driven from nature to the safe confines of the mind.[27]

Pierre Gassendi "traveled the same intellectual path as Descartes and Mersennes," Ashworth noted; "he too was profoundly affected by the skeptical revival of the period and was led ultimately to embrace a thoroughly mechanical philosophy of nature." A doctor of theology, a priest, and canon of Grenoble, Gassendi came to Paris to assume the chair of mathematics at the Collège Royale and became friends with the Minim monk Mersenne. After Mersenne, in the midst of his debate with Fludd, asked for Gassendi's assistance, Gassendi joined earnestly and energetically in the campaign against occult teaching and alchemy. At the same time, he participated in the orthodox quest for a mechanical philosophy of nature, bringing ancient atomic theory into accord with Christian doctrine. This work, later introduced in England by Walter Charleton, influenced the thinking of Boyle and Newton. After the Minim's death, Gassendi presided over the weekly meetings of the Mersenne circle, paving the way for the French Academy of Sciences.[28]

Mersenne's circle made Paris the scientific center of Europe. What Henry Oldenburg, secretary of the Royal Society in England, was to the 1660s, Mersenne was thirty years earlier in France. He was a "universal correspondent," keeping in touch with academic and non-academic scientific investigators throughout Europe. "From all parts of Europe," wrote one historian of scientific societies, "news of the advancement of the sciences came to the convent, *dès pères Minimes, proche la Place Royale*." In addition to his far-flung correspondence, Mersenne held conferences in Paris, bringing together most of the leading lights of the new movement, including Galileo's disciple Torricelli. He held weekly meetings, sponsored translations and explications of the latest work, and otherwise oversaw what was for him a vast, coordinated, and urgent intellectual campaign. He created "a mutually supportive social group, begun to construct a mechanical philosophy that ultimately presented a solution to the problems of certainty, social stability, and individual responsibility. Together, this group criticized ideas associated with social disorder and anarchy, such as uncontrolled passion and spontaneity, individual criteria for religious truths, control over the spirits of nature by ordinary people, and 'subversive' secret sects. . . ." As in Italy, such intellectual activity was of a piece with political consolidation.[29]

"In France," as Carolyn Merchant has pointed out, "the rise of the mechanical world view was coincident with a general tendency toward central government controls and the concentration of power in the hands of the royal ministries. The rationalization of administration and of the natural order was occurring simultaneously." This convergence explains the appeal of the new philosophy to royal authority, at a time of intense religious strife and a wave of peasant uprisings. Mersenne's Minim order was a staunch defender of the king and maintained close ties to his court. "God sets up mathematical laws in nature," Descartes wrote to Mersenne, "as a king sets up laws in his kingdom." "God is not the soul of the world," echoed Gassendi, "but its governor or director." The man who most clearly expressed the political implications of the new philosophy was another of Mersenne's circle, Thomas Hobbes. An English royalist and for a time secretary to Lord Chancellor Francis Bacon, he had met both Galileo and Mersenne during a visit to Europe in 1634. Exiled during the Civil War, he became a part of the Paris circle. In his famous *Leviathan* (subtitled *The Matter, Forme, and Power of a Commonwealth Ecclesiastical and Civil*), Hobbes, metaphorically constructing the world as a machine, proposed a "mechanical model of society as a solution to social disorder." In such a manner, "he sought an answer to the disorder of the Civil War in the reassertion of sovereign power, a French solution to a English problem." England in the 1650s was not yet ready for such ideas, but the French monarchy welcomed them.[30]

Under Gassendi's direction, the Paris circle continued to meet after Mersenne's death in 1648, eventually moving to the house of Henri-Louis Habert de Montmort, patron of Descartes and Gassendi, among others. The so-called Montmort Academy was formally established in 1657, the same year as the Accademia del Cimento. In 1666, Louis XIV's minister Jean Baptiste Colbert reorganized the Montmort Academy into the French Academy of Sciences. Like its Italian counterpart, the French scientific society was the result of a "political and religious campaign to create a stable social and ecclesiastical order throughout Europe." Moreover, in keeping with its monastic origins and inherited hostility to heresy and enthusiasm—now both identified with women—the new academy from the start excluded women. Largely through the efforts of Mersenne and his colleagues, all legitimate study of nature would now once again be an academic, and a male, monopoly. Six years after the academy was created, the playwright Molière published his popular and influential satire *Les Femmes savantes*. In the manner of Juvenal in Hellenistic Rome, Molière ridiculed the intellectual pretensions of noble and bourgeois women, bidding them to attend to their wifely and domestic duties. "It isn't decent, for many reasons," the bourgeois gentleman Chrysale explains to his sister, Belise, "that womankind should study and know too much."[31]

Whereas the Italians and French organized, Francis Bacon still just dreamed. In 1603, the same year Heckius and Cesi formed the Accademia del Lincei, Bacon became "learned counsel" (he would go on to become lord chancellor) to the new king of England, James I. That same year, he wrote two short fragments entitled "The Masculine Birth of Time" (subtitled "The Great Instauration of Man's Dominion over the Universe") and "Three Books Concerning the Interpretation of Nature." In these short pieces, addressed rhetorically to "my son" and "my dearest son," Bacon proposed a means of restoring mankind's rightful dominion over nature, which had been lost, at the bidding of woman, with the Fall. Outlining the themes that would be elaborated in his fuller works, Bacon criticized the alchemists and the scholastics alike, offering a more directly instrumentalist method "to bind, and place at your command, nature with her offspring about her." In truth, Bacon was a transitional thinker, midway between magic and mechanism, but the masculinist orientation of his writing well reflected the setting in which it was composed.[32]

The court of James I was notoriously homosocial and misogynous—not that the two necessarily go together. King James I was a homosexual whose lovers included the earl of Somerset and the marquis of Buckingham. Bacon himself, though later joined in a marriage of convenience to the daughter of a London alderman, was a well-known pederast whose intimacies with his male servants probably led to his ultimate disgrace. The biographer John Aubrey wrote of Bacon after his death, "he was a pederast. His Ganymedes and favourites took bribes." Before he assumed the English throne, then King James VI of Scotland had written a book on witchcraft entitled *Daemonologie*. In the first year of his reign as king of England, he replaced the relatively mild Elizabethan laws against witchcraft with a statute that condemned all witches to death. Bacon was directly involved in the king's persecution of heresy and was well aware of the witch trials then taking place; as a number of recent studies have shown, his language discussing the investigation of nature is replete with metaphors of inquisition and torture. As witches were female, so too was Bacon's conception of nature. (William Harvey, King James' royal physician and discoverer of the circulation of blood, apparently played a role in the witchcraft trials. Though married, he held women in low regard. According to Aubrey, "he would say that we Europeans knew not how to order or govern our women, and that the Turks were the only people who used them wisely.") In 1620, the same year Lord Chancellor Bacon wrote his famous *Novum Organum*, King James called upon the clergy for aid in keeping his female subjects in their proper place. According to one contemporary account, "the bishop of London had express commandment from the king to will [the clergy] to inveigh vehemently against the insolence of our women. . . . The truth is the world is very much out of order." What had so aroused the king's wrath was a new fashion in women's dress, which made them look too masculine.[33]

Unfortunately for Bacon, King James displayed little interest in his scientific program. In 1624, after his disgrace and shortly before his death, Bacon wrote his utopia, *The New Atlantis*, in which he described a future scientific community designed, dedicated, and possessing the power to achieve mankind's dominion over nature. In Bacon's vision, this rational, experimental recovery from the Fall would be the exclusive privilege of men, the "Fathers of Salomon's House" and their "sons"; as Carolyn Merchant has noted, "the role of woman had been reduced to near invisibility." Though married, Bacon upheld the celibate ideal formulated earlier by the members of the Italian Accademia dei Lincei—and by so many clerics and monks before them. "He that hath wife and children hath given hostages to fortune, for they are impediments to great enterprises," Bacon wrote in an essay on "Marriage and the Single Life." "Certainly the best works, and of greatest merit for the public, have proceeded from the unmarried or childless men." Bacon's portrayal of the scientist "Father" was a composite of the clerical and the military, a history in imagery of the making of the modern scientist: "He was clothed in all the majesty of a priest, complete with a robe of fine black cloth with wide sleeves and a cape, an undergarment . . . of excellent white linen, and a girdle with a clerical scarf, also of linen. His gloves were set with stone, his shoes were of peach-colored velvet, and he wore a Spanish helmet." Bacon did not live to see his community of scientific patriarchs become a reality. That would be an accomplishment of later Englishmen.[34]

Like the French and Italian intellectuals who forged the new scientific academies, their English counterparts were devoutly religious. As Charles Webster has emphasized, "there existed the deepest interpenetration between science and religion in the English scientific movement, from the date of its origin to its full maturity." Indeed, he noted, "a long line of leading figures in [English] science were ordained clergymen, and many occupied important ecclesiastical positions." Among these were Henry More, Ralph Cudworth, Isaac Barrow, John Ray, John Wilkins, John Willis, William Turner, and Seth Ward. Ward, Wilkins, and Thomas Sprat, historian of the Royal Society, were bishops. Moreover, laymen such as Robert Boyle and Isaac Newton were, in their own way, religious zealots. As many scholars have noted, a good number of these men were Puritans, beginning with Francis Bacon. But Puritanism meant different things to different people; the fragmentation of Puritanism, first with the Separatists and then, during the Interregnum, with the sectarians, generated profound tensions within a superficially uniform faith. Thus those who during the Civil War gathered together under the unifying banners of religious conviction and Baconian philosophy proved in the end to have been, in Webster's phrase, an "unstable coalition."[35]

The passions of the Civil War, Thomas Sprat later wrote, "stirred up men's minds." The two-decade Interregnum, a period of revivalist fervor, widespread interest in occult learning, and unprecedented religious and intellectual toleration, proved fertile ground for natural philosophy. During this time, several groups of scientific-minded men coalesced in the continental manner. The Polish émigré Samuel Hartlib established a Baconian "Office of Address," which received some support from the Cromwell government, whereby he and his associates maintained contact with European educational and scientific reformers of the day. The so-called Invisible College centered at Oxford, which merged with the Hartlib circle, and the "1645 Group" formed around John Wilkins, likewise brought religiously motivated men together to discuss the theories and discoveries of natural philosophy.[36]

Although younger than many of his associates, a leading figure in these Civil War conclaves was the landed aristocrat Robert Boyle, the father of modern chemistry. After a sojourn on the continent, Boyle retired to the family estate to pursue his interest in natural philosophy. He learned about the Invisible College from Hartlib and William Petty, and his involvement with this group of self-styled savants was, in the estimate of one historian of the Royal Society, "historically of the greatest importance." In 1654, he took up residence in Oxford, where, together with his assistant Robert Hooke, an early English enthusiast of mechanism, he conducted some of his most famous experiments. Like other natural philosophers of the time, Boyle earnestly devoted himself to the study of alchemy. As Rattansi observed, "Robert Boyle himself was closely associated with Helmontians like George Starkey, Robert Child, and Hartlib's son-in-law Clodius." In a 1649 letter, Boyle confided to his sister Lady Ranelagh that "Vulcan has so transported and bewitched me, that, as the delights I taste in it make me fancy my laboratory a kind of Elysium . . . I there forget my standish and my books, and almost all things, but the unchangeable resolution I have made of continuing till death."[37]

Boyle's passion for his work was of a piece with his religious zeal, something he shared with his associates and with his sisters, Mary Boyle (Lady Warwick) and Lady Ranelagh. Boyle took his religious zeal a bit further than most, however (especially for a Protestant), even in that pious time. He was, in fact, a monk in earl's clothing, his passion for science the reverse side of his resolute sexual renunciation. In 1648, a year in which he experienced a profound spiritual crisis reminiscent of the lives of the saints, the twenty-one-year-old Boyle took a self-imposed vow of celibacy for "love of God," a vow he would adhere to for the rest of his life. He declared his commitment in a long treatise on "Seraphic love," in the form of an extended letter to a friend entitled *Motives and Incentives to the Love of God*. Armed with biblical allusion, Boyle, following St. Paul, laboriously contrasted the woes of earthly love of woman to the sublimity of angelic love of God. The treatise, which he at the time showed only to Mary Boyle, was made public eleven years later. At that time, his friend John Evelyn wrote to praise the work, mildly chastising Boyle for having kept it hidden so long. Though he was himself married and took exception to Boyle's antipathy toward women, Evelyn conceded that Boyle had indeed made "the worthiest choice."[38]

For Boyle, in the spirit of a millennium of monks, philosophy was a form of worship requiring purification from earthly desires. Only now the requisite monastic rites would be performed in a new setting, the "lab[or]oratory." Evelyn's deference to Boyle's superiority in this regard is striking, an indication that even in Protestant, antimonastic England the celibate ideal was very much alive among the natural philosophers. The revivalist spirit of the Reformation had kindled in the bosom of religious enthusiasts a profound affinity for ascetic devotion, and the devotees of the new learning were by no means exempt. In a subsequent letter, Evelyn proposed to Boyle that, in the spirit of "a Salomon's house," they should set up a scientific monastery "in the manner of the Carthusians," with "the promotion of experimental knowledge as the principal end of the institution." "Why might not some gentlemen, whose geniuses are greatly suitable, and who desire nothing more than to give a good example, preserve science, and cultivate themselves, join together in society, and resolve upon some orders and economy, to be mutually observed, such as shall best become the end of their union." Evelyn offered to devote his fortune to the project, "to assemble some small number together who would resign themselves to live profitably and sweetly together." In this altogether earnest proposal, Evelyn described in detail how the land would be obtained and the facilities secured. The scientific retreat would have a "pretty chapel" and "cells" for each member of the society. There would be a regular round of prayers, as well as fasts and communion, and, for attire, a "decent habit." Being married, Evelyn proposed that he and his wife would occupy separate cells— "for we are to be decently asunder"—with the assurance that she "shall be no impediment to the Society, but a considerable advantage to the economic part." Evelyn beseeched Boyle to give the matter his most careful attention. Explicitly likening their situation amid the strife of the Interregnum to that of the fathers of the church caught up in the turbulence of the fourth century, Evelyn asked Boyle, "is not this the same that many noble personages did at the confusion of the empire by the barbarous Goths, when Saint Jerome, Eustochius, and others retired from the impertinences of the world to the sweet recesses and societies in the East . . . ?"[39]

Boyle apparently never responded to Evelyn's proposals, but, as one historian of the Royal Society surmised, "in all probability they had some effect on hastening the establishment of the Royal Society." (Evelyn, who gave the society its name, was a founding member.) At any rate, by this time the fertile soil of the Interregnum had generated other schemes, not quite so monastic perhaps, "for the advancement of experimental philosophy," such as that proposed to Hartlib by William Petty. But by this time too, significant rifts had appeared within the "unstable coalition" of English natural philosophers, sending pioneers off in distinctly different directions. With their emphasis upon utility, artisan-based practical knowledge, universal antischolastic education, and utopian social reform, "Hartlib and his associates drifted into partnership with the separatists." "In contrast," according to Charles Webster's account, "their colleagues within the universities rapidly made common cause with other occupants of the middle ground within the church, many of whom had remained loyal to the monarchy." In addition, they had begun to appropriate the continental mechanical philosophy of Galileo, Gassendi, and Descartes. Charles Webster has suggested that the division which emerged within Puritan science might well be characterized as "a dichotomy between occultists and radicals on the one hand and the mechanists and conservatives on the other. . . . The one was eager to generate social change, the other to buttress social stability."[40]

The role of the established universities in the new learning was a central issue in this "realignment." John Wilkins and Seth Ward, both masters of Trinity College, Cambridge, and future bishops, were in the forefront of the defense of the universities against antischolastic critics such as Hartlib and John Webster. They "recognized the attack on the universities both as an assault on the idea of a learned ministry and the organized national church and as a threat to social stability." (As David Kubrin has suggested, such men, though allied with the Puritan cause in the Civil War—Wilkins married Oliver Cromwell's widowed sister—felt closer affinity with their Anglican and perhaps even papist peers than with the lower-class sectarians.) Thus a group of university-based churchmen had resolved to reappropriate natural philosophy for the academy and the clergy. It was they who would ultimately organize the Royal Society—Wilkins is recognized as its "chief founder," but Hartlib was never even invited to join—and "their protection of the fabric of essential institutions earned them rewards at the Restoration."[41]

Thus these descendants of the monks of Ely—who had first laid the foundation for Cambridge University—undertook in the second decade of the Interregnum to steer the ship of natural philosophy in a socially respectable direction. Before long, in the wake of increasing sectarian strife, even those who retained "residual links with the more radical Puritans"—among them Boyle, Petty, and Henry Oldenburg, later Royal Society secretary—drifted toward the Wilkins camp. In addition to their defense of the universities, the new mechanists were distinguished by their now vociferous condemnation of hermetic philosophy and alchemy. Donning the mantle of Bacon, they attacked the works of Paracelsus, van Helmont, and Fludd. John Baxter denounced Paracelsus as a "Drunken Conjuror, who had converse with Devils," and the Oxford don Henry More now condemned the work of the famous alchemist as "the wildest Philosophical Enthusiasms that ever were yet on foot." Walter Charleton, a former advocate of Paracelsian and Helmontian ideas, now introduced to England the work of Gassendi and likewise condemned Paracelsus as "harebrained and contentious." John Wilkins himself, aside from Robert Hooke perhaps the "most influential spokesman for the mechanical philosophy," associated the practitioners of alchemy with "the gang of vulgar Levellers." "There is no doubt at all," one biographer concluded, "that Wilkins was antagonistic to the sects. He disliked their separatism, their lower-class membership, and above all their mysticism and excessive zeal."[42]

"By the 1650's," Rattansi observed, "the doctrine of 'private illumination,' so widely invoked at the beginning of the Puritan Revolution, was proving a deep embarrassment and a source of danger to the authority established in Church and State after the overthrow of the monarchy. Those who keenly sensed that danger strove to curtail, as drastically as possible, the claims of sectarians who alleged divine inspiration." It is noteworthy that the most vociferous critics of sectarian enthusiasm and hermetic philosophy were those who had themselves earlier been associated with them. Much as Jerome and his fellow ascetics of the later fourth century strove to distance themselves from such heresies as Priscillianism by energetically disavowing their earlier beliefs and associations, men like More and Charleton decried the enthusiastic excesses of their former comrades. With regard to Charleton, Rattansi observed that "the changes in his views and his defection from Paracelsian and Helmontian doctrine offer a remarkable parallel to the revulsion of moderate opinion for the natural magic tradition as that tradition became identified, through the sectarians and their 'inner light' doctrines, with heretical religious and social opinions." Indeed, as Keith Thomas pointed out, "magic's very success during the Interregnum may have helped to accelerate its rejection afterwards by scientists, anxious to shake off overtones of sectarian radicalism." "The scientists themselves," Christopher Hill added, "were so anxious to cover up their revolutionary past that they [later] flooded the Royal Society with dilettante aristocrats who hated soiling their hands with experiments."[43]

Henceforth, and especially after the restoration of the monarchy in 1660, "those virtuosi who [openly] continued to search for occult virtues and correspondences were essentially outside the mainstream of scientific thinking." Most of the Royal Society membership energetically condemned such practice, while those who might have continued to harbor alchemical aspirations, took pains to conceal them. In an effort to guarantee the respectability of the new academically and clerically sanctioned scientific organization—the Royal Society was founded in 1660 and chartered by the king two years later—its anxious adherents had to guard themselves as much as possible against any and all outward signs of heresy, whether magic, alchemy, religious sectarianism, or political radicalism. And since heresy had come to be associated, through witchcraft and enthusiasm, with women, they had earnestly to emphasize that theirs was, above all, a reliably "masculine" endeavor. As Bacon had earlier heralded "the Masculine Birth of Time," so now Oldenburg, first secretary of the Royal Society, announced that the purpose of the society was "to raise a Masculine Philosophy . . . whereby the Mind of Man may be ennobled with the knowledge of Solid Truths." Likewise, Joseph Glanvill, the churchman and society propagandist who joined Henry More in the debate with Webster about the existence of witchcraft, wrote in 1661 that, "where the Will or Passion hath the casting voice, the case of Truth is desperate. . . . The Woman in us, still prosecutes a deceit, like that begun in the Garden; and our understandings are wedded to an

Eve, as fatal as the Mother of our Miseries." Walter Charleton, an early champion of the mechanistic philosophy and a founding member of the society, put the belatedly misogynous Jerome to shame with his own newfound conviction. With the shrill voice of a male character in his *Ephesian Matron* of 1659, Charleton evoked the anxious spirit of the new men of science toward women: "you are the true Hienas, that allure us with the fairness of your skins; and when folly hath brought us within your reach, you leap upon us and devour us. You are the traitors to Wisdom: the impediment to Industry . . . the clogs to virtue, and goads that drive us all to Vice, Impiety, and ruine. You are the Fools Paradise, the Wiseman's Plague, and the grand Error of Nature."[44]

In 1667, the year John Milton published his *Paradise Lost*, Margaret Cavendish paid a visit to the Royal Society. As patron with her husband of the "Newcastle circle," the brilliant autodidact duchess had once met regularly with Descartes, Gassendi, Mersenne, and Hobbes and had become an early critic of the new mechanical and experimental natural philosophy. But she too, like the blind poet of the Commonwealth, was now on the periphery. As the Restoration had reestablished the church and the monarchy, so the state sanction of the Royal Society had restored the clerical and academic, and hence male, monopoly over natural philosophy. Cavendish had long complained bitterly about her lack of a formal higher education, which was due to the fact that the universities excluded women. When the Royal Society received its charter in 1662, Cavendish wrote a play about a fictive "Female Academy," designed to serve the educational and philosophical purposes of learned women and their daughters. "Being a Woman," Cavendish wrote the following year, "I cannot publicly Preach, Teach, Declare or Explane [my works] by Words of Mouth, as most of the Famous Philosophers have done, who thereby made their Philosophical Opinions more Famous, than I fear Mine will ever be." Four years later, in 1667, perhaps in the hope of gaining such an audience for her work, Cavendish asked to attend a working session of the Royal Society. She made no bid to become a fellow or anything quite so bold—although, having written six books on natural philosophy, she was more qualified than many members—but her modest request prompted "a flood of controversy" among the membership. Samuel Pepys, a fellow and later president of the Royal Society, recorded at the time that there was "much debate, pro and con, it seems many being against it, and we do believe the town will be full of ballads of it." Members feared that a visit by Cavendish, being a woman, would "bring ridicule rather than honor," and perhaps worse. But Cavendish was also a duchess. Not wanting to offend a wealthy and well-connected aristocrat who had long been a generous patron of Cambridge University, the leaders of the society ultimately acceded to her request, arranging for her to visit several scientific demonstrations by, among others, Hooke and Boyle. Cavendish never recorded her impressions of the event, and there was no return visit. The controversy she had provoked, however, was later rekindled in a debate over the election of women to membership in the Royal Society, a debate which this time had more positive results. But that was in 1945, nearly three centuries later.[45]

As an exclusively male retreat, the Royal Society represented the continuation of the clerical ascetic culture, now reinforced by what might be called a scientific asceticism. The medieval monks believed that self-renunciation was essential to effective prayer and ultimate salvation; the scientists, following the magi as well as the monks, clerics, and schoolmen, believed that personal purification was essential to their new form of worship as well. This was hardly much of a leap for the churchmen who dominated the society; as C. G. Coulton long ago pointed out, when it came to asceticism, Protestantism and especially Puritanism had much in common with medieval Catholicism. But the laymen of the society, including the most ardent proponents of the new mechanistic philosophy, also readily adopted the celibate life. They too understood that close relations with women, especially in the repressive religious climate of the early Restoration, might easily bring suspicion of heresy. As Kearney observed, the Royal Society was really "Boyle's society." It was the lay aristocrat Boyle whose generosity and commitment to the new philosophy sustained the society in its early years. At the same time, it was the celibate Boyle, so revered by Evelyn, who served as the model of the new scientist. Boyle's lay assistant Robert Hooke, curator of experiments and later fellow and secretary of the society, was its most avid mechanist and experimenter, and for him too mechanics became "his first and last mistress." Like Boyle, and perhaps in emulation of him, Hooke vowed early in his life to remain a "bachelor, never to marry." Except for a troubling affair with his ward and niece, Grace, late in his life, Hooke remained faithful to his vow, and religiously reverent.

Even more than Boyle or Hooke, it was the layman Isaac Newton who epitomized both the mechanical philosophy and the ascetic scientist, the twin orthodoxies of the renewed world without women.[46]

Newton entered Trinity College, Cambridge, the year after the Restoration and his career and life fully reflected the demands of the new order. He led a remarkably schizophrenic existence, his outward aura of control matched by the most intense inner turmoil. Within his very person were replicated the tensions of his age. On the one hand, as the public personification of the new philosophy, he was the very paragon of orthodoxy; on the other, as a secret revivalist immersed in occultist, alchemist, and theological enthusiasms, he routinely indulged in heresy. No doubt as a result of this precarious double life, Newton developed a markedly paranoid personality, carefully hiding all evidence of his private preoccupations, suppressing publication of his voluminous alchemical and theological writings, and carefully censoring his published scientific work. All the while, he maintained an almost pathologically austere exterior, and he avoided women like the plague.

As an undergraduate, the young Newton came under the "decisive influence" of the Cambridge theologian Henry More, a fellow native of Grantham and a prominent member of the Royal Society. More was at the very moment engaged in his campaign against enthusiastic ideas, publishing his influential *Enthusiasmus Triumphatus* the year after Newton's arrival. More would soon also be embroiled in the controversy with Webster over the existence of witchcraft. The other major influence on Newton was the churchman and Royal Society member Isaac Barrow, who turned his attention to mathematics and natural philosophy. Newton became a fellow of Trinity College in 1667 and succeeded Barrow as Lucasian professor in 1669. Following the success of his work on optics, the results of which he had shared with the Royal Society, Newton was nominated for early membership in that august body. He was nominated by Royal Society founder Seth Ward, by then bishop of Salisbury and a "determined opponent of dissenters"; with the Restoration, Ward welcomed the imposition upon all clergy of an oath of loyalty to the state and church, and "vigorously supported" the notoriously repressive Five-mile and Conventicle Acts, which outlawed the activities of sectarians. Given his associations with More, Barrow, and Ward, Newton learned early and well the proper "code of behavior [that] had emerged to govern the still young study of natural philosophy in England." Enthusiasm, whether manifested in sectarian politics and religion or alchemical and hermetic preoccupations, had become heresy, to be avoided at all costs. The same year Newton became a fellow of Trinity College, Bishop Thomas Sprat, in his *History of the Royal Society*, proclaimed that the new natural science would serve further to restore social and religious order, thereby diminishing the "danger of Civil War."[47]

Newton, having learned these dire lessons well, nevertheless remained the ultimate revivalist, literally obsessed with unlocking the authoritative wisdom of the ancient past. He did not simply dabble in alchemy, occult learning, and the study of ancient prophecy as a diversion from his more serious scientific labors or as a way of occupying himself in his dotage. For thirty years, at the very prime of his scientific career, Newton immersed himself in such studies to an extent perhaps never before or since equaled. In his own time, however, he was forced to keep this half, the true heart, of his work totally hidden. Indeed, this most earnest devotee of revival had all the more to become, at the same time, the very model of orthodoxy.

Isaac Newton delved deeply and widely for signs of his Creator. If in his public work he sought them in the mathematical order of the physical universe, in his private work he sought them in the myriad sources of ancient wisdom. Certainly, as Kubrin observed, it was "as evident to Newton as it was to any student at Cambridge just after the Restoration . . . that Hermetic knowledge was widely viewed by his contemporaries as an inducement to enthusiasm, social chaos, and the rising up of the lower orders, and that extreme caution must be exercised with such ideas." Yet, for thirty years, alchemy was for Newton "a private passion." "For thousands of hours, he labored with his furnace or pored over alchemical books," tediously deciphering their mysterious codes in search of buried meanings. According to one historian of science, Newton's acquaintance with alchemical literature was of "unparalleled extent and intimacy. . . . Newton was probably better acquainted with the whole body of alchemical writing than anyone before him, and certainly than anyone since." It is estimated that in the course of his alchemical studies, which included both textual interpretation and actual experimentation, Newton wrote over one million words of commentary, most of it still in manuscript form.[48]

During the same time he was so assiduously pursuing his alchemical studies (and, of course, his public work, including the *Principia*), Newton was also actively involved in theological inquiry. Here too he was engaged in a task of revival, in pursuit of divine knowledge; he "believed that a pure ancient doctrine had been corrupted in the course of its transmission through history, but that it could be recovered by intensive interpretive effort. . . . Newton's researches in alchemy and theology were thus simultaneous and interconnected. In both cases [he] was engaged in a private process of textual interpretation, devoted to uncovering a secret truth that had been distorted" by subsequent commentary. "There are many respects in which he looked backwards rather than forwards," historian John Brooke has written of Newton's theological inquiries. Thus Newton spent enormous energy and considerable time reading and interpreting ancient pagan, Jewish, and Christian texts. Through tedious interpretation of the book of Ezekiel, for example, in Hebrew, Latin, and Greek, Newton tried to reconstruct the precise dimensions of the Temple of Solomon, which he believed to be a "blueprint of heaven." He studied the works of Clement of Alexandria, the third-century bishop who early helped to forge the orthodox church, "one of Newton's favorite authorities from antiquity." If there was a villain in Newton's account of the Christian past, it was Athanasius, the fourth-century bishop who formulated the doctrine of the Trinity, thereby perverting the pristine Christianity of the primitive church into a veritable polytheistic religion. Newton, the ardent monotheist, thus rejected the fourth-century Nicene Creed upon which Catholic orthodoxy had been built, including Arianism among his secret heresies.[49]

By the end of his life, Newton had produced many volumes of theological inquiry and reflection, among them *A Church History, A History of the Creation, A Historical Account of Two Notable Corruptions of Scripture, Paradoxical Questions Regarding Athanasius*, and several studies of ancient prophecy, including *Lexicon Propheticus* and *Observations on the Prophecies of Daniel and the Apocalypse of St. John*. In addition, he conducted intense and sustained studies of classical-Greek texts. To some extent, as Rattansi has suggested, Newton was searching for "anticipations of his own work in the writings of the ancients." But, more fundamentally, he aimed at "recovering the lost Adamic knowledge," in preparation for the millennium. Above all, Newton viewed himself as the last of the prophets. As Rattansi noted, "the various fields of activity which absorbed Newton's energies over a long and prodigiously creative life were, for him, consistent with the goal of tracing and recovering the wisdom of Creation. This wisdom was manifested not only in the lost knowledge of the structure and the processes of nature, but in divine mysteries which had prefigured the course of history as it progressively disclosed God's eternal purposes."[50]

But Newton's larger life project was lost to the public. If he labored at his alchemist's furnace and hermetic texts, "he communicated virtually nothing of what he was doing." Such works, he discreetly insisted to his fellow alchemist Boyle, were not "fit to be communicated to others." Boyle too held to their "high silence," alert, as he put it, to the "political inconveniences that may ensue" upon their disclosure. Newton likewise kept secret his theological investigations. When his treatise on Athanasius mistakenly got into the hands of a French publisher, Newton entreated his friend John Locke "to stop the translation and impression as soon as he could, for he designed to suppress them." Newton did well to be cautious. His successor as Lucasian professor, William Whiston, was later forced out of his position because of his declared rejection of the trinitarian doctrine. In addition to keeping his vast alchemical and theological work from public view, Newton engaged in careful self-censorship of his published works in order to avoid any suspicion of underlying heterodox opinion. As David Kubrin has shown, Newton re-edited portions of his *Optics* and the *Principia*, to avoid all hints of animistic assumptions or cosmogonic speculation. "Religion and philosophy are to be preserved distinct," wrote Newton. "We are not to introduce divine revelation into Philosophy, nor philosophical opinions into religion." "The uncomfortable similarity between some of his notions and those associated with radical religious and political ideologies," Kubrin suggests, "made it necessary for Newton to construct a body of philosophy that was deceptively one-sided and which conveyed only a part of his real vision." Thus "the specific social and political environment in which he lived—with its tremendous anxiety over radical political and religious movements—[encouraged] Newton to hide some of his most important ideas." That same anxiety encouraged him to stay away from women.[51]

"Ever since his nineteenth year [when he entered Cambridge], Newton had been confined to the company of males," his biographer Gale Christianson noted. "So far as is known, the only woman he saw regularly was his aged housekeeper." "Isaac Newton died a virgin," Frank E. Manuel, another Newton biographer, concluded. "The verdict would be upheld in an English court of law on the word of two witnesses—an elderly relative to whom he confided when already advanced in years that he had never violated chastity and who whispered intelligence of his moral victory to the poet Thomas Maude, and Dr. Richard Mead, his attending physician and friend, interrogated on the subject by Voltaire, who proclaimed it to the world." There are a number of probable explanations for Newton's self-imposed isolation from women and sexuality. Like the monk Peter Damian, the misogynous Gregorian reformer of the eleventh century, Newton felt abandoned by his mother early in life. His father had died before he was born, and when he was two his mother remarried and moved with her new husband to another town, leaving Isaac to be raised by relatives. She returned only following the death of her second husband, by which time Newton was eleven. It has been suggested that perhaps this early trauma contributed to Newton's distrust of women.[52]

Whatever his personal psychological proclivities, Newton's thirty years in the all-male environment of Cambridge University was certainly an indelibly formative experience. The university culture was by Elizabethan statute a world without women. There were, of course, no female students or professors; women were not permitted even to cross the threshold of this male sanctuary; and fellows were required to remain celibate. Following his graduation, Newton remained here as a fellow and then a professor for three decades. According to Manuel, "he inhabited a monastic cell at Trinity," the only Cambridge college with a true cloister (Thomas Neville's Great Court). "Newton lived there by his own rule, albeit a stricter regimen than prevailed in many a religious order. . . . The few accounts of Newton's behavior during the Cambridge period when his genius was most productive speak of an indifference to bodily needs and a divorcement from the world which, though hardly equal to the asceticism of mystics in the desert, had something of their denial of the flesh in a holy service. . . . The solitude of Isaac Newton . . . was rarely broken." In the light of Newton's patently monastic existence, there is some irony in his stalwart opposition to the abortive effort of the papist King James II to admit the Benedictine monk Alban Francis as a master of arts at Cambridge University. Despite Anglican statutes against the admission of members of regular orders to the universities, the monks had never really left. Newton labored in his cell much in the manner of the regular clergy, not far from the site where the monks of Ely had long before established their school for novitiates.[53]

Newton's asceticism was also no doubt reinforced by his strong personal identification with the Paracelsian magi and the ancient prophets, both of whom embraced the celibate ascetic life as an essential self-purifying aid to enlightenment. "Philosophical alchemy had a traditional morality and code of behavior not unlike that of the pious Puritans," Manuel pointed out, "and its asceticism was appreciated by Newton." Newton's understandable paranoia about his secret alchemical and theological obsessions certainly contributed even more to the inward turn of his life, now fully sanctioned by the new scientific ascetic ideal embodied by his alchemical collaborator Robert Boyle. At the same time, Newton's heroic public quest to illuminate the divine mathematical order of the universe served not only to mask his private preoccupations but also to facilitate his self-control. Newton had nothing but scorn for the hapless monks whose rigors of self-denial only ignited in their minds "apparitions of women . . . and of the Devil tempting them to lust." The only true "way to chastity," Newton insisted, "is not to struggle with incontinent thoughts but to avert the thoughts by some imployment [*sic*]." Thus, as Easlea noted, "for Newton, natural philosophy was the means of escape from women, carnality, and lust."[54]

Finally, Newton's ready identification of women with the devil well reflected not only the monastic inheritance of the academic culture but the contemporary identification of women with witchcraft and heresy. In the throes of his nervous breakdown of 1693, Newton, in a famous fit of feverish paranoia, lashed out at his friend John Locke for allegedly attempting to "embroil [him] with woemen [*sic*]," chiding him, " 'twere better if you were dead." The proximate reason for Newton's breakdown, aside from the stress of his work, the cumulative weight of his double life, and the accidental burning of a valuable manuscript, was his romantic involvement with Fatio de Duillier, a passion that momentarily rent his armor and rendered him vulnerable. The object of this singular affection was a young Swiss genius and fellow alchemist, enthusiast, and scientist, who had himself taken a vow of celibacy. According to Manuel, Newton's correspondence with Fatio "is touched with more earnest concern than he ever showed for any other human being." In Christianson's view, this correspondence, "with its lavish praise, requited loneliness at separation, and melancholy swings of mood"—distinctly reminiscent of the letters of Robert Grosseteste and Adam Marsh—"bears haunting overtones of an ill-fated romance." Apparently this relationship too fell prey to Newton's paranoia. As Christianson explained, "the final break itself appears to have been prefigured in their agonizing desire to share the same chambers, a desire quite possibly overridden by the fear of what might happen if they were to attempt it." Thus Newton pulled back from Fatio for "fear of further emotional involvement." Fatio thereupon joined up with the Prophets, a radical religious sect, and was eventually persecuted and prosecuted. Newton, meanwhile, utterly abandoned Fatio in his hour of trial, loath to "jeopardize his hard-won reputation by identifying himself in any way with a convicted enthusiast."[55]

Newton's breakdown lasted roughly a year and a half and signaled the end of his Olympian scientific creativity. His lasting recovery resulted largely from a dramatic change in his life, following his royal appointment as warden of the Mint in 1697 and his ultimate abandonment both of his Cambridge University cell and his private alchemical and theological preoccupations. "Newton's crisis," Manuel noted, "was followed by a dramatic reorganization of his personality, and a rechanneling of his capacities that enabled him to manage his existence successfully for more than three decades." In short order, Newton became master of the Mint, president of the Royal Society (from 1703 until his death in 1727), and a knight of the realm. From this point on, he turned his considerable energies outward, to achieve not only almost mythical fame but very real political power as well, in the interest of intellectual, religious, and social order. At the Mint he was responsible for the establishment of the gold standard, which lent order to the economic world for several centuries thereafter, and prosecuted to the gallows if necessary any and all counterfeiters. At the Royal Society, he imposed upon the fledgling community of science an unprecedented organization and structure; consolidating science "in one body, and under one head," he became an "autocrat" bending to his will all intellectual "insurgents." His knighthood, moreover, unprecedented for a scientist, gave "symbolic representation" to the "bond between science and the crown." In an imperial fashion,

> Newton devoted himself to the moral as well as the financial renovation of the Society, and made a ceremony of the sessions over which he presided, the first high priest of modern science officiating at its rites. His dread of disorder and tendency to ritualize his own behavior, along with his desire to imitate the elaborate manners of the great, led him to assign specific places to the officers who attended him at meetings like the members of a royal court.

Thus did the fervent revivalist transform himself into the august orthodox "dictator of the English scientific establishment." And "standing on that solid base he was apotheosized into the symbol of Western science."[56]

The deification of Newton symbolized the triumph of the mechanist philosophy as a bulwark against heterodoxy and social disorder. Within England, Newton's work was eagerly appropriated by Anglican churchmen intent upon maintaining their authority in the wake of the Glorious Revolution, which had deprived them of their exclusive religious authority. As James R. Jacob explained,

Newton's law of universal gravitation provided the mathematical demonstration of . . . God's working in the world. Here indeed was the ultimate weapon in the war against irreligion. . . . What a boon Newtonian natural philosophy turned out to be for the latitudinarians intent on preserving and advancing Church interests after the Revolution. . . . If God operated as intimately and dynamically in his world as Newton claimed he did, then the Church had a fundamental role to play in the world order, and the clergy could take a new lease on life, as the special interpreters of God's will. What the Church had lost as a result of the recent Revolution it might more than regain with Newton's help.

The Boyle lectures, established by Boyle's will and administered by John Evelyn (who "was much at Court after the Restoration") and Thomas Tenison, archbishop of Canterbury, became the chief forum for the dissemination of the new Newtonian apologetics. Here "science as interpreted by Newton and his followers offered a model of the stable, ordered, providentially guided universe." As Margaret C. Jacob has pointed out, "only in the nineteenth century did Darwinism deliver a severe blow, not to Christianity, but to science-supported and liberal Anglicanism." Thus "for nearly a century . . . Newton's science had provided the intellectual foundation for a unique version of European Protestantism, one particularly suited for the maintenance of political stability. . . ."[57]

Thus, as Frank Manuel observed, Newton, "with his extraordinary genius and energy, was able to impose on the Western world a personal scientific style and a movement that reflected his character." In the process, "Newton's early sense of the fluidity of science—the fantasies of the youth who dabbled freely in all forms of knowledge—[had] vanished with age," the range of respectable inquiry having become far more narrowly bounded. In essence, the triumph of mechanism, as Mersenne had hoped, signaled the reclericalization of natural philosophy. Earlier clerical champions of orthodoxy had strived to gain and extend their control over religion—and hence over church, state, and society—by insisting first and foremost upon their essential mediation between people and God, as theologians, churchmen, and priests. Now, in the wake of a religious and philosophical revival which had identified God with nature and had thereby afforded people a more immediate connection with God through nature itself, without clerical intervention, the re-establishment of orthodoxy required a new form of mediation between mankind and nature. This, above all, was the meaning of the so-called scientific revolution. Linked closely to religious institutions, the emergent scientific establishment constituted in effect a new layer of ecclesiastical (but increasingly lay) "clergy," interposed between mankind and nature, and thus between mankind and God.[58]

In the time-honored manner of the orthodox clergy, this new clerical caste established itself as mankind's exclusive agents for the study of nature, in the process disqualifying all others. Their natural philosophy now came to be identified with reason itself, and all others with the irrational; their knowledge was truth, all others were heresy. In their early development, the mechanical philosophers had mirrored their alchemical colleagues in looking to practical experience for insight and inspiration, even associating with artisans and craftsmen. But this proved only a moment of passage to a more sublime, and abstract, level of understanding. The appropriation of experiential knowledge was essential, but, as Bacon himself had foreordained, "man must forsake Vulcan in order to entrust himself to Minerva." Descartes tied the real progress of science to the theorists, not the practitioners. And Galileo, as Paolo Rossi has shown, "was certainly keenly aware of the fact that the elevation of a theory shifts to another level, or, as he said, 'far outweighs' the testimony and the observations of empiricists and technicians."[59]

For all the justificatory utilitarian rhetoric surrounding the emergence of science—which, as Westfall suggests, remained largely rhetoric until the nineteenth century—the essence of the new philosophy was transcendence. Artisan knowledge, like hermetic knowledge, alchemical knowledge, prophetic revelation, and popular magic, was imperfect, even subversive, knowledge. By design, the mechanization of nature, the abstraction of mind from matter, and the mathematical reconstruction of natural phenomena disqualified as inadequate (and possibly dangerous) all other modes of thought, yielding the desired means of escape from the unruly particulars of time and place, person and experience: a depoliticized, impersonal, disembodied, universal, absolute, and authoritative—God-like—knowledge, perfectly suited to ascetic clerical purpose. What the fourth-century church historian Eusebius said of the then ascendant orthodox ascetic clergy might well have been said of this new clergy of science: that they are "above nature, and beyond common human living. Like some celestial beings, [they] gaze down upon human life, performing the duty of a priesthood to Almighty God for the whole race."[60]

Indicative of this at once transcendent and conservative clerical resurgence was a remarkable Royal Society campaign to reform language itself, that it might better serve and reflect the new orthodoxy. As David Kubrin has demonstrated, the clerics and scientists viewed language as "the source of thinking and feeling," and thus believed that, "if language can be toned down, so too can peoples' [sic] ideas and passions." Among the leaders of this effort were John Wilkins, founder of the Royal Society and bishop of Chester, who in 1668 published his *Essay Towards a Real Character and a Philosophical Language*, and his son-in-law John Tillotson, who became the archbishop of Canterbury. As Kubrin explained, "the target of this campaign was, once more, 'enthusisam' [sic], which was seen to be encouraged by the use of figurative or visionary language." Thus "prose was lauded as truthful, poetry as fanciful, 'romantic,' worthless if not downright subversive. Even a prose which indulged in metaphoric and figurative language was suspect." The proponents of reform "eagerly sought languages containing only words which were direct reflections of concrete reality, and nothing else"; they "tried to reduce language to a one-to-one correspondence with 'real' objects—'so many things in the same number of words' was how [Bishop Thomas] Sprat put it—so as to make virtually impossible ambiguity and nuance." In 1670, Samuel Parker, bishop of Oxford and president of Magdalen College, Oxford, went so far as to introduce a bill in Parliament "to fine all divines caught using metaphors." Such clerical and scientific efforts to reform language, however bizarre, well reflected the expansive new spirit of clerical revitalization, which was perfectly in keeping with an ancient and bold tradition. Tillotson, a leader of the effort, otherwise devoted himself to the study of fourth-century patristic writers, particularly Basil and Chrysostom; drawing upon his father's work, Parker's son published a new translation of Eusebius.[61]

As a clerical reappropriation of nature, the scientific revolution signaled the removal of women from the realm of natural philosophy. If the scientific priesthood now defined what was science, they also defined, by their example, who was science. As they disqualified some kinds of knowledge, so they disqualified some kinds of knowledge-seekers, including women. Women were readily disqualified from orthodox natural philosophy by the reassertion of clerical and academic authority, and thus by the continuation of the inherited clerical ascetic, and Aristotelian, prejudice. Once again women were identified as exaggeratedly sexual beings, intellectually inferior by nature. The campaign to reclericalize philosophy, moreover, disqualified women as harbingers of heresy, witchcraft, and religious enthusiasm. Increasingly in the eighteenth century, women were characterized as creatures more of passion than of reason, emotional, irrational, and merely intuitive by nature (psychological terms for "religious enthusiasm," "heresy," and "unaided revelation"), and hence unfit for objective science. With the advance of science, then, the clerical culture gained new territory, extending even further its world without women.[62]

The social revolutions and "enlightenment" of the eighteenth century made no difference in this regard. The universities, the chief locus of this extended church, would remain exclusively male well into the nineteenth century, and the scientific academies would hold the line against female enthusiasm until the middle of the twentieth. In the interim, as increasing political control tightened guild regulations, artisan women were steadily displaced by their male counterparts and relegated to the "domestic sphere." At the same time, scientifically trained male professionals, competing for their function, at once denigrated and appropriated their craft knowledge, notably in medicine. As science thus absorbed art, the latter, so long disdained in classical and medieval culture, attained an unprecedented new dignity: it had become "masculine." In time, activities long associated with women and slaves—production and manufacturing—would become evocative of a new masculine ethos. In the hands of the clerical scientific elite, artisan understanding was put less to pecuniary or practical purpose than to such transcendent ends as theological speculation and the construction of ingenious toys for the mechanical simulation of life. Certainly there had already been some utilitarian advantage, in navigation, metallurgy, chemistry, and the military and mechanical arts—perhaps best evidenced by the fact that, by the middle of the eighteenth century, laws against witchcraft had been replaced by laws against machine-wrecking. But another century would pass before the scientific reconstruction of the arts would begin to yield results commensurate with the cost. Only then would this decidedly masculine activity get its own name: "technology."*[63]

In 1663, in the midst of the clerical resurgence, Margaret Cavendish had seen the writing on the wall; referring to the mythical female Muses of knowledge, she said of the new breed of natural philosopher, "could it be done handsomely, they would turn them all from Females to Males; so great is grown the conseit [*sic*] of the Masculine, and the disregard of the Female Sex." By the end of the century, Englishwomen had become so marginalized that some began even to wax nostalgic for the convent, as John Evelyn had done before the Restoration. In 1694, Mary Astell unsuccessfully petitioned the court to establish a Protestant female "monastery," wherein women might gain the education they were otherwise denied. "It shall not so cut you off from the world as to hinder you from bettering and improving it," she explained to her reader, "but rather qualify you to do it the greatest Good. . . ." Noting that "a Learned Education of the Women will appear so unfashionable," she reckoned that "the Ladies, I'm sure, have no reason to dislike this Proposal, but I know not how the Men will resent it to have their enclosure broke down, and Women invited to taste of that Tree of knowledge they have so long unjustly Monopoliz'd." A half-century later, in 1727—the year of Newton's death—Madame Lambert, *salonnière* of the Hôtel de Rambouillet, mourned the passing of a momentarily different world, now irrevocably lost. "There were, in an earlier time, houses where [women] were allowed to talk and think, where the muses joined the society of the graces. The Hôtel de Rambouillet, greatly honored in the past century, has become the ridicule of ours. . . . Cannot women say to men, what right have you to be the guardians of the sciences and fine arts?"[64]

---

*The connection between a world without women and the development of modern technology is the subject of a separate study currently under way, entitled *The Masculine Millennium*. It examines the masculinization of both production and reproduction as a transcendent project inspired, in part, by an enduring vision of Eden before Eve. According to this vision, which took shape within the clerical culture and became explicit in Reformation millenarianism, men could recover from the Fall and thus restore their original perfection by overcoming, through artifice and abstraction (as well as asceticism), both the curse of toil and the liabilities of women.

Ten · *Women in a World Without Women*

T HE CLERICAL CULTURE of Western science survived as a
world without women well into the nineteenth century, despite the anticlerical promise of the eighteenth-century European Enlightenment. Only in the nineteenth century did women
begin belatedly to gain access to the universities and the mainstream
of scientific learning. The site of this revolution was the United States,
at the farthest frontier of the established order. At its heart was yet
another lay-sponsored religious revival, confirming again Hastings
Rashdall's observation on the "close connection between great educational reforms and religious movements." Moreover, the revivalist
movement, which challenged clerical authority from within religion,
was coupled with a fundamental transformation in social production,
which challenged clerical authority from without. While the religious
movement revived ancient notions of the equality of male and female
souls before God, industrial capitalism, with its neutered and disembodied conception of labor as a commodity, theoretically abolished
distinctions between male and female in the labor market. If religious
revival once again provided openings for women, this time the new
expectations and demands of capitalist production kept them open.
The nineteenth-century transformation of education and science reflected both religious and commercial developments. Evolving in parallel, together they posed an unprecedented challenge to clerical
culture and its world without women.[1]

THE EUROPEAN PERSECUTION of radical reformation sects in the
seventeenth century had driven the movement farther west, to the
frontier of the New World. From the outset, America provided fertile
soil for anticlerical religious enthusiasm. The Pilgrims of Plymouth
had themselves been anticlerical Separatists from Leiden, while their
more theocratic Massachusetts Bay neighbors were confronted almost
from the start with challenges to their clerical authority. The expulsion

of Roger Williams led to the establishment of the first Baptist church on Narragansett Bay; persecuted as Anabaptist heretics, his followers proceeded farther south, into Virginia and the Carolinas. Like so many female enthusiasts in Europe, Anne Hutchinson and her largely female following claimed to be under a "covenant of Grace" which exempted them from clerical control. Espousing an antinomian heretical faith inherited from the ancient Gnostics and Marcionites, Hutchinson staunchly defied the authority of the clergy; tried for "traducing the ministers," she was excommunicated. In 1656, two Quaker women, Mary Fisher and Ann Austin, arrived in Boston, where their books were burned and they were imprisoned for heresy. The following year, Quakers were formally banned from the colony, under penalty of death. More Quakers arrived, however, and some were indeed executed. Only later did the anticlerical Quakers find sanctuary in Pennsylvania, refuge of the radical reformation. There they were eventually joined by the myriad revivalist sects ardently recruited by William Penn to populate his new colony, including the Hutterites, Mennonites, and Moravians.[2]

The Moravians were perhaps the most active missionaries of the radical reformist German Pietists; successors to the Labadists (who had attracted Mary Merian and her daughter), the evangelical Pietists, founded by Philipp Jacob Spener, emphasized the universality of the priesthood and the equality of all believers. With historical roots in the medieval millenarian Waldensian and Anabaptist movements, the Pietists constituted "the last great surge of the . . . Reformation." Their great teacher John Comenius, the last bishop of the Moravian Brethren, was one of the first educational reformers to advocate the teaching of science in the schools, for women as well as men, and had lasting influence upon Samuel Hartlib, John Dury, and other seventeenth-century educational reformers. In the 1730s, the Moravian Church was revived as an intensely missionary organization by Count Nicolaus Zinzendorf, who established its center at Herrnhut and from there dispatched missionaries throughout the world. Pennsylvania became one of the most important Moravian missionary outposts, with its center in Bethlehem. In addition to the Moravian settlements, radical Pietists under Conrad Beissel eastablished in the 1720s the Ephrata cloister in Lancaster County, a latter-day double monastery. Gnostic in orientation, the Ephrata commune attempted to imitate the practices of the early church and drew into its rigorously ascetic fold many women who were "rebaptized into virginity" upon leaving their husbands. It was such Pietist fervor that sparked the Great Awakening in the 1730s, the first mass movement in America. During the next two decades, the revival extended with celebrated consequence into New England and elsewhere, spreading the gospel of the "new light," causing division within established church institutions, and swelling the ranks of Baptists and other evangelical enthusiasts. The Pietists also significantly contributed to evangelical religion with their conversion at Herrnhut of John Wesley, founder of the Methodists, a new sect which was to have an enduring impact upon both England and, after 1769, America. "These groups were more experimental in their theology and social practices toward women," two historians of American religion recently observed. Such groups "suggested that women might claim equal spiritual authority and even become the chosen instruments of God to preach salvation and found churches of the new millennial order. . . . Women, unequal in society, were spiritually equal before God." Predictably, therefore, "women enthusiastically responded to and participated in the renewal movements." Methodist women, in particular, "would increasingly claim the right to preach."[3]

The European Enlightenment's deistic faith in natural law and reason was no match for American revivalism. Though it greatly influenced some elite thinkers and statesmen—including the Founding Fathers—and a small number of freethinking artisans, it was easily overshadowed by much more potent evangelical energies. "Very few Americans . . . became skeptics or deists," noted Henry F. May, a historian of the American Enlightenment. The ink was barely dry on the new nation's Constitution when these energies burst anew in the Second Great Awakening. In addition to the most radical Methodists, Baptists, and Quakers, who reaped the biggest harvest from the new wave of revivals, evangelical Congregationalists and New School Presbyterians embarked upon a revival campaign that exceeded the first Great Awakening in its zeal and missionary activity. The dawning of the nineteenth century thus appeared to many as the final dawning of the millennium itself.[4]

"In the first half of the nineteenth century militant Protestant Christianity saw itself marching to the conquest of America and the World," wrote Robert Samuel Fletcher, historian of Oberlin College.

Rank on rank they advanced with flying banners: the revivalists leading the way, the missionary societies, the Bible societies, the

Sabbath reformers, the religious education and sabbath school societies, and the tract societies. Combined in the same great army,
and under the same staff were the anti-slavery societies, the peace
societies, the Seaman's Friend Society, the temperance societies,
the physiological reform and moral reform societies. Closely allied
were the educational reformers whose task it was to train a generation
for utopia. In the heavens they saw the reflection of the glorious
dawn, which was just beyond the horizon, when all men should know
Christ, should serve him in body and in spirit, and acknowledge
their universal brotherhood. The movement was to some extent
international [with the Methodists, Quakers, and Evangelicals in
England and the Société de la Morale Chrétienne in France]. . . .
But it was in America that there was the greatest hope for success.
In America all things were being made new. In America where all
was progress, development, movement and hope, in America the
Millennium seemed about to begin, to be completely achieved by
one last tremendous effort by the organized hosts of Christian reform.

This, then, was the context in which women first gained a foothold,
albeit halting and restricted, to the heretofore closed world of higher
learning.[5]

"America's non-restrictive environment permitted an unexpected
and often explosive conjunction of evangelical fervor and popular
sovereignty," Nathan O. Hatch has suggested, which fostered in the
nineteenth century an unprecedented "democratization of American
Christianity." Baptists, Methodists, Disciples of Christ, Mormons, as
well as the new black churches, all reflected a veritable "populist"
upsurge within the church, fueled by a "virulent anti-clericalism."[6]

"The popular religious movements of the early republic articulated
a profoundly democratic spirit," Hatch explained. "First, they denied
the age-old distinction that set the clergy apart as a separated order of
men, and they refused to defer to learned theologians and traditional
orthodoxies. . . . Second, these movements empowered ordinary
people by taking their deepest spiritual impulses at face value rather
than subjecting them to the scrutiny of orthodox doctrine and the
frowns of respectable clergymen." Thus "potent strains of anti-clericalism welled up within the bounds of the church, challenging the
right of any special order to mediate the gospel. This virulent anti-
clericalism resembled the kinds of dissent that were endemic to Protestants from the English Civil War through the Great Awakening. . . .

Yet forms of anti-clericalism at the end of the eighteenth century gained sharper focus and broader appeal." "All of these movements," Hatch emphasized, "challenged common people to take religious destiny into their own hands, to think for themselves, to oppose centralized authority, and the elevation of the clergy as a separate order of men." In a Connecticut pamphlet of 1811, such sentiment was put to verse, "Aimed for the Final Destruction of Priestcraft":

> Why are we in such slavery, to men of that degree;
> Bound to support their knavery when we might all be free;
> They'r nothing but a canker, we can with boldness say;
> So let us hoist the anchor, let priest-craft float away.[7]

In its religious aspect, then, early-nineteenth-century America was remarkably reminiscent of earlier periods of Christian revival, going back to the dawn of Christianity itself. "The first third of the nineteenth century experienced a period of religious ferment, chaos, and originality unmatched in American history," Hatch noted, but its significance transcended merely an American reference. It was "a period of chaos and originality unmatched, perhaps, since the religious turbulence of seventeenth century England," Hatch suggested. As in earlier periods of religious upheaval, "wandering prophets appeared dramatically, supremely heterodox religious movements gained followings . . . and new and passionate causes sprang up within the church's walls." "The democratic winnowing of the church produced not just pluralism but also striking diversity," Hatch wrote; "religious options in the early republic seemed unlimited." In his view, "Christendom had probably not witnessed a comparable period of religious upheaval since the Reformation."[8]

Like the earlier episodes of religious ferment, this revival too spawned a movement for popular education. The new "democratic" Christianity posed a powerful challenge to the "clerical monopoly over learning" in that it was, by definition, "intellectually open to all." "Insurgent religious leaders," Hatch argued, "were not so much anti-intellectual as intent upon destroying the monopoly of classically educated and university-trained clergymen." Thus the religious movements "opened educational and leadership opportunities to common people." In the process, the increased diversity of religious organization and practice reawakened ancient possibilities for women.[9]

The crucial part played by women in the nineteenth-century American awakening, long noted by historians, has recently been confirmed in detail by Mary Ryan. In her close study of the religious ferment in Oneida County, the wellspring of the legendary revivals of Upstate New York, Ryan has described how "for nearly twenty years the women of Utica carefully prepared the soil" for the later campaigns, igniting a veritable "women's awakening" within the larger religious movement. In a manner strikingly reminiscent of early-Christian experience, Ryan observed, "the religious history of Oneida County contains hints of evangelical disregard for the distinctions of sex." Thus Deborah Pierce, from the nearby town of Paris, demanded that men "remove the yoke from my sisters' necks," and called upon other women to preach the gospel with her. Martha Howell likewise "toured the environs of Utica preaching against the practice of infant baptism." "Women were more than the majority of converts," Ryan wrote, "more even than the private guardians of Americans' souls. The combination and consequence of all these roles left the imprint of a women's awakening on American society as well as on American religion."[10]

In a similar vein, Barbara Epstein suggested that the early-nineteenth-century American revivals were, in essence, "female revivals" in which "women may have gained the confidence to explore issues that in a male-dominated atmosphere they would have left dormant." She pointed out that "women often regarded revivals . . . as victories, though they were careful to point out that in scoring such triumphs they were acting only as agents of Christ and not for themselves." "In many families," she found, "revivalism became a focus of conflict in which were at stake not only divergent religious convictions but also a woman's relative power in the family. . . ." Clerical critics of revival, echoing the alarms of Tertullian a millennium and a half earlier, observed such female temerity with grave concern. "A minister who opposed the revival in his town," Epstein recorded, "wrote that as a result of it 'there are many men who begin to doubt whether they hold that place in their houses, and in the affection and regard of their wives and daughters, which, by nature, by law and by gospel, belongs to them.' " This was no idle concern.[11]

In 1818, a New England schoolteacher named Nancy Towle experienced spiritual conversion and resolved to "put my hand to the Gospel plough, never more to turn again." She became an indefatigable itinerant preacher, traveling some fifteen thousand miles over the next ten years. Her memoirs chronicle her encounters with "a score of women preachers among Christians, Freewill Baptists, Universalists and Methodists," and she unceasingly "called for more female laborers in the Gospel harvestfield." Convinced that "the preaching of the Gospel by females was justifiable," she turned her back on "country and kindred" and proclaimed defiantly, "with the fond paternal roof, I now renounce you once for all."[12]

As in the past, religious revival held great appeal for women, because it defied the authority and misogynous precepts of the all-male clerical hierarchy, broke down social barriers between devout men and women, and enabled women to come to the fore on their own behalf to challenge existing institutions, on appeal to a higher authority. The evangelical ethos of spiritual equality before God translated readily into a call for greater social equality, including access to higher education. It is no mere accident, for instance, that pioneer women's-rights advocates Susan B. Anthony, Lucretia Mott, Elizabeth Chace, and Angelina and Sarah Grimke were all Quakers. (Elizabeth Cady Stanton reserved her most scathing criticism for the clergy, declaring that "our strongest enemies entrench themselves in the church.") The early-American pioneers of higher education for women, as founders of women's colleges and champions of coeducation, were imbued with a similar anticlerical spirit.[13]

The Quakers were among the first sects to establish schools for boys and girls together. As Thomas Woody pointed out, "the Friends accepted, in a most complete sense, the idea of equality of all men, inasmuch as they held that in all there dwelt a measure of the divine. All possessed the 'inner light,' whether male or female. And since men became ministers of the 'word' without the classical education obtained in the ecclesiastical colleges of the day, so also did women." The Quakers provided for the education of their own leadership, including women, and thus the Friends' coeducational schools later gave rise to coeducational colleges (among them Earlham, established as a college in 1859, and Swarthmore). The Moravians were likewise in the forefront of women's education, following the teachings of Comenius, who held that women were as capable as men. In 1742, Countess Benigna Zinzendorf opened a boarding school in Germantown which was subsequently moved to Bethlehem. For the first four decades, enrollment was restricted to Brethren, but in 1785 a sister institution was founded for women, the Moravian College for Women, which influenced the opening of the Young Ladies Academy of Philadelphia two years later. In 1794, another Moravian school for women was established at Lititz, Pennsylvania, and another, in 1802, in Salem, North Carolina.[14]

"In the nineteenth century there arose many prominent, influential schools [for women] that soon eclipsed the meagre record of the eighteenth," Woody noted, and these too were largely the product of "religious zeal." In their recent history of coeducation in American public schools, David Tyack and Elisabeth Hansot pointed out that

> in the nineteenth century, many advocates of the education of women were activists in the evangelical religious movements that swept the nation in the first half of the nineteenth century. Religious doctrine sanctified their cause and legitimated a more active role for women in the churches, in social reform, and in education. It was inconceivable that women, whose souls were thought to be immortal, like those of men, and who exercised a formative influence on their children and their husbands, should not share in the benefits of schooling.

Joseph Emerson was a fervent evangelical Congregationalist whose school at Byfield (and later Saugus, Massachusetts) became a training ground for the pioneers of women's education. He was the "teacher and inspirer" of Zilpah Grant, founder of the Adams Female Seminary; Mary Lyon, founder of Mount Holyoke—usually recognized as the first bona-fide college for women; and Alice Welch Cowles, first head of the Female Department at Oberlin—the first true coeducational institution of higher learning. According to Woody, Emerson emphasized the virtues of "practical education" and "foresaw the day when higher institutions for the education of women would be regarded as necessary as colleges for men." In addition to his essays on women's education, Emerson produced *The Evangelical Primer*. "His constant aim was, first of all, to fill the hearts of the pupils with reverence for the laws of God, whether revealed in the Scriptures or discovered by reason." Emma Willard, founder of the Troy Seminary for women and a staunch advocate of women's education, also betrayed a deeply religious purpose. In her "Plan for Improving Female Education," submitted to the New York Legislature in 1819, she emphasized that "a regular attention to religious duties would, of course, be required of the pupils by the laws of the institution. The trustees would be careful to appoint no instructors who would not teach religion and morality, both by their example, and by leading the minds of the pupils to perceive that these constitute the true end of all education." In the section on "Suitable Instruction," "Religious and Moral" is the first category. "Our highest responsibility is to God, and our highest interest is to please him," Willard wrote. "Therefore to secure this interest should our education be directed." Willard's sister, Mrs. Phelps, founder of the Ellicott Mills seminary in Maryland, was similarly inspired.[15]

Catherine Beecher, daughter of the evangelist Lyman Beecher, shared a sense of religious mission with her brother Henry Ward Beecher and her sister Harriet Beecher Stowe. Like Willard, she was intent upon securing higher education for women so that they might become teachers, and established the Hartford Academy for that purpose. She viewed teaching in decidedly missionary terms, describing her disciples as "missionary teachers" whose task it was to bring religion from the East to "the newly settled and ignorant sections of the West and the South." In her 1835 "Essay on the Education of Female Teachers," Beecher stressed above all the importance of "moral and religious education" as a bulwark against the "disenthralled intellect" of the skeptic.[16]

If Willard and Beecher viewed the education of women as a religious mission, Mary Lyon of Mount Holyoke saw it as a veritable crusade. Perhaps more than any other pioneer of higher education for women, Lyon embodied the evangelical fervor of her age. She was raised a Baptist and worshipped with her father in the meetinghouse he had founded in Ashfield, Massachusetts. It was through her contact with Joseph Emerson at Byfield, however, that Mary Lyon became truly devoted to a religious calling. Of Emerson's influence, she wrote to her mother in 1821, "such a spirit of piety is mingled with all Mr. Emerson's instructions, that the one thing needful is daily impressed on our minds." The following year, she became a member of the Congregational Church, and soon thereafter joined Zilpah Grant, another zealous evangelist, as her assistant at the Adams Female Seminary. After that, she established her own schools, first at Ipswich and then at Mount Holyoke.[17]

"Though religion played a prominent role in the life of most schools of the early part of the last century," Woody pointed out, "there is no exaggeration in saying that at Mount Holyoke there was probably more personal religious fervor than in any other single institution. Miss Lyon was prone to regard the success of her efforts to create the school as sealing a covenant with God for the advancement of His Kingdom." Here more than anywhere else religious instruction took the form of a "fervid missionary activity." Lyon devoted nearly half of her own salary to missionary work and urged her teachers and pupils to do likewise. In her 1832 plan for "New England Female Seminary for Teachers," her earliest appeal for support of the new school, she stressed at the outset that "its religious character is to be strictly evangelical." In an 1835 pamphlet, she declared that "the grand features of this Institution are to be an elevated standard of science, literature, and refinement, and a moderate standard of expense; all to be guided and modified by the spirit of the gospel. Here we trust will be found a delightful spot for those whose heart has stirred them up to use all their talents in the great work of serving their generation and of advancing the Redeemer's Kingdom."[18]

She wrote two years later in her "Principles and Design of the Mt. Holyoke Female Seminary,"

> this institution is sacredly consecrated to the great Head of the church. . . . [It] seeks to lay the foundation strong, on which, under God, the Temple, with all its increasing weight, is to rise, and be sustained, and to secure it from injury and decay. It looks abroad on a world lying in wickedness. It beholds with painful interest the slow progress of these United States in carrying the blessings of salvation to the two hundred millions, who are the estimated proportion of the inhabitants of this benighted world to be converted to God through our instrumentality.

Hence, she proclaimed,

> [we] consecrate this beloved Institution . . . to the Lord, to be devoted forever to his service. . . . The donors and benefactors of this Institution, with its trustees and teachers, have felt a united obligation to seek, in behalf of this beloved Seminary, first the kingdom of God and his righteousness. Endeavors have been made to raise the funds and to lay the whole foundation on Christian principles, to organize a school and form a family that from day to day might illustrate the precepts and spirit of the gospel. Public worship, the Bible lesson, and other appropriate duties of the Sabbath, a regular observance of secret devotion, suitable attention to religious instruction and social prayer meetings, and the maintaining of a consistent Christian deportment, are considered the most important objects of regard, for both teachers and scholars. The friends of this seminary have sought that this might be a spot where souls shall be born of God. . . .[19]

Just as the revivalist spirit pervaded this earliest of women's colleges, so too did it inspire the earliest experiment in collegiate coeducation, Oberlin. Oberlin's founder, John Jay Shipherd, underwent a religious conversion following a near-fatal acident in 1819 and came to believe that he had been called to preach the gospel. (His father, a lawyer and politician, had likewise become an enthusiastic follower of the revivalist Charles G. Finney, a future Oberlin president.) Shipherd moved west with the revival movement and settled in the Western Reserve. Here he established an experimental religious community modeled upon the earlier Oneida experiment, emphasizing manual labor and piety. Shipherd conceived the idea of "Oberlin Institute" in 1832, the same year Mary Lyon had envisioned Mount Holyoke, and he did so along the same evangelical lines. His first prospectus, written the following year, echoed Lyon: "The plan for this Seminary was projected in July, 1832. It owes its origins to the following facts. The growing millions of the Mississippi Valley are perishing through want of well qualified ministers and teachers, and the Great Head of the Church has latterly inclined multitudes of youth to preach his gospel and train the rising generation for his service; but his people have not yet adequately provided for their education. In view of these facts the founders of Oberlin Institute . . . resolved to rise and build."[20]

Oberlin was not merely a product of revival, it was "the embodiment of the movement." "Nowhere else was the vision quite so clearly seen," wrote Oberlin's official historian. "Nowhere else was consecration to the great cause quite so complete and fervent. And from the Oberlin center went out an influence whose power is beyond estimation, through the thousands of young men and women educated in the Institute, through publications like the Oberlin Quarterly and the Oberlin Evangelist, and through the preaching of [Presidents Asa] Mahan and Finney." First and foremost, Oberlin was a religious school. "You are not only educated, but educated in God's College," President Finney told the graduating class of 1851, "a college reared under God, and for God, by the faith, the prayers, the toils and the sacrifices of God's people. You cannot but know that it has been the sole purpose of the founders and patrons of this College to educate here men and women for God and for God's cause." Under Finney's influence, the spirit of revival was maintained at Oberlin for thirty years, along with coeducation. (Finney's revivals had been renowned for their "irregular methods," including "the active participation of women." Of the forty female students who announced their future intentions in 1836, nearly half had resolved to become missionaries. "Hot from the fires built by Finney," Fletcher recounted, "students . . . went to nearby settlements, to the East, to the Far West, to the West Indies, and to Africa to kindle new flames and finally, it was hoped, to set the world ablaze for Christ."[21]

From the outset, Shipherd had insisted upon education for women as well as men. In his oft-quoted 1834 circular, he declared that one of the prominent objects "of the school shall be the elevation of the female character, bringing within the reach of the misjudged and neglected sex, all the instructive privileges which hitherto have unreasonably distinguished the leading sex from theirs." At Oberlin, moreover, Fletcher noted, "the merely ornamental accomplishments, much emphasized in some female seminaries, were frowned upon. . . . Young women were to be educated primarily for 'future usefulness,' i.e. for the salvation of the world and the establishment of the Millennium." Toward this end, a Female Department was established under the direction, first, of Mrs. Cowles, another disciple of Joseph Emerson, and, thereafter, of Marianne Parker Dascomb, a former student of Zilpah Grant and Mary Lyon. "Oberlin's peculiar contribution to female education," Fletcher noted, "was the admission of young ladies to the complete college course and 'joint education of the sexes' for students of college grade." When women students attended some of the first college classes in 1834, Fletcher pointed out, "for the first time college students shared their classrooms and class instruction with women." By the following year, women constituted a quarter of the college enrollment, and by 1841 three women had received the A.B. degree, according to Fletcher, "the first bona fide college degrees ever granted to women."[22]

Coeducation constituted "an important part of the Oberlin Gospel," distinguishing its mission from that of the medieval "monastic" institutions against which it relentlessly railed. In 1836, the faculty wholeheartedly endorsed the institute's policy of "associating the sexes— which lies at the basis of the very idea of human society; which God himself has inserted in its structure . . . and the exceptions to which, as in the case of monasteries and nunneries have been attended with unparalleled and most disgusting licentiousness." A writer in the Oberlin *Evangelist* in 1854 harked back to the virtue of the study circles of early Christianity in defense of coeducation. "Similar studies, common recitations, the daily measuring of mental strength, conduce greatly to the practical impression on each sex that the other are to be held and deemed as intellectual and social beings. The relation of beau and belle is in good measure displaced by the more healthful one of fellow student. The idea that the young lady is a toy or a plaything is very thoroughly exploded by the practical working of intellectual competition on the College race ground—to say nothing of the influence of that higher nobler Christian life, in which united efforts for the salvation of souls deeply engross the heart." "Brothers in the monastic Colleges we pity you," wrote another defender of coeducation in an 1860 *University Quarterly* article. "The day of deliverance dawns. . . . Women are to be educated because we choose civilization rather than barbarism."[23]

Through the pioneering efforts of Oberlin and Mount Holyoke, religious revival paved the way for the establishment of both collegiate coeducation and colleges for women. Other evangelically inspired institutions soon followed Oberlin's coeducational example, among them the Quaker colleges of Earlham and Swarthmore, and the Methodist Wesleyan and Boston universities. At the same time, Mount Holyoke had a profound influence upon the development of other colleges for women, such as Wellesley in Massachusetts, the Michigan Seminary at Kalamazoo, and Mills College in California (which was established to do "for the West what Mt. Holyoke Seminary does for the East"). Nowhere was this influence greater than at Wellesley, which carried the revivalist inspiration of women's education well into the latter half of the nineteenth century.[24]

Wellesley founder Henry Durant received his early-childhood education first from an aunt who had been a pupil and great admirer of Mary Lyon and then from Mrs. Samuel Ripley, a self-taught teacher in Waltham. He went on to become a very prominent Boston lawyer and successful businessman. The traumatic early deaths of his only daughter and only son broke his spirit, however, and he underwent a religious conversion, becoming a fervent "disciple of Christ." According to his biographer, "his religious experience was henceforth his life." At the suggestion of a friend, he tried his hand at preaching, only to be scoffed at by the established clergy. He thus became an evangelist. "Once [he was] launched upon his labors as an evangelist," one contemporary recounted, "we quickly came to recognize in Mr. Durant a type of speaker not met with since the days of Finney." Perhaps influenced by fond recollections of his childhood teachers, Durant eventually resolved to devote his evangelical energies and

considerable fortune to the promotion of women's education. Inspired
most of all by Mount Holyoke, Durant in 1871 proposed to establish
the Wellesley Female Seminary (renamed Wellesley College in 1873)
on his family's country estate.[25]

"The great object we have in view," Durant wrote in 1871, "is the
appropriation and consecration of our country place and other property
to the service of the Lord Jesus Christ, by creating a Seminary on the
plan (modified by circumstance) of South Hadley [Mount Holyoke]."
(That same year, Durant became a Mount Holyoke trustee, and his
wife gave Mount Holyoke the foundation grant for its library building.) In her inscription of the dedicatory Bible buried at the site of
the first excavation for Wellesley College, Mrs. Durant wrote: "this
building is humbly dedicated to our Heavenly Father with the hope
and prayer that He may always be first in everything in this institution." Echoing Finney at Oberlin, her husband solemnly declared
that "this is God's college." According to article I of the Wellesley
College statutes,

> the College was founded for the glory of God and the service of the
> Lord Jesus Christ by the education and culture of woman. To realize
> this design it is required that every trustee shall be a member in
> good standing of some evangelical church; that every teacher shall
> be of a decided Christian character and influence, and in manifest
> sympathy with the religious spirit and aim with which the College
> was founded; and that the study of the sacred Scriptures by every
> student shall extend over the first three years. . . .[26]

Durant declared that "Wellesley College offers to young women
opportunities for education equivalent to those provided at Harvard
[his own alma mater] and the other leading educational institutions in
the land for young men." In keeping with his deep faith in the equal
abilities of women, Durant insisted upon a female faculty, which was
drawn largely from Mount Holyoke and Oberlin. All the while, he
insisted upon the paramount religious significance of the enterprise,
which he spelled out in his sermon to the first Wellesley class. Durant
noted,

> the Wellesley College plan of education may properly be made a
> lesson for the Sabbath Day because it is religious throughout. . . .
> The Higher Education of Women is one of the great world battle-
> cries for freedom; for right against might. It is the cry of the op-

pressed slave. It is the assertion of absolute equality. The war is
sacred, because it is the war of Christ against the principalities and
powers of sin, against spiritual wickedness in high places. . . . You
mistake altogether the significance of the movement of which you
are a part, if you think this is simply the question of a College
education for girls. . . . The higher education is but putting on
God's armor for the contest. . . . The one vital question of the
morning is: God first in the higher education of women. God first
in Wellesley College . . . Our strength is to come from union with
the Lord. . . . We must have God within our lives.

It was such revivalist spirit as this which gave rise to the epochal
movement for women's education. Resonating with a resolute anti-
clericalism, it challenged head-on the womanless world of the established ecclesiastical institutions of higher learning. This challenge was
perhaps nowhere more clearly spelled out than in Wellesley College's
own defiant motto: *"Non ministrari, sed ministrare"*—"Not to be minis-
tered to, but to minister."[27]

Just as religious enthusiasm generated new opportunities for women
in higher education, so it also fostered anew an intense interest in
science as an aid to revelation and salvation. In his study of nineteenth-century American science, Ronald L. Numbers observed that
there was a "prevailing . . . harmony between science and religion in
the antebellum period," which fostered a "doxological science, . . .
science pursued for the glorification of God." If piety occupied a
central place in the curriculum and vision of educational reformers,
so too did the study of nature. "Learning pleads for woman to bring
her energies and her charms to its exalted cause," Charles Burroughs
wrote in his spirited 1828 call for women's education in the *American
Journal of Education*. "Religion pleads for woman, that she may be
guided by its cheering light, and adorned with its precious ornament;
that she may be admitted to the temple of its sublime doctrines
and holy truths, to its chambers, decked with curious and glorious
workmanship by the hand of God. Science pleads for woman, to open
before her susceptible mind the mysterious and splendid exhibitions
of omniscience and infinite benevolence in the works of nature."
Reminiscent of the pious purpose of earlier religiously inspired women
of science, such as Maria Merian, the female pioneers of women's
education waxed eloquent about how natural philosophy might bring
them and their pupils closer to God.[28]

Emma Willard, Almira Phelps, and Mary Lyon all attended the lectures in chemistry offered at Troy by Amos Eaton, founder of the Rensselaer Polytechnic Institute. At her Troy Seminary, Willard introduced the study of mathematics, physiology, and physics. "A knowledge of natural philosophy," she wrote, "is calculated to heighten the moral taste, by bringing to view the majesty and beauty of order and design, and to enliven piety, by enabling the mind more clearly to perceive, throughout the manifold works of God, that wisdom, in which he hath made them all." Willard's sister Almira Hart Lincoln (later Phelps), an educational reformer in her own right and also the author of widely successful textbooks on chemistry, botany, and natural philosophy, sought also to introduce more science into the women's curriculum. "Especially does geology afford important aid to religion by confirming the truth of revelation," wrote Phelps. "Infidels are confounded by the undeniable truth, that as the structure of the earth is investigated, and the secrets of its interior brought to light, the strictest coincidence is observed, between them, and the facts recorded in Scripture." Such a decidedly religious approach to science was by no means atypical. In support of her views, Phelps quoted Benjamin Silliman (the elder), professor of chemistry at Yale: " 'I believe,' says Professor Silliman, 'the period is not far distant, when geology will be admitted into the train of her elder sister, astronomy, and that both will be eventually hailed as the friends and allies of revealed religion.' " Historian Margaret Rossiter has suggested that Phelps' religious orientation contributed immeasurably to the success of her textbooks. "Although [Phelps] also stated that the discipline of studying science would be good training for [young women's] minds, her stress on science's value in increasing their respect for nature and bringing them closer to God probably accounts for her books' wide popularity."[29]

Mary Lyon was also greatly inspired by Eaton's lectures at Troy, boarded with his family for a summer, and developed a lifelong interest in science, which she made the core of the curriculum at Mount Holyoke. She herself lectured in chemistry and performed laboratory experiments. Her approach to science was also profoundly religious, and in this she was inspired and encouraged by her true scientific mentor, Edward Hitchcock, professor of natural theology and geology, and later president of Amherst. Lyon had also boarded with Hitchcock and his family, and he became one of her closest advisers and, after her death, her biographer. In addition to his more technical works, Hitchcock was the author of several books on the religious significance of science, among them *Religious Truth, Illustrated from Science* (1857) and *The Religion of Geology* (1852). "The grand features of this Institution," Lyon wrote of her seminary, "are to be an elevated standard of science, literature, and refinement . . . all to be guided and modified by the spirit of the gospel."[30]

At Oberlin too the study of science was imbued with deep religious purpose. As had the study circles and double monasteries of old, here coeducation brought men and women together in chaste companionship to gain knowledge of God and do his service. "The day of deliverance dawns," the *University Quarterly* announced in 1860. "It is our happy experience, of a quarter century's growth, that it is better for both sexes to travel together along the paths of science." In his sermon to the first class at Wellesley, where science was also at the center of the curriculum (Wellesley set up the country's second laboratory for experiments in physics, after MIT), Durant bitterly derided the "modern self-styled educator" who claims "that all true, scientific education must be forever divorced from religion." "Now it is a joy to maintain—right in the face of this unreason and prejudice," Durant declared, "that education without religion is a rayless night without a star—a dead world without a sun."[31]

"Few people viewed science and religion as enemies before the Civil War," Ann Braude has recently pointed out. And if the intimate connection between religious enthusiasm and science challenged traditional notions about who constituted science, it also raised anew questions about what constituted science. In her intriguing study of the relationship between spiritualism and the women's-rights movement, Braude has demonstrated that spiritualism—communication with the dead through (mostly female) mediums—was widely considered " 'scientific' evidence of religious truth" in the mid-nineteenth century, no less scientific than telegraphy. Spiritualism appealed greatly to women—including many of the pioneers of the women's-rights movement (dissident Quakers formed the core of both movements)—not only as a powerful means of autonomous female expression but also as science in the service of religion. In Braude's apt description, "the American women's rights movement drew its first breaths in an atmosphere alive with rumors of angels." The same could be said of the related movement for women's access to education and science.[32]

BUT IF RELIGIOUS ENTHUSIASM initially ignited the movement which began finally to pry open the world without women, another major force added the necessary fuel to the fire and caused it to spread. Had this force not existed, the time-hardened clerical culture might well have survived intact yet another intense but ultimately unsuccessful assault. This other force was capitalist enterprise, increasingly dependent upon a reliable trained work force and a ready supply of useful knowledge which could be put to productive and pecuniary advantage. To meet these twin demands, the new self-consciously "revolutionary" masters of industry began in the early nineteenth century to try to turn the country's institutions of higher learning to their gainful purpose. They pressured the established institutions to create schools of industrial science, founded new technical institutions devoted to such purpose, and supported popular "democratic" efforts to develop public institutions for training in the useful arts—all the while railing vehemently against the backwardness of the established clerical and "monastic" institutions. In the process, the new educational reformers eventually widened further the breaches in the academic fortifications, enabling women more readily to enter (especially through the new portals of scientific education). In their quest for a disciplined and able work force, moreover, they welcomed the enrollment of women, viewing them either as just so much more potential labor or, better, as cheaper labor (or more able mothers or educators of labor). At the same time, they sponsored evangelical revival as a means of instilling moral discipline and temperance in their new work force. Finally, they made common cause with the pioneers of women's education, lending material support to their efforts and securing in turn their considerable energies, religious and otherwise, for the battle against the "backward" institutions. It was this unlikely alliance that eventually rendered women's access to higher education and science an enduring reality.[33]

In the seventeenth century, the Baconian reformer Samuel Hartlib, inspired by the religious and pedagogical teachings of Comenius, had called for a thoroughgoing reform of educational institutions along more scientific, practical, and utilitarian lines. He emphasized training in the arts and welcomed women to the new learning. Although the effort led to the establishment of Gresham College and to the teaching of the useful arts in the dissenting academies, the vision was premature. It was not until the nineteenth century that a class of men arose with both the vision and the sufficient power to put such sweeping reforms into full effect. In the United States, the Moravian colleges, following Comenius, early emphasized the useful arts, as did Mount Holyoke and Oberlin; such practical work was viewed as a means of material support, an aid to useful learning, and a stimulus to Christian piety. But it was the industrial rather than the religious impulse that put such learning squarely on the agenda of educational reform.[34]

For the industrial pioneer, science was capital, a factor of production; its value was not theological or intellectual, or even social, but economic. What counted was not the learning itself or the wisdom thereby gained but the practical and profitable result. Science had value, therefore, only insofar as it was wedded to the useful arts or manufactures (a union later christened "technology"). In the same vein, with regard to the graduate of the schools, these reformers desired not "laborious thinkers, but thinking laborers." In their view, the function of higher education should be the creation and distribution of useful knowledge and knowledgeable people—both of which could be bought and sold, patented and contracted, and applied to the pursuit of wealth, power, and further industrial development (called "progress"). In the vision of the industrialists, the primary functions of the schools were to be applied scientific research and the education of a work force destined not for the established hierarchies but for the labor market. "Educate labor and set knowledge to work" became a familiar cry of these reformers.[35]

This bold yet prosaic educational vision was predictably greeted with derision and disdain by the established institutions. Some wealthy industrialists attempted to force, or bribe, the universities into setting up courses or schools of industrial science, at Harvard, Columbia, Yale, Dartmouth, and the University of Pennsylvania. But these enterprises, embedded as they were in a hostile environment, were hardly true to the purposes of the benefactors, at least initially. "Where can we send those who intend to devote themselves to the practical applications of science?" the New England mill owner Abbott Lawrence asked Harvard in 1847. But Harvard was reluctant to move in such a patently practical direction, assigning most of the Lawrence funds for a school of industrial science to the zoologist Louis Agassiz. In the face of such resistance from the established institutions, the industrial-educational reformers, like the pioneers of women's education, resolved to set up their own.[36]

"I have established a school in Troy," Amos Eaton declared in 1824, in a letter he wrote on his patron's behalf, "for the purpose of instructing persons in the application of science to the common purposes of life." Thus, with the backing of Troy capitalist Stephen van Rensselaer, Eaton created the first engineering school in the United States (aside from West Point), Rensselaer Polytechnic Institute. The 1826 brochure of the new institution boldly proclaimed that the school "promises nothing but experimental science. . . . Its object is simple and unique, and nothing is taught at the school but those branches which have a direct application to the 'business of living.' " Eaton plainly had nothing but contempt for the clerics of the established institutions, whom his RPI colleague Samuel Warren dismissed as a "crew of disreputable divinities." It was the RPI graduate Eben Horsford who urged Lawrence to set up the scientific school at Harvard. The practical failure of that effort led to the establishment of a separate institution down the road, the Massachusetts Institute of Technology, which was likewise dedicated, as its motto indicated, to the practical-minded linking of "*mens et manus*," head and hand. The name of the new institution—"technology"—was proposed by Jacob Bigelow, the physician who first introduced the word in its modern usage in his 1826 *Elements of Technology*, to indicate that the study of science would here be directed toward decidedly utilitarian ends.[37]

MIT's school of industrial science opened in 1865. At the same time, the new orientation in higher education was given a decisive assist with the passage of the Morrill Act in 1862. Acknowledging the growing need for industrial knowledge and labor, and the democratic demand for education, this landmark legislation granted federal aid to the states for the support of colleges dedicated to the advancement of the practical agricultural and mechanic arts. In the first decade following passage of the act, the number of engineering schools jumped from six to seventy. Subsequent federal and state legislation in support of agricultural-extension and engineering-experiment stations strengthened further the connection between the worlds of learning and industry, between the study, the laboratory, the workshop, and the counting house. In relatively short order, therefore, higher learning in America had undergone a profound transformation. If the traditional course of study, clerical and classical, remained at the heart of the curriculum—the career path traveled by those men destined for the clergy and the law—a new space had now been created for more utilitarian inquiry and for those who would take their knowledge to the market. It was here that women made their earliest advance upon the established institutions.

Just as they were ahead of their time in their quest for a more practical scientific education, so the seventeenth-century reformers Comenius and Hartlib were out front in their advocacy of education for women. Hartlib's collaborator John Dury decried the "monkish constitutions and customs" of the established universities and insisted that equal education for women would enable them "to follow lawful callings for profitable use." But the proposals of such reformers had no more effect in their own time than had other such calls for women's education, from Hrotswitha to Christine de Pisan, from Cornelius Agrippa to Mary Astell to Mary Wollstonecraft. And the visions of nineteenth-century pioneers of women's education would no doubt have faced a similar fate had it not been for the emergence of a new class of science-minded industrialists whose view of education was expansive enough to include women. Evangelical religious fervor, much less democratic political ferment, though vital to the new movement, could never have been in and of itself decisive. In the end, it was industry that laid the material conditions and industrialists who shaped the ideological outlook of educational reform.[38]

From the beginning, the campaign for women's education reflected such industrial, as well as religious, motivation. Women, after all, were the mainstay of manufacturers in the age of household production, and they became a significant proportion of the industrial work force as well. By the time the factory system became firmly established in mid-century, in textiles, women constituted a third of the new industrial work force. At the same time, the growing limits on readily available land and the resulting postponement of marriage by sons of this still predominantly agrarian society created its correlate of "superfluous women," socially and economically adrift without husbands and a burden on their parents. Thus employers' eagerness to hire women at cheaper wages corresponded with women's own demands for independent employment. In the 1840s, reflecting both interests, legislation was passed in Massachusetts, New York, and Connecticut—all birthplaces of women's education—granting even married women the right to earn and keep their own wages (rather than give them to their spouses). The new social space of the market was thus viewed by women reformers and industrialists alike as the arena of social progress. Likewise, as science was identified as a vehicle of industrial prosperity, so women came to view it not only as a means of revelation and salvation but also as a preparation for labor and hence freedom and equality. If their call to science reflected their equality with men in the eyes of God, it also signaled their potential equality with men in the eyes of employers and the new society they represented.[39]

"The cry of 'give us labor' was raised especially in behalf of these 'superfluous women,' " Woody noted. The feminist reformer Caroline Dall became convinced that woman's status as a human being now depended upon her ability to produce goods and services, to buy and sell property. "Why be educated if not to labor?" she asked. "Why labor if not to acquire capital of some sort—including money, the great motive power. . . . Now I should rejoice to see a large Lowell Mill wholly owned and operated by women." Three decades later, Julia Tutweiler of Alabama wondered, in a similar vein, "in what way shall we make available the vast unused capital of womanly intellect and energy that now in defiance of all the precepts of political economy is going to waste among us? I answer, by the technical education of our surplus women." "I would give to all girls equal intellectual and industrial training with boys," declared another writer on the subject of "What Shall We Do with Our Daughters?" Such sentiments were shared by the early champions of women's education. It is hardly an exaggeration to suggest that the advocates of higher education for women and the promoters of higher education for industry marched arm in arm, despite their deeper differences, under the same banners of progress and science, as well as religion, and against the same entrenched enemies.[40]

This historic convergence was to a greater or lesser extent embodied by those pioneers of women's education who sought to upgrade the quality of the Jacksonian academies, which already reflected the aspirations of farmers and mechanics. Catherine Beecher aimed to secure for her pupils "a liberal education and remunerative employment." She focused her attention upon the creation of a cadre of scientifically educated teachers who would be prepared to educate new generations for the dawning industrial society. Emma Willard, Almira Hart Phelps, and Mary Lyon were all indelibly inspired along the same lines by their scientific mentor Amos Eaton, founder of RPI. According to one biographer, Eaton "wandered through the New England states and New York like a religious evangelist," preaching the truths of natural science. A "devout Christian," he placed equal emphasis upon "the study of the Word and of the Works of the Creator." This latter-

day Jerome found his itinerant lectures attended "mainly by ladies."
Indeed, he became a firm proponent of education for women as well
as for industry, and he decried the "monkish policy of the Dark
Ages" which characterized the established universities. He originally
intended that RPI would be open to women from the outset. (His
letter of 1824 explicitly proposed instruction for both "sons and daughters.") Although this did not happen, for reasons that remain obscure,
Eaton in his private capacity offered courses for women in chemistry
and natural philosophy. It was thus that he tutored Willard, Phelps,
and Lyon and subsequently assisted Willard in establishing the scientific curriculum for her nearby Troy Academy. For Eaton the purpose
of such instruction was industrial as well as religious. "The education
of all girls," he wrote, "should be adapted to some useful employment." Emphasizing the teaching of mathematics, chemistry, zool-
ogy, and botany, he proposed that women should do all the "light
operations required in manufactories" and that they alone should be
the teachers of boys and girls.[41]

Elmira College, which claimed to be the first women's college
proper (Mount Holyoke was called a "seminary" until the 1880s), was
founded in 1852 by Simeon Benjamin, a promoter of canals, railroads,
and industry. Here too emphasis was placed upon practical education
for useful employment. It was at the encouragement of Elmira's President Cowles, a former Oberlin professor, that Matthew Vassar decided
to found Vassar College. (Vassar considered Cowles "our most eminent practical educator.") Vassar was a brewing magnate at a time
when there were many women working in the breweries of Pough-
keepsie. Milo Jewett, a veteran educator of women whom Vassar had
recruited to be the college's first president, early fell out of the
founder's favor and was succeeded by J. H. Raymond, who actually
set up the college and the curriculum. Significantly, Raymond brought
to the task nine years' experience as the founding president of Brooklyn Polytechnic Institute, one of the premier institutions pioneering
in utilitarian scientific education. At Brooklyn Polytechnic, Raymond,
in his own words, sought "to adjust a complete system of education
to the actual present necessities of the public, rather than to abstract
philosophical ideals or the antiquated models of former times." "A
large proportion of those who attended the Institute," he pointed out,
"desired an education which should fit them for mercantile rather
than professional life."[42]

Predictably, as Mabel Newcomer noted, from the outset "Vassar was oriented toward science, as were the other women's colleges of the time." Fully half of the professors were in scientific fields, and the college's equipment for teaching science was among the best in the country, even compared with that of men's institutions. "What work, what profession does science offer to women?" asked Mary W. Whitney of Vassar's first graduating class. "A large number of young women in our colleges go out into the world and earn their own living, and the number is likely to increase. . . . A large number of young women seeking an education in our higher schools and colleges must begin to earn their living immediately upon closing the course of study. . . . The old prejudice against remunerative labor for women has not wholly died out . . . [yet] more girls join the worthy ranks of self-supporting women, who learn out of the beneficent necessity, . . . that the best living means usefulness."[43]

Smith College reflected similar tendencies. The guiding spirit behind its founding was John Morton Greene, a Hatfield pastor from whom Sophia Smith sought counsel about how to dispense her inherited fortune. Greene, an Amherst graduate, turned for advice to Edward Hitchcock, science educator and mentor of Mary Lyon. Predictably perhaps, Greene's first suggestion to Smith was to establish a scientific school in association with Amherst. (Smith rejected the suggestion, but Greene went ahead and included such a bequest in her will anyway, though Smith ultimately prevailed.) Greene next proposed the establishment of a women's college. "It is my opinion," he wrote in his original plan, "that by this highest and more thoroughly Christian education of women, what are called their 'wrongs' will be redressed, their wages will be adjusted, their weight of influence in reforming the evils of society will be greatly increased. . . ." "Some people are coming to feel that really women need a more complete education and preparation for the work of life. . . ." This theme was echoed in the first Circular of the College: "The chief aim of Smith College will be . . . to furnish young women with that general yet appropriate discipline of all their powers and faculties which will qualify them . . . to do the work of life for which God has made them, in any place to which in his providence they may be called." The Circular emphasized also that "all the physical sciences will be taught so as to keep pace with the scientific and material progress of the age."[44]

Henry Durant, the founder of Wellesley, was a fervent evangelist, but he was also an astute and successful "captain of industry." As a leading corporate attorney he early became associated with John H. Cheever in the New York Belting and Packing Company, pioneers in the manufacture of vulcanized rubber. He held interests in the original Goodyear patents and also advised the Goodrich Rubber Company and became a major stockholder in that firm. In addition, he invested heavily in iron and gold mines, steel production (Montauk Iron and Steel Company), and steam power (New York Steam Engine Company). If anyone embodied the convergence of the revivalist and industrial impulses which together brought about the higher education of women, it was the dedicated founder of Wellesley College. In practical terms, Durant was really the cofounder of Wellesley. Aside from his wife, who played a minor role, the other guiding spirit behind the college was Durant's closest friend, Eben Horsford, the RPI graduate who had persuaded Abbott Lawrence to establish the Lawrence Scientific School. In addition to his educational efforts, Horsford was president of the Rumford Chemical Works, a major manufacturer of industrial chemicals. (Durant, his collaborator at Wellesley, was also vice-president of the Rumford firm; at the same time, Durant was president of the St. Helena gold mine in Sonora, Mexico, while Horsford was vice-president.) Horsford, an avid industrial inventor and promoter, was U.S. commissioner at the Vienna World's Fair and chairman of the U.S. 1876 Centennial Exposition. It was Horsford above all who gave Wellesley its practical, scientific orientation, overseeing the establishment of the college's experimental laboratories, and otherwise fostering a scientific environment in which women could prepare themselves for future careers.[45]

Just as industrial motivations contributed decisively to the creation of colleges for women, so too did they foster the development of coeducation. At Oberlin, the first coeducational college, the religious emphasis upon the virtue of manual labor squared nicely with preparation for industrial employment, for women as well as men. "The sole aim will be to train them up for usefulness," John Shipherd insisted. *The First Annual Report of Oberlin Collegiate Institute* declared that "its grand object is the diffusion of useful science, sound morality, and pure religion among the growing multitudes of the Mississippi Valley." "The machine age released the daughters or sisters of doctors, ministers, teachers, farmers, small businessmen, thrifty tradesmen," Frances Horsford later wrote in her history of women at Oberlin. "By heritage and habit these girls took life in earnest. And now certain thoughtful souls were asking whether women were receiving their share of the enlarging world and whether they were being prepared for its responsibilities." In its practical orientation, Oberlin deliberately modeled itself on the so-called manual-labor schools, in particular Oneida Academy, later the Oneida Institute of Science and Industry, which combined religious instruction with the principles of science and practical training in the agricultural and mechanical arts, for women and men alike. Wealthy, pious Yankee merchants and industrialists of New York City, such as David and William Dodge, Anson Phelps, and Arthur and Lewis Tappan, had sponsored the evangelistic crusades of Charles Finney, who became professor of theology and second president of the college, and they provided the major financial backing for the new institution. The Tappan brothers, successful silk merchants, were the principal benefactors.[46]

In the 1850s, educational reformers joined with "machinists and manufacturers" to back the so-called People's College movement in Upstate New York. The curriculum of these coeducational colleges included systematic instruction in agricultural science and manufacturers as well as the liberal arts. Central College in McGrawville, a prime example, combined coeducation with a utilitarian scientific curriculum and enjoyed the enthusiastic support of women's-rights advocates Elizabeth Stanton, Lucy Stone (an Oberlin graduate), and Susan B. Anthony. It was out of this movement that Cornell University was established, on a coeducational basis. Cornell's founder was the Quaker Ezra Cornell, who had amassed his fortune developing the telegraph system with Western Union. The school's first president, Andrew Dickson White, was a director of the New York Central Railroad and a leading promoter of scientific and industrial education. He was also a staunch advocate of coeducation. (In his study of nineteenth-century feminism, William Leach points out that feminists favored such coeducational schools over women's colleges, because they felt that segregated cloisters turned the sexes in on themselves, fostering "diseases of the body" and "diseases of the imagination"; for this reason, Stanton sent her sons to Cornell.)[47]

Wesleyan University, a Methodist institution, also illustrated the close connection between coeducation and industrially oriented scientific education. Wesleyan was the first Eastern college to go coeducational, and it was also a leader in industrial science. Among the three founders of Wesleyan, Wilbur Atwater was perhaps the most influen-

tial. A German-trained chemist and promoter of scientific education—
and coeducation—he succeeded in 1873 in bringing to Wesleyan the
nation's first agricultural-experiment station and later founded the
Office of Experiment Stations of the U.S. Department of Agriculture.
At MIT, meanwhile, whose president, Francis Amasa Walker, was
another advocate of coeducation, the first woman student, Ellen S.
Richard (a Vassar graduate), was enrolled in the second class; a chemist, she later established the MIT Women's Laboratory in Chemistry.
By 1895, over 6 percent of the students were women.[48]

Such a relationship between utilitarian education and coeducation
was most significantly demonstrated in the experience of the land-
grant colleges, following passage of the Morrill Act. These new schools
of the Midwest and West, created to provide popular education in the
agricultural and mechanic arts, pioneered also in coeducation. The
universities of Iowa, Michigan, Wisconsin, California, Illinois, Kan-
sas, and Vermont were in the forefront of the coeducational movement. Between 1875 and 1900, the increase in the enrollment of
women in such schools was double that of men, and the schools
quickly became irretrievably dependent financially upon coeducation.
During the same time, moreover, women began finally to gain access
to the established men's schools, through the openings created by the
industrialists. The first women at the University of Pennsylvania, for
instance, enrolled in the Towne Scientific School, which had been
established by the manufacturer of heavy machinery. It was not without reason, therefore, that President John Vleck, of coeducational
Wesleyan University, could believe that "the progressive advancement of women . . . represented the true index of the scientific advancement of the race."[49]

In 1891, Drexel Institute of Technology opened in Philadelphia.
The founder of the new institution, banker Anthony Drexel, had
originally intended to establish a college for women. After exploring
the matter, however (including correspondence with Matthew Vassar), he opted instead for a coeducational college dedicated to science
and industry. At the dedication ceremony for the new college, the
dedicatory address was delivered by Chauncey Depew, president of
the New York Central Railroad (and college classmate and lifelong
friend of Cornell President Andrew Dickson White). Flanked on the
dais by Andrew Carnegie and Thomas Edison, Depew recounted the
role played by industry in breaking down the barriers to women's
education.

All the conservatism of centuries had crystallized about the university. Every radical effort to break up old systems and proceed upon new lines has met the combined hostility of faculty and alumni—that is, until steam, electricity, and invention hardened the conditions of competition. . . . The old education simply trained the mind. The old education gave the intellect a vast mass of information useless in the library and useless in the shop. The new trains the mind, the muscles, and the senses. . . . Our new education is a noble recognition of the needs of the youth of both sexes by placing before them the weapons and the armor for the battle of life. . . . One of the chief glories of the new education is the advantage it gives to women. It recognizes and enforces their equal rights to every intellectual and industrial opportunity which schools or colleges can give to men. . . . Our boasted progress has known neither age nor sex. . . . It is through the power they acquire here, in institutions like this, that women will be able to fight for and win their rights.[50]

In the wake of the evangelical and industrial assault upon the clerical bastions of American higher education, women began once again to join together with men in the pursuit of higher learning. They traveled this path as companions before Christ, before Christ in science, or before science alone (as a new kind of quasi-religious calling in and of itself). As the exalted virgins of old had been, they were more often than not expected in this new role to become "like men" and were required (now unlike their male counterparts) to lead a celibate life, leaving behind their (reproductive) lives as women for a more transcendent existence. But for many of these women, as for so many of their angelic ancestors, such dire costs were offset by a new freedom and the potential rewards of their calling. Thus, as the ranks of female university students swelled in the second half of the nineteenth century, so too did female participation in science. Certainly there were many constraints yet to be overcome on the kinds and degree of female participation in science, as Margaret Rossiter has amply demonstrated. But in light of the epoch-making gains already made, these appeared readily surmountable in time, as women continued to make their presence known and felt.[51]

Such confidence reflected not only a reassuring sense of momentum but also a real weakening of clerical influence. Anticlerical revivalism may have momentarily waned in the latter decades of the century, but so too did clericalism itself, and more permanently. By 1835, the law had already begun to rival the clergy as the career choice of graduates at Yale, Bowdoin, Brown, and Dartmouth, and the appeal of a religious career continued to decline throughout the century. At Williams, graduates joining the ministry dropped from 50 percent in 1826 to 20 percent in 1846 to 15 percent in 1866. At Yale, the proportion of graduates choosing clerical careers declined by half between 1821 and 1861. "Nor was the curve at these two institutions atypical," Burton J. Bledstein pointed out. "The combined figures for 37 representative colleges and universities showed that the ministry fell as a professional choice among graduates from 30% in 1820 to 20% in 1860. In contrast, the law held its own throughout the period, at first ranking below the ministry and then surpassing it. By 1860, commercial pursuits had risen most dramatically as a professional choice of graduates, placing only slightly below the law and the ministry." At the same time, a naturalistic deism, implicit in the work of Newton and explicit in that of Darwin, subtly shifted the dominant metaphysical focus of intellectuals from acts of God to the inherent logic of his works, from revelation of divine truth to the natural laws of the universe, evolution, society, and the market—all to be apprehended not by theology but by science, in the service of the new order. Industrially minded educational reformers such as Cornell's Andrew Dickson White sought to divorce science and education from any narrow religious orthodoxy, albeit within a larger, decidedly Christian framework, in order better to integrate them with the needs of the emergent order. In the process, they created the enduring myth of a history of "warfare" between religion and science. Thus, as the revivalist threat to clericalism from within religion diminished, the challenge from without widened dramatically. The spread of popular scientific lectures and literature kindled an unprecedented belief in scientific deliverance and a mass infatuation with invention—the makings of a different kind of religion—which fostered, among other things, the great expansion of higher education dedicated to improvements in the useful arts. In this sense, the gains made by women were but part of a broader effort to infuse the emergent industrial order with something of a republican spirit.[52]

BY THE END of the nineteenth century, the epochal changes first beheld in the New World began to take hold in the Old, as women haltingly gained access to the educational citadels of Europe. In the United States, meanwhile, the vacuum in ideological authority left by the relative decline in the prestige and influence of the clergy began to be filled by the newly organized professionals of science. Between 1876 and 1890, many of the new professional scientific (and engineering) societies were founded, including the American Chemical Society, the American Society of Naturalists, the Geological Society of America, the American Physical Society, and the American Mathematical Society, as well as the American Society of Civil Engineers, the American Society of Mechanical Engineers, and the American Institute of Electrical Engineers. As the nineteenth century came to a close, the new professionals undertook to refashion the universities, and science itself, in their own more exclusive, and exclusively male, image.[53]

The rise of the engineering and scientific professions paralleled the increasing consolidation of control over science and technology by the industrial corporation, which in turn transformed the nature of higher education. By the time Chauncey Depew, in his Drexel Institute address, proclaimed the expansive emancipatory promise of industrial progress, that promise had already begun to fade, as the presence of Edison and Carnegie on the dais mutely symbolized. In the closing decades of the nineteenth century, entrepreneurial artisans and lone inventors had given way to salaried employees and bureaucratic researchers, as scientific inquiry became an organized part of corporate operations and universities were increasingly integrated as research and training centers within the corporate industrial structure. The latter development rendered explicit the commodity orientation of the new higher education. "An educational institution resembles, in some respects, a manufacturing concern . . . ," declared Frederick Bishop, secretary of the Society for the Promotion of Engineering Education and dean of engineering at the University of Pittsburgh. "The good produced must be of such design, finish, material, etc. as to satisfy its patrons; likewise the graduates of educational institutions must meet the requirements of the concerns which are to employ them." The educational outlook of such employers was made clear by the director of training at Westinghouse, one of the leaders of the new wave of corporate educational reform. "We do not underrate knowledge and training but we want the graduates to be of use. We want men who can see the situation and fit themselves to it. The outcome depends upon the ability of the man for harmonizing himself

with his environment and the more complete and efficient this adjust-
ment the more useful the life. [College students must learn] to work
first for the success of the corporation, and only secondarily to consider
themselves, . . . to subordinate their own ideas and beliefs to the
wishes and desires of their superiors. Self-forgetfulness is what is
required."[54]

This change in the focus and objectives of higher education did not
go unnoticed by women, who had only just recently gained a first
foothold in the academy. In her *Reminiscences*, Catherine Beecher
decried "the fact that there is no university in the United States the
intellectual interests of which are managed by the professors, but
always by a corporation outside"—usually composed exclusively of
men. One particularly astute critic of the limits placed upon women's
potential by the new "commodity coeducation" was Anne Allinson,
writing from the perspective of the women's colleges. Allinson understood that women, though having gained entry into this new industri-
alized education, still remained at the margins of learned society.
"That technical education may be a desirable supplement to college
training we are not interested in denying," Allinson allowed, "but
that the four precious years of 'liberal pursuits' should be intruded
upon is an educational blunder of the first magnitude. Yet the intrusion
is stealthily made. Sweetness and light are unmarketable commodi-
ties." Allinson acknowledged that her "moralistic plea does not disregard the fact that many girls in this vast country will need later to
apply their powers to self-support." But, she noted insightfully, "the
world itself, for all its clamour, unconsciously demands something
better than mechanical equipment, for it gives its largest prizes,
whether of position or of favor, to those who possess a personal power
that is not the outcome of 'practical courses'. . . . Perhaps [men]
exercise a late revenge in offering the apple of 'practical knowledge'
to the Eves in their Garden."[55]

The commoditization of higher education was at first resisted but
later reinforced by the new professions of science and engineering,
especially as their organizations became dominated by corporate func-
tionaries and consultants. Professionalization itself, meanwhile, reflected an elite consolidation of control over the scientific enterprise
through its restrictive monitoring of the qualifications of entrants to
the fields and the imposition of its standards of acceptable training,
practice, and performance. Advanced degrees and professional career
positions in teaching and research came increasingly to mark the

"true" professional scientist and distinguish him from the popular crowd of amateurs. At the same time, the new "research universities," which were built upon such professional notions of scientific education and practice, became the "new ideal type" for higher education.[56]

Predictably perhaps, the professionalization of science increasingly restricted women to the margins of the enterprise. In 1882, Vassar's Mary Whitney felt compelled to acknowledge that the promise of earlier years was not being so readily fulfilled as she and other pioneers of women's scientific education had expected. "We are forced to admit that, in spite of the wonderful enlightenment of opinion which the last half century has produced in the public mind in reference to women's ability and position, there is still considerable unreadiness to believe that in the higher professions she either can or will make herself as proficient as a man." It appeared indeed that "women's education in science took them only to the vestibule of the Temple," not to its inner sanctum. Once again the world of science was becoming a world without women.[57]

The new obstacles confronted by women in science were not unique to science but, rather, reflected a more general academic and professional backlash against the advances of women. In 1873, the Harvard physician Edward H. Clarke had published his popular book *Sex in Education*, which asserted that women's health, and especially their reproductive capability, suffered as a consequence of the mental strains required by higher learning. Clarke's book, together with countless other medical treatises on women's inherent weaknesses and tendencies toward hysteria, brought to the fore unspoken but deep-seated anxieties about women's incursions into heretofore male enclaves. Such a climate of fear threw advocates of coeducation onto the defensive for over a decade. At Wesleyan coeducation was eliminated altogether, at MIT women's enrollment fell off precipitously, at Harvard and Columbia women's "coordinate colleges" were established to pre-empt and prevent coeducation, while within established coeducational institutions women found themselves increasingly ghettoized and marginalized. In a manner reminiscent of the monastic horror of insatiable female lust, the students at Amherst College vigorously decried the advance being made upon their academic citadel by female "thirsty knowledge seekers." (Catholic education, meanwhile, remained unmoved by the coeducation movement. "False also and harmful to Christian education is the so-called method of 'coeducation,'" Pope Pius XI declared in a 1929 Encyclical. "There is not in nature itself, which fashions the two quite different in organism, in temperament, in ability, anything to suggest that there can be or ought to be promiscuity, and much less equality, in the training of the two sexes.")[58]

Professionalization likewise mirrored the intense status anxieties of middle-class careerists, insecure in an unstable world, threatened by a menacing array of alien immigrant cultures, intensifying class warfare, aggressive industrial appropriations of knowledge and power, popular encroachments upon their inherited preserves and prerogatives, and grave economic uncertainty. Just as the leaders of the orthodox clergy of the fourth century or the founders of the scientific academies in the seventeenth anxiously strove to formalize their position and legitimize their authority through a process of exclusion, distancing themselves from any and all who might jeopardize their elite respectability, the professionals of the nineteenth century strove nervously to forge for themselves a similarly exclusive, exalted, and unassailable social identity. As in the earlier episodes, this entailed, among other things, a renewed distance from the undisciplined enthusiasm, impassioned iconoclasm, and supposed latent hysteria of women.[59]

Historian Margaret Rossiter, in her pathbreaking book *Women Scientists in America*, has recounted in great detail the "defeminization" of science in the wake of professionalization. In the 1880s and '90s, "in the midst of upgrading themselves into nationwide 'professional' societies by excluding or diminishing the influence of persons perceived pejoratively as 'mere amateurs,'" scientific organizations increasingly shunned women or relegated them to the unseen periphery of science. "An influx of women who rarely held important positions in science, if at all, usually was seen in these years as a threat to a group's precarious 'prestige' and triggered an intense discussion of the need to 'raise standards' for membership. Since the concepts of prestige, status, and professionalism were at the time closely intertwined with that of masculinity, the new membership requirements that were introduced . . . were often deliberately harder on women than on men. . . . [The] response to women's desire to join scientific societies [was] to relegate them to a secondary level of membership . . . , to exclude them for an extended period of time . . . , [or] to retreat to the higher ground of a more exclusive, more highly 'professional' (and so almost totally masculine) society." "In fact," Rossiter pointed out, "the very word *professional* was in some contexts a synonym for an all-masculine and so high-status organization." "By the 1890's," Rossiter found, "such defeminized national professional organizations had become the norm" in most scientific fields, including psychology, mathematics, the biological sciences, and physics. Moreover, "the highly qualified women who did belong to these professional scientific societies, including even those who held office in them, often felt ill at ease and unsure of their welcome."[60]

Women in science were caught in a "Sisyphean dilemma." Though they had apparently increased their opportunities over earlier times,

> many new barriers had arisen even faster than the best women of the time could scramble over them. They could thus in all sincerity think that women were making many important "advances" only to discover a few years later that it had all been a cruel illusion—that the men had moved so much higher than they that their "progress" was by contrast virtual stagnation or possibly even regression. The coming of professionalism in the 1880s and 1890s had contained and circumscribed the women and restricted them to the fringes of science, almost as far from the real involvement and leadership as they had been decades before, when they had to work through their fathers and brothers. . . . The main thrust of science was passing them by.[61]

Ideologically and culturally, this new "main thrust of science" was all too familiar. As professional scientists legitimized themselves as society's sole authorities in the understanding of life, nature, and the cosmos (and a now largely unspoken God), they assumed the "clerical" mantle of secular society. Displacing the now diminished clergy at center stage, they nevertheless carried forward their predecessors' proclivities for a world without women. Such a future was suggested, as its past was invoked, at the "Misogynist Dinner of the American Chemical Society." This remarkable affair was hosted in the summer of 1880 by two of its most prominent members, Henry Morton, president of the Stevens Institute of Technology and secretary of the Franklin Institute, and Thomas Sperry Hunt, professor at MIT and fellow of the Royal Society. Both were "leading figures in nineteenth century chemistry, founders and early officers of the American Chemical Society, respected and distinguished men with impeccable scientific, scholarly, and social credentials." The event was attended by the male members of the ACS, one of the first and largest of the new professional scientific societies, and the proceedings were duly recorded and published. According to this record, the evening was spent in song and merriment at the expense of women. One of the final recitations of the evening, appropriately enough, was "The Temptation of Saint Anthony." With such verse the brave new men of science betrayed their monastic heritage and its lingering legacy.

> *There are many devils that walk this world—*
> *Devils large and devils small;*
> *Devils so meagre and devils so stout;*
> *Devils with horn and devils without;*
> *Sly devils that go with their tails upcurled;*
> *Bold devils that carry them quite unfurled;*
> *Meek devils and devils that brawl;*
> *Serious devils and laughing devils;*
> *Imps for churches and imps for revels;*
> *Devils uncouth and devils polite;*
> *Devils black and devils white;*
> *Devils foolish and devils wise—*
> *But a laughing woman with two bright eyes*
> is the Worst Devil of All.[62]

Epilogue

THE WORD "SCIENTIST" first appeared in a review of a scientific book written by a woman. William Whewell, master of Trinity College, coined the new word in 1834 in his glowing, albeit anonymous, review of Mary Somerville's *On The Connection of the Physical Sciences*. Somerville tried to establish some underlying unifying principles and hence a common identity for practitioners in the various fields of natural philosophy. Whewell proposed the term "scientist" in the same spirit, to fulfill what he believed to be a pressing need; he noted that the members of the recently established British Association for the Advancement of Science had felt themselves handicapped "by the want of any name by which we can designate the students of knowledge of the material world collectively. . . . There was no general term by which these gentlemen could describe themselves with reference to their pursuits." As Whewell assumed, and Somerville understood all too well, this new collective identity, like the word invented to name it, had a decidedly masculine aspect.[1]

Mary Somerville was a self-taught master of mathematics and natural science who became "the premier scientific lady of the ages," her long life (1780–1872) spanning the great European epoch of political and industrial revolution. Although well born, she received little in the way of formal education and, despite her private intellectual ambitions, was early destined for the domestic life of wife and mother. But the death of her first husband left her the means and some leisure to advance her avid self-education, and the elite connections made available through her second marriage brought her into intimate association with the leading figures of nineteenth-century science. "Science was not yet professionalized," her biographer Elizabeth Patterson pointed out. "At that date no formal course of training had yet been designed or prescribed, and scientific men—safe from economic or professional threat from women—were cordially welcoming to serious students be they male or female." At the same time, there was a growing interest among scientific circles in the widest possible dissemination of the so-called useful knowledge needed by industry.[2]

Somerville conducted her own scientific investigations and wrote widely on scientific matters. A commission from Henry Brougham, founder of the Society for Diffusing Useful Knowledge, led to her greatest triumph; with her book *Celestial Mechanism of the Heavens* she rendered the mathematics and astronomy of the French philosopher Laplace accessible to the English and thereby helped to bring the then lagging British mathematics up to the more advanced French standards. In recognition of this achievement, Somerville was awarded a civil-list pension; her book was made a standard text for advanced students at Cambridge University—"the highest honour I ever received," Somerville wrote in her memoirs; and a bust of her was commissioned and put on prominent display by the Royal Society (still the only bust of a woman ever owned by the society). She became an honorary member of the Royal Astronomical Society, and there was also mounted on her behalf an ultimately unsuccessful effort to make her a member of the Cambridge Philosophical Society. Somerville continued her scientific labors up to the time of her death at the age of ninety-two, producing works of distinction and immense popularity. Throughout her career, she received many awards and honors, among them the coveted Victoria gold medal of the Royal Geological Society. Upon her death, the *Morning Post*, in its lengthy obituary, dubbed her the "queen of science." When colleges for women were finally established at Oxford, one bore her name.[3]

But, like so many women before and after her, Somerville understood all too well the gendered boundaries of science. Her book was used as a required text in a university in which she could not teach nor have her daughters study. Her bronze likeness was placed in the Royal Society's Great Hall, from which she herself was barred. (Although her nonscientist husband early became a fellow of the Royal Society, no such honor was ever even contemplated for her.) The mother of two talented daughters (as well as a son), and acutely conscious of the obstacles that had early blocked her own path because of her sex, Mary Somerville was a staunch advocate of women's rights and, especially, of higher education for women. Hers was the first signature on the parliamentary petition drawn up in 1868 by John Stuart Mill to demand voting rights for women, and in 1862 she unsuccessfully petitioned the University of London to offer examinations and grant diplomas to women. "Age has not abated my zeal," she wrote late in life, "for the emancipation of my sex from the unreasonable prejudice too prevalent in Great Britain against a literary and scientific education for women."[4]

Mary Somerville lived to see women educated in science at the University of London and elsewhere. But she continued to fear that the world of science would nevertheless remain in its essence a world without women. For she had herself internalized, albeit in a mirrored female form, the prejudices of this strange clerical culture now a thousand years in the making. In the second draft of her memoirs, written in the final years of her life, this celebrated "queen of science" poignantly betrayed her despair about what she believed were the true prospects of women among the heavenly host of Western science. "I have perseverance and intelligence, but no genius," she wrote. "That spark from heaven is not granted to the sex, we are of the earth, earthy, whether higher powers may be allotted to us in another existence God knows, original genius in science at least is hopeless in this." Her despair haunts us still.[5]

With the grace of God, and in the absence of women, the self-anointed apostles of science continue to extend their heavenly rule over earth. Despite its utilitarian rhetoric, and abundantly apparent consequences, science has carried forth what has been essentially a transcendent enterprise. For, in the eyes of its exclusively male inhabitants, the clerical culture always existed above and apart from society. It was a spiritual redoubt from within which the clergy could judge and guide the rest of humanity—as it were, from outside. In such a rarefied realm, masculinity readily came to be associated with separation and transcendence, manifested in the seemingly unambiguous authority of artifice and abstraction. The more "earthy" feminine, meanwhile, was disdained as disorder, dreaded as the embodiment of worldly corruption.

As an extension of clerical culture, Western science inherited and perpetuated such associations, which continue to mark the scientific mission and milieu. In what specific ways these associations have actually shaped scientific thought is now a matter of serious speculation, and the present study can offer only some suggestions. Several habits and characteristics of modern science have often been noted: the strict separation of subject and object, the priority of the objective over the subjective, the depersonalized and seemingly disembodied discourse, the elevation of the abstract over the concrete, the asocial self-identity of the scientist, the total commitment to the calling, the fundamental incompatibility between scientific career and family life, and, of course, the alienation from and dread of women with which this study opened. To what extent do these contemporary characteristics and habits of science betray its clerical legacy? To what extent might the overriding scientific obsession with infallible universal knowledge and artificial instrumentality reflect a long-standing clerical effort to subdue the feminine in society and nature, in order to effect man's recovery from the Fall—"as if he had never sinned"?

Such a bold quest was depicted, as yet without equal, by Mary Shelley in her science-fiction novel, *Frankenstein*; she aptly rooted its passion and excitement in male loneliness, desperation, and horror. Shelley understood also that the scientist's fear of female disorder and corruption fueled the effort not only to subdue the feminine but to substitute for it something more reliable, and hence more reliably masculine. Ironically, this effort, which entailed an appropriation by the male of female functions, produced for the scientist an even more ambiguous gender identity. Whereas in the early years of Christianity devout women "became" men, in later years, in the absence of women and in an effort to replicate their essential productive and reproductive functions, men "became" women. In this process of appropriation, moreover, they gradually but indelibly transformed beyond recognition these heretofore female functions of production and reproduction.[6]

In the Middle Ages, productive labor was generally associated with women, identified with the distaff and viewed with disdain. Women were the mainstay of the "inner economy" of the household and performed much of the labor essential to survival: food preparation, baking, brewing, animal husbandry, water portage, home repairs, horticulture, and, of course, spinning, sewing, and weaving, and other tasks involved in the production of clothing. In addition, women managed the property and worked the fields alongside their husbands (or alone, in their absence). Women were thus central to medieval economic life. What was true of the family economy of the laity was true also of that of the married clergy. Not only did the married clergy seek economically advantageous liaisons with propertied women, they depended upon the routine labor of their wives for their very survival. If in their preaching they rhetorically extolled the virtues of manual labor, in their own households they lived by the hands of their women. Thus, as David Hèrlihy noted, in clerical families too "women had assumed economic functions of central importance." It is no wonder, then, that the ecclesiastical campaign for clerical celibacy was so vigorously resisted: it posed a fundamental threat to the economic life of the clergy.[7]

At Vercelli, Ravenna, and Verona in the tenth century, as the campaign for celibacy intensified, married priests ordered to give up their wives insisted repeatedly that "unless they were maintained by the hands of their women they would succumb to hunger and nakedness." The medieval monasticization of the church, which swelled the ranks of the celibate regular orders and at the same time divorced the secular clergy from their traditional labor supply, compelled multitudes of men to do the work of women. Confronted with this dire prospect, they began almost at once to devise mechanical substitutes for human labor, giving rise to what has been called the "industrial revolution of the Middle Ages." In their abbeys, these celibate men pioneered in the mechanization of the inner economy, replacing woman power with water power. By the twelfth century, the Cistercians, who forbade women to cross the threshold of their monasteries, were running "the most modern factories in Europe. . . . Every monastery had a model factory . . . and waterpower drove the machinery of the various industries located on its floor." Surely this medieval industrial advance reflected the Benedictine elevation (and associated masculinization) of manual labor, the shortage of available labor given the press of priestly office, as well as the manorial pursuit of profit. But perhaps it also had something to do with the exclusion of women from clerical society, the crucial first step in what would become a familiar pattern of male appropriation and transformation of women's work. "The natural movement of our industry," Auguste Comte observed in 1843, in the wake of the next industrial revolution, "tends gradually to pass to men the professions long exercised by women."[8]

The celibate clerical effort to find substitutes for the productive labor of wives was matched by the effort to find substitutes for the reproductive labor of mothers. The barrenness of the monastery prompted a prolonged and pathetic quest for maternal surrogates. As Caroline Bynum has shown, in the Middle Ages "the males who popularized maternal and feminine imagery were those who had renounced the family and the company of women." The Cistercians especially, who emphasized "the renunciation of all family ties," metaphorically replicated the family and motherhood within their all-male communities. The Cistercians, who played a key role in fostering

Mariolatry, used maternal images in describing God, Christ, and the church, as well as their bishops and abbots. In their writings, "many male figures are referred to as mother, or described as nursing, conceiving, and giving birth." Again, whereas early Christian women, like Perpetua, sometimes referred to themselves as men, here "monks sometimes call themselves women."[9]

"I will show myself a mother by love and anxious care," wrote Guerric, abbot of Igny. "You too are mothers," he assured his brothers, "of the child who has been born for you and in you, that is, since you conceived from the fear of the Lord and gave birth to the spirit of salvation." "Gentle nurse, gentle mother," Anselm of Canterbury wrote of Jesus, "who are these sons to whom you give birth and nurture if not those whom you bear and educate in the faith of Christ by your teaching?" Bernard of Clairvaux was the monk whose "use of maternal imagery for male figures is more extensive . . . than that of any other twelfth century figure." He urged his fellow abbots to "show affection as a mother would. . . . Be Gentle, let your bosoms expand with milk not swell with passion." To a departed brother he lamented, "you too were torn from my breast, cut from my womb." Like Bernard, Francis of Assisi encouraged his associates to be as mothers to their friars and, according to David Knowles, "encouraged those nearest him to address him thus."[10]

Among the clerical ascetics, maternal metaphor was matched by maternal mimicry, an ersatz procreative effort to simulate life. In the tenth century, the learned monk Gerbert, Pope Sylvester II, is said to have constructed the first of the "oracular heads," brazen devices which appeared to speak. In the early thirteenth century, the Dominican Albertus Magnus apparently spent thirty years in the construction of a "mobile robot" which could answer questions and solve problems. Albertus' contemporary the Franciscan Roger Bacon is also reputed to have constructed a speaking head and was preoccupied with the possibilities of artificial instrumentality. Bacon's mentor Bishop Grosseteste is likewise said to have spent many years making a brazen head. In the fifteenth century, Regiomontanus constructed a much-celebrated artificial eagle.[11]

This medieval enchantment with the artificial simulation of life was carried to ingenious lengths by early-modern clockmakers. In the seventeenth century, Athanasius Kircher declared that "it was possible to make a figure endowed with the power of moving its eyes, lips, and tongue and which, by emitting sounds, would give all the signs of life." Valentine Merbitz, rector of a college at Desde, "was said to have made such a 'creature' which, according to contemporary reports, could reply to questions in several languages." The clockwork contrivances apparently aroused more than mere curiosity and amusement. At the end of the seventeenth century, they were the subject of papers before the Royal Society, and a century later the Academy of Sciences of St. Petersburg offered a prize for a speaking head that could pronounce the five vowels.[12]

Certainly among the greatest of the would-be mothers of mechanism was Jacques de Vaucanson. A century after Descartes pondered the difference between the living and the mechanical, Vaucanson aimed at their seeming resolution. His celebrated mechanical duck could simulate not only a duck's movement but also the acts of drinking, digesting, and eliminating. Vaucanson also masterfully devised a mandolin player which sang and tapped its foot in time, and a piano player which moved its head to the music and appeared to be breathing. According to one student of the history of automata, Vaucanson "is said to have cherished a secret ambition to make an artificial man"; he apparently began to make a model, with heart, veins, and arteries, but died before its completion. Though Vaucanson was only one of many makers of automata, there is no evidence that any of them was a woman. Nor are there noticeably many women among their equally earnest descendants, the robot-engineers of the age of automation, whose extravagant "pseudo-maternal" efforts, as James Lighthill has described them, blindly play out the mechanized couvade ritual of industrial society. Typically portrayed as men playing God, they might perhaps more appropriately be described as men playing women.[13]

The male mothers of the Western past "were not all content with logical machines or heads of brass," or even remarkably refined mechanical androids, for that matter. As John Cohen suggested, "they dreamt of making a creature of flesh and blood." There are numerous medieval accounts of the magical conception of living creatures by men, perhaps the best known being the legend of the golem created of clay by Rabbi Low of Prague. In the sixteenth century, such fantasy took a seemingly more scientific turn in the work of Low's contemporary Paracelsus. Paracelsus argued that it was possible and not at all unnatural "that a man may be born without the natural mother." In his *De Generatione Rerum*, Paracelsus actually offered a recipe—which entailed incubating semen in horse dung—for generating the homunculus, a motherless child. This new being was "a true and living infant, having all the members of a child that is born from a woman, but much smaller."[14]

The idea of the homunculus, based upon spermist theory of conception, continued for some time to hold great attraction for men of science. As James Hillman has pointed out,

> during the seventeenth and eighteenth centur[ies] reasonable scientific men (Delpatius, Hartsoeker, Gardin, Bourget, Leeuwenhoek, Andry), while empirically studying the problems of fertility, conception, and embryology, asserted that they had seen exceedingly minute forms of men, with arms, heads and legs complete, inside the spermatozoa under the microscope. . . . We encounter a long and incredible history of theoretical misadventures and observational errors in male science regarding the physiology of reproduction. These fantastic theories and fantastic observations are not mere apprehensions, the usual and necessary mistakes on the road of scientific progress; they are recurrent deprecations of the feminine phrased in the unimpeachable, objective language of the science of the period.[15]

The new technologies of reproduction and genetics have brought us closer to this ancient dream than many of us care to think about. Already, as the diligent disciples of the monk Gregor Mendel continue methodically, if not magically, to bring their bold imaginings into being, the very word "mother" has become a scientific anachronism. "The definition of mother doesn't work with these new technologies," one practitioner recently explained; "we need to develop a new definition of the word." He might well have added: a masculine definition. *In vitro* fertilization and embryo transplant are, after all, only steps toward the artificial womb—a womb for men. After a thousand years, the obsessive scientific pursuit of a motherless child remains the telltale preoccupation of a womanless world.[16]

Notes

INTRODUCTION

1 Sandra Harding, *The Science Question in Feminism* (Ithaca, N.Y.: Cornell University Press, 1986), p. 31.

2 *Successful Women in the Sciences, Annals of the New York Academy of Sciences*, vol. 208 (March, 1973), pp. 15, 23.

3 Naomi Weisstein, "Adventures of a Woman in Science," in Sara Ruddick and Pamela Daniels, eds., *Working It Out* (New York: Pantheon, 1977), pp. 242, 44, 46; Evelyn Fox Keller, "The Anomaly of a Woman in Physics," in Ruddick and Daniels, *Working It Out*, pp. 85, 86.

4 Carolyn Merchant, *The Death of Nature* (New York: Harper & Row, 1980); Brian Easlea, *Science and Sexual Oppression: Patriarchy's Confrontation with Woman and Nature* (London: Weidenfeld and Nicolson, 1981); Brian Easlea, *Fathering the Unthinkable: Masculinity, Scientists, and the Nuclear Arms Race* (London: Pluto Press, 1983); Brian Easlea, *Witch-Hunting, Magic, and the New Philosophy* (Brighton: Harvester Press, 1980); Evelyn Fox Keller, *The Life and Work of Barbara McClintock* (New York: W. H. Freeman, 1983); Evelyn Fox Keller, *Reflections on Gender and Science* (New Haven: Yale University Press, 1985); Harding, *The Science Question in Feminism*; Londa Schiebinger, *The Mind Has No Sex? Women in the Origins of Modern Science* (Cambridge, Mass.: Harvard University Press, 1989).

5 Henry Lea, *A History of Sacerdotal Celibacy* (London: Williams and Norgate, 1907), vol. I, p. 17.

CHAPTER ONE

1 R. W. Southern, *Western Society and the Church in the Middle Ages* (New York: Penguin, 1985), p. 310; Bede, *A History of the English Church and People* (London: Penguin, 1956), pp. 218–22, 238–52, 335, 184, 187.

2 Pliny, quoted in A. Powell Davies, *The Meaning of the Dead Sea Scrolls* (New York: New American Library, 1956), p. 138; Paul, quoted in Peter Brown, *The Body in Society* (New York: Columbia University Press, 1988), p. 51.

3 Charles A. Frazee, "The Origins of Clerical Celibacy in the Western Church," *Church History*, vol. 41 (1972), p. 150; Brown, *Body in Society*, p. 44. See also David Herlihy, *Medieval Households* (Cambridge, Mass.: Harvard University Press, 1985), pp. 2–28.

4 JoAnn McNamara, "Chaste Marriage and Clerical Celibacy," in Vern Bullough and James Brundage, eds., *Sexual Practices and the Medieval Church* (Buffalo: Prometheus Books, 1982), p. 23.

5 Frazee, "Origins of Clerical Celibacy," p. 151; McNamara, "Chaste Marriage," p. 23; Henry Lea, *A History of Sacerdotal Celibacy* (London: Williams and Norgate, 1907), vol. I, pp. 13, 59; Anne Barstow, *Married Priests and the Reforming Papacy* (New York: Edwin Mellen Press, 1980), p. 1.

6 Lea, *History of Sacerdotal Celibacy*, vol. I, p. 91; Suzanne Wemple, *Women in Frankish Society* (Philadelphia: University of Pennsylvania Press, 1981), pp. 134–5.

7 Frazee, "Origins of Clerical Celibacy," p. 158; Barstow, *Married Priests*, pp. 37, 44, 31; Lea, *History of Sacerdotal Celibacy*, vol. I, p. 179.

8 Wayne Meeks, *The First Urban Christians* (New Haven: Yale University Press, 1983), pp. 70–1.

9 Ibid., pp. 179, 200; Brown, *Body in Society*, p. 50.

10 McNamara, "Chaste Marriage," p. 23.

11 Brown, *Body in Society*, pp. 140, 143, 144, 145, 146.

12 Ibid., p. 150. See also Sarah Pomeroy, "The Education of Women in the Fourth Century and in the Hellenistic Period," *American Journal of Ancient History*, vol. II (1977), pp. 51–62.

13 Brown, *Body in Society*, pp. 151–2; Pomeroy, "Education of Women," p. 61.

14 Luke 17:21; "Panel: Jesus Didn't Speak of Second Coming," Philadelphia *Inquirer*, March 6, 1989, p. A1; Brown, *Body in Society*, pp. 53, 64; Wayne Meeks, "The Image of the Androgyne," *History of Religions*, vol. 13 (February, 1974).

15 Meeks, "Androgyne," p. 206.

16 Meeks, "Androgyne," pp. 166–7; Brown, *Body in Society*, pp. 51, 31.

17 Brown, *Body in Society*, p. 61; JoAnn McNamara, *A New Song: Celibate Women in the First Three Christian Centuries* (New York: Hawthorn, 1983). See also Herlihy, *Medieval Households*, pp. 20–3; Elizabeth Clark, *Ascetic Piety and Women's Faith* (Lewiston, N.Y.: Edwin Mellen Press, 1986), p. 42.

18 McNamara, *New Song*, pp. 1, 32; Stevan Davies, *The Revolt of the Widows: The Social World of the Apocryphal Acts* (Carbondale: Southern Illinois University Press, 1980), p. 16.

19 Brown, *Body in Society*, pp. 80, 83.

20 Ibid., pp. 76, 80–81, 87–89; Clark, *Ascetic Piety*, p. 33.

21 Brown, *Body in Society*, pp. 99–101.

22 Ibid., pp. 104, 111, 119.

23 Bailey, quoted in Clark, *Ascetic Piety*, p. 265; Brown, *Body in Society*, p. 119; Clark, *Ascetic Piety*, p. 282. See also Rosemary Rader, *Breaking Boundaries: Male/Female Friendship in Early Christian Communities* (New York: Paulist Press, 1983).

24 Pierre Payer, *Sex and the Penitentials* (Toronto: University of Toronto Press, 1984), p. 46; Hans Achelis, quoted in Clark, *Ascetic Piety*, pp. 268, 566; Roger E. Reynolds, "Virgines Subintroductae in Celtic Christianity," *Harvard Theological Review*, vol. 61 (1968), pp. 547–66; McNamara, *New Song*, p. 113; McNamara, "Chaste Marriage," p. 27.

25 Brown, *Body in Society*, pp. 152, 177.

26 Ibid., pp. 167, 168.

27 Ibid., pp. 99, 168–9.

28 Ibid., pp. 169, 171.

29 Ibid., pp. 53, 372; Daniel Callam, "Clerical Continence in the Fourth Century: Three Papal Decretals," *Theological Studies*, vol. 44 (March, 1980), pp. 16, 22, 23.

30 Brown, *Body in Society*, p. 202.

31 Georges Duby, *The Knight, the Lady, and the Priest* (New York: Pantheon, 1983), pp. 108–9; Zoe Oldenbourg, *Massacre at Montségur: A History of the Albigensian Crusade* (New York: Pantheon, 1961), pp. 60–1; R. I. Moore, *The Origins of European Dissent* (Oxford: Basil Blackwell, 1977), pp. 51, 77, 88–9, 195–6, 227–8.

32 Brown, *Body in Society*, p. 208.

33 Ibid., pp. 263, 266; Clark, *Ascetic Piety*, pp. 179, 188; Jan Willem Drijvers, "Virginity

and Asceticism in Late Roman Western Elites," in Josine Blok and Peter Mason, *Sexual Asymmetry: Studies in Ancient Society* (Amsterdam: J. C. Gieben, 1987); Mary Bateson, "Origins and Early History of Double Monasteries," *Transactions of the Royal Historical Society*, vol. XIII (1899), passim.

34 Brown, *Body in Society*, pp. 244–5, 264, 244, 278, 289; Bateson, "Double Monasteries," pp. 139, 141; Herbert Workman, *The Evolution of the Monastic Ideal* (London: Epworth Press, 1927), p. 177.

35 Brown, *Body in Society*, pp. 280–1, 282.

36 Ibid., p. 342; Ross S. Kraemer, "The Conversion of Women to Ascetic Forms of Christianity," *Signs* (Winter, 1980), pp. 298–307.

37 Drijvers, "Virginity and Asceticism," pp. 241–6; Brown, *Body in Society*, pp. 366–7; Anne Yarbrough, "Christianization in the Fourth Century: The Example of Roman Writers," *Church History*, vol. 45 (1976).

38 Brown, *Body in Society*, p. 369; Clark, *Ascetic Piety*, p. 47.

39 Brown, *Body in Society*, p. 371; Eleanor Duckett, *Women and Their Letters in the Early Middle Ages* (Northampton, Mass.: Smith College Press, 1965), p. 8.

40 Augustine, quoted in Count de Montalembert, *The Monks of the West* (Boston: Marlies, Callanan and Co., 1847), vol. I, pp. 256–7.

CHAPTER TWO

1 Derek Bailey, *The Man-Woman Relation in Christian Thought* (London: Longmans, Green and Co., 1959), p. 69; Suzanne Wemple, *Women in Frankish Society* (Philadelphia: University of Pennsylvania Press, 1981), p. 149.

2 Elizabeth Clark, *Ascetic Piety and Women's Faith* (Lewiston, N.Y.: Edwin Mellen Press, 1986), p. 216; JoAnn McNamara, "Chaste Marriage and Clerical Celibacy," in Vern Bullough and James Brundage, eds., *Sexual Practices and the Medieval Church* (Buffalo: Prometheus Books, 1982), p. 21.

3 Mary Bateson, "Origins and Early History of Double Monasteries," *Transactions of the Royal Historical Society*, vol. XIII (1899), p. 138; Sharon K. Elkins, *Holy Women of Twelfth Century England* (Chapel Hill: University of North Carolina Press, 1988), p. xvii.

4 Bateson, "Double Monasteries," pp. 144, 197.

5 Ibid., p. 144; Robert H. Trone, "A Constantinopolitan Double Monastery of the Fourteenth Century," *Byzantine Studies*, vol. 10 (1983), pp. 81–7.

6 Trone, "Constantinopolitan Double Monastery," p. 82; Bateson, "Double Monasteries," p. 145; R. W. Southern, *Western Society and the Church in the Middle Ages* (New York: Penguin, 1985), p. 96.

7 David Herlihy, "Land, Family, and Women in Continental Europe," in Susan Stuard, ed., *Women in Medieval Society* (Philadelphia: University of Pennsylvania Press, 1976), pp. 13, 15, 30; Wemple, *Women in Frankish Society*, pp. 189–97; Thorstein Veblen, "The Barbarian Status of Women," *American Journal of Sociology*, vol. IV, no. 4 (1899), p. 503.

8 Herlihy, "Land, Family, and Women," pp. 25–6; David Herlihy, *Medieval Households* (Cambridge, Mass.: Harvard University Press, 1985), pp. 43, 53.

9 Jean-Michel Picard, "The Marvelous in Irish and Continental Saints' Lives of the Merovingian Period," in H. B. Clarke and Mary Brennan, eds., *Columbanus and Merovingian Monasticism* (Oxford: BAR International Series 113, 1981), p. 100; Heinrich Zimmer, *The Irish Element in Medieval Culture* (New York: G. P. Putnam's Sons, 1891), pp. 13, 129; Wemple, *Women in Frankish Society*, p. 159; Roger E. Reynolds,

"Virgines Subintroductae in Celtic Christianity," *Harvard Theological Review*, vol. 61 (1968), p. 550; Bateson, "Double Monasteries," p. 168; Herbert Workman, *The Evolution of the Monastic Ideal* (London: Epworth Press, 1927), p. 178.

10 Patrick J. McCormick, *Education of the Laity in the Early Middle Ages* (Washington, D.C.: Catholic University Press, 1912), p. 17; Zimmer, *Irish Element*, p. 14.

11 Mary Pia Heinrich, *The Canonesses and Education in the Early Middle Ages* (Washington, D.C.: Catholic University Press, 1924), pp. 90–3; Margaret MacCurtain, "The Religious Image of Woman," *The Crane Bag* (Dublin: Blackwater Press, 1980), vol. IV, no. 1, p. 539.

12 Heinrich, *Canonesses and Education*, p. 62; Wemple, *Women in Frankish Society*, pp. 159, 178.

13 Lina Eckenstein, *Women Under Monasticism* (Cambridge: Cambridge University Press, 1896), pp. 96, 100, 46, 57; Bateson, "Double Monasteries," pp. 141, 145–7; Heinrich, *Canonesses and Education*, p. 66.

14 Friedrich Prinz, "Columbanus, the Frankish Nobility, and the Territories East of the Rhine," in Clarke and Brennan, eds., *Columbanus and Merovingian Monasticism*, p. 76; Heinrich, *Canonesses and Education*, p. 50; Wemple, *Women in Frankish Society*, p. 194.

15 Wemple, *Women in Frankish Society*, pp. 159–60; Eckenstein, *Women Under Monasticism*, p. 98.

16 Bateson, "Double Monasteries," passim; Heinrich, *Canonesses and Education*, passim.

17 Bateson, "Double Monasteries," pp. 158, 662.

18 Ibid., pp. 158, 640; Heinrich, *Canonesses and Education*, pp. 87, 88, 178; McCormick, *Education of the Laity*, p. 14; Wemple, *Women in Frankish Society*, p. 177.

19 Heinrich, *Canonesses and Education*, pp. 60, 70.

20 Doris Stenton, quoted in Christine Fell, *Women in Anglo-Saxon England* (Bloomington: Indiana University Press, 1984), p. 13; Fell, *Women in Anglo-Saxon England*, pp. 56, 57, 59.

21 Ibid., pp. 61–2, 75, 94–5; Eckenstein, *Women Under Monasticism*, p. 79.

22 Angela Lucas, *Women in the Middle Ages* (London: Harvester Press, n.d.), p. 32; Joan Nicholson, "Feminae Gloriosae: Women in the Age of Bede," in Derek Baker, ed., *Medieval Women* (Oxford: Basil Blackwell, 1978), p. 21; Bateson, "Double Monasteries," p. 168.

23 Peter Levi, *The Frontiers of Paradise: A Study of Monks and Monasteries* (New York: Weidenfeld and Nicolson, 1987), pp. 100–1; Bateson, "Double Monasteries," pp. 169, 170; Alfred Clapham, *Whitby Abbey* (London: Historic Buildings and Monuments Commission for England, 1952).

24 Bateson, "Double Monasteries," p. 171; Nicholson, "Feminae Gloriosae," p. 17; Lucas, *Women in the Middle Ages*, p. 35; Heinrich, *Canonesses and Education*, p. 71; H. J. Mozans, *Women in Science* (New York: Appleton, 1913), p. 36; Helen Leibell, *Anglo-Saxon Education of Women* (New York: Burt Franklin, 1971), pp. 60–5; Eckenstein, *Women Under Monasticism*, p. 91; M. L. W. Laistner, *Thought and Letters in Western Europe, A.D. 500 to 900* (Ithaca, N.Y.: Cornell University Press, 1957), pp. 136–66.

25 Eckenstein, *Women Under Monasticism*, p. 112; Fell, *Women in Anglo-Saxon England*, p. 109; Laistner, *Thought and Letters*, pp. 136–66.

26 Nicholson, "Feminae Gloriosae," p. 27.

27 Edward Miller, *The Abbey and Bishopric of Ely* (Cambridge: Cambridge University Press, 1951), p. 14; Joan Morris, *The Lady Was a Bishop* (New York: Macmillan, 1973), p. 25; Lucas, *Women in the Middle Ages*, p. 35; C. J. Stranks, *St. Ethelreda: Queen and Abbess* (Ely, England: The Dean and Chapter of Ely, 1975); Eckenstein, *Women Under Monasticism*, p. 98.

28 Fell, *Women in Anglo-Saxon England*, pp. 111–13; Bateson, "Double Monasteries," p. 180.
29 Leibell, *Anglo-Saxon Education*, pp. 108–9; Bateson, "Double Monasteries," pp. 183–7; Wemple, *Women in Frankish Society*, pp. 177, 182.
30 Southern, *Western Society*, p. 312; Elkins, *Holy Women*, pp. 57–8; E. A. Livingstone, *The Concise Oxford Dictionary of the Christian Church* (Oxford: Oxford University Press, 1975), p. 196.
31 Elkins, *Holy Women*, pp. 89, 125, passim.
32 Ibid., pp. 125, 131, 133, 134.
33 Ibid., p. 158; Wemple, *Women in Frankish Society*, p. 192.

CHAPTER THREE

1 Elizabeth Clark, *Ascetic Piety and Women's Faith* (Lewiston, N.Y.: Edwin Mellen Press, 1986), p. 29; Robin Scroggs, "Paul and the Eschatological Woman," *Journal of the American Academy of Religion*, vol. 40 (1972), pp. 282–303; Elaine Pagels, "Paul and Women," *Journal of the American Academy of Religion*, vol. 42 (1974), pp. 548–9; Averil Cameron, "Neither Male nor Female," *Greece and Rome*, vol. 27 (1980), pp 60–8.
2 Elaine Pagels, *The Gnostic Gospels* (New York: Random House, 1979), pp. 63–4; G. E. M. de Ste. Croix, *The Class Struggle in the Ancient Greek World* (Ithaca, N.Y.: Cornell University Press, 1981), pp. 100–1.
3 Elaine Pagels, *Adam, Eve, and the Serpent* (New York: Random House, 1988), p. 57; Henry Chadwick, *The Early Church* (New York: Penguin, 1967), p. 41.
4 Elizabeth Schussler Fiorenza, *In Memory of Her* (New York: Crossroad Publishing Company, 1983), p. 286; JoAnn McNamara, *A New Song: Celibate Women in the First Three Christian Centuries* (New York: Hawthorn, 1983), p. 89; Chadwick, *Early Church*, p. 41; Pagels, *Adam, Eve, and the Serpent*, p. 58.
5 Pagels, *Adam, Eve, and the Serpent*, p. 77; Ste. Croix, *Class Struggle*, p. 452; Peter Brown, *The Body in Society* (New York: Columbia University Press, 1988), pp. 104–5.
6 Chadwick, *Early Church*, pp. 42, 52; Pagels, *Adam, Eve, and the Serpent*, p. 60; Brown, *Body in Society*, p. 125.
7 Pagels, *Adam, Eve, and the Serpent*, p. 58; Fiorenza, *In Memory of Her*, pp. 301–2.
8 Brown, *Body in Society*, pp. 68, 138, 137; Fiorenza, *In Memory of Her*, pp. 302, 304.
9 Clark, *Ascetic Piety*, pp. 33, 37. See also Ida Raming, *The Exclusion of Women from the Priesthood* (Metuchen: Scarecrow Press, 1976), passim.
10 McNamara, *New Song*, p. 89; Pagels, *Gnostic Gospels*, p. 59; Pagels, *Adam, Eve, and the Serpent*, p. 77.
11 Pagels, *Gnostic Gospels*, p. 60.
12 Brown, *Body in Society*, pp. 138, 139.
13 McNamara, *New Song*, pp. 124, 88–9; Mary Douglas, *Purity and Danger* (London: Routledge and Kegan Paul, 1966), pp. 186–7.
14 Brown, *Body in Society*, p. 14.
15 McNamara, *New Song*, pp. 100–1; Brown, *Body in Society*, p. 78; Charles A. Frazee, "The Origins of Clerical Celibacy in the Western Church," *Church History*, vol. 41 (1972), p. 151.
16 Brown, *Body in Society*, pp. 153, 80–2; McNamara, *New Song*, pp. 57–8.
17 Cameron, "Neither Male nor Female," p. 65; Brown, *Body in Society*, pp. 192–5.
18 Brown, *Body in Society*, pp. 202–7.
19 Ibid., p. 208.
20 Herbert Workman, *The Evolution of the Monastic Ideal* (London: Epworth Press, 1927), pp. 10–14, 23, 15.

21 Ibid., pp. 20, 21, 22.
22 See, for example, Gilbert H. Herdt, ed., *Rituals of Manhood* (Berkeley: University of California Press, 1982); Gilbert H. Herdt, *Guardians of the Flutes* (New York: McGraw-Hill, 1981); Marvin Harris, *Cannibals and Kings* (New York: Random House, 1977); Barton Hacker, "The Invention of Armies: Origins of Military Institutions, Gender Stratification, and the Labor Process," talk presented to Society for the Study of Social Problems, Chicago, Ill., August, 1987.
23 Chadwick, *Early Church*, pp. 125–6.
24 Philippe Cantamine, *War in the Middle Ages*, trans. Michael Jones (Oxford: Basil Blackwell, 1984), pp. 263, 264, 302; Adolph Harnack, *Militia Christi: The Christian Religion and the Military in the First Three Centuries*, trans. David M. Gracie (Philadelphia: Fortress Press, 1981), p. 49. See also Charles M. Odahl, "Constantine and the Militarization of Christianity," Ph.D. dissertation, University of California, San Diego, 1976.
25 Workman, *Evolution of the Monastic Ideal*, pp. 31, 65, 66, 83; Chadwick, *Early Church*, p. 178; Count de Montalembert, *The Monks of the West* (Boston: Marlies, Callanan and Co., 1847), vol. I, p. 179; George Ovitt, *The Restoration of Perfection: Labor and Technology in Medieval Culture* (New Brunswick, N.J.: Rutgers University Press, 1986), p. 94; Clark, *Ascetic Piety*, p. 277.
26 Lewis Mumford, *The Myth of the Machine* (New York: Harcourt Brace Jovanovich, 1968), vol. I, p. 266; Brown, *Body in Society*, p. 262.
27 Brown, *Body in Society*, p. 243; Montalembert, *Monks of the West*, vol. I, pp. 177, 195, 235.
28 Brown, *Body in Society*, pp. 242, 243, 244.
29 Ibid., pp. 243, 245, 267.
30 Ibid., pp. 254, 267; Workman, *Evolution of the Monastic Ideal*, p. 61; Cassian, quoted in Michel Foucault, "The Battle for Chastity," in Philippe Aries and Andre Bejin, eds., *Western Sexuality* (Oxford: Basil Blackwell, 1985), p. 16.
31 Clark, *Ascetic Piety*, pp. 273, 277; Brown, *Body in Society*, pp. 230, 246, 308; Pierre Payer, *Sex and the Penitentials* (Toronto: University of Toronto Press, 1984), passim.
32 Brown, *Body in Society*, pp. 206, 250, 270; Workman, *Evolution of the Monastic Ideal*, p. 153; Peter Levi, *The Frontiers of Paradise: A Study of Monks and Monasteries* (New York: Weidenfeld and Nicolson, 1987), p. 64.
33 McNamara, *New Song*, pp. 121, 124.
34 Chadwick, *Early Church*, pp. 266–7, 275. See also Carol Neuls-Bates, *Women in Music* (New York: Harper & Row, 1982), pp. xii, 3.
35 Workman, *Evolution of the Monastic Ideal*, p. 152; Henry Lea, *A History of Sacerdotal Celibacy* (London: Williams and Norgate, 1907), vol. I, p. 91.
36 Lea, *History of Sacerdotal Celibacy*, vol. I, p. 116.
37 Montalembert, *Monks of the West*, vol. I, p. 219; Lea, *History of Sacerdotal Celibacy*, vol. I, p. 119.
38 Judith Herrin, *The Formation of Christendom* (Princeton: Princeton University Press, 1987), pp. 285–6; Ian C. Hannah, *Christian Monasticism* (London: Allen & Unwin, 1924), pp. 42–57.
39 "Celibacy," *New Catholic Encyclopedia*, vol. 3, p. 371.

CHAPTER FOUR

1 Henry Chadwick, *The Early Church* (New York: Penguin, 1967), pp. 237, 240.
2 Peter Levi, *The Frontiers of Paradise: A Study of Monks and Monasteries* (New York: Weidenfeld and Nicolson, 1987), p. 55.

3 Herbert Workman, *The Evolution of the Monastic Ideal* (London: Epworth Press, 1927), pp. 115, 119.
4 Peter Brown, *The Body in Society* (New York: Columbia University Press, 1988), pp. 338, 364, 348, 346.
5 Ibid., pp. 347, 348, 356.
6 Ibid., p. 343.
7 Charles A. Frazee, "The Origins of Clerical Celibacy in the Western Church," *Church History*, vol. 41 (1972), pp. 155–6.
8 Brown, *Body in Society*, pp. 362, 357, 359; Chadwick, *Early Church*, pp. 238, 240; Daniel Callam, "Clerical Continence in the Fourth Century: Three Papal Decretals," *Theological Studies*, vol. 44 (March, 1980), p. 49.
9 Brown, *Body in Society*, pp. 365, 383; Chadwick, *Early Church*, p. 240.
10 Elaine Pagels, *Adam, Eve, and the Serpent* (New York: Random House, 1988), p. 89; Brown, *Body in Society*, p. 382.
11 Brown, *Body in Society*, p. 372.
12 Ibid., pp. 377, 379; Pagels, *Adam, Eve, and the Serpent*, p. 95.
13 Brown, *Body in Society*, pp. 379, 385, 383; Workman, *Evolution of the Monastic Ideal*, p. 117; Elizabeth Clark, *Ascetic Piety and Women's Faith* (Lewiston, N.Y.: Edwin Mellen Press, 1986), p. 74; *The Concise Oxford Dictionary of the Christian Church* (Oxford: Oxford University Press, 1975), p. 372.
14 Brown, *Body in Society*, pp. 387–8; Chadwick, *Early Church*, pp. 217–20. See also Peter Brown, *Augustine of Hippo* (Berkeley: University of California Press, 1967).
15 Brown, *Body in Society*, p. 389.
16 Ibid., pp. 390, 395; Chadwick, *Early Church*, p. 217; Henry Chadwick, "The Ascetic Ideal in the History of the Church," in W. J. Sheils, ed., *Monks, Hermits and the Ascetic Tradition* (Oxford: Basil Blackwell, 1985), p. 22.
17 Chadwick, "Ascetic Ideal," pp. 22, 20.
18 Workman, *Evolution of the Monastic Ideal*, pp. 22, 59, 254; Chadwick, "Ascetic Ideal," p. 22; Brown, *Body in Society*, p. 388.
19 Brown, *Body in Society*, p. 388; Brown, *Augustine of Hippo*, pp. 159–63; Chadwick, *Early Church*, p. 234.
20 Pagels, *Adam, Eve, and the Serpent*, pp. xxvi, 100, 114; Brown, *Body in Society*, pp. 123, 399, 400; Brown, *Augustine of Hippo*, p. 138.
21 Pagels, *Adam, Eve, and the Serpent*, p. 125; Chadwick, "Ascetic Ideal," p. 12.
22 Chadwick, *Early Church*, pp. 226–31; Pagels, *Adam, Eve, and the Serpent*, pp. xxvi, 125.
23 Brown, *Body in Society*, pp. 425, 426.
24 JoAnn McNamara, *A New Song: Celibate Women in the First Three Christian Centuries* (New York: Hawthorn, 1983), p. 109; Brown, *Body in Society*, p. 122; T. C. Lawler, "Melania the Elder," *Traditio*, 1947, p. 59; Elizabeth Schussler Fiorenza, *In Memory of Her* (New York: Crossroad Publishing Company, 1983), pp. 278–85.
25 Samuel Laeuchli, *Power and Sexuality: The Emergence of Canon Law at the Synod of Elvira* (Philadelphia: Temple University Press, 1972), p. 95; Brown, *Body in Society*, pp. 357–8. See also Workman, *Evolution of the Monastic Ideal*, p. 6; Henry Lea, *A History of Sacerdotal Celibacy* (London: Williams and Norgate, 1907), vol. I, p. 60; JoAnn McNamara, "Chaste Marriage and Clerical Celibacy," in Vern Bullough and James Brundage, eds., *Sexual Practices and the Medieval Church* (Buffalo: Prometheus Books, 1982), p. 24.
26 Callam, "Clerical Continence," p. 3. See also A. W. W. Dale, *The Synod of Elvira and Christian Life in the Fourth Century* (London: Macmillan, 1882); Laeuchli, *Power and Sexuality*, p. 95.

27 Laeuchli, *Power and Sexuality*, pp. 95–97.
28 Frazee, "Origins of Clerical Celibacy," p. 154; Lea, *History of Sacerdotal Celibacy*, vol. I, p. 59; Anne Barstow, *Married Priests and the Reforming Papacy* (New York: Edwin Mellen Press, 1980), p. 21.
29 Brown, *Body in Society*, p. 357; Lea, *History of Sacerdotal Celibacy*, vol. I, pp. 60–1; Callam, "Clerical Continence," pp. 5, 13.
30 Lea, *History of Sacerdotal Celibacy*, vol. I, p. 60; Callam, "Clerical Continence," pp. 5–16.
31 Callam, "Clerical Continence," p. 26; Lea, *History of Sacerdotal Celibacy*, pp. 62, 64, 66; Frazee, "Origins of Clerical Celibacy," p. 156.
32 Callam, "Clerical Continence," pp. 24, 40, 43, 44.
33 Ibid., p. 27; Frazee, "Origins of Clerical Celibacy," p. 156; Lea, *History of Sacerdotal Celibacy*, vol. I, p. 64.
34 Lea, *History of Sacerdotal Celibacy*, vol. I, p. 79; Brown, *Body in Society*, pp. 432, 443.
35 Frazee, "Origins of Clerical Celibacy," p. 157; Callam, "Clerical Continence," p. 48.
36 Brown, *Body in Society*, pp. 429, 430–2, 443; Frazee, "Origins of Clerical Celibacy," pp. 158–61.
37 Frazee, "Origins of Clerical Celibacy," p. 158; Lea, *History of Sacerdotal Celibacy*, vol. I, p. 79; Workman, *Evolution of the Monastic Ideal*, p. 156; Barstow, *Married Priests*, p. 56.
38 Friedrich Kempf, *The Church in the Age of Feudalism* (New York: Crossroad Press, 1982), p. 341.
39 Workman, *Evolution of the Monastic Ideal*, pp. 164–5; Suzanne Wemple, *Women in Frankish Society* (Philadelphia: University of Pennsylvania Press, 1981), p. 127.
40 Wemple, *Women in Frankish Society*, pp. 131–33, 141, 138–9.
41 Georges Duby, *The Early Growth of the European Economy* (Ithaca, N.Y.: Cornell University Press, 1978), pp. 43, 37; Wemple, *Women in Frankish Society*, p. 67.
42 Wemple, *Women in Frankish Society*, pp. 141–3.
43 Ibid., pp. 134, 142; Frazee, "Origins of Clerical Celibacy," p. 160.

CHAPTER FIVE
1 Count de Montalembert, *The Monks of the West* (Boston: Marlies, Callanan and Co., 1847), vol. I, p. 309; Herbert Workman, *The Evolution of the Monastic Ideal* (London: Epworth Press, 1927), pp. 141–3; Henry Chadwick, *The Early Church* (New York: Penguin, 1967), pp. 182–3.
2 Workman, *Evolution of the Monastic Ideal*, pp. 144, 146, 148, 153; R. W. Southern, *Western Society and the Church in the Middle Ages* (New York: Penguin, 1985), p. 219.
3 Charles A. Frazee, "The Origins of Clerical Celibacy in the Western Church," *Church History*, vol. 41 (1972), p. 157; Workman, *Evolution of the Monastic Ideal*, p. 169.
4 Henry Lea, *A History of Sacerdotal Celibacy* (London: Williams and Norgate, 1907), vol. I, p. 39; Peter Levi, *The Frontiers of Paradise: A Study of Monks and Monasteries* (New York: Weidenfeld and Nicolson, 1987), p. 56.
5 Frazee, "Origins of Clerical Celibacy," p. 157; Colin McEvedy, *The Penguin Atlas of Medieval History* (New York: Penguin, 1984), p. 40; Workman, *Evolution of the Monastic Ideal*, p. 168.
6 Southern, *Western Society*, pp. 217–19; Workman, *Evolution of the Monastic Ideal*, pp. 168–9, 170–2; Levi, *Frontiers of Paradise*, pp. 5, 6.
7 Workman, *Evolution of the Monastic Ideal*, pp. 206–7, 175–6; Southern, *Western Society*, p. 56.

8   Suzanne Wemple, *Women in Frankish Society* (Philadelphia: University of Pennsylvania Press, 1981), p. 76.
9   Ibid., p. 79.
10 Ibid., pp. 79–80, 81; Eleanor Duckett, *Carolingian Portraits* (Ann Arbor: University of Michigan Press, 1962), p. 23.
11 Wemple, *Women in Frankish Society*, pp. 87, 94–5.
12 Ibid., pp. 88, 108, 121; David Herlihy, "Land, Family, and Women in Continental Europe," in Susan Stuard, ed., *Women in Medieval Society* (Philadelphia: University of Pennsylvania Press, 1976), pp. 13–45. See also David Herlihy, *Medieval Households* (Cambridge, Mass.: Harvard University Press, 1985).
13 Wemple, *Women in Frankish Society*, pp. 121, 111, 95, 105.
14 Duckett, *Carolingian Portraits*, p. 25.
15 Southern, *Western Society*, pp. 218–19, 173, 74; Wemple, *Women in Frankish Society*, p. 143.
16 Workman, *Evolution of the Monastic Ideal*, p. 167; Southern, *Western Society*, p. 175.
17 Philippe Cantamine, *War in the Middle Ages*, trans. Michael Jones (Oxford: Basil Blackwell, 1984), pp. 269, 24, 270; Geoffrey Barraclough, *The Crucible of Europe* (London: Thames and Hudson, 1976), p. 15.
18 Barraclough, *Crucible of Europe*, p. 28.
19 Herbert E. J. Cowdrey, "Anglo-Norman Laudes Regiae," *Viator*, vol. XII (1981), pp. 43–4; Michael McCormick, "The Liturgy of War in the Early Middle Ages," *Viator*, vol. XV (1984), pp. 2, 8.
20 McCormick, "Liturgy of War," pp. 10, 16, 12, 15.
21 Ibid., p. 11; Barraclough, *Crucible of Europe*, pp. 22, 26–8.
22 Barraclough, *Crucible of Europe*, p. 27; Wemple, *Women in Frankish Society*, pp. 143–4.
23 Wemple, *Women in Frankish Society*, pp. 144, 147; Friedrich Kempf, *The Church in the Age of Feudalism* (New York: Crossroad Press, 1982), p. 211.
24 Wemple, *Women in Frankish Society*, pp. 143, 165.
25 Eleanor Duckett, *Saint Dunstan of Canterbury* (London: Collins, 1955), p. 12; John Chamberlain, ed., *The Rule of St. Benedict: The Abingdon Copy* (Toronto: Pontifical Institute of Medieval Studies, 1982), p. 4.
26 McCormick, "Liturgy of War," pp. 3, 21.
27 G. E. M. de Ste. Croix, *The Class Struggle in the Ancient Greek World* (Ithaca, N.Y.: Cornell University Press, 1981), p. 266.
28 Thomas F. X. Noble, "The Monastic Ideal as a Model for Empire: The Case of Louis the Pious," *Revue Bénédictine*, vol. 86 (1976), pp. 236–88.
29 Ibid., pp. 242–50.
30 Workman, *Evolution of the Monastic Ideal*, pp. 225–7; Ardo, *Emperor's Monk*, trans. Alan Cabaniss (London: Arthur H. Stockwell, 1979), passim.
31 Ardo, *Emperor's Monk*, pp. 86–8. See also Workman, *Evolution of the Monastic Ideal*, p. 227; Duckett, *Dunstan*, p. 16.
32 Ardo, *Emperor's Monk*, p. 88; Duckett, *Dunstan*, p. 16; Workman, *Evolution of the Monastic Ideal*, p. 227.
33 Workman, *Evolution of the Monastic Ideal*, p. 227; Duckett, *Dunstan*, p. 16; George Zarnecki, *The Monastic Achievement* (New York: McGraw-Hill, 1972), p. 25.
34 Zarnecki, *Monastic Achievement*, p. 25; Jean Leclercq, "On Monastic Priesthood According to the Ancient Medieval Tradition," *Studia Monastica*, vol. III (1961), pp. 138–55.
35 Ardo, *Emperor's Monk*, pp. 85, 95; Cantamine, *War in the Middle Ages*, pp. 275, 296–7.
36 Wemple, *Women in Frankish Society*, p. 165.

37 Ibid., p. 166.
38 Ibid., p. 143.
39 Ibid., pp. 147, 144, 145; JoAnn McNamara and Suzanne Wemple, "Sanctity and Power: The Dual Pursuit of Medieval Women," in Renate Bridenthal and Claudia Koonz, eds., *Becoming Visible* (Boston: Houghton-Mifflin, 1977), pp. 100–1.
40 McNamara and Wemple, "Sanctity and Power," p. 101; Wemple, *Women in Frankish Society*, p. 145.
41 Duckett, *Carolingian Portraits*, p. 23; Ardo, *Emperor's Monk*, pp. 75–6.
42 Wemple, *Women in Frankish Society*, pp. 165–8.
43 Ibid., pp. 168–70.
44 Ibid., pp. 167–9.
45 Southern, *Western Society*, p. 310; Wemple, *Women in Frankish Society*, p. 168.
46 Wemple, *Women in Frankish Society*, p. 187.
47 Sara Lehrman, "The Education of Women in the Middle Ages," in Douglas Radcliff-Umstead, *The Roles and Images of Women in the Middle Ages and Renaissance* (Pittsburgh: University of Pittsburgh Press, 1975), p. 135. The term "malestream" is from Mary O'Brien, *The Politics of Reproduction* (London: Routledge and Kegan Paul, 1981). Wemple, *Women in Frankish Society*, p. 188.
48 Johan Huizinga, *Homo Ludens* (Boston: Beacon Press, 1950), p. 154.
49 Erigena, quoted in Georges Duby, *The Knight, the Lady, and the Priest* (New York: Pantheon, 1983), pp. 50–1.
50 Wemple, *Women in Frankish Society*, p. 95. See also Peter Dronke, *Women Writers of the Middle Ages* (Cambridge: Cambridge University Press, 1984), pp. 36–8.
51 Wemple, *Women in Frankish Society*, p. 99.
52 Dronke, *Women Writers*, p. 38.

CHAPTER SIX
1 Eleanor Duckett, *Carolingian Portraits* (Ann Arbor: University of Michigan Press, 1962), p. 46; Geoffrey Barraclough, *The Crucible of Europe* (London: Thames and Hudson, 1976), pp. 84–94.
2 Barraclough, *Crucible of Europe*, p. 94; R. W. Southern, *Western Society and the Church in the Middle Ages* (New York: Penguin, 1985), pp. 177–80.
3 Charles A. Frazee, "The Origins of Clerical Celibacy in the Western Church," *Church History*, vol. 41 (1972), p. 160; Friedrich Kempf, *The Church in the Age of Feudalism* (New York: Crossroad Press, 1982), p. 211.
4 Suzanne Wemple, *Women in Frankish Society* (Philadelphia: University of Pennsylvania Press, 1981), pp. 121, 146, 173, 194–5; Peter Dronke, *Women Writers of the Middle Ages* (Cambridge: Cambridge University Press, 1984), p. 55.
5 Christopher Brooke, *Europe in the Central Middle Ages* (London: Longman, 1975), p. 242.
6 Eleanor Duckett, *Saint Dunstan of Canterbury* (London: Collins, 1955), p. 18; Georges Duby, *The Three Orders: Feudal Society Imagined*, trans. Arthur Goldhammer (Chicago: University of Chicago Press, 1980), p. 169.
7 Herbert Workman, *The Evolution of the Monastic Ideal* (London: Epworth Press, 1927), pp. 227, 228.
8 Duckett, *Dunstan*, p. 29; W. Lourdaux and D. Verhelst, eds., *Benedictine Culture, 750–1050* (Leuven, Belgium: Leuven University Press, 1983), p. vii; Adrian H. Bredero, "Cluny et le monarchism carolingien," in Lourdaux and Verhelst, eds., *Benedictine Culture*, pp. 50–75; Brooke, *Europe in the Central Middle Ages*, pp. 240–2; Workman, *Evolution of the Monastic Ideal*, pp. 227–8; Southern, *Western Society*, p. 228.

9 Southern, *Western Society*, p. 224.

10 Duby, *Three Orders*, pp. 54–5; Philippe Cantamine, *War in the Middle Ages*, trans. Michael Jones (Oxford: Basil Blackwell, 1984), p. 275; G. E. M. de Ste. Croix, *The Class Struggle in the Ancient Greek World* (Ithaca, N.Y.: Cornell University Press, 1981), p. 266; Barbara H. Rosenwein, "Feudal War and Monastic Peace: Cluniac Liturgy as Ritual Aggression," *Viator*, vol. II (1971), pp. 153–4; Barbara Rosenwein, "Rules and the 'Rule' at Tenth Century Cluny," *Studia Monastica*, vol. XIX (1977), pp. 307–20.

11 Southern, *Western Society*, pp. 310–11; Peter Levi, *The Frontiers of Paradise: A Study of Monks and Monasteries* (New York: Weidenfeld and Nicolson, 1987), p. 101. See also Mary Bateson, "Origins and Early History of Double Monasteries," *Transactions of the Royal Historical Society*, vol. XIII (1899).

12 Southern, *Western Society*, pp. 310–11.

13 Ibid., p. 311; Georges Duby, *The Knight, the Lady, and the Priest* (New York: Pantheon, 1983), pp. 50–1.

14 Lourdaux and Verhelst, eds., *Benedictine Culture*, p. vii; Mary Bateson, "Rules for Monks and Secular Canons After the Revival Under King Edgar," *English Historical Review*, vol. IX (1894), p. 690.

15 Brooke, *Europe in the Central Middle Ages*, pp. 244–6, 251; D. A. Bullough, "The Continental Background of the Reform," in David Parsons, ed., *Tenth Century Studies* (Phillimore, n.d.), pp. 20–8; Bernard Hamilton, "The House of Theophylact and the Promotion of the Religious Life Among Women in Tenth Century Rome," *Studia Monastica*, vol. XII (1970), p. 216; Bernard Hamilton, "The Monastic Revival in Tenth Century Rome," *Studia Monastica*, vol. IV (1962), pp. 35–65; Charles Julian Biskho, "Liturgical Intercession at Cluny for the King-Emperor of Laon," *Studia Monastica*, vol. III (1961), pp. 53–4, 76.

16 D. H. Farmer, "The Progress of the Monastic Revival," in Parsons, ed., *Tenth Century Studies*, p. 17; H. R. Loyn, "Church and State in England in the Tenth and Eleventh Centuries," in Parsons, ed., *Tenth Century Studies*, p. 95; Arnold William Klukas, "Liturgy and Architecture," *Viator*, vol. XV (1984), pp. 82–3.

17 Duckett, *Dunstan*, p. 10; John Chamberlain, ed., *The Rule of St. Benedict: The Abingdon Copy* (Toronto: Pontifical Institute of Medieval Studies, 1982), p. 6.

18 Duckett, *Dunstan*, pp. 41, 137; Klukas, "Liturgy and Architecture," p. 83; Thomas Symons, "Regularis Concordia: History and Derivation," in Parsons, ed., *Tenth Century Studies*, p. 93.

19 Duckett, *Dunstan*, pp. 111–17, 137; Chamberlain, *Rule of St. Benedict*, p. 6; Barbara Yorke, "Ethelwold and the Politics of the Tenth Century," unpublished manuscript (courtesy Barbara Yorke). See also B. Yorke, ed., *Bishop Aethelwold: His Career and Influence* (Woodbridge, England: Boydell Press, 1988).

20 Duckett, *Dunstan*, pp. 42, 116, 59; Chamberlain, *Rule of St. Benedict*, pp. 6, 8; Klukas, "Liturgy and Architecture," pp. 84–5; Levi, *Frontiers of Paradise*, p. 60; Bullough, "Continental Background," p. 30; Parsons, ed., *Tenth Century Studies*, p. 46; Farmer, "Progress of the Monastic Revival," p. 11; Frederick Tupper, Jr., "History and Texts of the Benedictine Reform of the Tenth Century," *Modern Language Notes*, June, 1893, p. 344; E. John, "The King and the Monks in the Tenth Century Reformation," *Orbis Britanniae*, 1966, pp. 154–80.

21 Klukas, "Liturgy and Architecture," p. 84; Parsons, ed. *Tenth Century Studies*, pp. 44, 46; Bateson, "Rules for Monks," p. 701; Duckett, *Dunstan*, p. 161.

22 Bateson, "Rules for Monks," p. 170; Parsons, ed., *Tenth Century Studies*, p. 44; Farmer, "Progress of the Monastic Revival," pp. 13–15; R. R. Darlington, "Ecclesiastical Reform in the Late Old English Period," *English Historical Review*, vol. LI (1936), pp. 389, 396, 405–46.

23 Parsons, ed., *Tenth Century Studies*, p. 44; Loyn, "Church and State in England," pp. 95, 99; D. J. V. Fisher, "The Anti-Monastic Reaction in the Reign of Edward the Martyr," *Cambridge Historical Journal*, vol. X (1952), pp. 262–3; Farmer, "Progress of the Monastic Revival," p. 12; Bullough, "Continental Background," p. 28.

24 Duckett, *Dunstan*, pp. 111, 121–23, 227; Darlington, "Ecclesiastical Reform," pp. 407–8; Farmer, "Progress of the Monastic Revival," p. 10; Parsons, ed., *Tenth Century Studies*, p. 49.

25 Loyn, "Church and State in England," pp. 98–9; Parsons, ed., *Tenth Century Studies*, p. 44; Levi, *Frontiers of Paradise*, p. 91; Klukas, "Liturgy and Architecture," p. 85; Southern, *Western Society*, pp. 224–5.

26 Duckett, *Dunstan*, pp. 44, 121; Yorke, "Ethelwold," p. 20; Farmer, "Progress of the Monastic Revival," pp. 14, 16.

27 Bullough, "Continental Background," p. 23; Marc Anthony Meyer, "Women and the Tenth Century English Monastic Reform," *Revue Bénédictine*, vol. 87 (1977), pp. 34–61; Duckett, *Dunstan*, p. 112.

28 Meyer, "Women and the Tenth Century," p. 45; Duckett, *Dunstan*, p. 129.

29 Duckett, *Dunstan*, pp. 74, 134; *Ely Cathedral* (Ely, England: Friends of Ely Cathedral, 1973), p. 6.

30 Fisher, "Anti-Monastic Reaction," p. 265; Duckett, *Dunstan*, p. 230; Cecily Clark, "After 1066," in Christine Fell, *Women in Anglo-Saxon England* (Bloomington: Indiana University Press, 1984), pp. 148–70; Darlington, "Ecclesiastical Reform," pp. 398–406; Farmer, "Progress of the Monastic Revival," p. 19.

31 Southern, *Western Society*, pp. 180, 95–7; R. W. Southern, *The Making of the Middle Ages* (London: Hutchinson, 1967), pp. 136–7; Colin McEvedy, *The Penguin Atlas of Medieval History* (New York: Penguin, 1984), pp. 56, 70; Frazee, "Origins of Clerical Celibacy," p. 160; Workman, *Evolution of the Monastic Ideal*, p. 233; Ephraim Emerton, ed., *The Correspondence of Pope Gregory VII* (New York: Columbia University Press, 1960), p. xi.

32 Southern, *Western Society*, pp. 100–10; Southern, *Making of the Middle Ages*, pp. 136–7; R. I. Moore, "Family, Community, and Cult on the Eve of the Gregorian Reform," *Transactions of the Royal Historical Society*, May, 1979, p. 59; David Herlihy, *Medieval Households* (Cambridge, Mass.: Harvard University Press, 1985), pp. 79–88; Workman, *Evolution of the Monastic Ideal*, p. 234.

33 Anne Barstow, *Married Priests and the Reforming Papacy* (New York: Edwin Mellen Press, 1980), p. 175; Georges Duby, *The Knight, the Lady, and the Priest* (New York: Pantheon, 1983), pp. 50–1; Workman, *Evolution of the Monastic Ideal*, p. 235; Frazee, "Origins of Clerical Celibacy," p. 163.

34 Emerton, ed., *Correspondence of Pope Gregory VII*, pp. xiv, xv; Frazee, "Origins of Clerical Celibacy," pp. 161–2.

35 Frazee, "Origins of Clerical Celibacy," p. 164; Brooke, *Europe in the Central Middle Ages*, pp. 257–62.

36 Workman, *Evolution of the Monastic Ideal*, p. 235; Southern, *Western Society and the Church*, p. 115.

37 Cantamine, *War in the Middle Ages*, p. 270; Brooke, *Europe in the Central Middle Ages*, pp. 253, 285; Emerton, *Correspondence of Pope Gregory VII*, p. xxix; Southern, *Making of the Middle Ages*, p. 54.

38 Brooke, *Europe in the Central Middle Ages*, p. 254.

39 Moore, "Family, Community, and Cult," p. 65.

40 Herlihy, *Medieval Households*, pp. 85, 86.

41 David Herlihy, "Land, Family, and Women in Continental Europe," in Susan Stuard, ed., *Women in Medieval Society* (Philadelphia: University of Pennsylvania Press, 1976), p. 21; Brooke, *Europe in the Central Middle Ages*, p. 254.

42 Henry Lea, *A History of Sacerdotal Celibacy* (London: Williams and Norgate, 1907), vol. I, pp. 212, 235.

43 Ibid., pp. 244–6.

44 C. N. L. Brooke, "The Gregorian Reform in Action," in Sylvia Thrupp, ed., *Change in Medieval Society* (New York: Appleton-Century-Crofts, 1964), p. 49; Lea, *History of Sacerdotal Celibacy*, vol. I, p. 247; Emerton, *Correspondence of Pope Gregory VII*, p. 52.

45 Brooke, "Gregorian Reform," p. 49; Frazee, "Origins of Clerical Celibacy," pp. 164–5; Workman, *Evolution of the Monastic Ideal*, p. 234; Moore, "Family, Community, and Cult," p. 60; Lea, *History of Sacerdotal Celibacy*, vol. I p. 247.

46 Lea, *History of Sacerdotal Celibacy*, vol. I, pp. 247, 255. Barstow, *Married Priests*, p. 172.

47 Lea, *History of Sacerdotal Celibacy*, vol. I, pp. 249, 210, 219, 232, 239, 241, 243, 208; Barstow, *Married Priests*, pp. 57, 132–3.

48 JoAnn McNamara, "Chaste Marriage and Clerical Celibacy," in Vern Bullough and James Brundage, eds., *Sexual Practices and the Medieval Church* (Buffalo: Prometheus Books, 1982), p. 32; Brooke, "Gregorian Reform," p. 49; James A. Brundage, *Law, Sex and Christian Society in Medieval Europe* (Chicago: University of Chicago Press, 1987), pp. 214–18.

49 Brooke, "Gregorian Reform," p. 62; Frazee, "Origins of Clerical Celibacy," p. 167.

50 Brooke, *Europe in the Central Middle Ages*, p. 254; Moore, "Family, Community, and Cult," pp. 65–7; Barstow, *Married Priests*, pp. 178–9; Kaufman, quoted in Barstow, *Married Priests*, p. 178. See also Susan Stuard, ed., *Women in Medieval Society* (Philadelphia: University of Pennsylvania Press, 1976), p. 8.

51 JoAnn McNamara and Suzanne Wemple, "Sanctity and Power: The Dual Pursuit of Medieval Women, in Renate Bridenthal and Claudia Koonz, eds., *Becoming Visible* (Boston: Houghton-Mifflin, 1977), p. 110; Lea, *History of Sacerdotal Celibacy*, vol. I, pp. 193, 238; Frazee, "Origins of Clerical Celibacy," p. 163; Zoe Oldenbourg, *Massacre at Montségur: A History of the Albigensian Crusade* (New York: Pantheon, 1961), p. 40; Jean Leclercq, "S. Pierre Damien et les femmes," *Studia Monastica*, vol. XV (1973), pp. 43–55.

52 Moore, "Family, Community, and Cult," p. 67; McNamara and Wemple, "Sanctity and Power," p. 111; Herlihy, *Medieval Households*, p. 87; Stuard, ed., *Women in Medieval Society*, p. 8.

53 Levi, *Frontiers of Paradise*, p. 91; Lea, *History of Sacerdotal Celibacy*, vol. I, p. 255.

54 Natalie Zemon Davis, "Introduction," in Duby, *The Knight, the Lady, and the Priest*, p. xi. See also Pierre Payer, *Sex and the Penitentials* (Toronto: University of Toronto Press, 1984); Michael Goodich, *The Unmentionable Vice: Homosexuality in the Late Medieval Period* (New York: Dorset Press, 1979); John Boswell, *Christianity, Social Tolerance, and Homosexuality* (Chicago: University of Chicago Press, 1980).

55 R. W. Southern, *Saint Anselm and His Biographer* (Cambridge: Cambridge University Press, 1963), p. 72; Brian Patrick McGuire, "Love, Friendship, and Sex in the Eleventh Century: The Experience of Anselm," *Studia Theologica*, vol. XXVIII (1974), pp. 111–52; Boswell, *Christianity*, p. 221; Brian Patrick McGuire, "Monastic Friendship and Toleration in Twelfth Century Cistercian Life," in W. J. Sheils, ed., *Monks, Hermits and the Ascetic Tradition* (Oxford: Basil Blackwell, 1985), pp. 147–60; Thomas Stehling, "To Love a Medieval Boy," *Journal of Homosexuality*, vol. VIII (Spring/Summer, 1983), pp. 151, 166.

56 David F. Greenberg, "The Construction of Homosexuality," manuscript, p. 653. See *The Construction of Homosexuality* (Chicago: University of Chicago Press, 1988).

57 Boswell, *Christianity*, pp. 216–18; Davis, "Introduction," p. xi.

58 E. Ann Matter, "Review of Boswell," *Journal of Interdisciplinary History* (Spring, 1982)

See also Judith C. Brown, *Immodest Acts: The Life of a Lesbian Nun in Renaissance Italy* (Oxford: Oxford University Press, 1985).

59 Abbot Conrad, quoted in Southern, *Western Society*, p. 314. See also Sharon K. Elkins, *Holy Women of Twelfth Century England* (Chapel Hill: University of North Carolina Press, 1988), pp. 117–24.

60 Dronke, *Women Writers*, p. 135; R. I. Moore, *The Formation of a Persecuting Society* (Oxford: Basil Blackwell, 1987), pp. 4, 5, 153.

CHAPTER SEVEN

1 Friedrich Heer, *The Medieval World*, trans. Janet Sondheimer (London: Weidenfeld and Nicolson, 1962), p. 265.

2 Margaret Deansby, "The Medieval Schools to c. 1300," *Cambridge Medieval History*, vol. V, p. 777; Hastings Rashdall, *The Universities of Europe in the Middle Ages* (Oxford: Oxford University Press, 1895), vol. I, p. 29. See also Georges Duby, *The Early Growth of the European Economy* (Ithaca, N.Y.: Cornell University Press, 1978).

3 Charles A. Frazee, "The Origins of Clerical Celibacy in the Western Church," *Church History*, vol. 41 (1972), p. 167; Achille Luchaire, *Social France in the Time of Philip Augustus*, trans. Edward B. Krehbiel (New York: Frederick Ungar, 1957), p. 65; Rashdall, *Universities of Europe*, vol. I, p. 29.

4 Heer, *Medieval World*, pp. 265, 261–2; Alexander Murray, *Reason and Society in the Middle Ages* (Oxford: Oxford University Press, 1985), pp. 50–107; Duby, *Early Growth*, pp. 177–80; David Herlihy, "Land, Family, and Women in Continental Europe," in Susan Stuard, ed., *Women in Medieval Society* (Philadelphia: University of Pennsylvania Press, 1976), pp. 33–4. See also Meg Bogin, *The Woman Troubadours* (New York: Norton, 1980); Peter Dronke, *Women Writers of the Middle Ages* (Cambridge: Cambridge University Press, 1984), ch. four.

5 George Ovitt, *The Restoration of Perfection: Labor and Technology in Medieval Culture* (New Brunswick, N.J.: Rutgers University Press, 1986), p. 187.

6 Penny Schine Gold, *The Lady and the Virgin: Image, Attitude, and Experience in Twelfth Century France* (Chicago: University of Chicago Press, 1985), p. 82. See also Sharon K. Elkins, *Holy Women of Twelfth Century England* (Chapel Hill: University of North Carolina Press, 1988); Lester K. Little, *Religious Poverty and the Profit Economy in Medieval Europe* (Ithaca, N.Y.: Cornell University Press, 1978); Jerome Taylor and Lester K. Little, *Nature, Man, and Society in the Twelfth Century* (Chicago: University of Chicago Press, 1968).

7 R. W. Southern, *Western Society and the Church in the Middle Ages* (New York: Penguin, 1985), pp. 312–20, 317; Dronke, *Women Writers*, pp. 148–9; JoAnn McNamara and Suzanne Wemple, "Sanctity and Power: The Dual Pursuit of Medieval Women," in Renate Bridenthal and Claudia Koonz, eds., *Becoming Visible* (Boston: Houghton-Mifflin, 1977), p. 111. See also Sabina Flanagan, *Hildegard of Bingen: A Visionary Life* (London: Routledge and Kegan Paul, 1989).

8 Gold, *Lady and Virgin*, p. 90; Heer, *Medieval World*, p. 264; Southern, *Western Society*, p. 321.

9 James Westphal Thompson, *The Literacy of the Laity in the Middle Ages* (New York: Burt Franklin, 1960), pp. 69, 124, 138, 162. See also M. T. Clanchy, *From Memory to Written Record in England, 1066–1307* (London: Edward Arnold, 1979).

10 Bernard, quoted in R. I. Moore, *The Formation of a Persecuting Society* (Oxford: Basil Blackwell, 1987), p. 118; Betty Radice, ed., *The Letters of Abelard and Heloise* (London: Penguin, 1974); James Brundage, *Law, Sex and Christian Society in Medieval Europe* (Chicago: University of Chicago Press, 1987) p. 187; Heer, *Medieval World*, pp.

110–14; M. M. McLaughlin, "Peter Abelard and the Dignity of Women," in *Pierre Abélard, Pierre le Vénérable* (Paris: Centre National de la Recherche Scientifique, 1975), pp. 287–333; D. E. Luscombe, ed., *Peter Abelard's Ethics* (Oxford: Clarendon Press, 1971), pp. 15, 19, 21, 23.

11 Radice, ed., *Letters of Abelard and Heloise*, p. 130.

12 D. E. Luscombe, *The School of Peter Abelard* (Cambridge: Cambridge University Press, 1969), frontispiece.

13 C. N. L. Brooke, "The Gregorian Reform in Action," in Sylvia Thrupp, ed., *Change in Medieval Society* (New York: Appleton-Century-Crofts, 1964), p. 62.

14 Luchaire, *Social France*, pp. 63–64, 65, 70–71; C. G. Coulton, *Medieval Panorama* (Cambridge: Cambridge University Press, 1938), p. 385; Paul Oskar Kristeller, "Learned Women of Early Modern Italy: Humanists and University Scholars," in Patricia A. Labalme, ed., *Beyond Their Sex: Learned Women of the European Past* (New York: New York University Press, 1980), p. 105; J. K. Hyde, "Universities and Cities in Medieval Italy," paper delivered at the Symposium on the University and the City, New York University, November 20, 1986.

15 Luchaire, *Social France*, pp. 72–3; Herbert Workman, *The Evolution of the Monastic Ideal* (London: Epworth Press, 1927), p. 259; Stephen C. Ferruolo, "Parisius-Paradisus: The City, Its Schools and the Origins of the University of Paris," paper delivered at the Symposium on the University and the City, New York University, November 20, 1986, p. 2 (courtesy of Stephen Ferruolo).

16 Ferruolo, "Parisius-Paradisus," p. 6; Luchaire, *Social France*, pp. 103, 102, 86.

17 Lynn Thorndike, *University Records and Life in the Middle Ages* (New York: Columbia University Press, 1949), pp. 25, 32; Luchaire, *Social France*, p. 75.

18 Radice, ed., *Letters of Abelard and Heloise*, pp. 58, 61; Murray, *Reason and Society*, p. 231; Walter J. Ong, *Fighting for Life* (Ithaca, N.Y.: Cornell University Press, 1981), pp. 126, 143; Walter J. Ong, "Agonistic Structures in Academia," *Interchange*, vol. V, p. 7.

19 Ferruolo, "Parisius-Paradisus," pp. 17, 21; Luchaire, *Social France*, pp. 82–3.

20 Walter J. Ong, "Latin Language as a Renaissance Puberty Rite," *Studies in Philology*, vol. LVI (April, 1959), pp. 106–9; Ong, *Fighting for Life*, pp. 130–2.

21 Marilyn French, *Beyond Power* (New York: Summit Books, 1985), p. 160; Murray, *Reason and Society*, pp. 265, 350, 367–8.

22 Robert A. Pratt, "Jankyn's Book of Wikked Wyves: Medieval Antimatrimonial Propaganda in the Universities," *Annuale Medievale*, vol. III (1962), pp. 5–27 (see especially 9, 14); Geoffrey Chaucer, *Canterbury Tales* (New York: Bantam Books, 1964), pp. 213–19; Ruth Dean, "Unnoticed Commentaries on the Dissuasio Valerii of Walter Map," *Medieval and Renaissance Studies*, vol. II (1950), pp. 128–50; Walter Map, "The Advice of Valerius to Rufinus the Philosopher Not to Marry," in his *De Nugis Curialum (Courtier's Trifles)*, trans. Frederick Tupper and Marbury Ogle (London: Chatto and Windus, 1924), pp. 192–3.

23 Charles Homer Haskins, *Studies in Medieval Culture* (New York: Frederick Ungar, 1929), p. 20; Thorndike, *University Records*, p. 119.

24 Workman, *Evolution of the Monastic Ideal*, p. 311; Henry Lea, *A History of Sacerdotal Celibacy* (London: Williams and Norgate, 1907), vol. I, pp. 306–7; Michael Goodich, "The Cycle of Life," paper presented at Drexel University, November, 1985.

25 Thorndike, *University Records*, pp. 210, 217–18.

26 French, *Beyond Power*, p. 161; Lea, *History of Sacerdotal Celibacy*, vol. I, p. 503; Jack Goody, *The Development of the Family and Marriage in Europe* (Cambridge: Cambridge University Press, 1983), p. 109; Levi, *Frontiers of Paradise*, p. 15.

27 Michael Goodich, *The Unmentionable Vice: Homosexuality in the Late Medieval Period*

(New York: Dorset Press, 1979), p. 21; Heer, *Medieval World*, pp. 90, 210; Thomas Stehling, "To Love a Medieval Boy," *Journal of Homosexuality*, vol. VIII (Spring/ Summer, 1983), p. 151; Philippe Aries, "Thoughts on the History of Homosexuality," in Philippe Aries and Andre Bejin, eds., *Western Sexuality* (Oxford: Basil Blackwell, 1985), p. 74; James McEvoy, *The Philosophy of Robert Grosseteste* (Oxford: Oxford University Press, 1982), pp. 40–1; Murray, *Reason and Society*, p. 238.

28 Thorndike, *University Records*, p. 78; Luchaire, *Social France*, pp. 82–3; Ferruolo, "Parisius-Paradisus," pp. 17.

29 Ferruolo, "Parisius-Paradisus," pp. 22, 23; Murray, *Reason and Society*, pp. 245, 263, 282.

30 David Knowles, *Evolution of Medieval Thought* (New York: Alfred A. Knopf, 1962), pp. 185, 191; Frances Gies and Joseph Gies, *Women in the Middle Ages* (New York: Barnes and Noble, 1980), pp. 50–1; Aristotle, *Generation of Animals*, trans. A. L. Peck (Cambridge, Mass.: Harvard University Press, 1943), p. 459; Thomas Aquinas, *Summa Theologica* (New York: McGraw-Hill, 1964), vol. XIII (question 92), p. 37; Paul E. Sigmund, ed., *Thomas Aquinas on Politics and Ethics* (New York: Norton, 1988), pp. 37–8; Vern L. Bullough, "Medieval Medical and Scientific Views of Women," *Viator*, vol. IV (1973), p. 486; Helen Lemay, "Some Thirteenth and Fourteenth Century Lectures on Female Sexuality," *International Journal of Women's Studies*, vol. I (1978); Londa Schiebinger, *The Mind Has No Sex? Women in the Origins of Modern Science* (Cambridge, Mass.: Harvard University Press, 1989), pp. 217, 162, 215, 234, 273.

31 E. I. J. Rosenthal, ed., *Averroë's Commentary on Plato's Republic* (Cambridge: Cambridge University Press, 1956), pp. 164, 165, 267.

32 Coulton, *Medieval Panorama*, pp. 623–4, 484; Thorndike, *University Records*, pp. 138–48; Shulamith Shahar, *The Fourth Estate* (London: Methuen, 1983), pp. 155–7; Heer, *Medieval World*, pp. 340, 299; Murray, *Reason and Society*, pp. 253–5.

33 Vern Bullough, "Postscript, Heresy, Witchcraft, and Sexuality," in Vern Bullough and James Brundage, eds., *Sexual Practices of the Medieval Church* (Buffalo: Prometheus Books, 1982), pp. 210–11; James A. Brundage, *Law, Sex and Christian Society in Medieval Europe* (Chicago: University of Chicago Press, 1987), p. 459.

34 Knowles, *Medieval Thought*, pp. 272–8; Thorndike, *University Records*, p. 148; Michael H. Shank, "A Female University Student in Late Medieval Krakow," *Signs*, vol. XII (1987), pp. 374–5.

35 Susan Groag Bell, "Christine de Pisan: Humanism and the Problem of a Studious Woman," *Feminist Issues*, vol. III (1979), p. 183; Joan Kelly, "Early Feminist Theory and the Querelle des Femmes," *Signs*, vol. V (1982), p. 14.

36 Kelly, "Early Feminist Theory," p. 14; Bell, "Christine de Pisan," p. 179.

CHAPTER EIGHT

1 Frederick B. Artz, *The Mind of the Middle Ages* (Chicago: University of Chicago Press, 1953), p. 319; Pearl Kibre and Nancy G. Siraisi, "The Institutional Setting: The Universities," in David C. Lindberg, ed., *Science in the Middle Ages* (Chicago: University of Chicago Press, 1978), p. 120.

2 Friedrich Heer, *The Medieval World*, trans. Janet Sondheimer (London: Weidenfeld and Nicolson, 1962), p. 303; David C. Lindberg, "The Transmission of Greek and Arabic Learning to the West," in Lindberg, ed., *Science in the Middle Ages*, pp. 52–90; Edward Grant, "Science and Theology in the Middle Ages," in David C. Lindberg and Ronald L. Numbers, eds., *God and Nature* (Berkeley: University of California Press, 1986), pp. 67, 69, 49, 50; John Murdock and Edith Sylla, eds., *The Cultural Context of Medieval Learning* (Dordrecht: D. Reidel, 1975).

3 William A. Wallace, "The Philosophical Setting of Medieval Science," in Lindberg, ed., *Science in the Middle Ages*, pp. 91–119; James McEvoy, *The Philosophy of Robert Grosseteste* (Oxford: Oxford University Press, 1982), passim; David Lindberg, "Science as Handmaiden: Roger Bacon and the Patristic Tradition," paper presented to the Colloquium on Late Medieval Science and Technology, Rutgers University, April 18, 1986. See also David Lindberg, "On the Applicability of Mathematics to Nature: Roger Bacon and His Predecessors," *British Journal for the History of Science*, vol. XV (1982), pp. 3–26.

4 Wallace, "Philosophical Setting," pp. 96, 102.

5 Ibid., p. 103; Alexander Murray, *Reason and Society in the Middle Ages* (Oxford: Oxford University Press, 1985), p. 250.

6 Grant, "Science and Theology," pp. 57, 62–8; Wallace, "Philosophical Setting," pp. 91–119.

7 Wallace, "Philosophical Setting," pp. 91–119. See also William A. Wallace, *Prelude to Galileo: Essays on Medieval and Sixteenth Century Sources of Galileo's Thought* (Dordrecht: D. Reidel, 1981), p. 44.

8 Wallace, *Prelude to Galileo*, pp. 44–46; Kibre and Siraisi, "Institutional Setting," pp. 135, 139–40; Hastings Rashdall, *The Universities of Europe in the Middle Ages* (Oxford: Oxford University Press, 1895), vol. I, pp. 251–2.

9 Rashdall, *Universities of Europe*, vol. I, pp. 214, 223–4, 215–16; Kibre and Siraisi, "Institutional Setting," pp. 139–40.

10 Paul Oskar Kristeller, "Learned Women of Early Modern Italy: Humanists and University Scholars," in Patricia A. Labalme, ed., *Beyond Their Sex: Learned Women of the European Past* (New York: New York University Press, 1980), pp. 91–117; Rashdall, *Universities of Europe*, vol. I, pp. 79, 83; vol. II, p. 745; Kate Campbell Hurd-Mead, *A History of Women in Medicine* (Haddam, Conn.: Haddam Press, 1938).

11 Heer, *Medieval World*, p. 254; Rashdall, *Universities of Europe*, vol. I, p. 214; Ian Maclean, *The Renaissance Notion of Women* (Cambridge: Cambridge University Press, 1980), p. 92; Joan Kelly-Gadol, "Did Women Have a Renaissance?," in Renate Bridenthal and Claudia Koonz, eds., *Becoming Visible* (Boston: Houghton-Mifflin, 1977), pp. 148, 154, 160.

12 Lawrence Stone, "Sex in the West," *New Republic*, July 8, 1985, p. 34; Judith C. Brown, "A Woman's Place Was in the Home: Women's Work in Renaissance Tuscany," in Margaret Ferguson et al., eds., *Rewriting the Renaissance* (Chicago: University of Chicago Press, 1986), p. 224; Patricia Labalme, "Introduction," in Labalme, *Beyond Their Sex*, pp. 4, 5.

13 Margaret L. King, "Book-Lined Cells: Women and Humanism in the Early Italian Renaissance," in Labalme, ed., *Beyond Their Sex*, pp. 68, 69, 71, 76, 78; Margaret L. King, "Thwarted Ambitions: Six Learned Women of the Italian Renaissance," *Soundings*, vol. LIX (1976), pp. 280–304; Margaret L. King, "The Religious Retreat of Isotta Nogarola," *Signs*, vol. III (1978), pp. 807–22, (see especially 811); Mary Beth Rose, *Women in the Middle Ages and the Renaissance* (Syracuse: Syracuse University Press, 1986), pp. 12–14.

14 Heer, *Medieval World*, p. 254; Kibre and Siraisi, "Institutional Setting," pp. 135–9.

15 Kibre and Siraisi, "Institutional Setting," p. 135; Wallace, *Prelude to Galileo*, pp. 44–6; Heer, *Medieval World*, p. 254; Artz, *Mind of the Middle Ages*, p. 244.

16 Paul O. Kristeller, "The Contribution of Religious Orders to Renaissance Thought and Learning," in his *Medieval Aspects of Renaissance Learning* (Durham, N.C.: Duke University Press, 1974), pp. 95–114.

17 James M. Saslow, *Ganymede in the Renaissance: Homosexuality in Art and Society* (New Haven: Yale University Press, 1986), pp. 205, 48, 116, 121.

18 Ibid., pp. 85–8, Freud quoted on p. 87.
19 Charles B. Schmitt, "Philosophy and Science in the Sixteenth Century University," in Murdock and Sylla, eds., *Cultural Context*, p. 500; Joseph S. Freedman, "Discussion of Women Within Academic Philosophical Writings of the High and Late Renaissance," paper presented to Renaissance Society of America, 1987 (courtesy of Georgianna Ziegler, Furness Shakespeare Library, University of Pennsylvania); Susan Groag Bell, *Women from the Greeks to the French Revolution* (Belmont, Calif.: Wadsworth Publishing Co., 1973), pp. 181–2; Diane Bornstein, ed., *The Feminist Controversy of the Renaissance* (Delmar, N.Y.: Scholars' Facsimiles and Reprints, 1980), pp. v–xiii; Carlos Norena, *Juan Luis Vives* (The Hague: Martinus Nijhoff, 1970), pp. 194–7; Constance Jordan, "Feminism and the Humanists," in Ferguson et al., eds., *Rewriting the Renaissance*, pp. 244, 257–8; Foster Watson, *Vives and the Renaissance Education of Women* (New York: Longman, Green, 1912), pp. 1, 11; Richard Marius, *Thomas More* (New York: Alfred A. Knopf, 1984), pp. 223–4; Charles G. Nauert, *Agrippa and the Crisis of Renaissance Thought* (Urbana: University of Illinois Press, 1965), p. 27.
20 Norena, *Juan Luis Vives*, pp. 195, 196; Bell, *Women from the Greeks*, p. 188; Marius, *Thomas More*, p. 223.
21 Keith Thomas, *Religion and the Decline of Magic* (London: Penguin, 1973), p. 321; Nauert, *Agrippa*, pp. 17–18. See also Frances A. Yates, *The Rosicrucian Enlightenment* (Boulder: Shambhala Publishers, 1978).
22 Thomas, *Decline of Magic*, p. 321; Walter Pagel, *Paracelsus* (Basle, Switzerland: S. Karger, 1958), p. 349; John Hargrave, *The Life and Soul of Paracelsus* (London: Victor Gollancz, 1951), p. 17; Anna Stoddart, *The Life of Paracelsus* (New York: David McKay, 1971), p. 42; Franz Hartmann, *The Life and Doctrines of Philippus Theophrastus* (New York: Theosophical Publishing Company, 1910), p. 140; Nauert, *Agrippa*, pp. 187, 50.
23 Hargrave, *Life and Soul*, p. 17; Pagel, *Paracelsus*, p. 30; Hartmann, *Theophrastus*, p. 140; Thomas, *Decline of Magic*, p. 320.
24 Nauert, *Agrippa*, pp. 90, 40, 71, 174–9.
25 C. G. Jung, *Psychology and Alchemy* (Princeton: Princeton University Press, 1968), pp. 23, 25; Sally G. Allen and Joanna Hibbs, "Outrunning Atalanta: Feminine Destiny in Alchemical Transmutation," *Signs*, vol. V (1980), p. 220; Paracelsus, quoted in Hartmann, *Theophrastus*, pp. 99–101.
26 Allen and Hibbs, "Outrunning Atalanta," pp. 219, 220; Jung, *Psychology and Alchemy*, pp. 23, 25.
27 Raleigh, quoted in Thomas, *Decline of Magic*, p. 320; Chiara Crisciani, "Alchemy in the Pretosa Margarita Novella," *Ambix*, vol. XX (1973), p. 177; Pagel, *Paracelsus*, p. 53; Allen G. Debus, *The Chemical Philosophy* (New York: Science History Publishers, 1977), pp. 206, 225; P. M. Rattansi, "Paracelsus and the Puritan Revolution," *Ambix*, vol. XI (1964), p. 26.
28 Nauert, *Agrippa*, pp. 45–6, 50, 49, 297.
29 Ibid., pp. 237, 73.
30 Hargrave, *Life and Soul*, p. 30; Pagel, *Paracelsus*, pp. 23, 40, 13.
31 Pagel, *Paracelsus*, pp. 53–4, 231.
32 Thomas, *Decline of Magic*, pp. 270–2.
33 Nauert, *Agrippa*, pp. 243, 226; Thomas, *Decline of Magic*, p. 264.
34 Paolo Rossi, *Philosophy, Technology, and the Arts in the Early Modern Era* (New York: Harper & Row, 1970), ch. one; Edgar Zilsel, "The Sociological Roots of Science," *American Journal of Sociology*, vol. XLVII (1942), passim; Carolyn Merchant, *The Death of Nature* (New York: Harper & Row, 1980), ch. three.

35 Brian Easlea, *Witch-Hunting, Magic, and the New Philosophy* (Brighton: Harvester Press, 1980), p. 102; Pagel, *Paracelsus*, pp. 15, 21.

36 Evelyn Fox Keller, *Reflections on Gender and Science* (New Haven: Yale University Press, 1985), pp. 51, 45.

37 Nauert, *Agrippa*, pp. 43, 239, 54, 92, 95, 174, 188.

38 Pagel, *Paracelsus*, pp. 19, 23, 231, 17, 311.

39 Christopher Hill, *The World Turned Upside Down* (London: Maurice Temple Smith, 1972), pp. 73–4, 77; Thomas, *Decline of Magic*, pp. 148, 165.

40 Hill, *Upside Down*, pp. 74, 293; Thomas, *Decline of Magic*, pp. 177–8, 16.

41 P. M. Rattansi, "Paracelsus and the Puritan Revolution," p. 26; Thomas, *Decline of Magic*, p. 323; Winstanley, quoted in Merchant, *Death of Nature*, p. 123.

42 Thomas, *Decline of Magic*, p. 269; Rattansi, "Paracelsus and the Puritan Revolution," p. 27; Hill, *Upside Down*, pp. 233–4.

43 Thomas, *Decline of Magic*, pp. 252–64; Barbara Ehrenreich and Dierdre English, *For Her Own Good* (New York: Doubleday, 1978), p. 38; Alice Clark, *Working Life of Women in the Seventeenth Century* (New York: Dutton, 1919), pp. 253–65.

44 Thomas, *Decline of Magic*, pp. 252, 678, 519, 16, 17.

45 R. A. Knox, *Enthusiasm: A Chapter in the History of Religion* (Oxford: Oxford University Press, 1950), p. 20; Sherrin Marshall (Wyntjes), "Women in the Reformation Era," in Bridenthal and Koonz, eds., *Becoming Visible*, p. 186; Merry E. Wiesner, "Nuns, Wives, and Mothers: Women and the Reformation in Germany," in Sherrin Marshall, ed., *Women in Reformation and Counter-Reformation Europe* (Bloomington: Indiana University Press, 1989), p. 15.

46 Wiesner, "Nuns, Wives, and Mothers," pp. 16, 20–1; Marshall, "Women in the Reformation Era," pp. 174, 175.

47 Marshall, "Women in the Reformation Era," pp. 174, 175.

48 Ibid., pp. 169, 175; Wiesner, "Nuns, Wives, and Mothers," p. 19; George Huntston Williams, *The Radical Reformation* (Philadelphia: Westminster Press, 1962), pp. 506–7; Claus-Peter Clasen, *Anabaptism: A Social History* (Ithaca, N.Y.: Cornell University Press, 1972).

49 Wiesner, "Nuns, Wives, and Mothers," pp. 16, 17; Marshall, "Women in the Reformation Era," p. 176; Sherrin Marshall, "Protestant, Catholic, and Jewish Women in the Early Modern Netherlands," in Marshall, ed., *Women in Reformation and Counter-Reformation Europe*, pp. 120, 126.

50 Marshall, "Women in the Reformation Era," p. 179; Natalie Zemon Davis, *Society and Culture in Early Modern France* (Palo Alto: Stanford University Press, 1975), p. 65.

51 Davis, *Society and Culture*, pp. 79, 80, 81, 82.

52 F. Ellen Weaver, "Erudition, Spirituality, and Women: The Jansenist Contribution," in Marshall, ed., *Women in Reformation and Counter-Reformation Europe*, pp. 190, 191, 196, 198.

53 Diane Willen, "Women and Religion in Early Modern England," in Marshall, ed., *Women in Reformation and Counter-Reformation Europe*, pp. 146, 141, 144, 149.

54 Ibid., pp. 144, 148, 156, 146, 151.

55 Ibid., pp. 147, 142; Hill, *Upside Down*, p. 250; Thomas, *Decline of Magic*, p. 69; Keith Thomas, "Women in the Civil War Sects," *Past and Present*, no. 13 (1958), p. 50.

56 Thomas, "Women in the Civil War Sects," pp. 44, 47; Ethyn Morgan Williams, "Women Preachers in the Civil War," *Journal of Modern History*, vol. I (1929), pp. 566–8.

57 Thomas, "Women in the Civil War Sects," p. 47; Hill, *Upside Down*, p. 251.

58 Hill, *Upside Down*, pp. 255, 59, 60.

59 Moira Ferguson, ed., *First Feminists* (Bloomington: Indiana University Press, 1985), pp. 10, 11; Hill, *Upside Down*, p. 259.

60 Thomas, "Women in the Civil War Sects," pp. 44, 45, 47.

61 Londa Schiebinger, *The Mind Has No Sex? Women in the Origins of Modern Science* (Cambridge, Mass.: Harvard University Press, 1989), pp. 17, 23, 44; Margaret Alic, *Hypatia's Heritage* (Boston: Beacon Press, 1986), p. 78.

62 Schiebinger, *The Mind Has No Sex?*, p. 45; Alic, *Hypatia's Heritage*, p. 9.

63 Schiebinger, *The Mind Has No Sex?*, pp. 44, 45.

64 H. J. Mozans, *Women in Science* (New York: Appleton, 1913), pp. 152–3; Alic, *Hypatia's Heritage*, pp. 139, 147.

65 Alic, *Hypatia's Heritage*, p. 100.

66 Schiebinger, *The Mind Has No Sex?*, p. 175; Merchant, *Death of Nature*, pp. 253, 68; Alic, *Hypatia's Heritage*, pp. 6–7, 192.

67 Schiebinger, *The Mind Has No Sex?*, pp. 47–58; Cavendish, quoted in Ferguson, *First Feminists*, p. 85.

68 Schiebinger, *The Mind Has No Sex?*, pp. 52, 53.

69 Schiebinger, *The Mind Has No Sex?*, pp. 67, 68; Alic, *Hypatia's Heritage*, pp. 99–101.

70 Alic, *Hypatia's Heritage*, pp. 99–100, 95–96; Schiebinger, *The Mind Has No Sex?*, pp. 113–14.

71 Schiebinger, *The Mind Has No Sex?*, pp. 67, 79.

72 Alic, *Hypatia's Heritage*, p. 123; Mozans, *Women in Science*, p. 171; Schiebinger, *The Mind Has No Sex?*, pp. 79–93.

73 Schiebinger, *The Mind Has No Sex?*, pp. 68–72.

74 Ibid., pp. 72–3.

CHAPTER NINE

1 Sherrill Cohen, "Asylums for Women in Counter-Reformation Italy," in Sherrin Marshall, ed., *Women in Reformation and Counter-Reformation Europe* (Bloomington: Indiana University Press, 1989), pp. 166, 167, 174, 175.

2 Natalie Zemon Davis, *Society and Culture in Early Modern France* (Palo Alto: Stanford University Press, 1975), p. 65; Merry E. Wiesner, "Nuns, Wives, and Mothers: Women and the Reformation in Germany," in Marshall, ed., *Women in Reformation and Counter-Reformation Europe*, p. 15; Keith Thomas, "Women in the Civil War Sects," *Past and Present*, no. 13 (1958), pp. 50–1; Ethyn Morgan Williams, "Women Preachers in the Civil War," *Journal of Modern History*, vol. I (1929), p. 562.

3 Keith Thomas, *Religion and the Decline of Magic* (London: Penguin, 1973), pp. 521–3; Starhawk, *Dreaming the Dark* (Boston: Beacon Press, 1982); pp. 183–219; Edward Peters, *The Magician, the Witch, and the Law* (Philadelphia: University of Pennsylvania Press, 1978), pp. 91–2.

4 Starhawk, *Dreaming the Dark*, p. 213; Rosemary Reuther, *New Woman, New Earth* (New York: Seabury Press, 1975), pp. 97, 98; Thomas, *Decline of Magic*, pp. 679, 621; Grethe Jacobsen, "Nordic Women and the Reformation," in Marshall, ed., *Women in Reformation and Counter-Reformation Europe*, pp. 48, 60; Carolyn Merchant, *The Death of Nature* (New York: Harper & Row, 1980), p. 142.

5 Thomas, *Decline of Magic*, pp. 671, 678; Merchant, *Death of Nature*, p. 142; Jacobsen, "Nordic Women," p. 60.

6 Barbara Ehrenreich and Dierdre English, *For Her Own Good* (New York: Doubleday, 1978), pp. 35–36; Starhawk, *Dreaming the Dark*, p. 187; Thomas, *Decline of Magic*, pp. 518, 523, 540, 542, 671.

7 Thomas, *Decline of Magic*, pp. 23, 764; Peters, *Magician, Witch and Law*, p. xiv.

8 Ibid., pp. 164–6. See also D. P. Walker, *Spiritual and Demonic Magic from Ficino to Campanella* (Notre Dame, Ind.: University of Notre Dame Press, 1975).

9 Charles G. Nauert, *Agrippa and the Crisis of Renaissance Thought* (Urbana: University of Illinois Press, 1965), p. 59; P. M. Rattansi, "Paracelsus and the Puritan Revolution," *Ambix*, vol. XI (1964), p. 29; "Robert Fludd," *Encyclopaedia Britannica*, vol. IX, p. 493; Merchant, *Death of Nature*, p. 125; Ehrenreich and English, *For Her Own Good*, p. 35.

10 Evelyn Fox Keller, *Reflections on Gender and Science* (New Haven: Yale University Press, 1985), p. 57.

11 See Merchant, *Death of Nature*, passim; David Kubrin, *How Sir Isaac Newton Helped Restore Law and Order to the West* (San Francisco: Kubrin, 1972); David Kubrin, "Newton's Inside Out!," in Harry Woolf, ed., *The Analytic Spirit* (Ithaca, N.Y.: Cornell University Press, 1981), pp. 96–121; Morris Berman, *The Reenchantment of the World* (Ithaca, N.Y.: Cornell University Press, 1981).

12 Ada Alessandrini, "Giovanni Heckius Linceo e la sua controversia contro i protestanti," *Revista di Storia della Chiesa in Italia*, vol. XXX (1976), pp. 365–6; William R. Shea, "Galileo and the Church," in David C. Lindberg and Ronald L. Numbers, eds., *God and Nature* (Berkeley: University of California Press, 1986), pp. 114–18; William B. Ashworth, "Catholicism and Early Modern Science," in Lindberg and Numbers, eds., *God and Nature*, pp. 148–9.

13 Ashworth, "Catholicism and Early Modern Science," pp. 152–5.

14 Ibid., pp. 153–5; John L. Heilbron, *Electricity in the Seventeenth and Eighteenth Centuries* (Berkeley: University of California Press, 1979), p. 2.

15 Alessandrini, "Giovanni Heckius Linceo," p. 363; Richard S. Westfall, "Galileo and the Accademia dei Lincei," in P. Galluzzi, ed., *Novita celesti e crisi del sapere* (Florence: Giunti Barbera, 1984), pp. 194–5; Ada Alessandrini, *Documenti Lincei e Cimeli Galileiani* (Rome: Accademia Nazionale dei Lincei, 1965), p. 9.

16 Westfall, "Galileo," pp. 194–5; A. Rupert Hall, "Introduction," in Richard Waller, *Essay on Natural Experiments* (New York: Johnson Reprint Corporation, 1964), p. 3; Pietro Redondi, *Galileo: Heretic* (Princeton: Princeton University Press, 1987), p. 29.

17 Westfall, "Galileo," pp. 194–5; Redondi, *Galileo: Heretic*, pp. 100, 44, 71, 177.

18 Marie Boas, *The Scientific Renaissance 1450–1630* (New York: Harper & Row, 1962), p. 243; Martha Ornstein, *The Role of Scientific Societies in the Seventeenth Century* (Chicago: University of Chicago Press, 1928), pp. 74–5; Redondi, *Galileo: Heretic*, pp. 82–3; Alessandrini, "Giovanni Heckius Linceo," p. 374.

19 Shea, "Galileo and the Church," pp. 118, 119, 128, 132; Redondi, *Galileo: Heretic*, passim.

20 Shea, "Galileo and the Church," p. 119; Ludovico Geymonat, *Galileo Galilei* (New York: McGraw-Hill, 1965), p. 42; James Broderick, *Galileo: The Man, His Work, His Misfortunes* (London: Geoffrey Chapman, 1964), pp. 19–21.

21 Geymonat, *Galileo Galilei*, p. 41; Shea, "Galileo and the Church," p. 118.

22 Mary Allan Olney, *The Private Life of Galileo* (London: Macmillan, 1870), pp. 68–70; Broderick, *Galileo*, p. 21; Geymonat, *Galileo Galilei*, p. 55.

23 Broderick, *Galileo*, p. 123; Geymonat, *Galileo Galilei*, p. 55; Olney, *Private Life*, pp. 68–70, 106, 271.

24 Ornstein, *Scientific Societies*, pp. 76–7; "Marin Mersenne," *Encyclopaedia Britannica*, vol. IX, p. 694.

25 Ashworth, "Catholicism and Early Modern Science," p. 138; P. J. S. Whitmore, *The Order of Minims in Seventeenth Century France* (The Hague: Martinus Nijhoff, 1967), pp. 61–7; Berman, *Reenchantment of the World*, p. 110; Peter Dear, *Mersenne and the Learning of the Schools* (Ithaca, N.Y.: Cornell University Press, 1988), p. 3.

26 Robert Lenoble, quoted in Dear, *Mersenne*, pp. 3, 64; Carolyn Merchant, *Death of Nature*, pp. 196–7; Ashworth, "Catholicism and Early Modern Science," p. 138; Hugh Kearney, *Science and Change* (New York: McGraw-Hill, 1971), p. 150.

27 Merchant, *Death of Nature*, pp. 203–4; Kearney, *Science and Change*, pp. 152, 153, 160. See also Karl Stern, *The Flight from Women* (New York: Farrar, Straus & Giroux, 1965); Susan R. Bordo, *The Flight to Objectivity* (Albany: State University of New York Press, 1987); Ashworth, "Catholicism and Early Modern Science," p. 139.

28 Ashworth, "Catholicism and Early Modern Science," p. 141; Merchant, *Death of Nature*, p. 202.

29 Harcourt Brown, *Scientific Organizations in Seventeenth Century France* (Baltimore: Williams and Wilkins, 1934), pp. 32, 76.

30 Merchant, *Death of Nature*, pp. 194–5, 206–14; Dear, *Mersenne*, p. 3.

31 Berman, *Reenchantment of the World*, pp. 110–12; Molière, quoted in H. J. Mozans, *Women in Science* (New York: Appleton, 1913), p. 82.

32 Francis Bacon, "The Masculine Birth of Time," in Benjamin Farrington, ed., *The Works of Francis Bacon* (Philadelphia: Carey and Hart, 1848), vol. VIII, pp. 533–4.

33 H. L. Rowse, *Homosexuals in History* (New York: Carroll & Graf, 1977), p. 67; Vern Bullough, *Homosexuality: A History* (New York: New American Library, 1979), p. 143; Susan Griffith, *Women and Nature* (New York: Harper & Row, 1978), p. 17; Carolyn Merchant, *Death of Nature*, pp. 165–8, 172; Keller, *Gender and Science*, ch. two.

34 Merchant, *Death of Nature*, pp. 172–4, 181; Francis Bacon, "Of Marriage and the Single Life," in Richard Whateley, ed., *Essays* (Boston: Lee and Shepard, 1887).

35 Charles Webster, "Puritanism, Separatism, and Science," in Lindberg and Numbers, eds., *God and Nature*, pp. 198, 200; Robert K. Merton, "Science, Technology and Society in Seventeenth Century England," *Osiris*, vol. IX, pt. two (1938).

36 Sprat, quoted in Christopher Hill, *The Century of Revolution* (New York: Norton, 1961), p. 280; Webster, "Puritanism, Separatism, and Science," p. 210.

37 Harold Hartley, *The Royal Society: Its Origins and Founders* (London: Royal Society, 1960), p. 24; Dorothy Stimson, *Scientists and Amateurs: A History of the Royal Society* (New York: Henry Schuman, 1948), p. 44; Boyle, quoted in Flora Masson, *Robert Boyle: A Biography* (London: Constable, 1914), p. 169. Rattansi, "Paracelsus and the Puritan Revolution," p. 29.

38 Robert Boyle, *Motives and Incentives to the Love of God* (London: Henry Herrington, 1661); Masson, *Robert Boyle*, p. 181; John Evelyn to Robert Boyle, September 29, 1659, in William Bray, ed., *John Evelyn: Diary and Correspondence* (London: Bell and Daldy, 1872), vol. III, p. 124.

39 John Evelyn to Robert Boyle, September 3, 1659, in Bray, ed., *John Evelyn*, vol. III, pp. 116–20.

40 Charles R. Weld, *A History of the Royal Society* (London: Royal Society, 1848), vol. I, p. 49; Stimson, *Scientists and Amateurs*, p. 53; Webster, "Puritanism, Separatism, and Science," pp. 210, 211.

41 Webster, "Puritanism, Separatism, and Science," pp. 210, 211–12; "John Wilkins," *Encyclopaedia Brittanica*, vol. XXVIII, p. 646; Mary Boas Hall, "Salomon's House Emergent: The Early Royal Society," in Woolf, ed., *Analytic Spirit*, p. 179; Kubrin, *How Isaac Newton*, p. 34.

42 Webster, "Puritanism, Separatism, and Science," pp. 211; Rattansi, "Paracelsus and the Puritan Revolution," pp. 29, 30; Kubrin, *How Isaac Newton*, p. 21, 22.

43 Rattansi, "Paracelsus and the Puritan Revolution," pp. 29, 31; Thomas, *Decline of Magic*, p. 270; Hill, *Century of Revolution*, p. 248.

44 Thomas, *Decline of Magic*, p. 270; Oldenburg and Glanvill, quoted in Keller, *Gender*

and Science, p. 52; Charleton, quoted in Brian Easlea, *Witch-Hunting, Magic, and the New Philosophy* (Brighton: Harvester Press, 1980), p. 242.

45 Stimson, *Scientists and Amateurs*, pp. 82–4; Londa Schiebinger, *The Mind Has No Sex? Women in the Origins of Modern Science* (Cambridge, Mass.: Harvard University Press, 1989), pp. 25–6, 37, 48–54; Merchant, *Death of Nature*, pp. 206, 270–2.

46 Kearney, *Science and Change*, p. 178; G. G. Coulton, "The High Ancestry of Puritanism," in his *Medieval Studies* (London: Simpkin, Marshall, Hamilton, Kent, 1915), pp. 37–45.

47 Kubrin, "Newton's Inside Out!," pp. 97, 98, 108.

48 Ibid., p. 109; Jan Golinsky, "The Secret Life of an Alchemist," in John Fauvel et al., eds., *Let Newton Be!* (Oxford: Oxford University Press, 1988), pp. 147, 150, 157. Richard H. Popkin, "Some Further Comments on Newton and Maimonides," in James E. Force and Richard H. Popkin, eds., *Essays on the Context, Nature, and Influence of Isaac Newton's Theology* (Dordrecht: Kluwer Academy Publishers, 1990), p. 1.

49 Golinski, "Secret Life," pp. 158, 160; John Brooke, "The God of Isaac Newton," in Fauvel et al., eds., *Let Newton Be!*, pp. 170, 177, 179. See also Richard H. Popkin, "Newton and Fundamentalism," and James E. Force, "Newton's God of Dominion: The Unity of Newton's Theological, Scientific, and Political Thought," in Popkin and Force, eds., *Essays on the Contextaa's*.

50 Piyo Rattansi, "Newton and the Wisdom of the Ancients," in Fauvel et al., eds., *Let Newton Be!*, pp. 187, 200.

51 Golinsky, "Secret Life," p. 150; Brooke, "God of Isaac Newton," p. 177; Kubrin, "Newton's Inside Out!," p. 116; Newton, quoted in Frank E. Manuel, *A Portrait of Isaac Newton* (Cambridge, Mass.: Harvard University Press, 1968), p. 119.

52 Gale E. Christianson, *In the Presence of the Creator: Isaac Newton and His Times* (New York: Free Press, 1984), p. 349; Manuel, *Portrait*, pp. 191, 26, 39.

53 Manuel, *Portrait*, pp. 100–1, 64, 66, 87.

54 Ibid., p. 172; Easlea, *Witch-Hunting*, p. 245.

55 Manuel, *Portrait*, pp. 216, 195, 211; Christianson, *In the Presence of the Creator*, pp. 349, 224.

56 Manuel, *Portrait*, pp. 231, 265, 281.

57 James R. Jacob, "Newtonian Theology and the Defense of the Glorious Revolution," in Robert P. Maccubbin and Martha Hamilton-Phillips, eds., *The Age of William III and Mary III* (Williamsburg, Va.: College of William and Mary, 1989), pp. 161–3; Margaret C. Jacob, "Christianity and the Newtonian Worldview," in Lindberg and Numbers, eds., *God and Nature*, pp. 242, 252; "John Evelyn," *Chambers Biographical Dictionary* (Edinburgh: W & R Chambers, 1978), p. 452.

58 Manuel, *Portrait*, pp. 290, 280.

59 Paolo Rossi, *Philosophy, Technology, and the Arts in the Early Modern Era* (New York: Harper & Row, 1970), pp. 87, 95, 109, 112–13.

60 Richard S. Westfall, "Flood Along the Bisenzio: Science and Technology in the Age of Galileo," *Technology and Culture*, vol. XXX (1989), pp. 905–7. Eusebius, quoted in Peter Brown, *The Body in Society* (New York: Columbia University Press, 1988), p. 207.

61 Kubrin, *How Isaac Newton*, p. 38; Kubrin, "Newton's Inside Out!," p. 108.

62 Schiebinger, *The Mind Has No Sex?*, p. 158.

63 Jacob Bigelow, *The Elements of Technology* (Boston: Boston Press, 1831), p. iv; Easlea, *Witch-Hunting*, p. 240; John Cohen, *Human Robots in Myth and Science* (New York: A. S. Barnes, 1967), ch. five and six; George Ovitt, "The Status of the Mechanical Arts in the Medieval Classification of Learning," *Medieval and Renaissance Studies*, vol.

XIV (1983), pp. 89–105; George Ovitt, "The Cultural Context of Western Technology," *Technology and Culture*, vol. XXVII (1986), pp. 477–500. See also Martha C. Howell, ed., *Women, Production, and Patriarchy in Late Medieval Cities* (Chicago: University of Chicago Press, 1986.)

64 Mary Astell, "A Serious Proposal to the Ladies," in Moira Ferguson, ed., *First Feminists* (Bloomington: Indiana University Press, 1985), pp. 187, 188, 190; Cavendish, Lambert, quoted in Schiebinger, *The Mind Has No Sex?*, pp. 146, 159.

CHAPTER TEN

1 Hastings Rashdall, *The Universities of Europe in the Middle Ages* (Oxford: Oxford University Press, 1985), vol. I, p. 265.

2 "Quakers," *Encyclopaedia Britannica* (tenth ed.), vol. XI, p. 226.

3 "Pietism," *Dictionary of the History of Ideas*, vol. III, pp. 493–5; "Moravians," *Encyclopaedia Britannica* (tenth ed.), vol. XVIII, p. 819; Rosemary Radford Reuther and Rosemary Skinner Keller, eds., *Women and Religion in America* (New York: Harper & Row, 1983), vol. II, pp. xx, xix, xxi; E. G. Alderfer, *The Ephrata Commune* (Pittsburgh: University of Pittsburgh Press, 1985), pp. 46–7.

4 Henry F. May, "The Decline of Providence?," in his *Ideas, Faiths, and Feelings* (New York: Oxford University Press, 1983), pp. 130–46; Sean Wilentz, *Chants Democratic* (New York: Oxford University Press, 1984), pp. 78–9; "Presbyterians," *Encyclopaedia Britannica* (tenth ed.), vol. XXII, p. 293.

5 Robert Samuel Fletcher, *A History of Oberlin College* (Oberlin, Ohio: Oberlin College, 1943), vol. I, pp. 207–8.

6 Nathan O. Hatch, *The Democratization of American Christianity* (New Haven: Yale University Press, 1989), p. 9.

7 Ibid., pp. 9, 44–5, 58; Timothy Waterous, "The Battle-Axe and Weapons of War: Discovered by the Moving Light; Aimed for the Final Destruction of Priestcraft," quoted in Hatch, *The Democratization of American Christianity*, p. 45.

8 Hatch, *The Democratization of American Christianity*, pp. 64–65, 80, 226–8.

9 Ibid., pp. 162, 209, 216, 64–5.

10 Whitney R. Cross, *The Burned-over District: The Social and Intellectual History of Enthusiastic Religion in Western New York 1800–1850* (Ithaca, N.Y.: Cornell University Press, 1950), p. 84; Mary P. Ryan, "A Woman's Awakening: Evangelical Religion and the Families of Utica, New York 1800–1840," in Janet Wilson James, ed., *Women in American Religion* (Philadelphia: University of Pennsylvania Press, 1980), pp. 90, 95, 110.

11 Barbara Leslie Epstein, *The Politics of Domesticity: Women, Evangelism, and Temperance in Nineteenth Century America* (Middletown, Conn.: Wesleyan University Press, 1981), pp. 65, 48, 61.

12 Nancy Towle, quoted in Hatch, *Democratization*, p. 58.

13 Opal Thornburg, *Earlham: The Story of the College* (Richmond, Ind.: Earlham College Press, 1963), p. 25; William Leach, *True Love and Perfect Union* (New York: Basic Books, 1980), p. 7.

14 Thomas Woody, *A History of Women's Education in the United States* (New York: Octagon Books, 1980), vol. I, pp. 177, 179, 330; Thornburg, *Earlham*, p. 16.

15 Woody, *Women's Education*, vol. I, pp. 341, 398; David Tyack and Elisabeth Hansot, *Learning Together: A History of Coeducation in American Public Schools* (New Haven: Yale University Press, 1990), p. 36; Fletcher, *Oberlin*, p. 374; Joseph Emerson, *Female Education* (Boston: Samuel T. Armstrong, 1822); Emma Willard, "Plan for Improving

Female Education (1819)," in Willystine Goodsell, *Pioneers of Women's Education in the United States* (New York: AMS Press, 1970), p. 60; Willard, quoted in Tyack and Hansot, *Learning Together*, p. 37.

16 Goodsell, *Pioneers*, p. 129; Catherine Beecher, "An Essay on the Education of Female Teachers (1835)," in ibid., p. 177.

17 Edward Hitchcock, *The Power of Christian Benevolence Illustrated by the Life and Labor of Mary Lyon* (Northampton, Mass.: Hopkins, Bridgman & Co., 1852), pp. 8, 14; Mary Lyon to her mother, May 13, 1821, quoted in ibid., p. 18.

18 Woody, *Women's Education*, vol. I, p. 362; Goodsell, *Pioneers*, pp. 223–5, 249; Mary Lyon, "New England Female Seminary for Teachers (1832)," quoted in Goodsell, *Pioneers*, p. 254; Mary Lyon, "Mt. Holyoke Female Seminary (1835)," quoted in Goodsell, *Pioneers*, p. 263.

19 Mary Lyon, "Principles and Design of the Mt. Holyoke Seminary (1837)," quoted in Goodsell, *Pioneers*, pp. 279, 283, 284, 286–7.

20 Fletcher, *Oberlin*, pp. 58–9, 61, 118–19.

21 Ibid., pp. 119, 208, 210, 213; Hatch, *Democratization*, p. 196.

22 Fletcher, *Oberlin*, pp. 373, 374, 375, 377; Frances J. Horsford, *Father Shipherd's Magna Charta* (Boston: Marshall Jones, 1937), pp. 1–3.

23 Fletcher, *Oberlin*, pp. 377, 379, 383.

24 Woody, *Women's Education*, vol. I, p. 458; Leach, *True Love*, pp. 70–7; Carl F. Price, *Wesleyan's First Century* (Middletown, Conn.: Wesleyan University Press, 1932), pp. 121, 172–5.

25 Florence Morse Kingsley, *The Life of Henry Fowles Durant* (New York: Century, 1924), pp. 24, 40, 77, 130, 131, 149, 159, 165.

26 Ibid., pp. 167, 174–5, 235.

27 Ibid., pp. 197, 193, 238, 189.

28 Burroughs, quoted in Woody, *Women's Education*, vol. I, p. 314; Ronald L. Numbers, "Science and Religion," *Osiris*, 2nd ser., vol. I (1985), p. 69. See also Theodore Bozeman, *Protestants in the Age of Science* (Chapel Hill: University of North Carolina Press, 1977).

29 Willard, quoted in Goodsell, *Pioneers*, p. 62; Phelps, quoted in Woody, *Women's Education*, vol. I, pp. 318–19; Margaret W. Rossiter, *Women Scientists in America* (Baltimore: Johns Hopkins University Press, 1982), p. 7.

30 Lyon, quoted in Goodsell, *Pioneers*, pp. 263, 239; Philip J. Lawrence, "Edward Hitchcock: The Christian Geologist," *Proceedings of the American Philosophical Society*, vol. 116 (1972), pp. 21–34; Beth Bradford Gilchrist, *The Life of Mary Lyon* (Boston: Houghton-Mifflin, 1910), p. 117.

31 Fletcher, *Oberlin*, p. 384; Kingsley, *Henry Fowles Durant*, pp. 241–2.

32 Ann Braude, *Radical Spirits* (Boston: Beacon Press, 1989), pp. 4–5, 58.

33 Wilentz, *Chants Democratic*, pp. 145–53; David F. Noble, *America by Design* (New York: Alfred A. Knopf, 1977), passim.

34 Charles Webster, *Samuel Hartlib and the Advancement of Learning* (Cambridge: Cambridge University Press, 1970), pp. 3, 7, 11, 54, 59, 65, 69.

35 J. B. Turner, quoted in Charles R. Mann, *A Study of Engineering Education* (Boston: Merrymount Press, 1918), p. 10; "The Inventor," quoted in Hugo Meier, "The Technological Concept in American Social History," unpublished Ph.D. dissertation, University of Wisconsin, 1950, p. 352.

36 Abbott Lawrence to Samuel A. Eliot, June 7, 1847, quoted in Ian Braley, "The Evolution of Humanistic-Social Courses for Undergraduate Engineers," unpublished Ph.D. dissertation, Stanford University, 1961, p. 65.

37 Ethel M. McAllister, *Amos Eaton: Scientist and Educator* (Philadelphia: University of Pennsylvania Press, 1941), p. 368; Warren, quoted in Braley, "Evolution," p. 24; Jacob Bigelow, *The Elements of Technology* (Boston: Boston Press, 1831), passim.

38 Webster, *Samuel Hartlib*, pp. 65, 149, 191.

39 Woody, *Women's Education*, vol. II, pp. 6–10, 339; Mabel Newcomer, *A Century of Higher Education for American Women* (New York: Harper & Row, 1959), p. 17.

40 Caroline Dall, quoted in Leach, *True Love*, p. 283; Julia S. Tutweiler, "The Technical Education of Women," *Education*, vol. VIII (1882), p. 201; Woody, *Women's Education*, vol. II, pp. 2, 65.

41 Catherine Beecher, "True Remedy for the Wrongs of Women (1851)," quoted in Woody, *Women's Education*, vol. II, p. 143; Anne Firor Scott, "The Ever Widening Circle: The Diffusion of Feminist Values from the Troy Female Seminary, 1822–1872," *History of Education Quarterly*, vol. XIX (1979), pp. 7, 8; Louise Schutz Boas, *Women's Education Begins* (Norton, Mass: Wheaton College Press, n.d.), pp. 185–90; McAllister, *Amos Eaton*, pp. 368, 491, 490, 485, 488, 180, 183, 59–63, 64; Lois Barber Arnold, *Four Lives in Science* (New York: Schocken Books, 1984), pp. 43–52.

42 Woody, *Women's Education*, vol. II, pp. 174, 175, 185; Gilbert Meltzer, *The Beginnings of Elmira College* (Elmira: Commercial Press, 1941), pp. 1, 5; James Monroe Taylor, *Before Vassar Opened* (Boston: Houghton-Mifflin, 1914), pp. 101, 221, 254; Harriet Gardener Raymond, *The Life and Letters of John Howard Raymond* (New York: Fords, Howard, and Hulbert, 1881), pp. 307, 309; J. H. Raymond to H. R. Worthington, May 29, 1855, quoted in Raymond, *Life and Letters*, p. 307.

43 Newcomer, *Century of Higher Education*, pp. 80–1; Mary W. Whitney, "Scientific Study and Work for Women," *Education*, vol. III (1882), pp. 58, 64.

44 Elizabeth Deering Hanscom and Helen French Greene, *Sophia Smith and the Beginnings of Smith College* (Northampton, Mass.: Smith College, 1925), pp. 32, 42, 60–1, 117, 119.

45 Jean Glasscock, ed., *Wellesley College 1875–1975* (Wellesley, Mass.: Wellesley College, 1976), pp. v, 18, 19; Patricia Palmieri, "In Adamless Eden: A Social Portrait of the Academic Community at Wellesley College, 1875–1920," unpublished Ed.D. dissertation, Harvard University, 1981, pp. 25, 28, 30; Kingsley, *Henry Fowles Durant*, pp. 109, 130.

46 Fletcher, *Oberlin*, pp. 38, 130, 25–6; Horsford, *Father Shipherd's Magna Charta*, p. 3; Wilentz, *Chants Democratic*, pp. 145–6.

47 Glenn C. Altschuler, *Andrew D. White* (Ithaca, N.Y.: Cornell University Press, 1979), pp. 58, 172. Leach, *True Love*, pp. 70–1. See also A. D. White, "On Scientific and Industrial Education in the United States (1874)," "Scientific Education (1869)," "A Report on the Admission of Women to the University (1870)," all cited in Altschuler.

48 Leach, *True Love*, pp. 74–5; Price, *Wesleyan's First Century*, pp. 121, 172–5.

49 Woody, *Women's Education*, vol. II, pp. 252, 251, 224, 256; Jill Conway, "Perspectives on the History of Women's Education in the United States," *History of Education Quarterly* (Spring, 1974) p. 8; Leach, *True Love*, p. 73.

50 Taylor, *Before Vassar Opened*, p. 221; Edward D. McDonald and Edward M. Hinton, *Drexel Institute of Technology* (Philadelphia: Drexel Institute, 1942), pp. 28–9.

51 Rossiter, *Women Scientists in America*, pp. 15–16; Patricia Albjerg Graham, "Expansion and Exclusion: A History of Women in American Higher Education," *Signs*, vol. III (1978), p. 771.

52 Burton J. Bledstein, *The Culture of Professionalism* (New York: Norton, 1976), pp. 198–9; Ronald L. Numbers, "Science and Religion," pp. 59–65; Andrew Dickson

White, "History of the Warfare of Science in Christendom (1896)," discussed in Numbers, "Science and Religion," *passim*. See also David Martin, *The Religious and the Secular: Studies in Secularization* (New York: Schocken Books, 1969); James A. Beckford, *Religion and Advanced Industrial Society* (London: Unwin Hyman, 1989).
53 Bledstein, *Culture of Professionalism*, pp. 85–7; Arnold, *Four Lives in Science*, p. 10.
54 Frederick L. Bishop, "The Cooperative System of Engineering Education at the University of Pittsburgh," *Society for the Promotion of Engineering Education Bulletin*, vol. II (1911), p. 141; Charles F. Scott, "The Engineering College and the Electric Manufacturing Company," *Society for the Promotion of Engineering Education Proceedings*, vol. XV (1907), p. 468.
55 Catherine Beecher, "Reminiscences (1874)," quoted in Woody, *Women's Education*, vol. II, p. 217; Anne Allinson, quoted in ibid., vol. II, p. 196.
56 Graham, "Expansion and Exclusion," p. 761.
57 Whitney, "Scientific Study and Work for Women," p. 67; Arnold, *Four Lives in Science*, p. 58.
58 Braude, *Radical Spirits*, pp. 160–1; Rossiter, *Women Scientists in America*, p. 13; Leach, *True Love*, pp. 74–5, 349; Woody, *Women's Education*, vol. II, p. 268; Pope Pius XI, quoted in "Coeducation," *Dictionary of the History of Ideas* (New York: Scribner's, 1973), vol. IV, p. 527.
59 Christopher Lasch, "The Moral and Intellectual Rehabilitation of the Ruling Class," in his *The World of Nations* (New York: Alfred A. Knopf, 1974).
60 Rossiter, *Women Scientists in America*, pp. 73, 82, 83, 88, 99, 91.
61 Ibid., p. 99.
62 Ibid., p. 78; *The Misogynist Dinner of the American Chemical Society, Boston, August 27, 1880* (New York: Russell Brothers Printers, 1880), p. 15 (American Philosophical Society Collection); George B. Kauffman, "The Misogynist Dinner of the ACS," *Journal of College Science Teaching* (May, 1983) pp. 381–3.

EPILOGUE
1 William Whewell, "*On the Connection of the Physical Sciences*, by Mrs. Somerville," *Quarterly Review*, vol. LI (1834), p. 59; Elizabeth Chambers Patterson, *Mary Somerville and the Cultivation of Science, 1815–1840* (Boston: Martinus Nijhoff Publishers, 1983), pp. 138, xii.
2 Patterson, *Cultivation of Science*, pp. 146, xi, 42–3.
3 Ibid., pp. 89–91, 48–9; Elizabeth C. Patterson, *Mary Somerville* (Oxford: Oxford University Press, 1979), pp. 5, 38; Martha Somerville, *Personal Recollections from Early Life to Old Age of Mary Somerville* (Boston: Roberts Brothers, 1876), p. 173.
4 Somerville, quoted in Patterson, *Mary Somerville*, pp. 40–1.
5 Somerville, quoted in Patterson, *Cultivation of Science*, p. 89.
6 Mary Shelley, *Frankenstein* (New York: Bantam Books, 1967).
7 George Ovitt, *The Restoration of Perfection: Labor and Technology in Medieval Culture* (New Brunswick, N.J.: Rutgers University Press, 1986), p. 183; David Herlihy, "Land, Family, and Women in Continental Europe," in Susan Stuard, ed., *Women in Medieval Society* (Philadelphia: University of Pennsylvania Press, 1976), pp. 25, 26.
8 Herlihy, "Land, Family, and Women," p. 26; Jean Gimpel, *The Medieval Machine: The Industrial Revolution of the Middle Ages* (London: Penguin, 1977), pp. 9, 14, 46, 49, 67–8; Auguste Comte to J. S. Mill, October 5, 1843, in L. Lévy-Bruhl, ed., *Lettres inédites de J. S. Mill á A. Comte avec les résponses de Comte* (Paris, 1899), p. 250.
9 Caroline Bynum, *Jesus as Mother* (Berkeley: University of California Press, 1982), pp. 144, 138.

10 Ibid., pp. 120, 121, 117, 115, 113; David Knowles, *The Religious Orders in England* (Cambridge: Cambridge University Press, 1948), pp. 122–3.

11 John Cohen, *Human Robots in Myth and Science* (New York: A. S. Barnes, 1966), pp. 83–4.

12 Ibid., p. 87.

13 Ibid., pp. 36–9; Sir James Lighthill, *Artificial Intelligence* (London: Science Research Council, April, 1983). See also Christine Woesler de Panafiere, "Automata—a Masculine Utopia," in Everett Mendelsohn and Helga Nowotny, eds., *Nineteen Eighty-four: Science Between Utopia and Dystopia* (Dordrecht: D. Reidel, 1984), pp. 127–45.

14 Cohen, *Human Robots*, pp. 42–4.

15 James Hillman, *The Myth of Analysis* (Evanston, Ill.: Northwestern University Press, 1972), pp. 221–4.

16 Kathleen Hart, "In-Vitro Program and Infertile Couples," *Quill* (Pennsylvania Hospital, Philadelphia, Spring, 1988), p. 5.

Index

Index

Artz, Frederick B., 163
asceticism
  androgynous cast, 12, 13–16, 19–20, 49
  appeal for women, 11, 13, 20–1
  ascetic communities, 14–15
  Christian apologists' endorsement of, 13
  church fathers' embrace of, 61–2
  identification with women, 23–4
  noble women, involvement of, 20–3
  origins of, 11–13
  popularization of, 20
  sexual transcendence ideal, 17–20
  study circles (*didaskaleion*), 16
  syneiactism (spiritual marriage), 16–17, 50
  see also clerical asceticism; monasticism
Ashworth, William B., 212, 213, 220
Astell, Mary, 197, 243
astrology, 171
astronomy, 202–3
Athanasius of Alexandria, St., 20, 22, 52–3, 56, 62, 243
Athenagoras, 13
Atwater, Wilbur, 269–70
Aubrey, John, 223
Augustine, St., 34
Augustine of Hippo, St., 23–4, 67–72
Augustus, emperor of Rome, 6
Austin, Ann, 245
automata, 284–5
Averroës, 157–8, 166

Bacon, Francis, 188, 222–4, 240
Bacon, Roger, 164–5, 284
Bailey, Derek, 16, 25
Barking double monastery, 35
Barraclough, Geoffrey, 92, 93–4, 108
Barrow, Isaac, 232
Barstow, Anne, 7, 8, 74, 79
Basil of Ancyra, 56
Basil of Caesarea, 21, 26
Bassi, Laura, 169
Bateson, Mary, 26, 27, 28, 30, 31, 32, 34, 37
Bathilde, Queen, 32
Baxter, John, 228
Baxter, Richard, 210
Beausoleil, baroness de, 203–4
Bede, St., 4, 34, 35, 121
Beecher, Catherine, 252, 265, 274
Beguine movement, 142
Beissel, Conrad, 245
Bellarmino, Robert, 214
Benedict Biscop, St., 86

Benedict VIII, Pope, 124
Benedictine Order, 83–4, 85
Benedictine Rule, 83–4, 85, 86, 91, 95, 97, 100
Benedict of Aniane, 97–9, 102, 111
Benedict of Nursia, St., 83–4
Benivieni, Gerolamo, 172
Benjamin, Simeon, 266
Bercarius, 32
Bernard of Clairvaux, St., 144, 145, 284
Bernard of Septimania, 89, 105–6
Berno of Cluny, 111
Bertile of Chelles, 32
Besançon double monastery, 31
Bigelow, Jacob, 263
Bischofsheim double monastery, 37
Bishop, Frederick, 273
bishops, spiritual duties of, 91
Blanche of Castile, 139, 156
Bledstein, Burton J., 272
Boas, Marie, 214
Bodenham, Anne, 209
Bodin, Jean, 208
Bonaventure, St., 165
Boniface, St., 36–7, 86–8, 91, 92, 95, 100
Bonosus, 75
Book of Gomorrah (Damian), 132
The Book of the City of Ladies (Christine de Pisan), 160
Bora, Katherine von, 189
Boswell, John, 135
Bowes, Elizabeth, 194
Boyle, Robert, 199, 225–7, 231, 235, 237
Bradwardine, Thomas, 167
Braude, Ann, 260
Brendan, St., 29
brides of Christ, 58
Brie double monastery, 31
Brigit, St., 29
Brihtnoth, Abbot, 122
Brinsley, John, 206
Brooke, Christopher, 110, 111, 125, 129, 130–1
Brooke, John, 234
Brooklyn Polytechnic Institute, 266
Brougham, Henry, 280
Brown, Judith C., 169
Brown, Peter, 6, 9, 10, 11–12, 13, 14–15, 16, 17–18, 19, 20–1, 22, 23, 45, 46, 48, 49, 50, 51, 52, 54, 55, 56, 57, 63, 64, 65, 66, 67–8, 69, 72, 73, 75, 77, 78
Brundage, James, 145
Bruno, Giordano, 212
Bucer, Martin, 188
Burgundofara, 31

Macrina, 21, 26
Mactefeld, Abbess, 31
magic, *see* alchemical movement
Makin, Bathsua, 197
Malleus Maleficarum, 207
Manichean Elect, 19
Manuel, Frank E., 235, 236, 237, 238, 239
Map, Walter, 152
Marcella, 17, 22, 23, 62
Marcellina, 22, 63
Marcigny nunnery, 114
Marcionites, 14, 15, 47
Margaret of Austria, 174
married household tradition, 5–8, 10
Marsh, Adam, 155
Marshall, Sherrin, 189, 190, 191
Martin of Tours, St., 29, 54, 100
martyred women, 191
Massachusetts Institute of Technology
    (MIT), 263, 270, 275
Matter, E. Ann, 135
Maude, Thomas, 236
Maximilla, 14
May, Henry F., 246
McCormick, Michael, 93, 96
McEvoy, James, 155
McNamara, JoAnn, 6, 9, 13–14, 47, 48,
    49–50, 58
Mead, Richard, 236
mechanics of motion, science of, 167
mechanistic conception of nature, 212,
    218–23, 228–9, 239–41
medical cookery, 201–2
medicine, 168, 170–1
    alchemical movement and, 181, 183,
        187–8, 201–2
    female practitioners, 201–2
    folk medicine, 181–2
Meeks, Wayne, 8, 9, 12
Melania the Elder, 21, 26, 67
Merbitz, Valentine, 285
Merchant, Carolyn, 221, 224
Merian, Maria Sibylla, 204
Merovingian Church, 80–2
Mersenne, Marin, 210, 218, 219, 220–1, 222
Merton College, 167
Methodists, 246
Meurdrac, Marie, 202
militarization
    of bishops and abbots, 91–3
    of church fathers, 63
    of clerical asceticism, 53–4, 57
    of ecclesiastical culture of learning,
        149–51

of monasticism, 53–4, 57, 96–100, 102–4
of papacy, 125–6
of scientific inquiry, 214
Mill, John Stuart, 280
Minims, order of, 218–19, 221
"Misogynist Dinner of the American
    Chemical Society," 277–8
Molière, 222
monastic cathedrals, 120
monasticism
    Benedict's influence on, 83–4
    Carolingian reforms, 93–4, 109–10
    church fathers' advocacy of, 68, 72
    clerical asceticism, alliance with, 51–3
    communal monasticism, 21–2, 23
        see also double monasteries
    Eastern Church and, 58–60
    evangelistic function, 85–8
    female monasticism, 25, 100–4, 109–10,
        113–14, 121–3
    homoerotic ethos, 57
    imperial transformation of, 94–100
    militarization of, 53–4, 57, 96–100, 102–4
    papal support for, 84–5
    priesthood for monks, 99
    sexual avoidance ethos, 54–8
    West, introduction in, 62
monasticization of the church
    alliance of royalty and church leadership,
        118–19, 120–1, 122–3
    background to, 108–10
    Benedictine revival, 110
    Cluniac reforms, 110–23
    in England, 115–23
    female monasticism and, 113–14, 121–3
    "knight" identity for monks, 112–13, 121
    lay dominion over church properties,
        elimination of, 119–20, 126–7, 133
    liturgical reform, 111–12, 120–1
    popular antimonastic reaction, 122
    scholarship and, 120
        see also papal revival
monogamy, advent of, 88, 89–90
Montalembert, Charles, 34, 59
Montanists, 14
Montierender double monastery, 32
Montmort, Henri-Louis Habert de, 222
Moore, R. I., 20, 126, 132, 137
Moravians, 245, 250–1
More, Henry, 199, 210–11, 228, 229, 232
More, Thomas, 173, 174
Morrill Act of 1862, 263
Morton, Henry, 277
motherless child, scientific pursuit of, 284–6

Index

Premonstratensian Order, 38, 136
Presbyterians, 246
priesthood for monks, 99
primogeniture, 127, 133, 155
Principles of the Most Ancient and Modern
   Philosophy (Conway), 200
Prinz, Friedrich, 30
Priscilla, 9, 13, 14
Priscillian, 19, 63, 65
procreation, ecclesiastical views on, 157
professionalization of science, 274–8
property rights, 27, 33
   inheritance of property, 75, 78–9, 94
   monogamy and, 89–90
prophetess role for women, 10, 190–1
puberty rites, 151
Puritanism, 194, 224

Quakers, 195, 196, 197, 200, 245, 250, 260
Quini-Sext canons, 60

Radegund, St., 30
Raemond, Florimond de, 191, 206
Raleigh, Sir Walter, 179
Rashdall, Hastings, 138, 139, 167–8, 244
Rattansi, Pietro M., 186, 187, 225, 228,
   229, 234
Raymond, J. H., 266
Rebstock, Barbara, 190
Redondi, Pietro, 214
Reformation, 171, 173
   alchemical movement and, 183–6
   women's role in, 188–97
Regiomontanus, 284
Regularis Concordia, 118, 120
religious revivals of late eleventh and early
   twelfth centuries, 140–3
Remiremont double monastery, 31
Renaissance, *see* humanist movement
Renaudot, Théophraste, 198
Rensselaer, Stephen van, 263
Rensselaer Polytechnic Institute (RPI), 263,
   266
reproductive function of women, substitutes
   for, 154, 282–6
Reuther, Rosemary, 207
Richard, Ellen S., 270
Robert d'Abrissel, 37–8
Roberts, Alexander, 208
Rohault, Jacques, 198
Roman Church, *see* Latin Church

Romanianus, 68
Romaric, 31
Rosenblatt, Wibrandis, 189
Rosenwein, Barbara, 113
Rosicrucians, 219
Rossi, Paolo, 182, 240
Rossiter, Margaret, 259, 271, 276–7
Royal Society, 226–7, 228, 229–31, 232,
   238, 241, 280
Rufinus of Aquileia, 21–2, 26, 65, 67, 152
Ruggiero, Guido, 169
Ryan, Mary, 249

Salaberga, 32
Saslow, James M., 172–3
Scala, Alessandra, 168, 170
Schiebinger, Londa, 197, 198, 200, 202
scholarship
   Carolingian Renaissance, 93–4, 104–5
   cathedral schools, 138–9
   celibate culture of learning, origins of,
      136–7
   double monasteries and, 28–9, 32–3,
      34–5
   government support for, 263, 270
   monasticization of the church and, 120
   papal revival and, 131
   professional choice of scholars, changes
      in, 271–2
   see also ecclesiastical culture of learning;
      education for women; scientific inquiry
Schurman, Anna Maria von, 197, 204
scientific inquiry
   Aristotelian heritage, 166–7
   artisans' contributions, 201–4
   ascetic impulse and, 214–15, 225–7,
      231–2, 235–7
   church-approved inquiry, 212
   clergy of science, emergence of, 239–43
   clerical legacy, 281–6
   doxological science in America, 258–60
   economic view of, 262, 273–4
   faith, conflict with, 166
   Galileo's role, 215–18
   Jesuits and, 212–13
   language reform and, 241
   male domination, 205–6, 273–8
      see also scientific restoration
   mechanistic conception of nature, 212,
      218–23, 228–9, 239–41
   militarization of, 214
   misogyny of scientific establishment,
      229–30, 242–3, 277–8

325

University of Bologna, 168, 169, 170
University of Padua, 171
University of Paris, 143, 147, 148–9, 156, 165
University of Pennsylvania, 270
University of Salerno, 168
Urban II, Pope, 126, 133
Urban VIII, Pope, 215–16

Valentinian I, emperor of Rome, 75
Valerius, 152
Varano, Costanza, 170
Vassar, Matthew, 266, 270
Vassar College, 266–7
Vaucanson, Jacques de, 285
Vaughan, Thomas, 183
Verecundus, 68
virgines subintroductae, 16
virginity, ideology of, 48, 51, 62, 64, 66
Vives, Juan Luis, 173, 174
Viviani, Vincenzio, 218
Vleck, John, 270
Voltaire, 199, 236

Waldensians, 142
Walker, Francis Amasa, 270
Wallace, William A., 165–6, 167
Walpurga of Heidenheim, 37
Waltilda, 32
Ward, Seth, 227, 232
Warren, Samuel, 263
Watson, Foster, 173
Weaver, F. Ellen, 192–3
Webster, Charles, 224, 227
Webster, John, 183, 210–11, 227
Weisstein, Naomi, xi
Wellesley College, 256–8, 260, 268
Wemple, Suzanne, 25, 30, 32, 39, 80, 82, 87, 90, 91, 95, 100, 103, 104–5, 106
Werburga, 3, 36
Wesley, John, 246

Wesleyan University, 269–70, 275
Western Church, *see* Latin Church
Westfall, Richard, 213–14, 217, 218, 240
Whewell, William, 279
Whiston, William, 235
Whitby double monastery, 34–5
White, Andrew Dickson, 269, 272
Whitney, Mary W., 267, 275
Wiesner, Merry, 189, 190
Wilfrid, archbishop of York, 36
Wilfrid of Ripon, 86
Wilkins, John, 225, 227, 228, 241
Willard, Emma, 251–2, 259, 265
Willen, Diane, 193
William, archdeacon of Paris, 150
William IX, duke of Aquitaine, 111
William of Ockham, 166
Williams, Roger, 245
Wimbourne double monastery, 36
Winkelmann, Maria, 203, 204
Winstanley, Gerrard, 186
The Wise-Woman of Hogsdon, 188
wise women, 187–8, 210
witchcraft, 89, 106, 188, 223
    alchemical movement and, 209–11
    women associated with, 206–9
Withburga, 122
Women Scientists in America (Rossiter), 276–7
Woody, Thomas, 250, 251, 252, 265
Wooley, Hannah, 197
Workman, Herbert, 28, 52–3, 54, 58, 62, 68–9, 80, 83, 85, 98, 111, 123, 124, 148
Wycliffe, John, 190

Zacharias, Pope, 90, 92
Zell, Katherine, 189
Zell, Matthew, 188
Zilsel, Edgar, 182
Zinzendorf, Countess Benigna, 250
Zinzendorf, Count Nicolaus, 245
Zosimus, Pope, 71
Zwingli, Ulrich, 188

Permissions Acknowledgments

Grateful acknowledgment is made
to the following for permission to reprint
previously published material:

American Society of Church History: Excerpts from "The Origins of Clerical Celibacy in the Western Church" by Charles A. Frazee (*Church History*, Vol. 41). Reprinted from *Church History* by permission of the American Society of Church History.

Columbia University Press: Excerpts from *University Records and Life in the Middle Ages* by Lynn Thorndike, copyright 1944 by Columbia University Press; excerpts from *The Body and Society* by Peter Brown, copyright © 1988 by Columbia University Press. Reprinted by permission.

Epworth Press: Excerpts from Herbert Workman: *The Evolution of the Monastic Ideal* (Epworth Press, London, 1927). Reprinted by permission.

Harvard University Press: Excerpts from *A Portrait of Isaac Newton* by Frank Manuel, Cambridge, Mass.: The Belknap Press of Harvard University Press, copyright © 1968 by the President and Fellows of Harvard College; excerpts from *The Mind Has No Sex? Women in the Origins of Modern Science* by Londa Schiebinger, Cambridge, Mass.: Harvard University Press, copyright © 1989 by Londa Schiebinger. Reprinted by permission.

Johns Hopkins University Press: Excerpts from *Women Scientists in America: Struggles and Strategies to 1940* by Margaret W. Rossiter. The Johns Hopkins University Press, Baltimore/London, 1982. Reprinted by permission.

S. Karger: Excerpts from *Paracelsus: An Introduction to Philosophical Medicine in the Era of the Renaissance*, 2nd, revised edition by W. Pagel (Kager, Basel, 1982). Reprinted by permission.

Macmillan Publishing Company and *Weidenfeld and Nicolson*: Excerpts from *Religion and the Decline of Magic* by Keith Thomas. Copyright © 1971 by Keith Thomas. Rights outside the U.S. controlled by Weidenfeld and Nicolson, London. Reprinted by permission of the publishers.

Oberlin College: Excerpts from *A History of Oberlin College* by Robert Samuel Fletcher (Oberlin College, 1943, reprinted 1971). Reprinted by permission of Oberlin College.

Octagon Books: Excerpts from *A History of Women's Education in the United States* by Thomas Woody (1980). Reprinted by permission of Octagon Books, a division of Hippocrene Books, Inc.

Pantheon Books: Excerpts from *The Knight, the Lady and the Priest* by Georges Duby, translated by Barbara Bray. Translation copyright © 1983 by Barbara Bray. Reprinted by permission of Pantheon Books, a division of Random House, Inc.

Penguin Books Ltd.: Excerpts from *Western Society and the Church in the Middle Ages* by R. W. Southern (Penguin Books, 1970). Copyright © 1970 by R. W. Southern. Reprinted by permission of Penguin Books Ltd., London.

Random House, Inc.: Excerpts from *Adam, Eve and the Serpent* by Elaine Pagels. Copyright © 1988 by Elaine Pagels. Reprinted by permission.

Society for the History of Alchemy and Chemistry: Excerpts from "Paracelsus and the Puritan

Revolution" by P. M. Rattansi (*Ambix*, XX, 1973). Reprinted from *Ambix* by permission of the Society for the History of Alchemy and Chemistry.

University of California Press Journals: Excerpts from "The Liturgy of War in the Early Middle Ages" by Michael McCormick. Copyright © 1984 by the Regents of the University of California. Reprinted from *Viator* XV, 1984, pp. 1–23, by permission of the University of California Press Journals.

University of Illinois Press: Excerpts from *Agrippa and the Crisis of Renaissance Thought* by Charles G. Nauert. Copyright © 1965 by the Board of Trustees of the University of Illinois. Reprinted by permission of the author and the University of Illinois Press.

University of Pennsylvania Press: Excerpts from *Women in Frankish Society* by Suzanne Wemple (1981). Reprinted by permission of the University of Pennsylvania Press, Philadelphia.

Viking Penguin: Excerpts from *The World Turned Upside Down* by Christopher Hill. Copyright © 1972 by Christopher Hill. Reprinted by permission of Viking Penguin, a division of Penguin Books USA Inc.

Weidenfeld and Nicolson: Excerpts from *The Medieval World* by Friedrich Heer (1962). Reprinted by permission of Weidenfeld and Nicolson, London.

Yale University Press: Excerpts from *The Democratization of American Christianity* by Nathan O. Hatch (1989). Reprinted by permission.